THE NEW CAMBRIDGE SHAKESPEARE

GENERAL EDITOR
Brian Gibbons

ASSOCIATE GENERAL EDITOR
A. R. Braunmuller, *University of California, Los Angeles*

From the publication of the first volumes in 1984 the General Editor of the New Cambridge Shakespeare was Philip Brockbank and the Associate General Editors were Brian Gibbons and Robin Hood. From 1990 to 1994 the General Editor was Brian Gibbons and the Associate General Editors were A. R. Braunmuller and Robin Hood.

CYMBELINE

This new edition of Shakespeare's *Cymbeline* takes full account of recent critical and historical scholarship. It foregrounds the elements of romance, tragicomedy and Jacobean stagecraft which together shape the play; it also acknowledges the post-modern indeterminacy of the play's key moments. Martin Butler presents a refreshingly unsentimental reading of the heroine, Innogen, and gives a greater place than his predecessors to the politics of 1610, especially to questions of British union and nationhood. There is a full and detailed commentary on the play's language, and discussion and illustration of the play's history of performance from 1610 to the present.

THE NEW CAMBRIDGE SHAKESPEARE

All's Well That Ends Well, edited by Russell Fraser
Antony and Cleopatra, edited by David Bevington
As You Like It, edited by Michael Hattaway
The Comedy of Errors, edited by T. S. Dorsch
Coriolanus, edited by Lee Bliss
Cymbeline, edited by Martin Butler
Hamlet, edited by Philip Edwards
Julius Caesar, edited by Marvin Spevack
King Edward III, edited by Giorgio Melchiori
The First Part of King Henry IV, edited by Herbert Weil and Judith Weil
The Second Part of King Henry IV, edited by Giorgio Melchiori
King Henry V, edited by Andrew Gurr
The First Part of King Henry VI, edited by Michael Hattaway
The Second Part of King Henry VI, edited by Michael Hattaway
The Third Part of King Henry VI, edited by Michael Hattaway
King Henry VIII, edited by John Margeson
King John, edited by L. A. Beaurline
The Tragedy of King Lear, edited by Jay L. Halio
King Richard II, edited by Andrew Gurr
King Richard III, edited by Janis Lull
Love's Labour's Lost, edited by William C. Carroll
Macbeth, edited by A. R. Braunmuller
Measure for Measure, edited by Brian Gibbons
The Merchant of Venice, edited by M. M. Mahood
The Merry Wives of Windsor, edited by David Crane
A Midsummer Night's Dream, edited by R. A. Foakes
Much Ado About Nothing, edited by F. H. Mares
Othello, edited by Norman Sanders
Pericles, edited by Doreen DelVecchio and Antony Hammond
The Poems, edited by John Roe
Romeo and Juliet, edited by G. Blakemore Evans
The Sonnets, edited by G. Blakemore Evans
The Taming of the Shrew, edited by Ann Thompson
The Tempest, edited by David Lindley
Timon of Athens, edited by Karl Klein
Titus Andronicus, edited by Alan Hughes
Troilus and Cressida, edited by Anthony B. Dawson
Twelfth Night, edited by Elizabeth Story Donno
The Two Gentlemen of Verona, edited by Kurt Schlueter
The Two Noble Kinsmen, edited by Robert Kean Turner and Patricia Tatspaugh
The Winter's Tale, edited by Susan Snyder and Deborah T. Curren-Aquino

THE EARLY QUARTOS
The First Quarto of Hamlet, edited by Kathleen O. Irace
The First Quarto of King Henry V, edited by Andrew Gurr
The First Quarto of King Lear, edited by Jay L. Halio
The First Quarto of King Richard III, edited by Peter Davison
The First Quarto of Othello, edited by Scott McMillin
The First Quarto of Romeo and Juliet, edited by Lukas Erne
The Taming of a Shrew: The 1594 Quarto, edited by Stephen Roy Miller

CYMBELINE

Edited by
MARTIN BUTLER
University of Leeds

CAMBRIDGE
UNIVERSITY PRESS

CONTENTS

ILLUSTRATIONS

Illustration 1 is from the Devonshire Collection, Chatsworth, and is reproduced by permission of the Duke of Devonshire and the Chatsworth Settlement Trustees; photograph from the Photographic Survey, Courtauld Institute of Art. Illustration 2 is reproduced by permission of Warwick Castle Ltd; 3 and 4 by permission of the Brotherton Collection, University of Leeds; 5 by permission of the British Library (shelfmark G3687); 6 by permission of the Folger Shakespeare Library; 8 and 9 are by Gordon Goode (Shakespeare Centre Library, Stratford-upon-Avon); 10 is reproduced by permission of Ivan Kyncl; 11 by permission of John Haynes; 12 by permission of Martha Swope; 13 by permission of Clive Barda; 14 by permission of Shakespeare Santa Cruz; and 15 by permission of Kneehigh Theatre and Steve Tanner.

ACKNOWLEDGEMENTS

In the eighteenth and nineteenth centuries, *Cymbeline* was one of Shakespeare's most popular plays, but in modern times it has moved to the edges of the canon and received comparatively little attention from editors. There are, though, three outstanding twentieth-century editions: the New Variorum by H. H. Furness (1913), J. C. Maxwell's 'old' New Cambridge edition (1960), and Roger Warren's Oxford World's Classics text (1998). The present edition is deeply indebted to these three. Each has saved me from a multitude of errors, and their textual notes and commentaries have been endlessly useful. The New Cambridge *Cymbeline* differs from its predecessors in several ways. I have attempted to foreground the richness of the literary relationships that shape the play (romance, tragicomedy, Jacobean stagecraft), and to acknowledge the post-modern indeterminacy of its key moments; I have tried to break with the legacy of the sentimental Victorian reading of Innogen, which still exerts some hold on production and interpretation even today; and I have given greater space than previous editors to the play's engagement with the politics of 1610, and especially to questions of British union and nationhood. Each of these themes underpins sections of the Introduction.

This edition has been far longer in the making than I intended, and I am deeply grateful to Sarah Stanton for not losing faith that some day it would arrive. Brian Gibbons has been an exemplary general editor and prompt, detailed and critical, while Al Braunmuller has waved me on from afar. I am especially indebted to three good friends, David Fairer, David Lindley and Gordon McMullan, each of whom read drafts of the Introduction. The final version has benefited greatly from their responses, and from Brian Gibbons's firm hand. David Lindley further contributed by transcribing the music. I am especially grateful to Lesley Johnson for sharing her expertise in the play's medieval background with me, to Gail Marshall and Francis O'Gorman for advising me on the Victorian stage history, and to John Jowett for commenting on my textual analysis. In sourcing images I was particularly helped by Kate Belsey, Dennis Kennedy, Danny Scheie and the staff of the Shakespeare Centre Library, Stratford-upon-Avon.

Finally, I am grateful beyond measure to Jane, James and Emily for suffering the presence of this play in their lives for so long; and I cannot neglect the opportunity that these acknowledgements allow for thanking Donald Coleman, whose inspirational teaching, thirty years ago, set me on the road to Shakespeare.

M. H. B.

ABBREVIATIONS AND CONVENTIONS

1. Shakespeare's plays

The abbreviated titles of Shakespeare's plays used in this edition have been modified from those in the *Harvard Concordance to Shakespeare*. All quotations and line references to plays other than *Cymbeline* are to G. Blakemore Evans (general editor), *The Riverside Shakespeare*, 1974, on which the *Concordance* is based.

Ado	*Much Ado About Nothing*
Ant.	*Antony and Cleopatra*
AWW	*All's Well That Ends Well*
AYLI	*As You Like It*
Cor.	*Coriolanus*
Cym.	*Cymbeline*
Err.	*The Comedy of Errors*
Ham.	*Hamlet*
1H4	*The First Part of King Henry the Fourth*
2H4	*The Second Part of King Henry the Fourth*
1H6	*The First Part of King Henry the Sixth*
2H6	*The Second Part of King Henry the Sixth*
3H6	*The Third Part of King Henry the Sixth*
JC	*Julius Caesar*
John	*King John*
LLL	*Love's Labour's Lost*
Lear	*King Lear*
Luc.	*The Rape of Lucrece*
Mac.	*Macbeth*
MM	*Measure for Measure*
MND	*A Midsummer Night's Dream*
MV	*The Merchant of Venice*
Oth.	*Othello*
Per.	*Pericles*
R2	*Richard the Second*
R3	*Richard the Third*
Rom.	*Romeo and Juliet*
Shr.	*The Taming of the Shrew*
Son.	*The Sonnets*
Temp.	*The Tempest*
TGV	*The Two Gentlemen of Verona*
Tim.	*Timon of Athens*
Tit.	*Titus Andronicus*
TN	*Twelfth Night*
Tro.	*Troilus and Cressida*
Ven.	*Venus and Adonis*

| Wiv. | The Merry Wives of Windsor |
| WT | The Winter's Tale |

2. Editions, adaptations and textual commentary

Alexander	*William Shakespeare: The Complete Works*, ed. P. Alexander, 4 vols., 1951
Boswell	*The Plays and Poems of William Shakespeare*, ed. J. Boswell, 21 vols., 1821
Brooks	H. F. Brooks, conjectures reported in Nosworthy
Cambridge	*The Works of William Shakespeare*, eds. W. G. Clark, J. Glover and W. A. Wright, 9 vols., 1863–6 (The Cambridge Shakespeare)
Capell	*Mr William Shakespeare His Comedies, Histories and Tragedies*, ed. E. Capell, 10 vols., 1767–8
Chambers	*William Shakespeare*, ed. E. K. Chambers, 1930
Collier	*The Works of William Shakespeare*, ed. J. P. Collier, 8 vols., 1842–4
Collier [2]	*The Works of Shakespeare*, ed. J. P. Collier, 8 vols., 1853
Collier [3]	*Shakespeare's Comedies, Histories, Tragedies and Poems*, ed. J. P. Collier, 8 vols., 1876–8
Craig	*The Complete Works of Shakespeare*, ed. W. J. Craig, 1905
Daniel	P. A. Daniel, *Notes and Conjectural Emendations of Certain Doubtful Passages in Shakespeare's Plays*, 1870
Deighton	K. Deighton, *The Old Dramatists: Conjectural Readings*, 1896, 2nd series, 1898
Delius	*The Complete Works of William Shakespeare*, ed. N. Delius, 1854
Dover Wilson	J. Dover Wilson, conjectures reported in Maxwell
Douce	F. Douce, *Illustrations of Shakespeare*, 1807
Dowden	*Cymbeline*, ed. E. Dowden, 1903 (The Arden Shakespeare)
Durfey	T. Durfey, *The Injured Princess, or the Fatal Wager* (1682)
Dyce	*The Works of William Shakespeare*, ed. A. Dyce, 6 vols., 1857
Dyce [2]	*The Works of William Shakespeare*, ed. A. Dyce, 9 vols., 1864–7
F	*Mr William Shakespeare's Comedies, Histories, and Tragedies*, 1623 (The First Folio)
F [2]	*Mr William Shakespeare's Comedies, Histories, and Tragedies*, 1632 (The Second Folio)
F [3]	*Mr William Shakespeare's Comedies, Histories, and Tragedies*, 1663 (The Third Folio)
F [4]	*Mr William Shakespeare's Comedies, Histories, and Tragedies*, 1685 (The Fourth Folio)
Furness	*The Tragedie of Cymbeline*, ed. H. H. Furness, 1913 (The New Variorum Shakespeare)
Globe	*Works*, ed. W. G. Clark and W. A. Wright, 1864 (The Globe Edition)
Hanmer	*The Works of Shakespeare*, ed. T. Hanmer, 6 vols., 1743–4
Herford	*The Works of Shakespeare*, ed. C. H. Herford, 1899
Hudson	*The Works of Shakespeare*, ed. H. N. Hudson, 11 vols., 1851–9
Hudson [2]	*The Complete Works of William Shakespeare*, ed. H. N. Hudson, 20 vols., 1880–1
Ingleby	*Shakespeare's 'Cymbeline'*, ed. C. M. Ingleby, 1886

Johnson	*The Plays of William Shakespeare*, ed. S. Johnson, 8 vols., 1765
Keightley	*The Plays of William Shakespeare*, ed. T. Keightley, 6 vols., 1864
Knight	*The Pictorial Edition of the Works of Shakspere*, ed. C. Knight, 8 vols., 1838–43
Knight [2]	*The Comedies, Histories, Tragedies, & Poems of William Shakspere*, ed. C. Knight, 12 vols., 1842–4
Malone	*The Plays and Poems of William Shakespeare*, ed. E. Malone, 10 vols., 1790
Maxwell	*Cymbeline*, ed. J. C. Maxwell, 1960 (The New Cambridge Shakespeare)
Neilson-Hill	*The Complete Plays and Poems of William Shakespeare*, eds. W. A. Neilson and C. J. Hill, 1942
Nosworthy	*Cymbeline*, ed. J. M. Nosworthy, 1955 (The New Arden Shakespeare)
Pope	*The Works of Shakespear*, ed. A. Pope, 6 vols., 1723–5
Pope [2]	*The Works of Shakespear*, ed. A. Pope, 8 vols., 1728
Rann	*The Dramatic Works of Shakspeare*, ed. J. Rann, 6 vols., 1786–94
Ritson	J. Ritson, *Remarks, Critical and Illustrative, on the Text and Notes of the Last Edition of Shakespeare*, 1783
Riverside	*The Riverside Shakespeare*, gen. ed. G. Blakemore Evans, 1974
Rowe	*The Works of Mr William Shakespear*, ed. N. Rowe, 6 vols., 1709
Rowe [2]	*The Works of Mr William Shakespear*, ed. N. Rowe, 8 vols., 1714
Singer	*The Dramatic Works of William Shakespeare*, ed. S. W. Singer, 10 vols., 1826
Singer [2]	*The Dramatic Works of William Shakespeare*, ed. S. W. Singer, 10 vols., 1856
Sisson	*William Shakespeare: The Complete Works*, ed. C. J. Sisson, 1954
Staunton	*The Works of William Shakespeare*, ed. H. Staunton, 15 vols., 1881
Steevens	*The Plays of William Shakespeare*, eds. S. Johnson and G. Steevens, 10 vols., 1773 (the Johnson-Steevens Variorum)
Steevens-Reed	*The Plays of William Shakespeare*, eds. G. Steevens and I. Reed, 15 vols., 1793
Taylor	*William Shakespeare: The Complete Works*, eds. S. Wells and G. Taylor, 1986 (in which *Cymbeline* is edited by G. Taylor)
Taylor, *Textual Companion*	G. Taylor and S. Wells, *William Shakespeare: A Textual Companion*, 1987
Theobald	*The Works of Shakespeare*, ed. L. Theobald, 7 vols., 1733
Thirlby	Styan Thirlby's unpublished conjectures (used by Theobald and Johnson)
Thiselton	A. E. Thiselton, *Some Textual Notes on the Tragedie of Cymbeline*, 1902
Tyrwhitt	T. Tyrwhitt, *Observations and Conjectures upon Some Passages of Shakespeare*, 1766
Vaughan	H. H. Vaughan, *New Readings and New Renderings of Shakespeare's Tragedies*, 3 vols., 1886
Walker	W. S. Walker, *A Critical Examination of the Text of Shakespeare*, 1860
Warburton	*The Works of Shakespear*, ed. W. Warburton, 8 vols., 1747
Warren	*Cymbeline*, ed. R. Warren, 1998
Wyatt	*Cymbeline*, ed. A. J. Wyatt, 1897

3. Other works cited and abbreviations used in the Commentary

Abbott   E. A. Abbott, *A Shakespearian Grammar*, new edn, 1875
(references are to numbered sections)

Adelman   J. Adelman, *Suffocating Mothers*, 1992

Bacon   F. Bacon, *Essays*, ed. B. Vickers, 1999

Baldwin   T. W. Baldwin, *William Shakespeare's Small Latin and Less Greek*,
1944

Barton   A. Barton, *Essays, Mainly Shakespearean*, 1994

B&F   *The Dramatic Works in the Beaumont and Fletcher Canon*, gen. ed.
Fredson Bowers, 10 vols., Cambridge, 1966–96

Bennett   J. W. Bennett, 'Britain among the Fortunate Isles', *SP*, 53 (1956),
114–40

Bindoff   S. T. Bindoff, 'The Stuarts and their style', *English Historical
Review*, 60 (1954), 192–216

Bullough   G. Bullough, *Narrative and Dramatic Sources of Shakespeare*,
8 vols., 1957–75

Chapman, *Tragedies* G. Chapman, *The Plays of George Chapman: The Tragedies*, ed.
A. Holaday et al., 1987

Chapman, *Homer's Iliad* G. Chapman, *Homer's Iliad*, ed. A. Nicoll, 1957

CJ   *Journals of the House of Commons*

CompD   *Comparative Drama*

Corin   F. Corin, 'A note on the dirge in *Cymbeline*', *English Studies*, 40
(1959), 173–9

Cromwell   O. Cromwell, *Letters and Speeches*, ed. T. Carlyle, 1871

Dekker   *The Dramatic Works of Thomas Dekker*, ed. F. Bowers, 4 vols.,
1955

Dent   R. W. Dent, *Shakespeare's Proverbial Language: An Index*, 1981

Donne   J. Donne, *Ignatius his Conclave*, ed. T. S. Healy, 1969

Drayton   M. Drayton, *Works*, ed. J. W. Hebel, 5 vols., 1931–41

Edelman   C. Edelman, *Brawl Ridiculous*, 1992

Edwards   P. Edwards, *Threshold of a Nation*, 1979

EiC   *Essays in Criticism*

ELR   *English Literary Renaissance*

Freer   C. Freer, *The Poetics of Jacobean Drama*, 1981

Galloway and Levack *The Jacobean Union*, eds. B. R. Galloway and B. P. Levack,
1985

Gordon, *Enotikon* J. Gordon, *Enotikon, or a Sermon of the Union of Great Brittanie*,
1604

Harris   B. Harris, '"What's past is prologue": *Cymbeline* and
Henry VIII', in *Later Shakespeare*, eds. J. R. Brown and
B. Harris, 1966, 203–34

Henslowe   *Henslowe's Diary*, eds. R. A. Foakes and R. T. Rickert, 1961

Herbert   E. Herbert, *Autobiography*, ed. J. S. Shuttleworth

Heywood   T. Heywood, *Dramatic Works*, ed. J. Pearson, 1874

Hill   G. Hill, '"The true conduct of human judgment": some
observations on *Cymbeline*', in *The Morality of Art*, ed.
D. Jefferson, 1969, 18–32

Hunt   M. Hunt, 'Fourteeners in Shakespeare's *Cymbeline*', *N&Q*,
(2000), 458–61

G. K. Hunter	G. K. Hunter, 'The spoken dirge in Kyd, Marston and Shakespeare', *N&Q*, 209 (1964), 146–7
R. G. Hunter	R. G. Hunter, *Shakespeare and the Comedy of Forgiveness*, 1965
James	H. James, *Shakespeare's Troy*, 1997
Jonson	*Ben Jonson*, eds. C. H. Herford, P. Simpson and E. Simpson, 11 vols., 1925–53
Jordan	C. Jordan, *Shakespeare's Monarchies: Ruler and Subject in the Romances*, 1997
Kane	R. J. Kane, '"Richard du Champ" in *Cymbeline*', *SQ*, 4 (1953)
Knight	G. W. Knight, *The Crown of Life*, 1947
Kyd	T. Kyd, *The Spanish Tragedy*, ed. P. Edwards, 1959
Lawrence	W. W. Lawrence, *Shakespeare's Problem Comedies*, 1931
Leishman	J. B. Leishman, ed., *Three Parnassus Plays*, 1949
Long	J. H. Long, *Shakespeare's Use of Music: The Final Comedies*, 1961
Lyly	J. Lyly, *Euphues*, ed. M. W. Croll and H. Clemons, 1916
Mahood	M. M. Mahood, *Bit Parts in Shakespeare's Plays*, 1992
Marlowe, *Poems*	C. Marlowe, *Complete Poems and Translations*, ed. S. Orgel, 1971
Marston	*Antonio's Revenge*, ed. G. K. Hunter *The Insatiate Countess*, ed. G. Melchiori
Matthews	C. M. Matthews, 'The true Cymbeline', *History Today* (1957), 755–9
Merrill	R. V. Merrill, 'Eros and Anteros', *Speculum*, 19 (1944), 265–84
Middleton	*The Changeling*, ed. N. W. Bawcutt, 1958 *Women Beware Women*, ed. J. R. Mulryne, 1975
Miola, *Rome*	R. S. Miola, *Shakespeare's Rome*, 1983
Miola, *Tragedy*	R. S. Miola, *Shakespeare and Classical Tragedy*, 1992
Milton	J. Milton, *Paradise Lost*, ed. A. Fowler, 1968
MLQ	*Modern Language Quarterly*
Moffet	R. Moffet, '*Cymbeline* and the nativity', *SQ*, 13, 1962, 207–18
Nashe	T. Nashe, *The Works*, eds. R. B. McKerrow and F. P. Wilson, 5 vols., 1958
Nearing	H. Nearing, 'The legend of Julius Caesar's British conquest', *PMLA*, 64, 1949, 889–929
Nevo	R. Nevo, *Shakespeare's Other Language*, 1987
Nitze	W. A. Nitze, 'On the derivation of the Old French Enygeus', *Zeitschrift fur Franzosische Sprache und Literatur*, 66, 1956, 40–2
N&Q	*Notes and Queries*
OED	*Oxford English Dictionary*, 2nd edn
Onions	C. T. Onions, *A Shakespeare Glossary*, 2nd edn, enlarged, 1953
Ovid	*Ovid's Metamorphoses*, transl. A. Golding, ed. J. F. Nims, 1965
Parker	P. Parker, 'Romance and empire: anachronistic *Cymbeline*', in *Unfolded Tales: Essays on Renaissance Romance*, eds. G. M. Logan and G. Teskey, 1989, 189–207
Pitcher	J. Pitcher, 'Names in *Cymbeline*', *EiC*, 43 (1993)
PMLA	*Publications of the Modern Language Association of America*
RES	*Review of English Studies*
Rogers	H. L. Rogers, 'The prophetic label in *Cymbeline*', *RES*, new series, 11 (1960), 296–9
Root	R. K. Root, *Classical Mythology in Shakespeare*, 1903
SDS	stage directions

Sidney   P. Sidney, *The Countess of Pembroke's Arcadia*, ed. V.
                Skretkowicz, 1987
Simonds   P. M. Simonds, *Myth, Emblem and Music in Shakespeare's
                'Cymbeline': An Iconographic Reconstruction*, 1992
Spenser, *FQ*   E. Spenser, *The Faerie Queene*, ed. A. C. Hamilton
Spenser, *Minor Poems*   E. Spenser, *Minor Poems*, ed. E. de Selincourt, 1910
SLI   *Studies in the Literary Imagination*
SP   *Studies in Philology*
SQ   *Shakespeare Quarterly*
S.St.   *Shakespeare Studies*
S.Sur.   *Shakespeare Survey*
Stone   L. Stone, *The Crisis of the Aristocracy 1558–1641*, 1965
Strong   R. Strong, *Henry Prince of Wales and England's Lost Renaissance*,
                1986
Thompson   A. Thompson, '"Making him speak true English": grammatical
                emendations in some eighteenth-century editions of
                Shakespeare, with particular reference to *Cymbeline*', in *Reading
                Readings: Essays on Shakespeare Editing in the Eighteenth Century*,
                ed. J. Gondris, 1998, 71–85
Tilley   M. P. Tilley, *A Dictionary of Proverbs in England in the Sixteenth
                and Seventeenth Centuries*, 1950
Venezky   A. Venezky, *Pageantry on the Shakespearean Stage*, 1951
Wayne   V. Wayne, 'The career of Cymbeline's manacle', *Early Modern
                Culture*, 1 (2000), 1–21
Webster   J. Webster, *Works*, eds. D. Gunby, D. Carnegie and A.
                Hammond, 3 vols., in progress (1995——)
Wells   S. Wells, *Staging Shakespeare's Apparitions and Dream Visions*,
                1990

INTRODUCTION

Cymbeline is one of Shakespeare's longest and richest plays. Its capaciousness is its great virtue. It ranges from the nightmare claustrophobia of Innogen's bedroom to the epic violence of Romano-British battle; it juxtaposes the innocent prude Posthumus, the refined brute Cloten, and the nonchalant hero Guiderius; it accommodates Iachimo's corrosive cynicism and Jupiter's transcendental affirmations. Its stagecraft is multi-levelled, and its texture is densely allusive, reflecting the bewildering array of sources on which it draws; its generic affinities link it with all parts of the canon. Yet despite this astonishing variety, its narrative grips and compels, rising inexorably from a naive tale of sundered lovers to a peripeteia of dazzling artfulness. The Victorian critics who supposed the ageing Shakespeare was writing in a mood of philosophic calm or cata-tonic boredom could scarcely have been more mistaken. *Cymbeline* was produced by a dramatist working at the height of his powers.[1]

These days *Cymbeline* has no shortage of able advocates, but it remains a difficult play to see whole, and has frequently been dismissed as muddled and overcomplicated. The most disparaging appraisal came, famously, from Dr Johnson:[2]

This play has many just sentiments, some natural dialogues, and some pleasing scenes, but they are obtained at the expense of much incongruity. To remark the folly of the fiction, the absurdity of the conduct, the confusion of the names and manners of different times, and the impossibility of the events in any system of life, were to waste criticism upon unresisting imbecility, upon faults too evident for detection, and too gross for aggravation.

Johnson's formidable censure shows the problems that rationalism has with romance, but his objection was less to *Cymbeline*'s implausibility than to its disunity – the feel-ing that while good in parts, as an entity it fails. Other critics echoed this charge of incoherence: notably F. R. Leavis, who complained that it lacked 'unifying significance such as might organize it into a profound work of art',[3] and George Bernard Shaw who, though admiring Innogen, Cloten and the princes, thought the play as a whole 'exasperating beyond all tolerance'. Shaw even suggested that Innogen's role should be altered, to disentangle the 'real woman divined by Shakespeare without his knowing it clearly' from the 'idiotic paragon of virtue' clad in the bombazine of a bishop's wife.[4]

---

[1] For Shakespeare 'on the heights', see Edmund Dowden, *Shakspere* (1877); for catatonia, see Lytton Strachey, 'Shakespeare's final period', in *Books and Characters* (1922; originally written 1904). William Archer thought Shakespeare wrote *Cymbeline* in a fit of 'morbid ingenuity': *The Theatrical World of 1896* (1897), p. 263.

[2] *Dr Johnson on Shakespeare*, ed. W. K. Wimsatt (1969), p. 136.

[3] Leavis, *The Common Pursuit* (1952; originally published 1942), p. 178. For a positive Leavisite reading, see Derick Marsh, *The Recurring Miracle* (1962).

[4] Shaw, *Plays and Players*, ed. A. C. Ward (1952), p. 115; and C. St John, ed., *Ellen Terry and Bernard Shaw: A Correspondence* (3rd edn, 1949), pp. 42, 45.

This sounds like typical Shavian bravado, but comparable sentiments go back to Charles Gildon in the early eighteenth century: 'Though the usual absurdities of irregular plots abound . . . yet there is something in the discovery that is very touching.'[1] Such praise of *Cymbeline*'s isolated beauties suggests that the problem is not implausibility so much as the difficulty of identifying the play's inner dynamic.

Cymbeline's pleasures differ from those anticipated by readers trained to admire singularity of effect. Its structure is a series of narratives that seem to stand apart from each other but which ultimately prove to be interconnected, although the exact nature of those connections often remains elusive. Actions at one level are affected by events at another, each sequence nesting within patterns of which the characters are unconscious but in which they need to find their places, so that the more local difficulties that preoccupy them can be resolved. The seemingly self-sufficient story of marital fidelity with which events open is absorbed into larger narratives that pull the simpler tale into their orbit, a design that is fully apparent only from the retrospect of the final scene. What makes the structure seem diffuse is the absence of a hero, and the consequent uncertainty about what is driving the action. Although the king is structurally central (he alone links the three plots: the wager, the Romans, and the lost princes), theatrically he is a blank; and while Posthumus, Innogen and Iachimo have, at different times, each been taken for the star part, none of them exactly dominates, and all disappear for long periods, even including Innogen, who after 4.2 is virtually silent. This makes the play's design remarkably decentred, and although the resolution is powerful when it comes, it arrives almost by accident, after coincidences that seem mysterious, if not frankly arbitrary. This dynamic opens out the play by counteracting its drive towards closure, creating sudden shifts of gear between its various levels and strong tensions that pull it in different directions. Modern readers and directors have shown more relish than did Dr Johnson for the play's outrageous crossovers between ancient Rome and modern Italy, its ostentatious disguises, confusions and chances. Such fractures appeal to post-modern tastes for fictions that reveal their engineering and question the terms of their own mimesis.

The other critical stumbling-block has been the play's politics. Although all Shakespeare's writing after 1603 registers the impact of the new cultural dispensation that arrived with James I, *Cymbeline*'s kingly families, masque-like revelations and praise of imperial peace make it seem more directly engaged with the circumstances of the new reign than any other play. Inevitably, this has caused difficulties, since *Cymbeline*'s Jacobean dimensions cannot easily be generalized: its allusions to half-forgotten issues get in the way of the usual appeals to Shakespeare's timelessness. At worst, its topicalities have been seen as a puzzle to be cracked, a code that could be broken were the right cryptographic key found. In general, allegorical readings have been a distraction, for they freeze the play into a deadly antiquarian past. But approaches that neglect its Jacobean contexts are just as problematic, since they risk seeming historically impoverished. The most remarkable instance of inattention to history was the Victorians'

---

[1] B. Vickers, ed., *Shakespeare: The Critical Heritage 1623–1801* (6 vols., 1974–81), VI, p. 261. Arthur Murphy, in 1771, called the play 'a wild chase of heterogeneous matter', yet 'amidst all its imperfections, a number of detached beauties would occur to surprise and charm the imagination' (Vickers, II, p. 359).

overindulgent attitude to Innogen (see pp. 58–9 below): only readers completely indifferent to anachronism could take her for Shakespeare's ideal woman and the play's only important character. But even in later times, more historically sensitized approaches have been inhibited by the assumption that too much politics damages the play's roots in myth. As the archetypal critic Northrop Frye put it, '*Cymbeline* is not, to put it mildly, a historical play: it is pure folktale'.[1] Yet politics and folktale are not incompatible, and in many ways the play inhabits the rich border zone where they meet. One aim of this Introduction will be to explore *Cymbeline*'s unique interplay between politics and aesthetics, history and myth.

DATE

Cymbeline is first mentioned in 'The Book of Plays and Notes Thereof', a small manuscript volume kept by the astrologer and quack doctor Simon Forman (1552–1611). Forman apparently began this as a collection of memoranda based on plays he had seen, but he abandoned it after listing only four: *Cymbeline, Macbeth, The Winter's Tale* and a play of Richard II that, from his account, was written by someone other than Shakespeare. The summary of *Cymbeline* runs as follows:[2]

Of Cymbeline, King of England

Remember also the story of Cymbeline, King of England in Lucius' time. How Lucius came from Octavius Caesar for tribute, and, being denied, after sent Lucius with a great army of soldiers; who landed at Milford Haven, and after were vanquished by Cymbeline, and Lucius taken prisoner, and all by means of three outlaws; of the which two of them were the sons of Cymbeline, taken from him when they were but two years old by an old man whom Cymbeline banished, and he kept them as his own sons twenty years with him in a cave. And how one of[3] them slew Cloten, that was the queen's son, going to Milford Haven to seek the love of Innogen the King's daughter. And how the Italian that came from her love conveyed himself into a chest, and said it was a chest of plate sent from her love and others to be presented to the King. And in the deepest of the night, she being asleep, he opened the chest and came forth of it. And viewed her in her bed and the marks of her body and took away her bracelet, and after accused her of adultery to her love, etc. And in the end how he came with the Romans into England and was taken prisoner, and after revealed to Innogen, who had turned herself into man's apparel and fled to meet her love at Milford Haven, and chanced to fall on the cave in the woods where her two brothers were; and how by eating a sleeping dram they thought she had been dead, and laid

---

[1] Frye, *A Natural Perspective: The Development of Shakespearean Comedy and Romance* (1965), p. 67. The seminal essays in recovering the play's politics were J. P. Brockbank's 'History and histrionics in *Cymbeline*', *S. Sur.*, 11 (1958), 42–8; and Emrys Jones's 'Stuart *Cymbeline*', *Essays in Criticism*, 11 (1961), 84–99. The first person to perceive that it could be read as a play about nationhood – albeit without much concern for the minutiae of Jacobean politics – was G. Wilson Knight, in *The Crown of Life* (1947).

[2] Bodleian Library, MS Ashmole 208, fo. 206r; reproduced in facsimile in S. Schoenbaum, *William Shakespeare: Images and Documents* (1981), pp. 3–20. I have modernized Forman's idiosyncratic spelling and added some punctuation. There is a slightly inaccurate literal transcription in E. K. Chambers, *William Shakespeare: A Study of Facts and Problems* (1930), II, pp. 337–40. The authenticity of Forman's 'Book' has sometimes been questioned, but its genuineness is proved by R. W. Hunt and J. D. Wilson in *Review of English Studies*, 23 (1947), 193–200.

[3] Most transcriptions read 'of of' and assume that Forman omitted 'one'; but what looks like the first 'of' is in fact the numeral '1'.

her in the woods and the body of Cloten by her, in her love's apparel that he left behind him, and how she was found by Lucius, etc.

Tantalizingly, Forman mentions neither the date of the performance nor the name of the playhouse at which he saw it. He did, though, date all the other plays between 20 April and 15 May 1611, and saw them 'at the Globe'. It seems plausible that *Cymbeline* was also staged at the Globe, and around the same time; it could not have been later than 8 September, which was when Forman died. If *Cymbeline* was current in the Globe repertory in spring 1611, it might have been written at any point in the previous two years. Company practice was to keep around twenty plays in the repertory and to alternate them daily. Plays continued to be performed until they ceased to attract spectators, at which point they were replaced: a successful play might have (say) thirty performances over two years.[1] So in spring 1611 *Cymbeline* must still have been new and popular enough to be making a profit.

Establishing a *terminus a quo* is complicated, for it is affected by the play's relationship with three other texts – Beaumont and Fletcher's *Philaster, The Winter's Tale* and Thomas Heywood's *The Golden Age* – and the nature of the debts and the dates involved are all disputed. To begin with *Philaster*, verbal resonances and situational similarities with *Cymbeline* indicate a significant genetic link between the two plays. Scholars have disagreed which way the debt runs: it is the view of this edition (argued below, p. 19) that *Philaster* preceded *Cymbeline* chronologically.[2] Unfortunately, the date of *Philaster* cannot be conclusively fixed. It was certainly written by October 1610, which was when a volume containing a poem praising it, by John Davies of Hereford, was licensed for the press. It was probably written much earlier than this: the Revels editor, Andrew Gurr, favours May 1609, on the basis of the Beaumont and Fletcher chronology, and because of an apparent allusion to a naval project then current.[3] This date may be near the truth, but without firmer evidence it is impossible to be absolutely certain.

The Winter's Tale raises similar questions of priority. It has clear links to *Cymbeline* through their shared romance motifs, jealousy theme and court setting, and there is one specific verbal borrowing: a detail that *The Winter's Tale* repeats from the story by Boccaccio that was one of *Cymbeline*'s sources (see p. 25 below). But again the dating is contested. Stephen Orgel believes that *The Winter's Tale* was brand new in 1611, on the basis of Forman's notebook and incorporation into the text of a dance of satyrs from Ben Jonson's court masque *Oberon* (staged 1 January 1611).[4] Against this is Stanley Wells's and Gary Taylor's case for 1609, based on the view that the borrowing from *Oberon* was a later interpolation, and that the Boccaccio allusion (which comes near the end of the play) shows that Shakespeare was beginning to explore the sources for

---

[1] See A. Gurr, *The Shakespearean Playing Companies* (1996), p. 101.

[2] Not all critics would agree with this, but the arguments boil down to little more than value judgements about the two plays' aesthetic merits (see p. 19, n. 1 below). The belief that *Cymbeline* must have preceded *Philaster* is the main sticking-point for those who assume it was written very early (1608, or early 1609): but as I argue here, all the other evidence points to a later date.

[3] Gurr, ed., *Philaster* (1969), pp. xxvi–xxix. The case is complicated by the fact that Gurr thinks *Cymbeline* came first: hence our combined arguments are circular, since his date for *Philaster* depends on locating *Cymbeline* early in 1609. However, if (as I believe) *Philaster* came first, the difference between our views disappears.

[4] Orgel, ed., *The Winter's Tale* (1996), pp. 79–80.

Cymbeline before he finished his previous project – a practice that can be paralleled in his working practices on other plays.[1] Wells's and Taylor's argument is the more persuasive; but once again complete certainty is elusive.

It has also been claimed that some of the details of Thomas Heywood's spectacular mythological play *The Golden Age* were imitated from *Cymbeline*. *The Golden Age* has scenes in which Jupiter descends on an eagle, and Roger Warren argues that there are verbal reminiscences of Iachimo's monologue in Innogen's bedchamber.[2] If there is a debt here – and it is far from obvious – the borrower must have been Heywood, but his play, too, is hard to date. It was registered for the press in October 1611, but this was some time after it was written, for there had already been two sequels, *The Silver Age* and *The Bronze Age*. Conceivably *The Golden Age* might have been staged as early as mid-1610, though Heywood was such an extraordinarily prolific writer that he may have produced sequels quicker than other, less industrious dramatists. This would push the date of his play back into early 1611.

To summarize: *Cymbeline* was probably written after *Philaster* (1609?) and before *The Golden Age* (late 1610 or 1611). The uncertainty over *The Winter's Tale* puts the sequence of Shakespeare's canon in doubt, but whichever way one comes at it, the result looks the same for *Cymbeline*: if Wells and Taylor are right, *Cymbeline* belongs to late 1609 or 1610; if Orgel is right, it could not be later than 1610, for with *The Winter's Tale* dated to Christmas 1610–11 there would scarcely be time to get *Cymbeline* into the Globe repertoire by the spring. Of course, these arguments are all circular. Since none of the plays is independently datable, assumptions that we make about each one depend on assumptions being made about the other two. But taken together, they do suggest the likeliest window for *Cymbeline* falls in 1610.

More helpful is the internal evidence that can be garnered from the play, for *Cymbeline* makes possible allusions to two events that happened in summer 1610. One was the investiture of Prince Henry as Prince of Wales (5 June 1610). This was the major ceremonial event of the year, and had been in preparation since Christmas. Since Henry was the first crown prince to be invested for nearly a century, and was given his own household and income, his coming of age put the political symbolism of Wales at a premium; and in one centrepiece of the celebrations, Samuel Daniel's masque *Tethys' Festival*, special attention was paid to Milford Haven as the 'port of union' at which Henry's ancestor, Henry Tudor, had landed on his journey to challenge Richard III at Bosworth (discussed on p. 41 below). Milford has similar prominence in *Cymbeline*, and the scenes set in Wales suggest that Shakespeare, too, had suddenly become preoccupied with the iconography and cultural significance of Welshness. It cannot be claimed that Shakespeare was reacting to Henry's investiture, nor that the play would necessarily have been any different had it not taken place. Nonetheless, the coincidence between the play's geography and the summer's political symbolism is very striking.

The other event was the assassination of Henri IV of France on 4 May 1610. This created an atmosphere of panic at Whitehall, especially in view of the impending

[1] Wells and Taylor, *A Textual Companion* (1987), p. 131.
[2] Warren, ed., *Cymbeline* (1998), pp. 66–7.

investiture, which would put the royal family in proximity to large crowds. On 8 and 21 May James asked parliament for new safety measures against fanatics, and parliament advised that Catholics not normally resident in London should be commanded to leave the city. The Privy Council ordered a close guard on recusants, and on 2 June James issued a proclamation that revoked licences permitting nonresident Catholics to come to London, required magistrates to disarm recusants, and commanded that the Oath of Allegiance, first instituted in 1606 in the wake of the Gunpowder Plot, be readministered.[1] There may be an echo of this last provision in Iachimo's claim that every touch of Innogen's hand would 'force the feeler's soul / To th'oath of loyalty' (1.6.100–1) – which is innocent enough in context but would have seemed more significant after the proclamation. More strikingly, these events (I suggest) colour Innogen's words at the reunion with her father when, having been knocked down by Posthumus, she resists the attempts of her servant, Pisanio, to revive her: 'O, get thee from my sight, / Thou gav'st me poison. Dangerous fellow, hence, / Breathe not where princes are' (5.4.236–8). Innogen reacts violently because she believes that Pisanio has tried to kill her with a feigned drug: still, one might have expected her first words on reviving would be to greet her father or husband, not to berate the treacherous servant and demand that he be kept from other vulnerable royal personages. Although Innogen makes no direct reference to Henri IV's assassination, one wonders whether her reason for reacting in this surprising way is because the news from France was still such a hot and shocking topic.

In short, *Cymbeline*'s possible topical allusions, plus Forman's notebook and the links to *Philaster*, *The Winter's Tale* and *The Golden Age*, suggest it was being written either in May/June 1610 or shortly after. And if, as Leeds Barroll argues, the playhouses were closed because of plague between June and November, then it seems likeliest that the first performances came in December 1610, followed by a court performance in the Christmas season 1610–11.[2]

FOLKTALE AND ROMANCE

In the 1870s Edward Dowden was the first to suggest that Shakespeare's life ended in a mood of philosophical calm and otherworldliness. This mood he detected in *Pericles*, *The Winter's Tale*, *Cymbeline* and *The Tempest*, plays he termed 'the romances':[3]

There is a romantic element about these plays. In all there is the same romantic incident of lost children recovered by those to whom they are dear – the daughters of Pericles and Leontes, the sons of Cymbeline and Alonso. In all there is a beautiful romantic background of sea or mountain.

[1] J. F. Larkin and P. L. Hughes, eds., *Stuart Royal Proclamations*, I, *James I* (1973), pp. 245–50. In summer 1610 there was a rash of prosecutions against Catholics who refused to swear the Oath of Allegiance.

[2] L. Barroll, *Politics, Plague, and Shakespeare's Theater* (1991), pp. 245–50. Barroll points out that the play was not staged at court in the 1611–12 season, full details of which are known to us (unlike the 1610–11 season, information about which is lost). He himself favours a date early in 1610.

[3] Dowden, *Shakspere* (1877), p. 32; developed from the less schematic discussion in his *Shakspere: A Critical Study of his Mind and Art* (1875). The term 'romance' had previously been used of *The Tempest* by Coleridge (*Lectures on Shakespeare*, 1818), and of *Cymbeline* by John Potter in 1772 and William Hazlitt in 1817 (Vickers, *Shakespeare: The Critical Heritage*, V, p. 432).

The dramas have a grave beauty, a sweet serenity, which seem to render the name 'comedies' inappropriate; we may smile tenderly, but we never laugh loudly as we read them. Let us, then, name this group consisting of four plays, Romances.

Today it is difficult to endorse Dowden's biographical fantasy, or the casualness with which he used that complex term 'romance'. Nonetheless, his label has been influential, for modern criticism still sees *Cymbeline*'s closest generic affinities as lying with the 'romances'. All four plays have similar motifs: families reunited after extremes of suffering and separation; recognition scenes in which characters reencounter each other in an atmosphere of amazement; oracles, dreams, revelations and deities; identities lost and marvellously restored; fathers weakened by a lack of male heirs and perilously dependent on the chastity of their daughters. And from such scenarios it is a short step to the openly miraculous events of wonder-story and folktale. The wager on a wife's chastity was a theme that reverberated through the literatures of medieval Europe,[1] while Innogen's story has parallels with Cinderella, Sleeping Beauty and, especially, Snow White. Like Snow White, she is forced from home by a stepmother, takes refuge with mysterious strangers and becomes their housekeeper, endures seeming death through a magic potion, and is finally reunited with a handsome lover. 'Snow White' was not written down until the eighteenth century, but its resemblances to *Cymbeline* tempt one to speculate that it must have been in oral circulation much earlier.

Modern anthropological and psychological criticism understands narratives like these as performing complex symbolic work. They stage collective desires and anxieties, and frequently invoke the politics of family life: the traumas of growing up, the difficult transition from childhood to adulthood, and the realization of the self as an entity separate from the family. With their orphaned children, domineering fathers and hostile stepmothers, they voice the pains of separation from one's past, and play out the conflict between the individual's inherited identity as a member of a group and their emerging self-definition as a personality in their own right. In *Cymbeline* Innogen's and Posthumus's problems are defined by Oedipal concerns. Innogen needs to establish herself as an autonomous adult, but her family exerts too tight a hold over her. She is resentful towards her parents, and the proposed marriage with her stepbrother has a whiff of incest that signals the dangers of endogamy and the need to marry beyond the tribe. By contrast, Posthumus lacks a family entirely and seems correspondingly insecure. He will not find himself as an individual until Jupiter provides him with his own kin.[2] More generally, with its nightmares and fantasies, its dismembered body, doubled husbands (Posthumus-Iachimo-Cloten), surrogate fathers (Belarius, Lucius,

[1] See Antti Aarne and Stith Thompson, *The Types of the Folktale* (2nd revision, 1961), Type 882. G. K. Hunter links Cloten to the witch's uncouth son of folktale, like the 'losel' in Spenser's *The Faerie Queene*, 3.7 (*English Drama 1586–1642*, 1996, p. 509). See also W. B. Thorne, '*Cymbeline*: "Lopp'd branches" and the concept of regeneration', *SQ*, 20 (1969), 143–59; and J. Carr, '*Cymbeline* and the validity of myth', *SP*, 75 (1978), 316–30. A later, famous version of the motif comes in Mozart's *Così fan Tutte*.
[2] See M. M. Schwartz, 'Between fantasy and imagination: a psychological exploration of *Cymbeline*', in F. Crews, ed., *Psychoanalysis and Literature* (1970), pp. 249–83; D. S. Brewer, *Symbolic Stories: Traditional Narratives of the Family Drama in English Literature* (1980), pp. 133–46; and M. Skura, 'Interpreting Posthumus' dream from above and below: families, psychoanalysts and literary critics', in M. M. Schwartz and C. Kahn, eds., *Representing Shakespeare: New Psychoanalytic Essays* (1980), pp. 203–16.

Jupiter), unpredictable transitions and punning condensations (from Iachimo's false trunk to Cloten's headless trunk), the story has the unsettling logic of a dream. Ruth Nevo suggests that although *Cymbeline* takes only a small part in the play named after him, he is the presiding ego whose psychic drama is enacted in his children's lives.[1]

Although such modern perspectives go a long way to explaining the story's mysterious power, the term 'romance' remains a problem. It does not denote a specific genre but a literary mode, and one that Renaissance readers did not yet recognize as a separate genre: when Shakespeare's friends assembled the Folio, they divided it into Comedies, Histories and Tragedies, and placed *Cymbeline* with the latter.[2] Moreover, Shakespeare's later 'period' was not confined to romance, but included *Antony and Cleopatra, Coriolanus, Henry VIII* and *The Two Noble Kinsmen*, as well as the revised *King Lear* and, perhaps, some of the sonnets.[3] With its Roman setting, sexual anxieties and historical theme, *Cymbeline* connects closely with these texts, too, and in many ways it unsettles romance assumptions, pulling against the conventions of the mode. It is important, then, to avoid homogenizing its genre, and to acknowledge the varieties of forms in which romance was available to Shakespeare.

HELLENISTIC ROMANCE

Cymbeline's ultimate literary prototypes are Greek romances such as Chariton's *Chaereas and Callirhoe*, Tatius's *Clitophon and Leucippe*, Xenophon of Ephesus's *Ephesiaca*, Longus's *Daphnis and Chloe*, and Heliodorus's *Ethiopica*. These long, rambling narratives were written in the first to third centuries AD for Hellenistic communities living under Roman rule, but came into vogue in sixteenth-century Europe and contributed indirectly to the rise of the novel. They present an ensemble of frequently reiterated motifs: Mediterranean settings; heroes raised by foster parents; lovers enduring hair-raising adventures after being separated by shipwreck or bandits; heroines threatened by rape; identities revealed in dreams and oracles; miraculous reunions of long-sundered partners. In *Chaereas and Callirhoe* the Syracusan Chaereas, persuaded that his wife has betrayed him, spurns her and seemingly causes her death. After her 'funeral' she wakes, is abducted, sold into slavery, and nearly raped. Meanwhile Chaereas learns the truth and pursues her, but he, too, is enslaved and presumed dead in a shipwreck; after many adversities they are eventually reunited. Similar misfortunes, with pastoral interludes and miraculous divine interference, afflict the heroes of the other romances. Such 'mouldy tales' (in Ben Jonson's disparaging phrase) were well known to the Elizabethans, who had translations of Heliodorus (1569), Longus (1587) and Tatius (1597). Shakespeare turned a related story, *Apollonius of Tyre*, into *Pericles*, having previously raided it for the reunion of Egeus's family in *The Comedy of Errors*.

---

[1] Nevo, *Shakespeare's Other Language* (1987), pp. 93–4.

[2] As Stanley Wells says, definitions tend to be circular, labelling as 'romantic' the sorts of motifs that appear in 'romances'; see his 'Shakespeare and romance', in J. R. Brown and B. Harris, eds., *Later Shakespeare* (1966), pp. 49–79.

[3] The New Arden editor of the sonnets, Katherine Duncan-Jones, argues that Shakespeare was still revising them down to their publication in 1609. For links with *Cym.*, see p. 25 below.

He also knew Heliodorus: in *Twelfth Night* Orsino compares himself to the *Ethiopica*'s 'Egyptian thief' (*TN* 5.1.107) who, in a tight corner, chooses to kill his lover.[1]

From Hellenistic romance Shakespeare inherited a structural combination of delay followed by epiphanic closure. In its labyrinthine plots narrative completion seems to be deferred by apparently endless complications; progress towards a goal is denied until a recognition scene (*anagnorisis*) eventually arrives and the proliferating digressions are triumphantly reined in. In *Cymbeline* the crucial deferrals come in Act 3. In 2.5 Posthumus's plot seems heading for tragedy, but is unexpectedly diverted: Posthumus disappears for two acts, and 3.1 and 3.3 introduce new characters with seemingly unrelated stories. This is less a 'slackening' of the design[2] than a subordination of the action to new trains of event, whose directions do not clarify until the final moments. The *anagnorisis* must absorb the apparently diverging plots and their possible endings, establishing an authoritative closure towards which everything turns out to have been working all along. However, the looseness of such narratives makes them prone to generic crossovers: as R. S. White observes, romance is 'a synthesizing genre, able to include in its structure a whole range of literary experiences which we normally try to isolate into other categories'.[3] In *Cymbeline* this undecidability is, until the final scene, unusually acute.

The *Ethiopica* has the combination of incidents closest to *Cymbeline*. Here Shakespeare would have found intertwined narratives, lost children, a wicked stepmother, an imprisoned hero, a sexually threatened heroine, and identities recovered through oracles and tokens. There is one suggestively parallel moment (though not in the same structural position), a pre-echo of Posthumus's reunion with Innogen, when Theagenes strikes Chariclea without realizing who she is:[4]

[Chariclea] ran to him like a mad woman, and, hanging by her arms about his neck, said nothing, but saluted him with certain pitiful lamentations. He, seeing her foul face (belike of purpose beblacked) and her apparel vile and all torn, supposing her to be one of the makeshifts of the city, and a vagabond, cast her off and put her away, and at length gave her a blow on the ear for that she troubled him in seeing Calasiris. Then she spake to him softly: 'Pithius, have you quite forgotten this taper?' Theagenes was stricken with that word as if he had been pierced with a dart, and by tokens agreed on between them knew the taper and, looking steadfastly upon her, espied her beauty shining like the sun appearing through the clouds, cast his arms about her neck.

Perhaps the *Ethiopica* also suggested *Cymbeline*'s most far-fetched incident, Innogen's mistaking of Cloten's corpse for Posthumus. This resembles the episode in which Theagenes, in a dark cave, confuses a corpse for Chariclea's body, falling on it 'and [holding] the same in his arms a great while without moving' – though comparable moments also occur in *Clitophon and Leucippe* and the *Ephesiaca*. Perilous and pathetic situations are the hallmark of these romances: sentimental and sensational by turns, they

---

[1] The *Ethiopica* was the source for several Elizabethan plays, now lost: *Cariclea* (1572), *The Queen of Ethiopia* (1578) and *The White Moor*.
[2] B. A. Mowat, *The Dramaturgy of Shakespeare's Romances* (1976), p. 72.
[3] R. S. White, *Let Wonder Seem Familiar: Endings in Shakespeare's Romance Vision* (2nd edn, 1985), p. 143.
[4] Quoted in S. Wells, 'Shakespeare and romance', p. 51.

manoeuvre their protagonists into extreme and emotionally charged situations, from which they are saved only by sudden revelation, coincidence or sheer happenstance.

In its own time Hellenistic romance reflected the preoccupations of a large-scale open society comfortable with its values but prone to anxiety about the individual's insignificance.[1] Their protagonists are noble but far from heroic. Helplessly driven by misfortune, they are dwarfed by the complex world and keep going only by faith that their sufferings will eventually be relieved. By contrast, *Cymbeline* is less permissive: its characters are on trial, and the happy ending is conditional on them showing evidence of virtue. This creates difficulties in the working out of plot. For example, Posthumus's conviction of his own worthlessness and his need to validate his status as a member of the Leonati are contradicted by the ghosts' complaints that he was unfairly treated and by Iachimo's frankly misleading recollections of how noble he had seemed at Rome. Such structural tensions show the play manoeuvring to square romance's miraculous consolations with the demands of a more ethically centred narrative. They introduce a moral accountancy which reflects the adjustments that romance received in the hands of Shakespeare's contemporaries.

SIDNEY AND SPENSER
Even had Shakespeare not known the *Ethiopica*, he would have encountered a narrative in the Heliodoran manner in Philip Sidney's *The Arcadia*. Shakespeare knew *The Arcadia* well, for he used it for the Gloucester plot in *King Lear*, in the process absorbing into his tragedy Sidney's romance motifs and interest in human suffering and the inscrutability of providence. J. F. Danby long ago suggested that *The Arcadia*'s lofty and philosophical narrative was the main English precursor of Shakespearean romance.[2] Although Danby's case is weakened by the idealizing aristocratic gloss that he puts on *The Arcadia*, it is true that *Cymbeline*'s weak king, power-hungry queen, cynical villain and high-minded heroes – enduring fortune's misprisions in the hope that their sufferings will some day be justified – could have stepped straight from Sidney's pages. It is hardly coincidental that *The Arcadia*'s equivalent character to *King Lear*'s Edgar is called Leonatus.

Cymbeline's clearest Sidneian allusion is to the wicked queen Cecropia.[3] Sister-in-law to the weak king Basilius, Cecropia wants to seize power by wedding her son to one of the two princesses and imprisons them in an attempt to force a marriage. Her son is no Cloten, but she has exactly the same hypocritical radiance as Cymbeline's consort. She treats her nieces with a teasing veneer of kindness, making 'courtesy the outside of mischief' (p. 444) and offering them 'such a smiling as showed no love and yet could not but be lovely' (p. 553).[4] An atheist and materialist, she holds the world to be ruled entirely by natural causes – an attitude perhaps echoed in the cruel scientific experiments of Shakespeare's queen. Her end, too, is similar: she dies in agony,

---

[1] See the excellent discussion by B. P. Reardon, *The Form of Greek Romance* (1991).
[2] *Poets on Fortune's Hill* (1952), pp. 74–107.
[3] Danby, *Poets on Fortune's Hill*, p. 61; White, *Let Wonder Seem Familiar*, pp. 139–41. Another possible literary source for Cecropia is the wicked queen Amata in Virgil's *Aeneid*.
[4] *Arcadia*, ed. M. Evans (1977).

confessing 'with most desperate but not repenting mind' that she had intended to poison the princesses, 'but everybody seeing, and glad to see her end, had left obedience to her tyranny' (p. 573). Cymbeline's queen is often regarded as a mere fairytale villain, but an audience versed in *The Arcadia* would have understood why Innogen calls her a 'tyrant / [Who] can tickle where she wounds' (1.1.84–5).

Against Cecropia's terrifying guile stands the passive but principled resistance of the two princesses. Their female heroism probably helped shape the conception of Innogen, who combines Pamela's courage and self-reliance with Philoclea's ready access to her emotions.[1] Innogen's polite but unyielding defence of her family also echoes Sidney's recurrent concern with the limits of obedience. This issue is explored at greater length in the role of the unfaithful servant Pisanio, whose decision to disobey his master is, remarkably, endorsed by the play. Posthumus's admission that 'Every good servant does not all commands; / No bond, but to do just ones' (5.1.6–7) has an aristocratic radicalism that is resonantly Sidneian. Of course, *Cymbeline* lacks any equivalent to the climactic confrontation with Cecropia and Pamela's apology for God's providence, but such concerns carry forward to the plot involving Posthumus, who, once imprisoned, voices much the same combination of self-doubt, desire for deliverance and resignation to the divine will as Pamela expresses in her famous prison prayer. Sidney's characters never quite receive such unequivocal assurances as Posthumus has from Jupiter that providence will protect them: proof that their sufferings have meaning is always just out of reach. Nonetheless, *Cymbeline*'s political and philosophical bearings are defined by framing situations that might have come straight from *The Arcadia*.[2]

The other Elizabethan romance important for *Cymbeline* is Spenser's *The Faerie Queene*. The first complete text, including the fragmentary seventh book, was printed in 1609, and traces of Spenser in *The Winter's Tale* suggest that its reissue affected Shakespeare profoundly. Cymbeline's name appears in *The Faerie Queene*'s chronicle of British kings (2.10), in a passage alluding to what was virtually the only historical 'fact' known about him, that he was king in Britain when Christ was born:[3]

> Next him [Cassibelan] Tenantius reigned, then Kimbeline,
> What time th'eternal lord in fleshly slime
> Enwombed was, from wretched Adams line
> To purge away the guilt of sinful crime:
> That heauenly grace so plenteously displayed;
> (O too high ditty for my sinful rime.)   (2.10.50)

---

[1] Danby, *Poets on Fortune's Hill*, p. 104.

[2] There is also a headless-body connection: Cecropia makes Philoclea's lover believe that he has seen her being beheaded. The 'golden chance' that Posthumus gets from Jupiter, but fears may only be like the 'fangled world, a garment/Nobler than that it covers' (5.3.226–9), has Sidneian resonances: it recalls Sidney's distinction, in the *Apology for Poetry*, between the brazen world of nature and the golden world created by the poets. The dirge, too, with its 'golden lads and girls' coming 'to dust' catches the same ambivalent Arcadianism.

[3] This circumstance was also noted in nonfictional historiography: see John Speed's *Theatre of the Empire of Great Britain* (1611), p. 189; and James I, *Works* (1616), p. 609. Symptomatically, it passes unmentioned in William Camden's *Britannia* (1586): see p. 37 below.

As we shall see (p. 23 below), this historical circumstance bears on the ending of the play, but Spenser's presence is most directly felt in the Welsh scenes, which explore the antithesis between court and country in a manner very reminiscent of Book 6, the legend of courtesy. Innogen's complaint that courtiers claim 'all's savage but at court' (4.2.33) recollects figures like Sir Satyrane, the satyr knight who is chivalrous despite his forest upbringing, and the 'savage man' who rescues Sir Calepine from the abusive Sir Turpine (*FQ*, 6.4). Such characters trouble *The Faerie Queene* by unsettling the link between social and moral hierarchies. The savage man lives like a beast, without home, clothes or language, yet his innate chivalry puts the discourteous Turpine to shame. Churlishly denying Calepine common civilities and attacking him when he is unhorsed, Turpine is appropriately defeated by a wild man who possesses naturally the compassion that the more courtly knight lacks. It is only a small step from this unmannerly knight to that civilized brute Cloten.

Of course, the princes are not wild men, for their life is far from savage, but their landscape is an austere life contrasting with court comforts, the 'hard' pastoral of the mountains rather than a 'soft' pastoral of fields. Here they exhibit an untaught civility which shows 'divine' Nature at work, an 'invisible instinct' fostering 'valour/That wildly grows in them' (4.2.168–82). Nature is the presiding goddess of *The Faerie Queene* Book 7, and Belarius's reflection 'How hard it is to hide the sparks of nature' (*Cym.*, 3.3.79) harks back to Spenser's savage man, whose 'sparkes of gentle mynd' break out despite being 'rudely borne' in 'desert wood' (*FQ*, 6.5.1–2). In the encounter between the princes' natural civility and Cloten's courtly boorishness, there is more than a hint of Spenserean allegory. Cloten takes the boys for 'mountaineers' – by which he seems to mean outlaws like those who frequently cause the separations of romance (in Spenser's Book 6 the shepherdess Pastorella is abducted by brigands and taken to their cave). But it is the prince who lacks civil graces, and his rudeness that provokes Guiderius, almost involuntarily, to violence. Reacting more to Cloten's insults than his physical threats, the noble savage responds to the courtly boor in the only way he knows, by killing him. The impression that Guiderius's inner clock runs on a separate time from everyone else's recurs in the final scene, when he confesses to Cloten's killing without embarrassment, despite the ripples of shock it causes. To courtly society he seems uncouth, but in this Spenserean dramaturgy the fact that he can behave no other way signals his status as the truly worthy prince. His presence renews Cymbeline's court, but on the basis of merit as much as status.[1]

Sidney and Spenser led complex afterlives, for their works were partly at odds with the cultural ethos of the post-Elizabethan state. Though foundational writers for early Stuart culture, they depicted aristocratic society ambivalently, their knightly tales being complicated with questioning and inner strain. This made them attractive to readers who were disenchanted with the unheroic Jacobean court, and nostalgic for the life they thought they remembered under James's predecessor. As we shall see, *Cymbeline*'s

---

[1] There are further similarities to forest-educated Sir Tristram who slays a scornful knight (*FQ*, 6.2); and to the aged hermit, a retired knight, who entertains Arthur and Serena with homely fare (*FQ*, 6.5.39) – a figure reminiscent of Belarius. See F. Kermode, *Renaissance Essays* (1971), p. 231; and W. G. Zeeveld, *The Temper of Shakespeare's Thought* (1974), pp. 191–7. 'Great Nature' is also the protector of Posthumus (5.3.134).

praise of peace and promulgation of British identity would have been congenial to James. Yet with its weak king, toadying courtiers, exiled heirs and suffering subjects, its representation of court politics is less than idealized, and it brings to mind anxieties about the conduct of power that were all too familiar in 1610, when king and parliament were at loggerheads over finance and prerogative. By harking back to romances from the last reign, *Cymbeline* occupied a double-edged relationship to the dominant culture, and remained internally detached from the Jacobean norms which, notwithstanding, it endorsed: it is a curious circumstance that its villain's name is 'James' in Italian. Its scepticism about courtly civility is a sign that its debt to Sidney and Spenser was political as well as literary.

DRAMATIC ROMANCE

If *Cymbeline*'s literary models came from the recent past, its theatrical prototypes were more remote, for in returning to romance Shakespeare was recoiling to dramas remembered from his childhood. Although only three such dramatic romances have survived (*Clyomon and Clamydes, c.* 1570; *Common Conditions,* 1576; and *The Rare Triumphs of Love and Fortune,* 1582), titles preserved in theatrical records show that romance was a staple of the early Elizabethan stage. Today the surviving examples seem desperately crude: Sidney had such plays in mind when he complained that English dramatists were incompetent, shifting their scenes unpredictably from country to country so that 'the player, when he cometh in, must ever begin with telling where he is'.[1] Even in 1610 such dramaturgy would have seemed very old-fashioned: when Ben Jonson poked fun at plays in which a 'Chorus wafts you o'er the seas . . . [and] creaking throne comes down, the boys to please', he was registering the gulf that separated his age's tastes from those of an earlier generation.[2] Yet the oracles, exiled princesses and sundered lovers of dramatic romance were surprisingly long-lived. In more developed forms romance lasted at the popular end of the market well into Stuart times, in plays such as *The Thracian Wonder* (1599?) or *Mucedorus* (1588?) – this last, revived in 1607 and in its thirteenth printed edition by 1639, perhaps the period's most popular play.[3] Dramatic romance appealed to citizen audiences whose tastes ran to novellas, spectacle and chivalry: Jonson's scorn for 'tales and tempests' expressed a social as well as aesthetic preference. Yet it was precisely this now-forgotten form that was the theatrical model for *The Winter's Tale* and *Cymbeline.*

    Cymbeline shares features with both *Clyomon and Clamydes* and *Love and Fortune.* *Clyomon* follows the adventures of two wandering knights whose improbable adventures blow them separately around a geographically imprecise Europe until surprising chances reunite them. The *Cymbeline* connection comes through Clyomon's lover, the princess Neronis. She is abducted but escapes, disguised as a page, and takes shelter

---

[1] See P. Russell, 'Romantic narrative plays 1570–1590', in J. R. Brown and B. Harris, eds., *Elizabethan Theatre* (1966), pp. 107–30; and L. G. Salingar, *Shakespeare and the Traditions of Comedy* (1974), pp. 73–5. Salingar demonstrates how ubiquitous these motifs were in popular Elizabethan drama.

[2] *Ben Jonson,* 3.303 (prologue to the revised *Every Man in His Humour, c.* 1610).

[3] Anne Barton speculates that Shakespeare was responsible for the revisions in the 1610 edition of *Mucedorus,* though arguably anyone could have done them (*Essays, Mainly Shakespearean,* 1994, pp. 198–9). *The Thracian Wonder* is interesting as a significant precursor for several motifs in *The Winter's Tale.* See also G. K. Hunter, *English Drama 1586–1642,* pp. 502–5.

with a shepherd, complaining of the hardness of her lot. Here she discovers a dead body, above which hangs Clyomon's emblem, a golden shield. Taking the body for Clyomon, she attempts suicide, but Providence descends and restrains her, revealing the corpse's true identity and promising that she will be reunited with her lover. Later she meets Clyomon, but since both are disguised, they fail to recognize each other. Calling herself 'Coeur d'Acier' (heart of steel) she becomes his page, until the *anagnorisis* in which identities are revealed.

Love and Fortune is even closer to *Cymbeline*. It concerns the love of Princess Fidelia for Hermione (a man's name in this play), an orphan brought up at her father's court. Her brother thinks their relationship is shameful and fights with Hermione, who wounds him. Hermione is banished and in the countryside he meets a hermit, who is really an exiled nobleman, driven from court by 'fawning friends' who procured his fall; he turns out to be Hermione's father. The ending finally comes through the intervention of the gods. Fortune and Venus have overseen events from the first, but when they fail to resolve them, Jupiter takes command and reveals the truth about Hermione and his father.

The parallels between Innogen and Neronis, and Posthumus and Hermione, and Shakespeare's use of the names Hermione and Fidelia (Fidele), are so striking that J. M. Nosworthy felt that *Love and Fortune* must have been *Cymbeline*'s starting-point.[1] But as Leo Salingar emphasizes, the specific debts are less significant than *Cymbeline*'s general resemblance to the whole species of dramatic romance of which these were representative examples.[2] Of course, Shakespeare's treatment cast the earlier romances into the shade: beside his play their sprawling form and clunking mechanics seem indiscriminate and inartistic. Yet *Cymbeline* does partially renew the older conventions, and it uses their technical freedoms to create a dramaturgy at once simple and sophisticated. It exploits the unpredictability of the romances and their telescoping of time and space, while its neofeudal anachronisms ('knights of the battle', and so forth) recall the earlier plays' fantasy medievalism. It adopts their naively explanatory devices, such as the expository monologues by Cornelius and Belarius (speeches that Victorian editors rejected as unworthy of Shakespeare), or daring moments such as Iachimo's emergence from the trunk or the brandishing of Cloten's empty head, devices which evoke the pared-down staging of plays like *Mucedorus*, in which traumatic events happen casually and with a certain grim humour. And in the pointedly archaic language spoken by the ghosts, *Cymbeline* resurrects the relentlessly stiff aural world of a theatre that had yet to unlock the fluency of blank verse. If in *A Midsummer Night's Dream* Shakespeare had mocked the lumbering fourteeners of mid-Tudor drama, fifteen years on his attitude was more

---

[1] Nosworthy, ed., *Cymbeline* (1955), p. xxv.

[2] Salingar, *Shakespeare and the Traditions of Comedy*, p. 38. Salingar also stresses *Cymbeline*'s structural debts to the miracle plays of medieval Europe. There are striking similarities to the fourteenth-century French miracle *Ostes, Roi d'Espaigne*, in which King Ostes wagers his kingdom on his wife's chastity and, persuaded she has been unfaithful, decides to kill her. The Virgin Mary intervenes and advises the wife to escape disguised as a boy; Ostes converts to the Saracens, but repents and is told by God – in another descent scene – to go to Rome, where he reencounters his wife. Of course, Shakespeare probably did not know this play directly, but the parallels in plot and stagecraft suggest how much *Cymbeline* owes to the underlying tradition of popular narrative theatre, a drama which has now almost completely disappeared from view. On *Cymbeline* and *Ostes*, see R. G. Hunter, *Shakespeare and the Comedy of Forgiveness* (1965).

complex, for the ghosts' archaic metre foregrounds their difference, making them seem like visitors from another, less spacious dramatic world. Their voices deepen the play by linking it with an older and harsher universe. Perplexed by sorrows that seem to them ineluctably tragic, the ghosts need Jupiter, and his more commanding speech, to show them that their sufferings are not meaningless. This edition acknowledges *Cymbeline*'s purposeful harking back to mid-Tudor drama by printing, for the first time, the ghosts' verses as the fourteeners that technically they are.

Such considerations qualify the often-repeated claim that Shakespeare's turn to romance was prompted by changes in the London theatres, and specifically by his company's acquisition of the Blackfriars playhouse which, after 1609, it operated in tandem with the Globe. A small indoor theatre, the Blackfriars was an intimate venue. It needed a quieter acting style than the open-air Globe, and its admission prices were higher, making for a select, even courtly audience. Its spectators would have known the elaborate spectacle of the Whitehall masques, and it is tempting to see moments like the descent of Jupiter as calculated for their tastes. Indeed, precisely this device was staged – albeit not until 1632 – in Aurelian Townshend's masque *Tempe Restored* (figure 1).[1] Some aspects of *Cymbeline* do seem designed for Blackfriars conditions. The intensity and focus of the first two acts – especially the wager at Rome and bedroom scenes – cry out for intimate staging, while the emphatic five-act structure matches the arrangements at indoor playhouses, where the custom was to perform music between the acts, requiring four clear pauses in the action. Yet the King's Men would have mounted *Cymbeline* at the Globe, too, and it was the open-air playhouses that provided most scope for stunning visual effects. *Cymbeline*'s spectacle is easily paralleled in other popular dramas, such as the four mythological plays written by Thomas Heywood for the Red Bull – *The Golden Age, The Silver Age, The Brazen Age* and *The Iron Age* (1611–13) – epic farragoes which utilized some of the same devices, including several descents by Jupiter on his eagle, with thunderbolt in hand. *Cymbeline* has sometimes been staged as a studio play, but it needs large spaces for its architecture to work, and its rising action means that without sufficient visual display the final act can seem anticlimactic: Jupiter has to be stunning to be effective. The play's literary self-consciousness may reflect a Blackfriars taste for tragicomedy, but its stagecraft belongs firmly to the popular theatre.[2]

TRAGEDY AND TRAGICOMEDY

When *Cymbeline* was published in the First Folio, it was placed with the tragedies, and titled 'The Tragedy of Cymbeline'. This looks like a category error, but arguably it is only our modern assumptions about romance that make the arrangement seem

---

[1] Although flying effects have been taken as typical of the court stage's elaborate mechanics, they were in fact relatively rare in early masques. Ben Jonson's *Haddington Masque* (1608) had Venus descending in a chariot, but only to the top of a cliff; in *The Golden Age Restored* (1616), Pallas descends completely from the 'heavens' to the stage. The Elizabethan court stage occasionally used flying machines; see J. Astington, *English Court Theatre 1558–1642* (1999), p. 41.

[2] See M. Lomax, *Stage Images and Traditions: Shakespeare to Ford* (1987).

Figure 1. Inigo Jones's design for Jupiter descending on an eagle, in Aurelian Townshend's masque *Tempe Restored* (1632)

unsuitable.[1] The editors had no space for 'romances', and by deeming *Cymbeline* a tragedy they acknowledged that its war, deaths and Augustan setting gave it greater amplitude than the other comedies. Its events may be unhistorical, but they are more founded in 'fact' than *King Lear*, and the acting tradition considered it a tragedy until surprisingly late. The adaptations by Marsh (1755), Hawkins (1759), Garrick (1761) and Kemble (1801) were all called tragedies, and not until the nineteenth century did terms begin to shift. *Cymbeline* was first called a 'historical' play in Mrs Inchbald's *British Theatre* (1808), and later editions of Kemble adopted this label. Only with Irving's adaptation of 1896 was it claimed for comedy.

Cymbeline's affinities lie more with the Tragedies than the Comedies. Innogen seems to be descended from the feisty comic heroines who circumvent their gender by cross-dressing, but disguise fails to liberate her.[2] She dwindles into the subordinated roles of housekeeper or page, and is less like the witty women chasing husbands than the suffering wives and daughters – the Juliets, Cordelias and Desdemonas. The one 'comic' prototype she resembles is Hero in *Much Ado*, whose rejection by her husband on her wedding day pushes that comedy to breaking-point. Like Posthumus, Claudio spurns Hero, believing that she has betrayed him, and the plan devised by Friar Francis – to pretend the accusation has killed her and hide her until Claudio comes to regret his actions – directly prefigures the scheme devised by Pisanio.[3] The connection is all the stronger since, in the intervening years, Shakespeare had written a fully tragic version of the slandered-wife scenario in *Othello*, which *Cymbeline* reproduces in compressed form. Iachimo's name links him to Iago, and the ghosts' complaint that Posthumus was made the 'geck and scorn' of a 'slight thing of Italy' (5.3.142) is a capsule version of the *Othello* plot.[4] Only the geographical separation of husband and wife, and the fact that Posthumus discovers an unexpected capacity for forgiveness, keep *Cymbeline* on this side of tragedy.

When the ghosts ask Jupiter not to 'show thy spite on mortal flies', they revise 'as flies to wanton boys are we to the gods' (*Lear*, 4.1.37–8), predicting that the action will eventually reenfold tragedy under the aegis of romance. The presence of tragic scenarios that threaten but are ultimately averted signals the play's connections with tragicomedy, a rising form in Stuart theatre. Jacobean tragicomedy developed partly in response to

---

[1] Nosworthy (*Cymbeline*, p. xiii) and W. W. Greg (*The Shakespeare First Folio*, 1955, pp. 80–81n.) speculated that the manuscript arrived late at the printing house, and that the play would otherwise have been placed with comedies. Leah Marcus offers the extreme view that *Cymbeline* was deliberately printed out of place (*Puzzling Shakespeare: Local Reading and its Discontents*, 1988, pp. 108–9). But it should be remembered that *Cymbeline* was not the last play to be printed, for *Troilus and Cressida* arrived later, and was positioned in a separate set of gatherings after the Histories. See Textual Analysis, p. 256 below.

[2] Nancy K. Hayles, 'Sexual disguise in *Cymbeline*', *MLQ*, 41 (1980), 230–47.

[3] There are further subterranean connections, since *Much Ado* and *Cymbeline* duplicate a name (Leonato/Leonatus) and *Much Ado* has a ghost character 'Innogen' (wife of Leonato) who is named in the opening stage direction but does not speak or reappear. The connection is explored in H. D. Swander, '*Cymbeline* and the "blameless hero"', *ELH*, 31 (1964), 259–70. For similarities between Innogen and Helena in *All's Well* – another heroine abandoned by her husband and wandering on her own – see C. Neely, *Broken Nuptials in Shakespeare's Plays* (1985), pp. 179–84.

[4] The parallels between Posthumus and Othello, and Innogen and Desdemona, are fully explored in A. C. Kirsch, *Shakespeare and the Experience of Love* (1981), pp. 144–73.

examples out of Italy, where dramatists led the way in exploring the possibilities of mixed genres. One key moment was the publication of *The Faithful Shepherd* (1602), Edward Dymock's version of Guarini's pastoral tragicomedy *Il Pastor Fido* (1590), English imitations of which quickly followed. With its slandered heroine, death-marked lovers and happy ending brought on by oracles and rediscovered identities, *Il Pastor Fido* provided an influential template. Its emphasis on the redemption of suffering through hidden providential ends is paralleled in *Cymbeline*: although *Cymbeline* lacks *Il Pastor Fido*'s love-lorn shepherds, Jupiter's axiom that 'Whom best I love, I cross; to make my gift, / The more delayed, delighted' (5.3.165–6) echoes several passages in Guarini.[1] More immediate models were presented by the native tragicomedy developing in the artful and aesthetically self-aware work of Marston and Beaumont and Fletcher. Such plays, which reflected a heightened English consciousness of the hybrid tendencies of inherited dramatic traditions, were increasingly common at the Jacobean indoor playhouses.[2]

It has been claimed that the emergence of tragicomedy went hand in hand with a vogue for experiment at the indoor theatres.[3] Certainly their audiences had adventurous tastes, and the boy companies, who before 1608 performed at these houses, were known for a sophisticated, even controversial style. They traded in fantastic and self-referential effects: burlesque, parody and pastiche, coups de théâtre and outrageous theatrical excess. Tragicomedy suited them, for it yoked conflicting materials, making for a kind of alienation effect. In Marston's tragicomedies the tonal clashes between lyric and satire are so violent that it is often unclear where seriousness ends and parody takes over. Beaumont and Fletcher's tragicomedies are more integrated, but the pleasure they give still comes from their artfulness in mingling kinds and managing generic options. Typically they present (in Guarini's words) '*il pericolo, non la morte*' ('the danger not the death'): they put characters into situations that seem heading for catastrophe, only for last-minute solutions to be found that redeem the action by discovering a comic pattern working below. With their protagonists ignorant of their circumstances, a double response is created: the rhetoric is tragic, but the spectators intuit that events will turn out more happily than the characters expect. In James Shirley's words, 'passions [are] raised to that excellent pitch and by such insinuating degrees that you shall not choose but consent and go along with them . . . and then stand admiring the subtle tracks of your engagement'.[4] This form trades on a combination of emotional involvement and aesthetic distance. The audience is moved by what happens, while it enjoys the theatrical skill with which anxieties are aroused and allayed.

---

[1] For some detailed verbal parallels, see A. C. Kirsch, *Jacobean Dramatic Perspectives* (1971), pp. 10–11; and Bernard Harris, '"What's past is prologue": *Cymbeline* and *Henry VIII*', in Brown and Harris, *Later Shakespeare*, p. 223.

[2] *Cymbeline*'s tragicomic dimensions are analysed in Joan Hartwig, *Shakespeare's Tragicomic Vision* (1972); Coburn Freer, *The Poetics of Jacobean Drama* (1981); R. Y. Young, 'Slander in *Cymbeline* and other Jacobean tragicomedies', *ELR*, 13 (1983), 182–202; and Robert Henke, *Pastoral Transformations: Italian Tragicomedy and Shakespeare's Late Plays* (1997).

[3] See Kirsch, *Jacobean Dramatic Perspectives*, pp. 1–6; and Hunter, *English Drama 1586–1642*, p. 284.

[4] From Shirley's preface to the 1647 Beaumont and Fletcher folio, quoted in Hunter, *English Drama 1586–1642*, p. 520.

The trace of Beaumont and Fletcher affects *Cymbeline* through its occasional echoes of the situations and stagecraft of their tragicomedy *Philaster*, performed by the King's Men *c*. 1609. Philaster is a dispossessed Sicilian prince, living unhappily in the court of his rival, the King of Calabria. He loves the king's daughter Arethusa, but her father intends her for a clownish suitor, the Spanish prince Pharamond. The two suitors fight, and an enemy of Arethusa's accuses her of sexual incontinence. Consumed with jealousy, Philaster repudiates Arethusa and tries to kill her in the woods, but he is himself hurt by a passer-by. He is condemned to death, but the princess stands by him and the citizens mutiny, at which point the King restores his lands. Critics have been reluctant to suppose that *Cymbeline* could have owed much to *Philaster*, even though Shakespeare's company had staged it barely months before.[1] The resemblances are mainly stock motifs – a fatherless prince, rivals for a princess's love, the princess slandered, rejected and threatened with murder – and *Philaster* is quite different dramaturgically. With its plot constructed as a series of sensational reversals, its protagonists are set on an emotional switchback, oscillating between contradictory feelings that stabilize only when the denouement uncovers hidden information. The subjectivity of Fletcher's characters is quite unlike that of Shakespeare's: their inner polarizations are so acute that as individuals they seem thoroughly dislocated. However, the texts do share a name (Bellario/Belarius), and there are some small but distinctive verbal echoes which suggest that, on the level of language at least, memories of *Philaster* were fossilized in *Cymbeline*.[2] Part of *Cymbeline*'s pleasure will come from the way it mines Fletcher's seam, drawing the tragic emotions of pity and fear into the tragicomic modes of admiration and wonder.

Cymbeline's engagement with tragicomedy is most evident in its stylistic sensitivity and self-awareness about its own art.[3] This is most apparent in its language, which often appears excessively mannered and compressed. Frequently its speakers seem divorced from their own verse, striving after notions that they can barely find words to articulate:

---

[1] The full case for *Philaster*'s priority was first made in Ashley H. Thorndike, *The Influence of Beaumont and Fletcher on Shakespeare* (1901); the case against is led by Harold S. Wilson, '*Philaster* and *Cymbeline*', in A. S. Downer, ed., *English Institute Essays 1951* (1952), pp. 146–67. It is difficult not to feel that the reluctance to see *Philaster* as the precursor is motivated by the assumption that Beaumont and Fletcher were 'decadents' and that it demeans Shakespeare to suppose he imitated them. But the case for *Philaster*'s chronological priority now seems unanswerable: see p. 4 above. The best modern comparison of the two plays is by Hunter, *English Drama 1586–1642*, pp. 508–12.

[2] At 2.1.31–2, *Cymbeline* repeats a pun on 'stranger/strange fellow' from *Philaster* 1.1.77–8; Philaster's words about the passer-by who wounds him – 'The gods take part against me, could this boor/Have held me thus else' (4.5.103–4) – are echoed by Iachimo (*Cym.* 5.2.2–6); and *Philaster*'s subtitle, 'Love Lies A-Bleeding' resonates with Posthumus's epistolary claim that 'Thy mistress, Pisanio, hath played the strumpet in my bed, the testimonies whereof lies bleeding in me' (3.4.21–2). More impressionistically, the dialogue with which *Cymbeline* opens resembles *Philaster* 1.1, and Cloten's approaches to Innogen's lady (2.3.68–80) are similar to Pharamond's attempted seduction of a waiting-woman (*Philaster* 2.2.1–56). However, the name Bellario could also have come from Bellaria in Robert Greene's *Pandosto* (the source for *The Winter's Tale*).

[3] For discussion of the play's language, see Anne Barton, *Essays, Mainly Shakespearean*, pp. 161–81; S. Palfrey, *Late Shakespeare: A New World of Words* (1997); and Harley Granville-Barker's interesting observations in his *Preface to Cymbeline* (1930).

FIRST GENTLEMAN He that hath missed the Princess is a thing
  Too bad for bad report; and he that hath her –
  I mean, that married her (alack, good man,
  And therefore banished!) – is a creature such
  As to seek through the regions of the earth
  For one his like, there would be something failing
  In him that should compare. I do not think
  So fair an outward and such stuff within
  Endows a man but he.
SECOND GENTLEMAN You speak him far.
FIRST GENTLEMAN I do extend him, sir, within himself,
  Crush him together, rather than unfold
  His measure duly.   (1.1.16–27)

The task, to introduce Posthumus's story, is simple enough, but the Gentleman's manner, awkwardly yoking comparison with hyperbole, is so convoluted that it unsettles faith in the antitheses that it asserts. Cloten's undesirability and Posthumus's perfection are, he says, so obvious as to be inexpressible, and comparisons inevitably fall short. This makes his praise seem redundant: his explanations are undone by their own disclaimers, and his attempt to gloss the failure, with its mind-bending paradox about 'extending' Posthumus within himself, only compounds the difficulty. The slide of positive and negative terms into each other is especially disconcerting, the praise being impeded by the syntax in which it is couched ('something failing . . . I do not think . . . rather'). Moreover, as events show, the Gentleman's views are quite wrong, for Posthumus turns out to be far less of a paragon than he predicts. His speech misdirects the audience, creating emotional and intellectual perplexity. It does not express his 'character' but (rather like the perspective trick that Innogen describes in 1.3) creates a dramatic puzzle that the ensuing action will unravel. The questions he asks of Posthumus will be answered in quite different ways than he foresees.

   A similar double vision is created by Arviragus's lament over Fidele's corpse:

              With fairest flowers,
  Whilst summer lasts and I live here, Fidele,
  I'll sweeten thy sad grave. Thou shalt not lack
  The flower that's like thy face, pale primrose, nor
  The azured harebell, like thy veins: no, nor
  The leaf of eglantine, whom not to slander,
  Outsweetened not thy breath. The ruddock would
  With charitable bill – O bill sore shaming
  Those rich-left heirs that let their fathers lie
  Without a monument! – bring thee all this,
  Yea, and furred moss besides, when flowers are none,
  To winter-ground thy corpse.
Guiderius.   Prithee have done,
  And do not play in wench-like words with that
  Which is so serious.
                  (4.2.217–30)

Generations of commentators have echoed Guiderius's rebuke, sensing a gap between the moment's emotion and Arviragus's artfulness. The poetic diction, the pathetic fallacy that takes the flower's pallor and the bird's charity as expressions of sympathy, and the moralizing parenthesis that steps aside from grief, all make Arviragus's words seem more ventriloquized than authentic. As Anne Barton says, they are 'hard to square with what we know about this princely rustic'.[1] In fact, we can track his language to his character – it advances the emerging distinction between the sentimental younger prince and his more heroic elder brother, whose eagerness for action proclaims him as Britain's heir – but the distancing of word and speaker underlines that the elegy is conditioned by generic factors. The elevation of pathos over passion, tenderness over torment, and sweetness over sorrow, is not peculiar to Arviragus but belongs to modes of pastoral lament that prepare for the funeral rites shortly to be performed. And, of course, Arviragus speaks truer than he knows, for Fidele is not really dead, and mourning is premature. Were his lament fully tragic, it would overwhelm the episode and make the resurrection moments later seem meretricious. His language alludes to patterns that the audience intuits but which are only subliminally apparent to him. It creates an aesthetic self-awareness, reassuring the spectators that at some level his pain is limited by the play's as yet incompletely disclosed design.

The character with the greatest self-consciousness is Iachimo. He is the play's great stylist, whose power lies in his ability to occupy different personae. He speaks the play's most developed tragic rhetoric, but it is rhetoric aware of itself as a pose:

> It cannot be i'th'eye – for apes and monkeys
> 'Twixt two such shes would chatter this way, and
> Contemn with mows the other; nor i'th'judgment –
> For idiots in this case of favour would
> Be wisely definite; nor i'th'appetite –
> Sluttery, to such neat excellence opposed,
> Should make desire vomit emptiness,
> Not so allured to feed.   (1.6.38–45)

The intellectual and moral disturbance of this language gives Iachimo's character a potentially tragic aspect. His speech is densely packed, rifted by syntactical hiatuses, and dominated by images selected for their meanness (apes, idiots, sluts) or paradox (the yoking of abstraction and materiality in 'desire vomit[ing] emptiness'): it implies that he sees further than the other characters, or in more complex ways. Yet this is not so much the language of tragedy as an ingenious simulacrum of it. Its difficulty is strategic, for Iachimo is attempting to wrong-foot Innogen and entangle her in a contrived scenario. Her immunity to his lies is an early hint that the story will end happily: his voice is less dominant than he supposes. But, unembarrassed, Iachimo simply switches to a new, equally persuasive voice, and when we next meet him (2.2) he has a third voice, cataloguing Innogen's body with a disconcerting mixture of envy and delight. His combination of worship and violation leaves the audience unsure of its bearings: by suggesting that he appreciates her more fully than her husband does, it makes it difficult not to admire the art with which he describes her body, even though it comes uncomfortably close to pornography. But none of these is Iachimo's natural voice, since when he first appears he speaks a cultivated prose quite unlike anything

[1] Barton, *Essays, Mainly Shakespearean*, p. 170.

we later hear, and his linguistic skill baffles Posthumus, who is at a loss to fathom his intentions: 'This is but a custom in your tongue; you bear a graver purpose, I hope' (1.4.112). In fact, all Iachimo's personae are performances, behind which no intrinsic self can be discerned. Even in the final scene, his long, self-advertising summary of the wager plot reaffirms his linguistic power, despite the moral censure under which he rests. Only Posthumus's equally masterful narrative of the battle (5.3.1–51) tells us that the play now has another character who might be his rhetorical match.[1]

If *Cymbeline*'s artfulness is apparent in its verse, its self-consciousness over situation is equally emphatic, most strikingly in those scenes where conflicting dramatic signals seem to collide with one another. Since plays in mixed genres inevitably present situations from which alternative plot options might unfold, they often involve moments of structural ambivalence: the audience's sense of its landmarks will be disrupted when events demand a double response, or when the underlying direction of the narrative is in doubt. *Cymbeline* is full of such moments. One capsule example is 'Hark, hark, the lark' (2.3), which is often met with as a delicate lyric, isolated in anthologies. But in context the song is problematized by the fact that Cloten presents it. His bawdy commentary sexualizes its compliments, activating their erotic undertow, and complicating the song's generic signals: is it an innocent aubade, or a sensual appreciation of Innogen's seductiveness? So, too, the revelations of the final scene are seen as if with a double eye. It is impossible to perform the sequence of cascading disclosures, each more astonishing than the last yet all somehow already known to us, without acknowledging at some level the tug of both irony and wonder.

But the most exquisite tensions are saved for Innogen's awakening beside the headless body, in which agony and absurdity are compressed into a single event. Like the comparable episode in *King Lear*, when Gloucester does and does not fall over Dover cliff, this scene trades on the ambiguities of the theatrical contract, the fact that theatre's realities are always understood at some level as illusions. Innogen's situation is clearly 'unreal' – the body is a prop and her error arises from elaborate contrivances – yet her language is laden with shock, and to read it as farce risks trivializing her sufferings. Undoubtedly it can be done farcically: one strand of modern criticism has felt that Shakespeare was 'playing' with Innogen, writing a sort of Jacobean theatre of the absurd for a sophisticated audience that would have found her error amusing.[2] But this is to simplify the scene's effect, for while her mistake over the body prevents full emotional identification, it cannot cancel the impact of her grief. On the contrary, her sorrow is full-throated though her circumstances tell a different tale; and the signs are just as mixed for her partner in 'death', for Cloten is a buffoon whose bluster is punished with more violence than comedy usually allows. It is as if two incompatible dramas had met in the same playing space, sending signals that prevent the spectators from lumping the action into a single, coherent generic category. *Cymbeline* foregrounds the provisionality of its own art more ostentatiously than any other play in the canon.

---

[1] The fullest discussion of Iachimo's verbal styles is in Freer, *The Poetics of Jacobean Drama*, pp. 103–35.
[2] See R. A. Foakes, *Shakespeare: The Dark Comedies to the Last Plays* (1971); and Kirsch, *Jacobean Dramatic Perspectives*.

Perhaps unsurprisingly, *Cymbeline*'s audiences often find themselves unsure about what kind of play they are witnessing, and spend much of the action trying to intuit the underlying direction of events, puzzling over what providence, if any, is moving the plot and whether the play's world is tragic or comic, meaningless or benign. These uncertainties are dramatized by the polarized attitudes of the characters themselves. At one extreme are Belarius and the princes, whose pagan naturalism, though pious, is far from encouraging. Their dirge over Fidele's corpse is much admired today, but its philosophy is chillingly materialist and offers no consolation for death beyond the grim idea that in returning to dust the body is at last insensible to pain. It is no coincidence that, in Samuel Beckett's *Happy Days* (1961), one of Winnie's treasured but self-deluding phrases is 'Fear no more'.[1] At the other extreme is Posthumus, whose upward trajectory is accomplished in a Pauline language of sin, penitence and forgiveness. He is convinced that self-sacrifice will redeem him and death will make him 'free' (5.3.250), but his affirmations have to compete with the worldly Jailer, who finds such faith incomprehensible. Between the two stands Jupiter, the deus ex machina himself, who replies to the ghosts' perplexities with promises that everything will work out happily; and since his predictions turn out to be true, his arrival seems to reveal the hidden hand that has been moving the action all along. However, his response to the ghosts' complaints that his justice is unjust is less than satisfactory. His reasons for neglecting Posthumus are frustratingly gnomic, and the explanation for the play's events remains elusive, hidden somewhere in his all-knowing but inscrutable will. His axiom 'Whom best I love, I cross' affirms that the world is divinely ordered but offers scant reassurance for mortals unsure about which of them his love will favour, while to modern ears his attitude to their sufferings sounds casual, or at best indifferent. Jupiter's god's-eye view ensures that at least one character sees the play's action as a coherent pattern, but for the rest, events continue to be shrouded in a mysterious arbitrariness.

Of course, the choice of Cymbeline's reign for the play's historical setting implicitly sets the conclusion in a proto-Christian framework. If for Spenser and other writers (see p. 11, n. 3 above), the main significance of Cymbeline's reign was that it coincided with the Incarnation, then the ending's universal peace resonates with intimations of redemptive purposes, a transcendent scheme in which little local difficulties simply evaporate. The closing reconciliations suggest that we are at the turning-point of year one, that watershed in human affairs when the eternal erupted into history and the secular was redeemed by the divine.[2] But unlike Guarini's Italianate tragicomedy, where resolutions unambiguously stage the accomplishment of the divine will, *Cymbeline*'s cosmic patterning remains unverified, present only in the background as hints and

---

[1] See also 'Missing God', Dennis O'Driscoll's poem on the emotional poverty of modern secularism in *Exemplary Damages* (2002): 'Miss Him when a choked voice/at the crematorium recites the poem/about fearing no more the heat of the sun'. The most sustained modern citation of the dirge's opening lines comes in Virginia Woolf's *Mrs Dalloway* (1925), where they are a leitmotif expressing Clarissa's confrontation with ageing and the withering away of her sexual identity (from reproductive 'heat' to barren 'winter').

[2] See Robin Moffet, '*Cymbeline* and the nativity', *SQ*, 13 (1962), 207–18; Hugh M. Richmond, 'Shakespeare's Roman trilogy: the climax in *Cymbeline*', *SLI*, 5 (1972), 129–39; and Cynthia Marshall, *Last Things and Last Plays: Shakespearean Eschatology* (1991).

dreams. Jupiter is structurally displaced, prevented by his position in the penultimate scene from dominating the ending, while the play's insistence on its own artifice ensures that the mood of wonder at these remarkable coincidences is shot through with recognition of their theatrical contrivance. When, in the final moments, the Soothsayer uses a series of ingenious but far-fetched puns to 'prove' that the oracle has been fulfilled, the play intrudes a scepticism about the providential ordering that, in other respects, the ending seems to affirm. This creates a rich but contradictory combination of wonder and disbelief that typifies tragicomedy's structural openness, with its power to accommodate contradiction, irony and the absence of resolution. As Stephen Orgel writes, 'the point about tragicomedy is not that it is both tragic and comic, but that it is neither: the comedy undercuts the tragedy, the tragedy subverts the restorations and reconciliations'.[1] Such double perception is intrinsic to *Cymbeline*: it manages to offer both a miraculous conclusion that surprises even the most hardened audiences with the emotionalism of its reunions, and a vein of scepticism that ensures we can never mistake its miracles for truth. In no other play are belief and disbelief – either aesthetic or ideological – thrust into a conjunction quite so acute.

THE WOMAN'S PART

The ninth tale of day two of Boccaccio's *Decameron* concerns Bernabo, a merchant of Genoa. In Paris on business, Bernabo falls into conversation with fellow-merchants about whether their wives stay chaste during their absence. Bernabo is confident that his wife, Zinevra, is faithful, but 'a young proper man', the Venetian Ambrogiuolo, argues that since all women are 'various and mutable', no amount of vigilance can discern their secret faults and Zinevra 'must needs do that which other women do'. He boasts that were they in private, he would 'find in her the selfsame frailty': Bernabo, overcome with anger, challenges him to prove it. Ambrogiuolo travels to Genoa and quickly realizes that she will not be seduced, but finding a poor woman who has access to her house, he bribes her to conceal him in a chest and entrust it to Zinevra's protection during her absence from the city. In the night, he leaves the chest, steals Zinevra's ring, purse and girdle, and memorizes details of her person, including 'a small wart upon her left pap, with some few hairs growing thereon, appearing to be as yellow as gold' – a detail that passed directly into *Cymbeline*. Returning to Paris, he claims the wager from Bernabo, who goes to his country house outside Genoa and sends a servant for Zinevra, commanding him to kill her on the way back. But Zinevra pleads so pitifully that the servant lets her go, giving her some man's clothes and telling Bernabo that wolves had devoured her body. In disguise, Zinevra travels to Alexandria and enters the Sultan's service, eventually becoming his favourite. One day she meets Ambrogiuolo at the Sultan's market in Acre, and recognizes the purse and girdle displayed in his booth. He tells her the story, though without admitting his trickery. She has Bernabo sent for, and the Sultan forces both men to tell the truth. Once the facts are out, Zinevra reveals

[1] Orgel, '*Cymbeline* at Santa Cruz', *SQ*, 52 (2001), 284.

her breasts and real identity, Bernabo is forgiven, and Ambrogiuolo is sentenced to a lingering death.[1]

By 1610 the tale of the man who wagered on his wife's chastity had been told in several languages and many different versions.[2] Shakespeare had already developed a related scenario in *The Rape of Lucrece*, based on the episode in Livy in which Sextus Tarquinius's lust for Lucretia is aroused by hearing her husband boast about her perfections (a fable to which Iachimo alludes at 2.2.13).[3] He seems to have known a German adaptation of Boccaccio's tale, *Frederick of Jennen* ('Jennen' is Genoa, and 'Frederick' the name that the wife adopts in disguise). This was printed in English in 1520 and 1560, and Shakespeare carried over several of its details, especially the crucial point that the husband chooses to forgive his wife before he realizes she was innocent all along.[4] But the primary source must have been Boccaccio, whose version was the most important literary treatment of the story and which Shakespeare read either in Italian or in French.[5] In adapting Boccaccio he trimmed the novella's sensational second half and discarded Zinevra's more exotic travels, keeping Innogen out of heroic adventures and displacing her from the centre of the story. Instead, the emphasis is thrown on to the triangular relationship between husband, wife and friend, and the psychology of jealousy that it involves. This suggests that what really interested Shakespeare was the struggle between the two men, and the recurrent anxiety about female chastity that it dramatized. It permitted him to return to the tragic territory he had explored with the poet, friend and dark lady of the sonnets, and with Othello, Iago and Desdemona.

In Shakespeare's early comedies marriage is the goal towards which plots move. Their emotional and structural objectives are the achievement of union in wedlock, and marriage's validity as an institution – on personal, social and symbolic levels – is taken as read. Although sometimes acknowledging that the future will be difficult, they treat wedded bliss as ending the story. But like *Othello*, *Cymbeline* begins with the marriage, and reverses its structural functions. With the plot taking wedlock as merely

---

[1] Quotations are from the 1620 translation of Boccaccio, reprinted in G. Bullough, ed., *Narrative and Dramatic Sources of Shakespeare*, VIII (1975), pp. 50–63. I have modernized spellings, and substituted the character names as they appear in the Italian.

[2] Bullough gives examples from three medieval French romances and a sixteenth-century Spanish play. See also W. W. Lawrence, *Shakespeare's Problem Comedies* (1931), chapter 5, and p. 7 n. 1 and p. 14 n. 2 above.

[3] Livy, *History of Rome*, I, 57–9; also in Ovid, *Fasti*, II, 685–856. See also p. 43 below.

[4] Other similarities are (i) the discussion takes place among a company of men from various nations (in Boccaccio they are all Italian); (ii) the wager is proposed by the Iachimo figure; (iii) the stakes are equal (not five to one, as in Boccaccio); (iv) the Iachimo figure has a preliminary meeting with the wife, instead of just seeing her from afar; (v) the chest is supposed to hold jewels and plate; (vi) the wife sleeps alone (in Boccaccio a girl sleeps with her); (vii) the wager is 'proved' in private, instead of before company; and (viii) the servant sends a bloody cloth as a token of her death. Roger Warren points out that Shakespeare knew *Frederick of Jennen* in the 1590s, when he used material from it for *The Comedy of Errors*.

[5] The clearest evidence that Shakespeare knew Boccaccio is the punishment to which Ambrogiuolo is condemned – to be tied to a stake, smeared with honey, and left for insects to devour – which crops up again in *The Winter's Tale*, 4.4.783–91. Other details from Boccaccio are the mole on the wife's breast (in *Frederick of Jennen* it is on her arm), and the conversation about female fidelity, which in *Frederick of Jennen* is only summarily treated. See also W. F. Thrall, '*Cymbeline*, Boccaccio and the wager story in England', *SP*, 28 (1931), 639–51. There is an English version of the tale, set against the Wars of the Roses, in *Westward for Smelts*; this was not printed until 1620, though Leo Salingar suggests that it perhaps reproduced a variant of the story that circulated independently (*Shakespeare and the Traditions of Comedy*, p. 58).

the starting-point, *Cymbeline* deconstructs assumptions that the earlier plays leave intact, calling into question the privileged status that, in them, marriage commands. This simple point is sometimes missed, in part because the Victorian legacy has been so strong. Romanticizing Innogen as the perfect wife, Victorian critics downplayed the negative aspects of her portrayal, and ignored the dysfunctional nature of her partnership with Posthumus.[1] Their idealization made it hard to see why her beauty – if it is so perfect – disrupts her world so much, and why – if the marriage is so good – she so spectacularly forfeits Posthumus's trust. Not surprisingly, in the nineteenth century Posthumus was often seen as a cad, but blaming the husband still leaves Innogen's loyalty to him unexplained. In an important recent essay, Anne Barton has put the marriage into truer historical perspective. She argues that the failures of trust seem perplexing because we have forgotten the different legal criteria by which marriage could be solemnized at this time, and which led to different degrees of certainty in marital union. She suggests that Posthumus and Innogen are clandestinely espoused: they have exchanged binding promises in private, but their marriage has not yet been ratified by public ceremonial or bodily intercourse. This leaves them caught between categories, not single but not yet fully joined, married but virginal, and it explains why Posthumus should seem so anxious and why Innogen's sexuality should seem so disruptive.[2] Yet however much the situation is inflected by legal niceties, one may still feel that the couple's problems remain considerable. *Cymbeline* is not *Measure for Measure*, where everything turns on a marriage's technical incompleteness, nor is it clear that Posthumus's doubts would have been allayed by legal consummation. Rather, it is the problem of marriage itself, and the impossibility of a totally reciprocal partnership, that drives the plot.

Everything in the first two acts leads to Posthumus's diatribe against women, with its remarkable slide into generalization. Posthumus attacks Innogen, then repudiates the female sex *en masse*: her betrayal calls his manhood into question, which leads to aspersions against his mother's chastity, and then against all women:

> Is there no way for men to be, but women
> Must be half-workers? We are all bastards,
> And that most venerable man which I
> Did call my father was I know not where
> When I was stamped.   (2.5.1–5)

---

[1] See p. 58 below. For many examples, see H. H. Furness's notes to the Variorum *Cymbeline* (1913), which struggle to reconcile his view of what Innogen should be with the less than saintly character he finds in the text. The Victorian Innogen continues to exert a hold: in Roger Warren's otherwise excellent Oxford edition, the whole story is seen as essentially focused on Innogen and her redeeming love.

[2] Barton, '"Wrying but a little": marriage, law and sexuality in the plays of Shakespeare', in *Essays, Mainly Shakespearean*, pp. 3–30. Barton persuasively shows that the union is shaped by complex legal distinctions between espousal and marriage, but she does not conclusively establish that it has only the limited validity of an espousal. By contrast, Jupiter's words are unequivocal – 'in / Our temple was he married' (5.3.169–70) – and Posthumus compares himself to '[y]ou married ones' in the audience (5.1.2), which suggests that he sees his marital ties as binding. There is also his complaint that Innogen restrained him 'of [his] lawful pleasure' (2.5.9), which suggests that sexual relations between the two were fully institutionalized. When, in *Measure for Measure*, Shakespeare presents a couple who are betrothed but not technically married, he makes the situation entirely unambiguous.

Even images of Innogen 'colted' by Iachimo (2.4.133) turn into a general rejection of
'[t]he woman's part' (2.5.20) and frustratingly nonspecific accusations of female vice:

            be it lying, note it,
    The woman's; flattering, hers; deceiving, hers;
    Lust and rank thoughts, hers, hers; revenges, hers;
    Ambitions, covetings, change of prides, disdain,
    Nice longing, slanders, mutability,
    All faults that earth can name, nay, that hell knows,
    Why hers, in part, or all . . .   (2.5.22–8)

A character-based reading would see this insane misogyny as a flaw that Posthumus
eventually learns to control, but it is properly part of a larger cultural problematic. Apart
from the central image of Innogen mounted by a boar – not a meaningful representation
of her but a fantasy projecting Posthumus's insecurities – the speech barely concerns
her at all. Its real subject is the man's humiliation, his loss of face and self-confidence,
and his feeling of disconnection from his community, here defined as a genetic tie
confirming biological descent from his father. Innogen's betrayal calls into question the
very basis of his manhood, the systems of inheritance and psychic order that structure
his masculinity. His conviction that, since she has betrayed him, his mother must
have failed his father, confirms a fear that all men are under threat of dethronement.
He lurches from betrayal by one female to betrayal by the Female – that category
against which Renaissance masculinity defines itself, and which always seems poised
to overwhelm it.

    Jacobean political culture invested immense symbolic capital in the idea of the hus-
band or the father.[1] An aggregation of households as well as a community of subjects,
the nation was often described as a great family, the politics of which reproduced the
structures of domestic life. King James liked to speak of himself as the father or husband of his realm, using analogies that presumed that the political world coordinated
seamlessly with the erotic. For example, in opening his first parliament, he described
his kingship in words from the marriage service: 'What God hath conjoined then, let
no man separate. I am the husband, and the whole isle is my lawful wife; I am the
head, and it is my body; I am the shepherd, and it is my flock.'[2] Such language was
echoed in masques and panegyric, which represented the king as political father to the
nation and genetic parent to his family. This rhetoric was different from the language
of Elizabethan sovereignty, which had emphasized the Queen's sexual invulnerability:
Elizabeth's power over her (male) people was embodied in her virgin immunity to
the desires to which everyone else was subject. By contrast, James's rhetoric foregrounded his commanding masculinity, and the correspondence between his sexual
power in the family and political power in the state. This trope was fed by a series of
culturally sanctioned assumptions about the proper subordination of wife to husband,

---

[1] See L. Danson, '"The catastrophe is a nuptial": the space of masculine desire in *Othello*, *Cymbeline* and
    The Winter's Tale', *S. Sur.*, 46 (1993), 69–79; and more generally, J. Goldberg, *James I and the Politics of
    Literature* (1983); E. Sedgwick, *Between Men: English Literature and Male Homosocial Desire* (1985); and
    M. Breitenberg, *Anxious Masculinity in Early Modern England* (1996).
[2] James VI and I, *Political Writings*, ed. J. P. Sommerville (1994), p. 136.

daughter to father, female to male, and the interconnectedness of sexual, domestic and political hierarchies. Equally important was its domestic corollary, that husbands had kingly authority within their households, and its sexualized variant, that proper political relations were figured in the husband's possession of his wife. Yet, as Shakespeare's preoccupation with scenarios of cuckolding or domestic rebellion shows, it bred a correspondingly intense anxiety about male insufficiency, the consequences of impotence, betrayal or loss of sexual control. If masculinity was a system of mastery that confirmed the husband's authority in his domestic kingdom, then the female was that which always threatened to dethrone him, the body of unruly desires by controlling which the husband's power manifested itself. The male's identity was thus in an ambivalent relationship to the female through which it constituted itself, for the subordination of wife to husband, or daughter to father, could never be taken for granted. The female as that which sanctioned male authority was also the rebellious Other that contested it, the weak spot through which power tended to seep away. So when Posthumus asks 'Is there no way for men to be, but women / Must be half-workers', his question is not the tautology that it seems. It is precisely this tension in Jacobean masculinity with which the wager plot engages.

Posthumus is insecure before the play begins. 'A fatherless youth whose very name orphans him',[1] he is already disconnected from what ought to be his sustaining male society, his identity conditional on a foster-father's unreliable love. When that link goes, his status (like Othello's) comes to rest on his wife's validation, and though sexually the dominant partner, subordination to a wife of superior rank puts him under threat of emasculation. Posthumus's anxieties are already apparent in his leave-taking, which is plagued by the need to keep down his 'tenderness' lest he be 'suspected' less than a man, and marred by his unhappy description of the bracelet as a 'manacle of love' (1.1.94, 122). His abrupt departure disappoints Innogen, and his exaggerated chivalry – 'My queen, my mistress!' (92) – sounds like a defensive response to perceptions of impotence. The claim by the First Gentleman that Innogen's love for him attests to his worth – 'his virtue / By her election may be truly read, / What kind of man he is' (52–4) – sounds appreciative but takes away more than it gives. When Iachimo arrives he seizes on just this point, in terms that demystify the social embarrassments hidden in the Gentleman's cloudy syntax:

This matter of marrying his king's daughter, *wherein he must be weighed rather by her value than his own*, words him, I doubt not, a great deal from the matter.   (1.4.10–12; my italics)

Iachimo's cutting remark helps to establish that Posthumus's touchiness in Rome is more than merely a traveller's discomfort: it betrays that his identity is ascribed rather than inherent and, crucially, that it is conditioned by sexual factors. Iachimo's plot is already immanent in these few words, but the underlying anxiety runs wider than Posthumus. Since his value resides not in himself but in his ability to command another, his story dramatizes the fragile sexual foundations of early modern masculinity. When his belief in Innogen collapses, so will his belief in himself.

[1] Nevo, *Shakespeare's Other Language*, p. 69.

Being an all-male world, Rome makes particularly evident the connection between Posthumus's subjectivity and the encompassing culture of manliness. In this environment social relations are structured as male-male competition. Amusingly, when Philario says of Posthumus, 'His father and I were soldiers together, to whom I have been often bound for no less than my life' (1.4.19), he momentarily forgets that Sicilius Leonatus was a Briton, and hence his enemy. Opposition or alliance seem to matter less than the underlying bonds that connect the two: being soldiers, Philario and Sicilius have a manly tie whatever their allegiance. Indeed, the play is structured around male-male encounters that blur boundaries of friendship and hostility. Posthumus is a kind of half-brother to his enemy Cloten, while Cymbeline's defiance of Lucius is oddly like imitation, and the brotherhood of Guiderius and Arviragus expresses itself as rivalry. In this state of filial warfare, Oedipal enmities are displaced into fraternal emulation, each 'brother' maintaining his place in an ongoing process as a competitor among his peers.

It is not surprising, then, that Posthumus's welcome to Rome should be a challenge, nor that the Frenchman should narrate a history of similar scrapes (1.4.43–9), for such sensitivities are the normal currency of masculine life. The fact that Iachimo makes Innogen the trigger for the quarrel underlines how much his wager is a challenge to Posthumus's manhood: what counts is not whether she is really virtuous, wise, chaste, and so forth, but whether Posthumus can claim her as his, and hence validate his identity. Indeed, Iachimo says as much: 'I make my wager rather against your confidence than her reputation' (1.4.89–90). In a sense, she is a trophy to be defended: when Posthumus says 'She holds her virtue still, and I my mind' (52), he admits how much his honour is at stake in hers. Simply by marrying above his rank he has initiated a contest, upsetting not only Innogen's father but Cloten, who had hoped to have her, and Cloten's anger about Innogen's preference for her lover's 'meanest garment' (2.3.144) emphasizes how much for him the social rebuff is always the main thing.[1] Iachimo's sardonic remark about Innogen 'taking a beggar without less quality' (1.4.17) shows that he, too, is piqued by Posthumus's social climbing, and by boasting that Innogen is 'less attemptable' (48) than any other lady, Posthumus himself admits that she is his social capital: his words imply that she is desirable to be possessed, and that others may want to 'attempt' her as well. By marrying her he has put her on the market, made her a prize that provokes the envy of his peers: Iachimo later says that she exceeded the 'shop of all the qualities' for which other gentlemen loved their wives (5.4.166). Iachimo's ploy in the wager is merely to make this marketability apparent, destroying Posthumus's manhood by proving that, contrary to what he thinks, anyone can possess her.

Boccaccio's story embodies the mechanisms of a mercantile economy: not only are his characters merchants, but the plot depends on the physical separations and confluences of the marketplace. In his tale the market works to the good, by promoting the flow of information that brings Ambrogiuolo to Acre and delivering to Zinevra the proof that she has been slandered. But in Cymbeline the economic undertow is unsettling, for it destabilizes the assumptions of Posthumus's world, exposing the fragility of his

---

[1] On this point, see Heather James, *Shakespeare's Troy* (1997), pp. 158–9.

notionally fixed categories of honour. Posthumus assumes that Innogen embodies an absolute value: she seems unique and therefore outside the currency of things, her price so high as to be incalculable. But ironically this is a market position, for it presumes a scarcity economy in which values are inflated. This allows Iachimo to shatter his confidence by proving she is just as marketable, and her worth just as negotiable, as anything else. Against the claim for her uniqueness, he replies that since the world is a large place, nothing can be beyond price:[1]

> If she went before others I have seen as that diamond of yours outlustres many I have beheld, I could not but believe she excelled many; but I have not seen the most precious diamond that is, nor you the lady.   (1.4.57–61)

If Iachimo can prove that Innogen is not transcendently outside the market as her husband believes, then all of Posthumus's assumptions about her inalienable value collapse: 'You may wear her in title yours; but, you know, strange fowl light upon neighbouring ponds' (72–3). The tendency of this ploy is to link Innogen's chastity to Posthumus's possession of her, exposing the hidden connection between his manliness and its manifestation in ownership. Shakespeare relieves Posthumus of some of the blame for what follows by making him seem backed into a corner, having the challenger initiate the bet (in Boccaccio the bet comes from the husband). Still, Posthumus is vulnerable to Iachimo's arguments because, in spite of his protestations about her pricelessness, he, too, sees her as a commodity, the wager arising remorselessly out of the assumptions about competitive masculinity that possession of her serves. The trap closes once Iachimo conflates her value with Posthumus's ring, since the ring has already been introduced as the symbol of fidelity, having belonged to Innogen's mother. Posthumus wears it now to display her value for him; but when he loses the bet, it passes to Iachimo in token of ownership. The ring thus embodies the contradictory meanings that female sexuality signifies in this male–male economy. Its value seems beyond price, yet it proves disconcertingly open to transfer.

It should be clear, then, why the Victorian Innogen is only half the story. Innogen may be a loyal wife, but male anxieties provoked by her sexuality poison her marriage. Like so many of Shakespeare's men (Oberon, Othello, Leontes), Posthumus is beset by doubts that his wife may betray him, and although this fear undermines his self-confidence, it cannot be easily discharged. Moreover, Innogen's status as his superior and Britain's heir makes control of her sexuality exceptionally fraught. When power came into female hands, it challenged all the usual assumptions about sexual subordination, that the woman's role was to be mastered. In recent history, Mary and Elizabeth Tudor had in their different ways exemplified the problems of female empowerment, but the issue also troubled Jacobean political discourse, for if power was imagined as passing smoothly from father to son, the nightmare scenario was the unmastered female. Like King Lear, Cymbeline's Achilles heel is his lack of male heirs, which creates a double instability: he can neither guarantee how power will be passed on, nor make his will

[1] See J. R. Siemon, '"Perplexed beyond self-explication": *Cymbeline* and early modern/postmodern Europe', in M. Hattaway, B. Sokolova and D. Roper, eds., *Shakespeare in the New Europe* (1994), pp. 294–309.

Figure 2. Marriage chest for Isaac Walton and Rachel Floud, 1626, at Warwick Castle

effective in the present. Innogen's choice of Posthumus looks heroic, but it sets her against her father, exposing a weakness in his authority and in the transfer of power to the next generation. Loyal to her husband, she is no rebel to male government, but since Posthumus is not her father's choice, her actions raise the problem of unruly female desire, the taint of which she cannot entirely escape. Inevitably, the play's praise of her fidelity will be shadowed by anxieties about the wilfully desiring female.

These contradictions in the presentation of Innogen are best seen in 2.2, Iachimo's invasion of her bedroom, and its follow-up in 2.4.[1] As Innogen lies unconscious, helpless and silent under Iachimo's gaze, her lack of control over her sexual identity could hardly be clearer. In the bedroom her reification is overwhelming: Iachimo has already called her a 'jewel' and sealed 'a covenant' with Posthumus as if bargaining for ownership (1.4.134), but now he makes an 'inventory' (2.2.30), itemizing her body as a list of objects waiting to be possessed. There is, too, an iconographic link between her bodily intactness and his penetration of her chamber, recalling early modern images of the chaste woman as a locked room or enclosed space, and playing ironically on the fact that decorated bridal chests often stood in the bedrooms of the wealthy, furniture which celebrated and commemorated marital union (see figure 2). The bedroom was the innermost space in the aristocratic household – as Cloten finds in 2.3, when he is

---

[1] On these scenes, see especially Patricia Parker, *Literary Fat Ladies: Rhetoric, Gender, Property* (1987), pp. 126–54; and Catherine Belsey, *Shakespeare and the Loss of Eden* (1999), pp. 55–83.

denied access to the same room – so that Iachimo's emergence from the trunk shockingly violates Innogen's privacy.[1] His uncovering of her bodily marks, 'secret' parts (2.2.40) which should remain hidden, seems like a symbolic rape, though his reluctance to touch her underlines how much his plan involves owning her rather than violating her.[2] His catalogue unnervingly dehumanizes her: it conflates her body with the room, treating her 'natural notes' (28) as just so much furniture, of which his inventory – now termed a 'voucher' (39) – proves his possession. Claiming to have 'picked the lock and ta'en / The treasure of her honour' (41–2), Iachimo reduces her to a token in a contest between men. He convinces Posthumus of her betrayal not by describing her yielding but by possessing her bracelet and the 'particulars' of her room (2.4.78). Little wonder that the exasperated husband tells him to '[s]pare [his] arithmetic' (142).

Innogen's entrapment within the struggle over Posthumus's masculinity helps to explain the play's double vision towards her, the way that she seems both attractive and disturbing. The iconography of her bedroom, with Diana on the fireplace and cherubs on the ceiling (2.4.82, 88), marks her out a chaste wife. To Iachimo she is a phoenix (1.6.17), the bird that reproduced without sex, or a lily (2.2.15), a flower linked with the Virgin Mary. Yet other images associate her with disruptively active female desire. In the bedroom there are blind Cupids in the fireplace, and the tapestries show Cleopatra meeting Mark Antony on the proudly swelling Nile (2.4.70, 89). Diana is depicted in her bath, a motif chosen for its link to Actaeon, the hunter who, stumbling across her when she was naked, was turned into a stag and killed by his own hounds. This myth could have several paranoid interpretations: it expressed the perils of prying into love's secrets; it represented man as emasculated and terrorized by his own desire; and it associated love with voyeurism and degrading lust. Of course, Iachimo's description of Innogen's bedroom plays on such anxieties by intensifying its sexual content, but even in the bedroom itself, his hypnotic response to her person evokes her erotic power and desirability. He calls her Cytherea (that is, Venus, 2.2.14), dwells on her physical coloration, and ventriloquizes the tug of desire that draws even the candle to 'underpeep' her eyelids (20). She may look like a monument in a chapel (33), but her breath is perfumed, and she is exhausted from reading Ovid's erotic tales: in the absence of a lover, her lips embrace each other (18). Iachimo comes from the trunk like a projection of her dreams, a sexual demon conjured by her imaginative identification with Philomel (46); even Innogen seems to fear her own sexuality, for she prays the gods to keep her from 'tempters of the night' (9). It is not surprising, then, that her bracelet proves to be 'slippery' (34), nor that her breasts hide a secret spot arousing the lusts of a sexual connoisseur. As Iachimo later tells Posthumus, her body truly does harbour the 'stain' of desire (2.4.140).

[1] The symbolism of bedroom furniture is discussed by Belsey. On the conflation of sexual and political 'secrets', see also Patricia Parker, *Shakespeare from the Margins* (1996), pp. 229–72.

[2] Directors have differed over whether Iachimo actually kisses Innogen. Granville-Barker said that 'a kiss is no more likely to wake her than is the stealing of the bracelet' (*Preface to Cymbeline*, p. 155n.), but arguably Iachimo's hesitation makes clearer how fetishistic his attitude is. There is an unresolved but symptomatic contradiction between what he tells us here (that he wants to kiss her lips) and what he later tells Posthumus (that he kissed her breasts).

Within the play only Cloten – who regards Innogen as a Diana whom Actaeon might get to rape by bribing her nymphs (2.3.62–5) – sees her entirely in these terms. Nonetheless, this ambiguity is more than Iachimo's fantasy, for the bedroom surrounds her with danger signals, making her beauty appear disturbingly sexualized. And her sexuality is more on show than that of other heroines, since throughout the play she functions as either the source or the object of male desire. The plot is driven by the men's need to control her body, but since she is usually in male disguise, mobile and alone, she occupies territory that neither husband nor father can police. Her sexual identity provocatively combines a married woman's self-awareness with the freedom of an unmastered female. This helps to explain Posthumus's frankly contradictory view of her:

> Oh vengeance, vengeance!
> Me of my lawful pleasure she restrained,
> And prayed me oft forbearance; did it with
> A pudency so rosy, the sweet view on't
> Might well have warmed old Saturn – that I thought her
> As chaste as unsunned snow.   (2.5.8–13)

Posthumus imagines Innogen as being prudish towards him but voracious behind his back: in his nightmare she is both frigid and a tease.[1] He is, too, confused about who the 'real' Innogen is, for her 'pudency' (modesty) excites him, and she seems both 'rosy' and 'snow'. Such confusion over her sexuality is not peculiar to him but an ambiguity the play fosters, for it arises from Innogen's overdetermined position. As a husbandless wife, her sexuality is legitimately active (hence she is chaste within marriage), yet she takes responsibility for her own desires (and hence may always turn out a 'counterfeit' [2.5.6]). Perhaps the surprise is not that Posthumus wagered on his wife's chastity, but that he ever thought the bet was winnable in the first place.

Innogen thus occupies a major pressure-point in the early modern 'construction of femininity'. She is required to guard her chastity, but has a sexuality that seems inherently in need of being mastered. And as is demonstrated by the suspension of Posthumus's role after 2.5, there is no easy mechanism by which this contradiction in the ideology of marriage can be discharged. Instead, Shakespeare uses Cloten to play out that hostility towards the female which, if developed through Posthumus, would destroy the ending.[2] Cloten and Posthumus are rivals, but they are oddly similar – as shown by the remarkable circumstance that Posthumus's clothes fit Cloten so well that Innogen cannot distinguish between them. Both are arrogant and self-confident, yet

---

[1] Anne Barton raises the possibility that Innogen may still be a virgin and that the refusal of which Posthumus complains was maiden modesty ('Wrying but a little', p. 24). However, the passage does seem to presume that the two have a prehistory of sexual relations within marriage ('my *lawful* pleasure'), and the simplest gloss seems to be that, for all her ardour, Innogen keeps her domestic sexuality in check ('oft forbearance', though not 'total forbearance'). The conflict between the demands of modesty and the endorsement of legitimate sexual pleasure as good in itself was one of the pressure-points in the ideology of Protestant marriage.

[2] For this parallel, see J. R. Siemon, 'Noble virtue in *Cymbeline*', *S. Sur.*, 29 (1976), 51–61; Hartwig, *Shakespeare's Tragicomic Vision*; and H. D. Swander, '*Cymbeline*: religious idea and dramatic design', in W. F. McNeir and T. N. Greenfield, eds., *Pacific Coast Studies in Shakespeare* (1966), pp. 248–62.

insecure and prone to violence. Neither has a father, both are given to wagers, and each desires Innogen but conceives violence against her. And it is crucial that Cloten's plan takes up where Posthumus's leaves off. Posthumus reacts to betrayal by proposing to 'tear her limb-meal . . . before / Her father' (2.4.147–9), and Cloten has the same idea: dress as her husband, rape her, then 'knock her back' to court, 'spurn her home to her father' (3.5.138, 4.1.15). On one level he is a parody, a clownish inversion of his rival's refined stupidity, but he is also a demystified repetition, carrying through vicariously, even down to his dress, the violence that Posthumus would do were he in Britain. In other words, Cloten and Posthumus parcel out the divided male response to Innogen's sexuality, Posthumus's misogynistic anger being acted out by his double. This makes evident why Cloten has to die, and in the husband's clothes: it kills a part of Posthumus, without which reunion is impossible.

When Posthumus returns in 5.1, the situation has completely changed and the old paranoia has gone. Believing Innogen to be dead, he is no longer prone to sexual doubts, and by dressing as a peasant he forgoes his social ambitions. With no woman to compete over or status to maintain, he is a new character, whose masculinity has been redrawn. To Posthumus Innogen is still the realm's 'mistress' (5.1.20) and he fights for her, but her 'death' means that his own political pretensions have lapsed. Her memory being public property, he can serve her as one patriot among many, and without the dangers that attended on marriage to the king's daughter. In battle he rediscovers ties to a community of brothers bound together by aggression in a common cause, and sublimates his competitiveness in the purifying and meritocratic violence of war.

Paradoxically, the loss of Innogen liberates him: free from paralysing anxieties, he acts with a new autonomy and self-possession. The final scene reunites him with Innogen, but in new terms: he has earned honour on his own account, and the likelihood that she will inherit Britain has gone. Were she Britain's heir, marriage would still be problematic, but since her brothers have been rediscovered she is free to wed whoever she wants. Significantly, although in the last scene her identity is the first to be discovered, Cymbeline does not acknowledge Posthumus or call him son-in-law until after Guiderius is revealed. The price of Innogen's happiness is abdication: she is saved by the rules of primogeniture, and ends the play subordinated to her brothers. The ending thus reinforces a gender divide that anticipates new social models that were starting to emerge in the seventeenth century. The woman is removed from the public world, safely consigned to the sphere of homemaking and domesticity, while the real business of politics and warfare is left to the men.

Some critics are disappointed that the condition of Innogen's happiness is the suppression of the characteristics that made her interesting in the first place – her lack of inhibitions and willingness to act on her emotions.[1] Undoubtedly she diminishes as the play proceeds. From a princess she dwindles to a 'franklin's housewife' (3.2.78), to a male youth, a 'cook to honest creatures' (4.2.299), and a mere page; she even contracts a cold. After the lament over the body, her role virtually ends: she falls silent and comes

---

[1] The main example is J. Adelman, *Suffocating Mothers: Fantasies of Maternal Origin in Shakespeare's Plays* (1992), pp. 209–11, 218.

to embody the hopeless fidelity signalled in her assumed name. The final scene brings a reunion with Posthumus, but its structural centrality is displaced by the far-reaching events caused by the recovery of her brothers. It is difficult not to feel that the Innogen who survives is chastened and domesticated, and that the reckless self-giving that was so endearing was also what made her problematic. The Victorians admired her eagerness to ride scores of miles each hour for Posthumus's sake, but Pisanio's more measured response – 'One score 'twixt sun and sun/Madam, 's enough for you' (3.2.69–70) – suggests that to Jacobean eyes such intense passions seemed dangerously unruly. Her headlong response to the letter, 'smothering . . . the sense' with a love that's 'beyond beyond' (3.2.56–9) makes her prone to take risks, and leaves her at sea when Posthumus proves untrue: all her big scenes in Act 3 emphasize her impulsiveness. So although her lament over the corpse is her role's climax, it also marks the end. Comparing herself to Hecuba grieving for Priam (4.2.312), Innogen becomes aligned with antiquity's most distraught female: her sorrows touch truly tragic despair.[1] But the parallel is fortunately false, and while it provokes pity, it is a relief when moments later she is taken into Lucius's care. For the rest of the play, Innogen has no shortage of fatherly protectors, and control of her future passes back to the men. Her disorientation is the point at which she forfeits responsibility for herself.

In 1937 George Bernard Shaw rewrote *Cymbeline*'s last scene, and made Innogen complain that Posthumus was a disappointment, implying that the play's problems stemmed from the excessive power that husbands had over wives.[2] Shakespeare's text never calls marriage itself into question: it remains the framework within which events are conducted. But if Innogen moves safely back into wedlock, the terms of that relationship have changed. Not only does Posthumus regret his jealousy, he has forgiven what he still, mistakenly, believes to be her betrayal:

> Yea, bloody cloth, I'll keep thee, for I wished
> Thou shouldst be coloured thus. You married ones,
> If each of you should take this course, how many
> Must murder wives much better than themselves
> For wrying but a little!   (5.1.1–5)

Anne Barton has eloquently articulated the huge mental leap involved in Posthumus's thought that adultery is only one of the 'little faults' (12).[3] By taking his wife's slip as venial, he rejects the contemporary assumption that female infidelity was unforgivable,

---

[1] Heather James, who explores this comparison, describes the later Innogen as 'post-tragic' (*Shakespeare's Troy*, p. 174). I cannot endorse her view that the corpse episode makes Innogen seem grotesque, but her complex account of the play's manoeuvres at this point is still helpful. See also Patricia Parker, 'Romance and empire: anachronistic *Cymbeline*', in G. M. Logan and G. Teskey, eds., *Unfolded Tales: Essays on Renaissance Romance* (1989), pp. 189–207; and Valerie Wayne, 'The career of *Cymbeline*'s manacle', *Early Modern Culture*, 1 (2000), 1–21.

[2] Shaw, *Cymbeline Refinished*. See R. Stamm, 'George Bernard Shaw and Shakespeare's *Cymbeline*', in D. C. Allen, ed., *Studies in Honor of T. W. Baldwin* (1958), pp. 254–66.

[3] Barton, 'Wrying but a little', pp. 29–30. See also Harley Granville-Barker, who praises Posthumus for reaching a point that Othello and Leontes fall short of (*Preface to Cymbeline*, pp. 165–6); and W. W. Lawrence, *Shakespeare's Problem Comedies*. Even Shaw acknowledged a hint of Ibsen in this passage; see *Plays and Players*, p. 153.

and rebuffs the double standard that condoned men's sexual freedom while censuring it in women. If to Posthumus Innogen still looks like Desdemona, he is an Othello who has internalized a more equal conception of marriage. Meanwhile, although Innogen's views about wifely 'obedience' (3.4.64) have taken some hard knocks, she has proved by her patience and fidelity how much she deserves Posthumus's love. Moreover, she has realized that part of the problem was the social imbalance between husband and wife, reflecting, on meeting the Welsh boys, that were they her brothers '[t]hen had my price / Been less, and so more equal ballasting / To thee, Posthumus' (3.6.74–6). This even weighting is finally delivered in the last scene, as her political demotion permits a new balance to emerge in which husband and wife take more equal roles in their marriage. The change is delicately underlined by the gender reversals of the language in which they greet one another: he may be her master but she is the 'rock', and he calls himself 'fruit' hanging from her sustaining 'tree' (5.4.263–4). If Innogen returns to domesticity, her consolation is that her status as wife has been upgraded, and her marriage reconstructed as a bourgeois partnership of equals. Moreover, as we shall see, she has a crucial function to play in resolving *Cymbeline*'s political dilemmas.

ROMANS AND BRITONS

One aspect of Innogen that modern spectators may overlook is that she bears the name of the mother of the Britons. Scholars now generally agree that the Folio's 'Imogen' is a scribal misreading of an unfamiliar name, and that Innogen is what Shakespeare originally called her.[1] This name he found in Raphael Holinshed's *First Volume of Chronicles*,[2] a source he consulted for information about early Britain. Holinshed's chronicles begin with several chapters of pseudo-history detailing the story of Britain before the arrival of the Romans, taking events back to Albion, son of Neptune, and the fanciful British kings who supposedly succeeded him. Much of this material came from the medieval annalists, especially the twelfth-century historian Geoffrey of Monmouth, who had synthesized the British myths into a grand narrative, the defining events of which were the Britons' conquest by Rome, and their resurgence under King Arthur. In Holinshed's story British history begins with the arrival of Brute, who was the great-grandson of Aeneas, the survivor of Troy and founder of Rome. Banished from Rome for accidental parricide, Brute dreamed that he had to raise a new Troy in an island in the west. Sailing to Albion, he cast out the aboriginal giants (mentioned at *Cym.* 3.3.5), founded Troynovant (Shakespeare's 'Lud's Town'),[3] and initiated several centuries of British kings. Shakespeare linked his play to this ancient myth of origin by

---

[1] See the notes to the play's characters, p. 79. The strongest case against 'Innogen' is made by John Pitcher, in 'Names in *Cymbeline*', *EiC*, 43 (1993), 1–16, but the only occurrence of 'Imogen' that he finds before 1623 is in a manuscript translation of Ralph Higden's fourteenth-century history of the world, *Polychronicon*. Almost certainly this, too, was a scribal misreading.

[2] First published in 1577; Shakespeare used the second edition, 1587.

[3] The historical Cymbeline had his court at Camulodunum (modern Colchester). Shakespeare foregrounds the Brutan connections, and maps them on to modern geography, by moving it to London.

borrowing some of its names. In the historically impossible combination of names that he uses, Cymbeline, Arviragus and Guiderius are from the first century AD and Cadwal is seventh-century, but three characters have names from the mythical past: according to Holinshed, Cloten was a British king in the direct line from Brute (ruling 413 BC), Brute's grandfather was called Posthumus, and Brute's wife was Innogen.[1] The fact that Shakespeare named his heroine after the mother of the British people makes the attack on her chastity all the more clearly an issue of nationhood.

In Shakespeare's time the Brutan myths were already regarded as historically unreliable. The medieval chroniclers who devised them wanted to enhance their nation's status by inventing a past in which Britain was more than an outlying colony of Rome, with an independent identity reaching back into time immemorial.[2] Their fictions had been criticized by the early Tudor historian Polydore Vergil – whose name is echoed in Guiderius's pseudonym, Polydore – and were ignored altogether by serious scholars such as William Camden, for whom recorded British history began with Julius Caesar's arrival in these islands.[3] Nonetheless, the British pseudo-history was well known, for it had long been used by Tudor propagandists. A Welsh dynasty, the Tudors exploited the coincidence that the remnants of defeated Britons described by Geoffrey of Monmouth had retreated into Wales, and found symbolic parallels between the return of Arthur and the establishment of their own line. In *The Faerie Queene* Britomart prophesies that, just as Aeneas remedied the fall of Troy by erecting a second empire at Rome, so a modern empire would emerge under his descendant in the west:

> But a third kingdome yet is to arise,
> Out of the Troians scattered of-spring,
> That in all glory and great enterprise,
> Both first and second Troy shall dare to equalise.
>
> (*FQ* 3.9.44)

It was, though, the combining of the kingdoms under James I, so as to recover the island's ancient geographic identity, that made these fictions particularly timely. James's arrival had turned England and Scotland into Britain, and Stuart panegyric repeatedly celebrated the new national name and the huge conceptual shift that it involved. In the pageantry for his entry into London, James was hailed as a new Brute, greater than the old:[4]

---

[1] For the relevant sections of Holinshed, see Bullough, *Narrative and Dramatic Sources*, VIII, pp. 38–46. Holinshed actually gives three conflicting genealogies for Brute; in two of them Posthumus is the name of either Aeneas's son or his grandson. See also W. G. Boswell-Stone, *Shakespeare's Holinshed: The Chronicle and the Plays Compared* (1907); and Geoffrey of Monmouth, *The History of the Kings of Britain*, trans. L. Thorpe (1966), pp. 53–74.

[2] L. Johnson, 'King Arthur at the crossroads to Rome', in E. Ni Cuilleanain and J. D. Pettifer, eds., *Noble and Joyous Histories* (1993), pp. 87–111.

[3] See T. D. Kendrick, *British Antiquity* (1950). Ben Jonson's panegyric for James's 1604 entry into London and John Speed's *Theatre of the Empire of Great Britain* (1611) both rejected the Brutan monarchs as unhistorical, but they are alive and well in William Slayter's poem *The History of Great Britain* (1621).

[4] T. Dekker, *Dramatic Works*, ed. F. Bowers (1955), II, p. 279. See also Thomas Heywood's *Troia Britannica, or Great Britain's Troy* (1609): 'three kingdoms, first by Brute divided, / United are, and by one sceptre guided' (Brute having divided England, Scotland and Wales between his three sons).

> Great Monarch of the West, whose glorious stem
> Doth now support a triple diadem,
> Weighing more than that of thy great grandsire Brute . . .

Brute himself appeared in the civic pageant *The Triumphs of Reunited Britannia* (1605) avowing his love for the island and explaining that Scotland had 'bred another Brute, that gives again / To Britain her first name'.[1] And in 1605 Ben Jonson's court entertainment *The Masque of Blackness* had as its culminating moment the disclosure of the name Britannia – the name that was debated in the 1604 parliament and adopted by proclamation in October.[2] Of course, *Cymbeline*'s Britain is only loosely historical: although a King Cunobelinus certainly existed, he ruled only in south-eastern Britain and there was no Roman invasion during his lifetime.[3] Nonetheless, by setting his play in early Britain, Shakespeare ensured that it alluded to a leading motif of James's political culture. When the Soothsayer envisions 'imperial Caesar' uniting his favour 'with the radiant Cymbeline, / Which shines here in the west' (5.4.475–6), he was echoing the royal entry and its idea of a westering empire, power passing from ancient Troy and Rome to James's new British *imperium*.[4]

Modern political readings of *Cymbeline* have seen the play as allegorizing James's new state, harking back to a mythical time when the island had been unified, a unity now remade in the Jacobean present.[5] It is important, though, not to telescope the course of future history back into 1610, nor to ignore the sedimented and incomplete union that James's 'Britain' was. Neither in Shakespeare's day nor for decades after would the multiple monarchy – English, Wales and Scottish peoples ruled by a single king – be translated into the single British state that James hankered after. Although under James the idea of Britain as a distinct political and cultural entity gained ground,[6] constitutional

[1] A. Munday, *Pageants and Entertainments*, ed. D. M. Bergeron (1985), p. 9.
[2] See B. Galloway, *The Union of England and Scotland 1603–1608* (Edinburgh, 1986); B. P. Levack, *The Formation of the British State* (1987); and S. T. Bindoff, 'The Stuarts and their style', *English Historical Review*, 60 (1945), 192–216.
[3] Holinshed says that after Julius Caesar's death, the Britons ceased payment of the tribute he had imposed in 54 BC; Augustus intended to reimpose it by force, but troubles nearer home prevented him from doing so. The next Roman invasion came in AD 55, under the command of the emperor Claudius, and was resisted by Cymbeline's successor, Guiderius. Shakespeare creates his own history by telescoping the Claudian invasion, on which Lucius's mission is indirectly based, back into the earlier period: the symbolic advantage of depicting a Romano-British war and reconciliation during the reign of Augustus outweighs other criteria of historical truth.
[4] In Jonson's masque *Love Freed* (1611), James was referred to as 'the sun throned in the west', 'these extreme parts of the world' (*Ben Jonson*, VII, pp. 362, 371). For another 'Jacobean' moment, compare Iachimo's account of Innogen as 'fastened to an empery/Would make the great'st king double' (1.6.119–20): this alludes passingly to the new status of the Stuart kingdoms as a multiple monarchy. See also Parker, 'Romance and empire'.
[5] See especially F. A. Yates, *Shakespeare's Last Plays: A New Approach* (1975); G. Wickham, 'Riddle and emblem: a study in the dramatic structure of *Cymbeline*', in J. Carey, ed., *English Renaissance Studies Presented to Dame Helen Gardner* (1980), pp. 94–113; and Marcus, *Puzzling Shakespeare*, pp. 106–59. The value of Yates's and Wickham's studies is undermined by their assumption that the Jacobean union was an achieved 'fact', and consequent simplification of the historical context. Yates is further flawed by attempting to read the play as a specific allegory of events in 1612, to achieve which she manipulates the date. For political accounts of the play more sensitized to the historical complexities, see J. Goldberg, *Voice Terminal Echo* (1986), and W. Maley, 'Postcolonial Shakespeare: British identity formation and *Cymbeline*', in J. Richards and J. Knowles, eds., *Shakespeare's Late Plays: New Readings* (1999), pp. 145–57.
[6] See Tristan Marshall, *Theatre and Empire: Great Britain on the London Stages under James VI and I* (2000).

union foundered on irreconcilable differences between his subject peoples, and royal attempts to promote integration by unifying elements of the English and Scots constitutions quickly ran into parliamentary sand. Calvin's Case (1608) established the principle that Scots born after 1603 (the *post-nati*) had the same rights under English law as did Englishmen, but on the basis of their common allegiance to a joint king, an argument that kept English and Scots law separate by stressing subjection rather than citizenship, vesting loyalty not in the state but in the person of the monarch. By contrast, the 1607 parliament rejected naturalization on the basis of statute, which would have compromised the separation of the two legal systems. In 1610, then, it was simply not possible for *Cymbeline* to endorse British union: politically, single nationhood was already dead, and would remain merely an aspiration until the realms were integrated by statute in 1707. Moreover, there were always significant gaps between the symbolism of union and the internal divisions of the British state – gaps that are all the more apparent from our twenty-first-century perspective, as a modern devolution of powers to Scotland and Wales has reversed some of the Jacobean process, bringing back into view regional faultlines that it was the aim of the British project to elide. Many English subjects were anxious about contamination by the 'beggarly' Scots, while Scots were unhappy with the precedent of Anglo-Welsh union, which had left Wales a colony of England, absorbed by the dominant power – a fate which the Scots wished to avoid. So James's apparently unified island was in fact an uncertain hybrid: three principalities in different degrees of dependence and autonomy, all ruled from England by a Scot.

In *Cymbeline* shortfalls between the rhetoric and reality of 'Britain' are clearly evident. For example, it is a striking fact that, although Innogen journeys from Lud's Town to Wales, she does not meet one genuine Welshman, while her intended destination is a strategically crucial harbour in Pembrokeshire – an area of the principality long under English dominance – which the play always refers to by its modern English name, Milford Haven, and never as Aberdaugleddyf or any other title more in keeping with the place or supposed period.[1] The Welsh are thus curiously absent from the play, yet Wales is still represented as problematically 'other', a place of mountains occupied by outlaws and weak coasts receptive to enemy infiltration (and at this date Milford was indeed regarded as the route through which any future Spanish invasion would come).[2] It is unclear whether Wales is part of Cymbeline's Britain or not: Lucius asks for a safe-conduct to Milford, but his escort leaves him at the Severn (3.5.8, 17) and the territory beyond seems lawless, a place of refuge in need of civilizing. As for the Scots, they, too, seem absent from the play, yet it is a striking coincidence that when Shakespeare needed to flesh out the battle in which Posthumus and the princes earn their spurs, he drew material from the account of the battle of Luncarty (AD 976) in Holinshed's *History of Scotland*, at which special service was done by the ancestors of James Hay, one of the king's closest Scottish favourites.[3] Leah Marcus and Mary

---

[1] Terence Hawkes discusses the absence of the Welsh in *Shakespeare in the Present* (2002), pp. 46–65. See also R. J. Boling, 'Anglo-Welsh relations in *Cymbeline*', *SQ*, 51 (2000), 33–66.
[2] See the evidence collected by Garrett A. Sullivan, 'Civilizing Wales: *Cymbeline*, roads, and the landscapes of early modern Britain', in *The Drama of the Landscape* (1998). Arviragus's pseudonym, Cadwal, echoes the name of the last British king of Wales (see note to List of Characters).
[3] See Bullough, *Narrative and Dramatic Sources*, VIII, pp. 46–50; Luncarty is in Fife.

Floyd-Wilson have argued that Shakespeare was more aware of Scottish views on union than is immediately apparent, and particularly that Posthumus's alienation dramatizes the sense of abandonment or internal exile felt by Scots after James went to London.[1] Posthumus – whose name perhaps echoes the legal term *post-nati*[2] – seems insecure even though he is a favoured member of the royal bedchamber. Lacking a father and unable to be 'delve[d] . . . to the root' (1.1.28), he is confused about his identity. He is in Cymbeline's court yet not of it, unsure whether his allegiance is to Cymbeline or the Leonati, and his enemy, Cloten, is an Englishman notable for xenophobia. Thus the stable and unified entity that the play celebrates as Britain is, in reality, an imaginary and not entirely secure construct. Its faultlines match the unresolved political and cultural tensions of James's state.

In 1610 British identity was complicated by its novelty, the fact that it was contentious and contested. Significant differences of attitude towards it coexisted within the English political nation. For James the value of Britishness was the peace that it promised, internally at home and externally across Europe (where he hoped his status as monarch of several peoples would give him weight as a political arbiter). He saw himself as Rex Pacificus, and the pageantry for his accession contrasted his firm government with the disturbances that had dogged his predecessor: unlike Elizabeth's unstable female rule, James's masculine state would bring peace and quietness. The speeches at his 1604 entry compared him to Augustus, under whom the whole world was at peace, and in later years court masques frequently alluded approvingly to Virgil's first *Eclogue*, with its reference to the island as a world 'divided from the world': a trope that Cloten echoes when he calls Britain a 'world by itself' (3.1.13).[3] Stuart poets took Virgil's passing but famous allusion to Britain's remoteness as testimony to the island's autonomy, its happy separation from Europe's troubles, and as powerful confirmation of the Union's geographical rationale, that James had restored a territorial integrity prescribed by nature. And James brought further security by his bodily fertility, being (like Cymbeline) a father to many heirs, a 'majestic cedar . . . whose issue / Promises Britain peace and plenty' (5.4.455–6).[4] When Cymbeline announces 'My peace we

---

[1] Marcus, *Puzzling Shakespeare*, pp. 106–59; Floyd-Wilson, 'Delving to the root: *Cymbeline*, Scotland and the English race', in D. J. Baker and W. Maley, eds., *British Identities and English Renaissance Literature* (2002), pp. 101–15. Floyd-Wilson's further suggestion that Cloten and the Queen are 'Pictish' characters (that is, ancient Scots) is less convincing: rather, Shakespeare invests Cloten with many of the habits of contemporary *English* aristocracy at Whitehall.

[2] Marcus, *Puzzling Shakespeare*, p. 125. The problem with this is that the fit is not quite exact: Posthumus's situation is closer to that of the *ante-nati*, the Scots born before 1603, who were not naturalized under English law. Posthumus's problem is not that his king has left him behind (like the Scots who remained in the north after 1603 and were in fact happy to do so) but that he is in a British court which he no longer feels is home.

[3] For this trope, see J. W. Bennett, 'Britain among the Fortunate Isles', *SP*, 53 (1956), 114–49; G. M. MacLean, *Time's Witness: Historical Representation in English Poetry 1603–1660* (1990), pp. 64–78; and more generally, H. Erskine-Hill, *The Augustan Idea in English Literature* (1983). King James called Britain 'a little world within itself' in his first speech to parliament: *Political Writings*, p. 136.

[4] Shakespeare uses this same image to describe James I directly in *H8*, 5.4.52–4, but it was also prominent in the literature of Union: compare C. Jordan, *Shakespeare's Monarchies: Ruler and Subject in the Romances* (1997), p. 83. James's peace credentials were strong in 1610, for he was currently acting as mediator between Spain and the Netherlands in the Cleves-Julich crisis.

will begin' (5.4.457), Jacobean audiences would have taken that possessive pronoun as echoing their own monarch's pride in the stable empire that he alone guaranteed.

Against this view of British priorities was that of James's heir, Prince Henry. Although only sixteen in 1610, Henry was already acquiring a reputation as an enthusiast for more aggressive policies than his father's. An athletic youth, who cut a figure on the tiltyard and maintained a circle of admirers, he wanted Britain to take a lead in Europe by cultivating alliances with Protestant states and he attracted followers who disliked James's pacifism. His cultural patronage was forward-looking but his political sympathies cast backwards, to the Protestant nationalism associated with the Tudors – an idea of empire as heroic enterprise rather than Augustan peace.¹ Such notions were at a premium in 1610, for this was when, politically, Henry came of age. His first solo appearance at court was in January 1610, demonstrating his skill at push of pike, with sixty-two assistants. These exercises were prefaced with speeches from Ben Jonson that hailed him as a new Prince Arthur and hymned the rebirth of British valour. Jonson praised the island's 'ancient name', and linked it with the tradition that before Julius Caesar subdued the Britons, they had twice defeated him: thus Britain was 'the only name made Caesar fly'.² Even more notable was Henry's investiture as Prince of Wales in June, the shows for which harked back to a past when Britain had been a nursery of heroes. The main court event was Samuel Daniel's masque *Tethys' Festival*, which featured a scene depicting Milford Haven, Wales's main port but also a spot identified with Tudor imperialism. As the masque explained, Milford was the place where Henry VII landed en route to defeat Richard III, from which event came the union of Lancaster and York, and, under Henry's great-great-grandson James, the greater union of England and Scotland. This made it the symbolic spot where Tudor Britain could be said to have begun:³

> The happy port of union, which gave way
> To that great hero Henry and his fleet,
> To make the blest conjunction that begat
> A greater, and more glorious far than that.

Although the masque warned Henry against excessive ambition, it presented him with Astraea's sword in token of his princely hopefulness. We need not see the prominence that Milford assumes in Cymbeline's topography as a direct allusion to Henry's neo-Tudor cult,⁴ but Henry's masques demonstrate that these associations were well known and were subject to conflicting investments. *Cymbeline* was written for a culture in which alternative versions of the national myth uneasily coexisted.

---

¹ See Roy Strong, *Prince Henry and England's Lost Renaissance* (1986).
² *Ben Jonson*, VII, pp. 323, 328.
³ D. Lindley, ed., *Court Masques* (1995), p. 59.
⁴ Rather, it was common stock; see Michael Drayton's *Poly-Olbion* (1612), V, ll. 49–56, and John Selden's note on this passage; the map of English and Welsh invasion points in John Speed's *Theatre of the Empire of Great Britain* (1611); and Camden's *Britannia* (transl. P. Holland, 1610), p. 651. It is tempting to associate *Cymbeline*'s lost princes living in their cave with Prince Henry's masque *Oberon* (1611), in which he made his entry from a fairy palace hidden inside a rock, were it not that the dates are against it. However, all Henry's masques traded in tropes that presented him as a sleeping Arthurian hero.

In *Cymbeline* these rival historiographies come together in 3.1, when the Britons refuse Lucius's demand for tribute. Critics have been perplexed that Cloten and the Queen, characters who are not respectfully treated, should be the mouthpieces of British defiance, but it is important to understand the contested nature of the history that the scene presents. Lucius's account of his mission derives from Julius Caesar's narrative of his two invasions (55–54 BC) in *The Gallic War*, which describes his encounter with Cassivelaunus (Shakespeare's Cassibelan) and the tactics that routed the Britons. But in Cloten's and the Queen's version, Caesar wins only after being 'twice beaten' (3.1.26), once by Cassibelan and once by the island itself, the seas of which wreck his ships. These details come from another, disparaging tradition, first found in anti-Caesarian writers such as Lucan, and vastly elaborated by Geoffrey of Monmouth, which held that Caesar conquered only by subterfuge and at great cost.[1] In the second invasion, says Geoffrey, Caesar needed help from a British traitor and lost his ships on caltrops hidden in the water, while in the first invasion Cassibelan beat him in hand-to-hand combat and captured his sword (compare *Cym.* 3.1.29–33). Shakespeare does not, then, dramatize a single source, for in Holinshed Geoffrey's story was anthologized side by side with material deriving from Caesar, presenting two versions of the same events. Shakespeare's Britons voice the Galfridian line, for Geoffrey represented Caesar as a braggart getting his comeuppance from the Britons. Geoffrey's Cassibelan deplores the invasion as a symptom of Caesar's insatiable ambition, and an insult to a free people. Not only are the Romans greedy, he says, 'they want us to surrender our liberty and to endure perpetual bondage by becoming subject to them', even though they share an inheritance through their common ancestor Aeneas (compare *Cym.* 3.1.46–51).[2] Moreover, *Cymbeline*'s anti-Roman rhetoric recollects a further passage in Geoffrey, in which, many generations later, the great hero Arthur refuses a renewed demand for the tribute originally imposed by Caesar.[3] Arthur retorts that Caesar's conquest was illegal, and anyway, these days his nation is stronger than it was (cf. *Cym.* 3.1.34–7 and 2.4.20–2). Perhaps not coincidentally, the name of the Roman procurator whose demand he refuses is Lucius.[4]

In 1610 a story displaying resurgent British heroism would have appealed to those for whom national identity was linked to national aspiration, but in representing the Britons as aggressively self-assertive and rebels to empire, it potentially conflicted with the more pacific and internationalist determinations of Jacobean kingship. It is all the more striking, then, that in *Cymbeline* the Queen's defiance of Lucius evokes not so much James's peaceful imperialism as the old Elizabethan rhetoric of English separateness. Praising the land's geographical defences – '[t]he natural bravery of your

---

[1] See Homer B. Nearing Jr., 'The legend of Julius Caesar's British conquest', *PMLA*, 64 (1949), 889–929.

[2] Geoffrey of Monmouth, *History of the Kings of Britain*, pp. 107–8 (*Historia Regum Britanniae*, 4.2).

[3] *History of the Kings of Britain*, pp. 232–3 (*Historia Regum Britanniae*, 9.16). I am grateful to Lesley Johnson for drawing this striking echo to my attention. See also J. E. Curran, 'Royalty unlearned, honor untaught: British savages and historical change in *Cymbeline*', *CompD*, 31 (1997), 277–303.

[4] Marshall (*Theatre and Empire*, pp. 73–5) and Donna B. Hamilton (*Shakespeare and the Politics of Protestant England*, 1992, p. 150) both argue that the name refers to Lucius, the first Christian king of Britain (*Historia Regum Britanniae*, 4.19–5.1), but there is nothing in the play to link Lucius with a Christian theology. The Arthurian Lucius is much likelier as a source for the name.

isle, which stands / As Neptune's park, ribbed and paled in / With oaks unscalable and roaring waters' (3.1.18–20) – the Queen expresses national difference in terms that recall the iconography of the Armada years, and such Shakespearean precursors as John of Gaunt's panegyric to the sceptred isle, nature's fortress and womb of kings. In this older, more militantly nationalistic language, the land was conflated with the body of the ruler, Elizabeth's virginity signifying her land's immunity to foreign encroachment – the famous example being the Ditchley portrait that showed her standing on the English map. In *Cymbeline* Britain's resistance to what Gaunt calls 'the envious siege of wat'ry Neptune' (*R2* 2.1.62–3) has its equivalent in the 'salt-water girdle' that Cloten evokes (3.1.77), warding off, like some topographical chastity belt, any pollution that might sully the national maidenhead.[1] Such sexualized resonances are inevitable once the Queen becomes the voice of British resistance – and seconded as she is by Cloten, an effeminized character obsessed with foreign fashions and who somehow seems to lack a father – but as a national mouthpiece she is clearly problematic. Not only is she a distorted memory of the Elizabethan past, a descendant of unruly Amazons like Shakespeare's Tamora, Joan of Arc and Queen Margaret, but her patriotism is tainted by her secret ambitions for power. One of the play's aims will be to disentangle British identity from the feminized and aggressive model of nationhood that she voices. Native valour is ultimately endorsed, but in terms distinct from the Queen's patriotic enthusiasms.

In the unfolding action competing models of political identity gradually crystallize around Innogen and the princes, characters whose views on nationhood pointedly reverse the Queen's assumptions about British exceptionality. There is, of course, a precise structural correlation between the Queen's response to Roman invasion and Innogen's exposure to Iachimo's sexual predation. The obsession with Innogen's bodily purity foreshadows the problems of political encroachment that occur in the other plot, for Iachimo's attempts to possess her parallel the imperial conquests of which the Britons complain. His sexual boasts neatly echo Caesar's political 'brag' of 'Came, and saw, and overcame' (3.1.23–4): Posthumus's nightmare image of Innogen being mounted by a boar crystallizes the underlying fear of pollution, monstrous contamination of the species. For a while it seems that the defence of her chastity will create a new, feminized focus for national identity, a symbolic rallying-point that expresses an opposition between national purity and foreign difference. Particularly, Innogen's association with the Roman Lucrece – signalled explicitly in Iachimo's comparison of himself to Tarquin (2.2.12) – seems to foreshadow that her fate will be tragic, and tied up with policing the boundary between the home and its enemies. In Livy's *History of Rome* (1.57–9), Lucrece is raped by Sextus Tarquinius, son of Rome's last king, when

---

[1] See L. Woodbridge, 'Palisading the body politic', *Texas Studies in Language and Literature*, 33 (1991), 327–54; J. Mikalachki, 'The masculine romance of Roman Britain: *Cymbeline* and early modern English nationalism', *SQ*, 46 (1995), 301–22; and R. Smallwood, 'We will nothing pay for wearing our own noses', in M. T. Jones-Davies, ed., *Shakespeare: Cosmopolitisme et Insularité* (1994), pp. 97–113. For a suggestive non-Shakespearean conflation of Elizabeth and her land, see George Peele's *The Battle of Alcazar*, ed. W. W. Greg (1907), ll. 722–62, which depicts the island as a shining fortress surrounded by the sea and crowned by the Queen's sacred person.

he becomes inflamed with desire for her after hearing her husband boasting about her beauty and chastity; her suicide is the trigger for the rebellion that expels the Tarquins from Rome. Lucrece's death is thus the moment of violence out of which the republic is made, a traumatic sacrifice that creates a new state. But Innogen's history takes a different turn, for though resisting her assailants at court, she joins with the Romans, and in doing so she pointedly rebuts Cloten's notion that 'Britain's /A world by itself':

> *Pisanio.*   If not at court,
>   Then not in Britain must you bide.
> *Innogen.*   Where then?
>   Hath Britain all the sun that shines? Day, night,
>   Are they not but in Britain? I'th'world's volume
>   Our Britain seems as of it, but not in't;
>   In a great pool a swan's nest. Prithee, think
>   There's livers out of Britain.   (3.4.133–9)

The idea of Britain as a swan's nest in a great pool conceptualizes nationhood in far less confident terms than the Queen's 'Neptune's park' image. The swan's nest may be peaceful, but it preserves its separateness at the cost of marginality to the larger world, the pool's edges from which it withdraws. Innogen's words revisit the famous trope from Virgil's first Eclogue, '*penitus toto divisus orbe Britannos*' ('Britain, that place cut off at the world's end'), but unlike virtually all other Stuart commentators, who see it as testifying to Britain's protective difference, she foregrounds its negative charge, its burden of longing and alienation. In the line's original context, the speaker Meliboeus – a farmer whose lands Augustus has seized for his veterans – voices his pain at being displaced to the wild north, to live with the coarse and uncivilized Britons. From this more truly Virgilian perspective, which registers the costs as well as the achievements of Augustan peace, Britain's isolation looks protective but means exile to the global periphery, far from the sunlight of the imperial south.[1] After this it is perhaps inevitable that despite Innogen's plans, she fails to reach Milford Haven, the sacred spot of Tudor nationalism. Instead of becoming the mother of the Britons, she is sidetracked into setting up home with princes whose stepmother, Euriphile, has a name that means 'Lover of Europe'.

Similar political adjustments are at work in the representation of the princes, characters who will eventually emerge as the embodiments of the British future. They are placed at the Welsh border – one of those places where Britain's constituent parts meet – and their life poses sharp ethnographic questions about British identity. James's accession had intensified interest in the character of the island's early peoples, but the topic had already been broached by Elizabethan historians, notably by William Camden,

[1] The only other writer to invoke the trope this way is Samuel Daniel. In *Musophilus* (1599), critiquing the suitability of English as a literary language, he asks, 'Is this the walk of all your wide renown, / This little point, this scarce discerned isle / Thrust from the world, with whom our speech unknown / Made never traffic of our style' (ll. 426–9); and in *The Civil Wars* (1599–1609), he has rebellious subjects complain that England's isolation makes it prone to tyranny: 'Why Neptune, hast thou made us stand alone / Divided from the world, for this, say they? / Hemmed in, to be a spoil to tyranny, / Leaving affliction hence no way to fly' (quoted in MacLean, *Time's Witness*, pp. 70–1). But both these references are ironic; only Shakespeare handles the trope in the Virgilian manner.

whose monumental work *Britannia* (Latin edition 1586; in English 1610) contained the first serious extended account of the pre-Roman inhabitants. Camden's description of the Britons is critical historiography of a very different stamp from Holinshed's. He ignored Geoffrey's imaginary kings and their fanciful achievements, and drew his evidence from Tacitus, Herodian and Diodorus Siculus. In Camden's view the Britons were not a sophisticated people but barbarians similar to the Gauls. Their lack of civility was marked: they wore skins or went naked, tattooed their bodies and painted them with woad, used iron rings as currency and held women in common. Their principal aspect was fierceness in battle: Caesar and other writers found them 'most warlike, and exceedingly given to slaughter' (p. 15).[1]

Camden imbibed from the classical historians an admiration of the Britons' spirit, but he welcomed the invasion for its cultural imperialism and civilizing influence. Reproducing a coin of Cunobelinus, or Cymbeline, 'who flourished in the days of Augustus and Tiberius', he remarked that its image – a two-headed Janus (see figure 3) – suited a time when 'Britons began to cast off and leave their barbarous rudeness. For we read how Janus was the first that changed barbarous manners into civil behaviour, and therein was depainted with two foreheads, to signify that he had of one shape made another' (p. 97). Although the Roman yoke was 'grievous', it was a 'saving health' to the Britons, for 'the brightness of that most glorious empire chased away all savage barbarism from [their] minds'. Bringing contact with civil life, arts and laws, it 'framed them to good manners and behaviour so as in their diet and apparel they were not inferior to any other provinces' (pp. 62–3). Whether or not Shakespeare read Camden,[2] he must have known that a more historically astute view of the Britons, as a people who benefited from colonization, was starting to develop. For example, the ancient Briton depicted on the title-page of John Speed's *Theatre of the Empire of Great Britain* (1611) was clearly a warlike barbarian (figure 4).[3]

Shakespeare's handling of the princes responds to these historiographical shifts and their consequences for the separatist and patriotic Tudor myths. Cymbeline defies Lucius by evoking the Galfridian king Mulmutius, and his laws and traditions (3.1.52), but the Welsh scenes quietly ignore Geoffrey's fantastic genealogies. Instead, the boys' suitability for rule is shown in the moral and physical benefits of austerity. Dwellers of cave and mountain, they are hunters rather than farmers, and their communal life, with its pagan religion and lack of comforts, seems like an early stage in the prehistory of civilization. Their tough, northern upbringing – 'freezing hours' in a 'pinching cave' untainted by society's luxuries (3.3.37–9) – breeds a self-confidence and fierce reckless-ness, what Shaw called their 'grave, rather sombre, uncivilized primeval strength and

---

[1] Quotations are from Philemon Holland's translation (1610).

[2] Shakespeare's friend Ben Jonson was Camden's pupil and he frequently drew historical information from *Britannia*. See also the note to *Cym.* 5.3.55.

[3] Polydore Vergil also says that the Britons were made 'more civil' by the Romans, and Milton's *History of Britain* says the Romans 'beat us into our civility: likely else to have continued longer in a barbarous and savage manner of life'; quoted in Thomas G. Olsen, 'Iachimo's drug-damn'd Italy and the problem of British national character in *Cymbeline*', in Holger Klein and Michele Marrapodi, eds., *Shakespeare and Italy* (1999), pp. 269–96. For other historians and the increasing currency of scholarly views, see Curran, 'Royalty unlearned, honor untaught'; and Kendrick, *British Antiquity*.

Figure 3. Coins struck in the reign of Cymbeline, from William Camden's *Britannia*, 1637 edition (first published 1586)

Figure 4. An ancient Briton, from the title-page of John Speed's *Theatre of the Empire of Great Britain*, 1611

Mohican dignity'.[1] But while their fortitude contrasts attractively with the pampered visitors from the 'spongy south' (4.2.349), the play stages an anxiety that their wildness is simply barbaric. The Romano-British encounters put British claims to civility in doubt, for in 'duller Britain' Iachimo's 'Italian brain' clearly has the edge (5.4.196–7). The boys' ethnic inferiority is seen in their skin colour, which is tanned and weathered by outdoor life (4.4.29–30),[2] and by their embarrassment over their mountain education, which teaches them manners from the wolf and fox (3.3.40–1). Their association with the cave is especially resonant, as it links them with notions of long-term social evolution that were coming to be entertained about the origins of nations. Particularly, once the American races were encountered, it was increasingly understood that modern societies had not declined from a prior Golden Age but developed from a state of nature.[3] The princes' troglodyte life and unsqueamishly violent treatment of Cloten pointedly evoke the spectre of barbarism. In particular, Guiderius's appearance with Cloten's clotpoll in his hand could have reminded audiences of Theodore de Bry's remarkable image of a naked and tattooed Pict, carrying weapons of war and an enemy's newly severed head. One of a set of engravings of ancient peoples that appeared as an ethnographical appendix to Thomas Hariot's *Brief and True Account of the New Found Land of Virginia* (1590), it was reprinted for Speed's *Theatre of . . . Great Britain*, to illustrate the nakedness and savagery of Britain's early inhabitants (see figure 5). These engravings exemplify the anxieties about lineage that were aroused by changing perceptions of the past. They suggest how unsettling must have been the relocation of national ancestry from heroic Trojans to such primitive forebears.[4]

Cymbeline's Welsh scenes adjudicate between the rival claims of civility and simplicity, and by emphasizing the princes' 'invisible instinct' (4.2.176), they assuage fears that their pre-civilized state marks them out as savages. The princes are at odds with their environment and eager to leave it: their impatience with the mountains signals their educability, their intuition towards culture and away from wildness. Milford may be the Tudors' iconographical home, but the princes' internal compass is Anglocentric: they dislike the barrenness of Wales and their affinities draw them to the centre. This is further underlined by Belarius's insistence on their innate virtue, that they have 'royalty unlearned, honour untaught, / Civility not seen from other' (4.2.177–8), which testifies to the promptings of nature. Shakespeare uses this trope elsewhere, especially in *The Winter's Tale*, but in *Cymbeline* it marks the boys out as ethnographically privileged, sequestering them from the discourse of barbarism that was applied to other supposedly inferior ethnic groups. In particular, it segregates them not only from the (absent)

---

[1] Shaw, 'Blaming the bard', in *Plays and Players*, p. 121.

[2] Shakespeare strikingly adjusts Camden in representing the British climate as hard and unforgiving (here and in the dirge). A major part of Camden's discussion of ancient British identity focuses on the softness of the climate, as reported by Caesar and other writers, making Britain the temperate nation *par excellence* (*Britannia*, pp. 1–15). By contrast, Shakespeare makes the British climate seem harsher and correspondingly inferior to the warmth of Rome.

[3] See A. B. Fergusson, *Utter Antiquity: Perceptions of Prehistory in Renaissance England* (1993), pp. 61–83.

[4] De Bry's engravings, and other ethnographic images, are discussed in Stuart Piggott's *Ancient Britons and the Antiquarian Imagination* (1989), pp. 73–86. Camden was one of the first historians to compare ancient Britons with New World races (see Piggott, p. 74).

Figure 5. Two ancient Picts by Theodore de Bry, from Thomas Hariot's *Brief and True Account of the New Found Land of Virginia*, 1590

native Welsh, but implicitly from the Irish, who in the early modern period were the people most relentlessly stigmatized as primitives in need of colonization. John Speed's account of the early Britons exemplifies how such anxieties took hold. While admiring the Britons' physical toughness, Speed is shocked to perceive similarities between their customs and those of modern peoples that he regards as 'savage', such as their habit of going naked:[1]

> The like patience [that is, tolerance of nakedness] we find even now not only in the wilder Irish and Virginians, but in rogues and wanderers of our own country, who often, pitiless of themselves, voluntarily deprive their bodies of their protection against the air's offence, to procure pity of others.

If Shakespeare's wild Britons are disturbingly similar to contemporary peoples that his society regarded as inferior, they are themselves travelling in the opposite direction from their 'primitive' counterparts on the Jacobean periphery. At the Welsh border British virtue is reconstituted in terms pointedly unlike the irredeemable savagery of Britain's own colonized or subjected races. For all that Cymbeline's sons will fight the invaders, their instinct is to eschew provinciality and assimilate the Roman values of empire.

[1] *Theatre of the Empire of Great Britain* (1611), pp. 179–80.

The princes' attitudes help to explain the play's magnificent but perplexing ending, in which Cymbeline resubmits Britain to Rome, and agrees to pay the tribute that had caused all the trouble. On the face of it, this quixotic submission reverses all that warfare had achieved. Although gaining the moral victory, Cymbeline hands the advantage back to Lucius. The invaders are forgiven, peace is proclaimed, and a 'Roman and a British ensign wave / Friendly together' (5.4.478–9). Solidarity with the Pannonians and Dalmatians is forgotten: Britain, it seems, cannot remain independent in the face of Rome's overwhelming preeminence. And yet the war is not totally pointless, for though Britain loses autonomy, she remains unconquered. Victory puts relations with Rome on a new footing, making Britain more a competitor than a colony. The future is projected in Philarmonus's second account of his vision:

> the Roman eagle,
> From south to west on wing soaring aloft,
> Lessened herself, and in the beams o'th'sun
> So vanished; which foreshowed our princely eagle,
> Th'imperial Caesar, should again unite
> His favour with the radiant Cymbeline,
> Which shines here in the west. (5.4.468–74)

When he first described this dream (4.2.346–52), Philarmonus thought that it predicted Rome's inexorable expansion, but his second account diminishes Rome's role. Not only does the eagle 'lessen' and turn female (becoming 'herself'), but by disappearing into Cymbeline's 'sun' she foreshadows a westering of empire, to British dynasties as yet unborn. Britain is not yet great, nor is Rome's status reduced: nonetheless, Cymbeline's control of the ending and Philarmonus's gloss on it suggest that Britain is the nation to which Rome's historic role will pass, the ultimate beneficiary of the Augustan legacy. It is Britain that will eventually inherit the Augustan *imperium*.

The resolution, then, suggests a new account of nationhood, a myth of origin that locates Britain in a chain of political paternity descending to Cymbeline from Augustus and Jupiter. Strikingly, this idea does not depend on fictitious genealogies like those boasted by Cloten and the Queen. Although British valour is vindicated, the shrill, insular patriots are not endorsed: Mulmutius and his laws are forgotten, the Queen is dead, and Cloten is dispatched by the same heroes who repel the invaders. The Romans are routed, but so are the Little Englanders: British virtue ends aligned with peace and empire, not militant separation. Moreover, this reconstituted nation is emphatically male-centred: power is left in the hands of fatherly monarchs. The final scene excludes unruly queens and their offspring, while the only woman on stage, Innogen, is dressed as a boy and using a pseudonym that expresses devotion to her husband. Female absence is underlined by Cymbeline's extraordinary response to his sons' return, calling himself father and mother at a triple birth:

> Oh, what am I,
> A mother to the birth of three? Ne'er mother
> Rejoiced deliverance more. (5.4.368–70)

Janet Adelman calls this startling remark a 'parthenogenesis fantasy', which imagines biological reproduction as happening without sexual congress: it clearly harks back to Posthumus's earlier wish that men could propagate themselves without women.[1] In fact, although Cymbeline may think he alone is father and mother, women remain crucial to his family in hidden ways. Guiderius is identified only through 'a most curious mantle wrought by th'hand / Of his queen mother', and by the foresight of 'wise nature', who stamped him with a wonderful mole, a genetic mark that exactly mirrors Innogen's bodily 'stain' (5.4.361–8). Cymbeline's world is thus more indebted to women than he chooses to admit. Nonetheless, behind these manoeuvres one senses the pressure of James's political culture and the emerging ideological configurations of a monarchy that was invested in the idea of the King as father to his people and ruler of a stable national family. Like James, Cymbeline is peaceful, cosmopolitan and a modernizer, but his kingship is no less potent for being pacific. In his state, authority is invested in a strong and self-authorizing fatherhood.

The conclusion focuses much that seems contradictory in the action, not least the split personalities of the Romans, whom the play depicts as at once predatory and benevolent.[2] Cymbeline seems as much Augustus's foster-child as his tributary king, proud of his education in Rome, and of being knighted by the emperor. Such anachronistic paternalism is repeated when Lucius adopts Innogen, promising rather to 'father thee than master thee' (4.2.395); this recalls Holinshed's remark that Cymbeline kept friends with Augustus 'because the youth of the Briton nation should not be deprived of the benefit to be trained and brought up among the Romans, whereby they might learn both to behave themselves like civil men, and to attain the knowledge of feats of war'.[3] But against these caring Romans stand the 'injurious' invaders (3.1.45), Caesar and Iachimo, whose actions show the oppressive aspect of Roman paternity. In British memory Julius Caesar was a vain despot, imposing his 'yoke' on the island without cause (3.1.49) and driven by a desire for mastery. The same drive reappears in Iachimo: his assault on Innogen replays Caesar's invasion, providing renewed grounds for British rebellion. Of course, the two Romes are flagrantly at odds. So marked is the disparity between Augustus and Iachimo that the play frequently seems disarticulated, as if competing stories were coexisting in the same text. But the split identity of the Romans stages an Oedipal scenario: it expresses the trauma of inheritance, that for Britain to emerge as a nation in its own right, the burden of resentment towards its political father must be discharged. British revolt is directed against Caesar and his surrogate Iachimo, who, as Augustus's evil twins, focus the anger felt towards the parent; but once they are defeated, friendship with the father is renewed. Although Rome's power remains intact, the Britons vindicate their place on the world stage, coming of age as an independent nation and as Rome's heir. As Posthumus predicts to Philario, Augustus does find the Britons a 'people such / That mend upon the world' (2.4.25–6).

---

[1] *Suffocating Mothers*, p. 202. A different view of this passage is argued in Wayne, 'The career of *Cymbeline*'s manacle'.
[2] The best recent discussion is Peter A. Parolin, 'Anachronistic Italy: cultural alliances and national identity in *Cymbeline*', *S.St.*, 30 (2002), 188–215.
[3] Bullough, VIII, p. 44.

This drama of inheritance frames the final act, which stages spectacular rites of passage to move Posthumus and the princes out of their subordinated pasts and into achieved social identities. The trajectory into manhood is clearest with the princes, who from the first appear as adolescents on the cusp of masculinity. Belarius thinks of them as 'boys', and they revere their mother's memory, but they are eager for the wider world and need to break their ties with home, their spirits 'fly[ing] out' (3.3.90) at tales of heroism in larger spaces. As is shown by their problems with the dirge, their biological clocks are just ticking into adulthood. Editors have speculated that Shakespeare inserted the dialogue in which they refuse to sing because their voices have 'got the mannish crack' (4.2.235) when he found himself writing for unsuitable actors, but their coyness is dramatically necessary: it shows their transitional status as maturing adolescents. That threshold is crossed in the battle, which confirms their coming of age by validating them as adult warriors, while Posthumus's narrative of the battle draws out its implications for British masculinity by wrapping it in eroticized language. The boys are 'striplings', with skins as delicate as a woman's and more suited to childish games, but so thrilling are their looks that they would turn a 'distaff to a lance' (5.3.19–22, 34). Inspiring their fellows to 'stand' (31), they beat the Roman eagles into chickens and inflict 'back door' wounds on them (45) – alluding to the shame of being hurt in flight, but perhaps suggesting a taint of effeminacy. Moreover, this encounter happens at a symbolic spot, a 'strait lane' (7) that is vulnerable to Roman penetration and intensely fought over by the men who crowd there. Critics have dwelt on this place's erotic geography, which echoes the larger anxiety about the endangered bodies of Innogen and the nation.[1] By leading the ejection of intruders from a weak territorial 'passage' (23), the princes prove their masculine valour and the collective bonds of national brotherhood. Their victory roots British identity in an emerging code of manliness: their leadership subordinates old heterosexual rivalries within a new homosocial kinship.

Much the same happens with Posthumus, who ends the battle with his masculinity reaffirmed. He defeats the person who cuckolded him, leaving Iachimo swordless, 'enfeeble[d]' and mourning his 'manhood' (5.2.2–4). Yet Posthumus's trajectory differs from the princes', for the final act relieves him of any public role in the emerging British state. As his obsessive costume changes show, from Roman to Briton and back again, he has lost his political moorings. He is also self-abnegating: convinced of his wrong in murdering Innogen, he takes up arms for oblivion, seeking a guiltless death in battle, suicide without self-slaughter (5.3.80–3). And crucially, although he redeems himself by valour, he ends disconnected from the high ambitions that were previously associated with him. This swerve is striking because thus far the play has ratcheted up expectations about him. Patricia Parker notes how frequently the lovers are framed by Virgilian echoes, epic resonances that link them to the founding of Rome: the hints that Juno is their enemy (3.4.164, 5.3.125, 131), that Posthumus's treachery is like Sinon's,

---

[1] Woodbridge, 'Palisading the body politic'; C. Kahn, *Roman Shakespeare: Warriors, Wounds, and Women* (1997), p. 164. On the play's shift between heterosexuality to homosociality, see Mikalachki, 'The masculine romance of Roman Britain'.

that the abandoned Innogen is a new Dido or Hecuba (3.4.56, 4.2.312).[1] Rather as Innogen seems to repeat Lucrece's story (p. 43 above), Posthumus looks like a new Aeneas, heading for empire – especially since Jupiter's promises to the ghosts that he will protect their son repeat what the same god told Aeneas's mother, Venus, in Book 1 of the *Aeneid*. Yet this trail is false, for though the prophecy implies that British fortunes hang on Posthumus's redemption, the events that follow – the return of Innogen's brothers – remove him from the prospect of rule to the role of private subject. His reward is not to achieve glory on his own account but to have his family restored and his self-worth renewed within the dynastic matrix of father, mother and brothers. And since the Leonati's main characteristic is a history of heroism in the 'country's cause' (5.3.146), Posthumus's recovery of family identity gives him both psychological and political resolution. His story affirms the duty of service to Britain while reasserting the independent value of the name which he bears as a member of a 'valiant race' (5.3.152). He becomes a British subject, but his otherness, his difference from Cymbeline's family, is respected – indeed, insisted on.

As we shall see (pp. 55–60), when the eighteenth- and nineteenth-century stages turned the play into a domestic romance, the lovers became the dramatic focus. But in Shakespeare's more politicized version, the king remains symbolically central, despite his slightness as a character. The ending vindicates his authority, by defeating external and internal threats to family and state, and this projects a model of power that mirrors the personalized monarchy of 1610: British sovereignty and nationhood inhere in the king's very person. But the play radically complicates the nature of that Britain over which he finally presides. His state and family are not so much unities as hybrids: their bodies are mongrelized and miscegenated. As is signalled by their double names, the young princes have dual citizenship. They are heirs to Cymbeline but are brought up as Welshmen, and their residual uncouthness extends and unsettles his court's idea of civility. Posthumus, too, remains half a stranger, an insider who is also an outsider and who has voyaged beyond the bounds. For all that the family accepts him, he ends dressed as a Roman and proud of his recovered link with the Leonati, an identity that suggests a different genetics of Britishness. As for Innogen, she has traversed the land, and in doing so she binds together the various components of Cymbeline's heterogeneous Britain. She comes from Lud's Town but makes herself at home in Wales, she finds friends among the Romans, and by her marriage she creates a place in her father's circle for Posthumus, the alienated insider. So while British identity is forged by defeating the enemy, it cannot happen without some kind of miscegenation. It is not a fait accompli dictated by the centre, nor a colonial absorption of subaltern bodies, but a process in which internal differences are accommodated and respected. And Innogen is the very embodiment of this. Shifting her identity from place to place, resisting the intruder yet marrying beyond her tribe, and embraced by Posthumus not as a conquest or possession but as the vine embraces the elm (5.4.263), she is the figure for a family constructed through partnership. It is, too, a remarkable testimony to *Cymbeline*'s dispersed image of the polity that events end not at Lud's Town but

---

[1] Parker, 'Romance and empire'. See also James, *Shakespeare's Troy*, p. 162.

at the periphery, where the boundaries between and among Britain's constituent parts are negotiated. Cymbeline may be King of Britain, but his realm is more than England writ large. The decentred, centrifugal nature of his story means that the king is only one component of the political process that the play has traced.

CYMBELINE ON STAGE

Although there must have been many early performances, records exist of only two. One was seen by Simon Forman in 1611, probably at the Globe (see pp. 3–4 above). The other was a revival taken to court on 1 January 1634, where it was 'well liked by the king'.[1] Probably it appealed to Charles I's interest in British origins, and it may have been popular at the Caroline court, for there are echoes of it in Walter Montagu's pastoral *The Shepherd's Paradise* (1633). No other early references survive, but its impact can perhaps be traced in a Jacobean vogue for plays on the Romano-British wars, such as Fletcher's *Bonduca* (*c.* 1612; on Boadicea), and R. A.'s *The Valiant Welshman* (printed 1615; on Caradoc) – though in both these examples the Romans beat the Britons.[2]

After the Restoration *Cymbeline* was among the plays assigned to the King's Company, but it regained currency only in an adapted version by Thomas Durfey, *The Injured Princess, or the Fatal Wager* (1682). Durfey turned it into a sentimental tragedy, high on thrills and pathos, and with some sensational coups de théâtre. Naming Posthumus and Innogen Ursaces and Eugenia, he restyled them after the protagonists of heroic drama, and made the Queen an electrifying villain and Cloten a block-headed debauchee; and he greatly increased the emotional temperature, turning the plot into a series of heart-stopping cliffhangers. Ursaces quarrels violently with Shatillion (= Iachimo, now a cynical French gallant), and Eugenia, unable to convince Pisanio of her innocence, is left alone to wander the desert. Meanwhile Pisanio has a daughter, whom Cloten attempts to rape: Pisanio saves her but is blinded for his pains. Ursaces eventually kills Shatillion in battle, but Shatillion's confession that he had slandered Eugenia sends Ursaces into a despair far more extravagant than anything Posthumus experiences. Durfey also coarsened the play's tone. Pisanio and Belarius endorse Ursaces's misogyny, and Eugenia's sexuality is treated very disrespectfully. In lines added to her interview with Shatillion, she ponders for a long time whether she should give in to him, only to recoil at the last moment. Her virtue is vindicated, but Durfey does little to dispel the idea that no woman can be trusted.[3]

---

[1] N. W. Bawcutt, *The Control and Censorship of Caroline Drama* (1996), p. 185.

[2] 'R. A.' may have been the clown Robert Armin. Echoes of *Cymbeline* in *The Valiant Welshman* include the Welsh king's defiance of Caesar's emissary, and a scene showing a sleeping Welsh princess sexually menaced by an intruding Roman. The first Roman invasions are also depicted in *Fuimus Troies, or the True Trojans* (published 1633) by the academic playwright Jasper Fisher, which presents Julius Caesar as a manifest tyrant who is initially humbled by British valour. A slightly earlier play on similar themes is William Rowley's *A Shoemaker a Gentleman* (1609?).

[3] J. I. Marsden, 'Pathos and passivity: Thomas Durfey's adaptation of Shakespeare's *Cymbeline*', *Restoration*, 14:2 (1990), 71–81; M. Dobson, *The Making of the National Poet: Shakespeare, Adaptation and Authorship, 1660–1790* (1992), pp. 85–90.

The Injured Princess was revived in 1698 and seen intermittently down to 1746. More adaptations of *Cymbeline* followed, by Charles Marsh (1755), William Hawkins (1759), David Garrick (1761), Henry Brooke (1778), Thomas Holcroft (1784) and Ambrose Eccles (1793). Only Garrick's and (briefly) Hawkins's versions reached the stage, but this flurry shows that, despite Dr Johnson's doubts about the play, it struck an eighteenth-century chord. Hawkins's preface discussed the aesthetic problem, praising *Cymbeline*'s sublimity while worrying that its style was too luxuriant and uncontrolled, and he attempted to improve the structure, introducing the Romans in the first act and compressing events into two days. But what really attracted him was the play's politics, which he turned into a fantasy of expansionist nationalism, showing what Britons could do if 'To king, to country, and to honour true'.[1] His Romans are tyrants and the Britons lovers of liberty, while Cymbeline is a strong ruler who defies the invader and leads his people to victory. For once he is the play's real centre, and Cloten is a serious villain, a fifth columnist who helps the Romans because he thinks Britain needs 'the heavy lash of government' (p. 14). By contrast, Innogen's role is severely cut: she is just the occasion for an international quarrel and sleeps through the most exciting events. An epilogue urging Britain to make war on Prussia leaves no doubts as to where Hawkins thought the play's relevance lay.

Much more successful was Garrick's version, which became a theatrical staple for generations. This, too, was patriotic – it praised George III and cut the promise to resume tribute – but its main achievement was to regularize the design, consolidating it into a form suited to current tastes. Garrick tightened the plot and built a balanced structure, reducing the number of locations, ironing out problems, and creating scenic sequences (for example, he combined all the pastoral scenes into one). He cut distracting dialogue and toned down the stagecraft: Cloten's severed head, Jupiter, the Soothsayer and the prison all disappeared, and the ending was much abbreviated. The effect was to privatize the play, subordinating the political to the domestic, and enhancing its seriousness. With no riddling providence set over them, Garrick's characters are responsible for their choices, and the politics are squeezed by the extension of the wager plot into Act 3: there is little quarrel between Cymbeline and Belarius, and at the end Rome is hardly mentioned. Instead, Posthumus and Innogen become central, and events culminate with Iachimo's defeat and their reunion. In battle Posthumus tells Iachimo to 'take thy life and mend it',[2] and once Iachimo expresses penitence the play swiftly ends. Innogen is important to this arrangement, but in schematic ways: she is more a fastidiously suffering wife than a strongly individualized personality. Garrick reduced her range, making her less rebellious, shortening her emotional speeches, reining in the dirge and the monologue over the corpse: she undergoes fewer humiliations and is less demeaned by rejection.[3] But the hero is Posthumus, the role that Garrick himself

---

[1] W. Hawkins, *Cymbeline: A Tragedy Adapted from Shakespeare* (1759), p. x.
[2] *The Plays of David Garrick*, eds. H. W. Pedicord and F. L. Bergmann, IV (1981), p. 159. See also G. W. Stone, 'A century of *Cymbeline*: Garrick's magic touch', *SP*, 54 (1975), 310–22. Later editions of Garrick, such as the 1777 text, abbreviate the political plot even more severely than described in Pedicord and Bergmann.
[3] In particular, the language about her is made less sexual: we lose Cloten 'penetrating' her with the musicians' fingers, Iachimo crying 'O!' and mounting, Posthumus being 'disedged' by a new mistress, and the hints of incest with her brothers. These bowdlerizations remained standard in the nineteenth-century adaptations.

played. His version has been called one of the century's most popular comedies, but despite the happy ending, its conception is firmly tragic. It is a bourgeois tragedy focused on the moral opposition between Iachimo and Posthumus (see figure 6).

Garrick's version was phenomenally successful. It was reprinted fourteen times before 1800 and had at least 163 performances. After Garrick's retirement, his role passed to William Powell and Samuel Reddish, then to John Philip Kemble, who in the 1780s had a famous partnership with Sarah Siddons as Innogen. Their reading remained very sombre, for Siddons was a tragic actress renowned for sublimity. Observers found her Innogen 'majestic', praising her dignified sorrow, her 'lightnings of scorn' against Iachimo, and 'absolute steadiness of affection, enduring all tests and pardoning all offences'. In comparison, Mrs Jordan, the previous Innogen, lacked 'natural dignity'.[1] Kemble later made his own acting version of the play,[2] but this followed Garrick's template, the only major change being the omission of Posthumus's diatribe against women: this was not spoken again until Irving partially restored it in 1896. Mrs Siddons last played Innogen in 1802, but Kemble kept Posthumus going until 1817. His brother Charles took the part in the 1820s, as did William Macready and, briefly, Edmund Kean; the role passed to Samuel Phelps in the 1830s. A fresh revision from the folio made for Phelps's 1864 revival was the last major production from this time, but in the Garrick-Kemble version the play had achieved a century of almost continuous stage life.[3]

In this period *Cymbeline* began to acquire pictorial trappings and a veneer of sentiment. In Kemble's staging the princes entered with a dead buck on their spears, and the end saw a display of British and Roman standards; his brother's revival added Iron Age details and a 'druidical scene'.[4] Macready's 1843 production had eleven spectacular sets, in which Britain was not primitive but elegantly Romanesque, and the wager took place at a banquet in an already decadent Rome. The battle was stunningly staged: Posthumus, dressed as a peasant, defeated a gorgeously armoured Iachimo, and at the end ninety people were on stage.[5] This vogue for archaeology moved Garrick's bourgeois tragedy in more fanciful and romantic directions, and attitudes to the characters were changing, too, particularly towards Posthumus, whom, as a hero, the Victorians found lacking in moral idealism. He was still the main part for Phelps in 1864, but Macready chose to play Iachimo, and salvaged the happy ending by giving it a moralistic twist, making Iachimo a good man gone bad, expressing sincere contrition and pain at his own

---

[1] J. Boaden, *Memoirs of Mrs Siddons* (1839), pp. 357–8; L. Kelly, *The Kemble Era* (1980), p. 60.

[2] *Cymbeline: A Historical Play in Five Acts* (1808); this removes many of Garrick's verbal 'improvements' but retains the overall shape. For the developing stock stage business, see the 1815 reprint of Kemble, *Shakespeare's Cymbeline, King of Britain.*

[3] *Lacy's Acting Edition*, LXIV (1865); Phelps printed part of Posthumus's diatribe, but it was not spoken on the stage. For detailed lists of nineteenth- and early twentieth-century productions, see C. B. Young's appendix to J. C. Maxwell's New Cambridge edition, pp. xliii–xlv.

[4] See *Cymbeline: A Tragedy*, in W. Oxberry, *The New English Drama*, XII (1821); S. Rosenfeld, 'The Grieves' Shakespearean scene designs', *S. Sur.*, 20 (1967), 107–12; and C. H. Shattuck, *The Shakespeare Promptbooks: A Descriptive Catalogue* (1965), p. 81. Phelps was still using the buck in 1865.

[5] C. J. Carlisle, 'Macready's production of *Cymbeline*', in R. Foulkes, ed., *Shakespeare and the Victorian Stage* (1986), pp. 138–52.

Figure 6. Samuel Reddish as Posthumus in David Garrick's *Cymbeline* (engraving by Robert Pine, 1771)

villainy. This view had already emerged in criticism: in 1847 George Fletcher explained that Iachimo had lost faith in women but regained it on encountering Innogen.[1]

The great beneficiary of this climate was Innogen, who in the Macready–Phelps years became the play's structural and emotional centre.[2] In the astonishing hagiographies written at this time, she rates as Shakespeare's ideal woman: someone with all the virtues of Isabella, Helena, Viola and Portia, but without Juliet's despair, Cressida's petulance, Desdemona's resignation and Hermione's aloofness.[3]

Helen Faucit, who was Innogen to Macready and Phelps, wrote a long essay on the part, calling her Shakespeare's 'woman of women', 'a noble, cultivated, loving woman and wife at her best'.[4] To George Fletcher she was Shakespeare's 'highest standard of female grace, virtue and intellect'; Anna Jameson, Shakespeare's earliest 'feminist' critic, said she united all 'those qualities which we imagine to constitute excellence in woman'.[5] The aspects that appealed were her spiritual delicacy – what Faucit called 'the purity and beauty of her soul' – and her 'conjugal tenderness', that (unlike the dangerously self-willed Rosalinds and Portias) she was a heroic wife.[6] Everyone dwelt on her domesticity, the fact that cave life brought out the homemaker in her, and that 'love is [her] ruling passion, but . . . love ratified by wedlock, gentle, constant and refined'.[7] Faucit praised her cookery and suggested that the boys hurried home to enjoy her meals: she made 'their cavern home as attractive and pleasant to them as only the touch and feeling of a refined woman could'.[8] Yet while idealizing her as the angel in the house, her admirers also dwelt on her courage and emotional range. Although outwardly domesticated, she was highly strung within, and her capacity for anger and rapture was as much admired as her fidelity. In this regard the Victorian love of Innogen involved a complex dialectic between policing female identity and liberating it. She allowed a fantasy of woman as both dutiful and free.

These emphases recur in reports of Helen Faucit's Innogen. Faucit, who built her career on the role, radiated purity and innocence, courage struggling against delicacy. All spectators remembered her approach to the cave, when she called out timidly then ran away to hide, but it was her emotionalism which was most praised, her variety and intensity of feeling. With Iachimo she swayed between agony, desolation and fierce indignation; she was ecstatic at Posthumus's first letter, and fainted hysterically at the second; there was a long anguished wail over the dead body, then 'grateful, tearful,

---

[1] G. Fletcher, *Studies in Shakespeare* (1847), p. 69. See also Ann Thompson, '*Cymbeline*'s other endings', in J. I. Marsden, ed., *The Appropriation of Shakespeare* (1991), pp. 203–20.

[2] An account of the play in *The Saturday Review* for 6 April 1872 discusses the tendency of audiences to applaud the heroine. Clement Scott's preview of Irving's 1896 production suggested that the play should really be called 'Imogen' (*Daily Telegraph*, 19 September 1896).

[3] I am summarizing Anna Jameson's *Shakespeare's Heroines* (1846). Gervinus's view in *Shakespeare Commentaries* (1849) is less sentimental but very similar. See also Ruskin's *Sesame and Lilies* (1893; written 1864), p. 93; and Judith Johnston, *Anna Jameson: Victorian, Feminist, Woman of Letters* (1997), pp. 73–99.

[4] H. Faucit, *On Some of Shakespeare's Female Characters* (1887 edn), pp. 160, 169.

[5] Fletcher, *Studies in Shakespeare*, p. 94; Jameson, *Shakespeare's Heroines*, p. 187.

[6] Faucit, *On Some of Shakespeare's Female Characters*, pp. 180, 192–3.

[7] *Cymbeline, An Historical Play* (*Cumberland's British Theatre*, 1829), p. 5.

[8] Faucit, *On Some of Shakespeare's Female Characters*, p. 208. See also G. Marshall, 'Helena Faucit: Shakespeare's Victorian heroine', in S. Chew and A. Stead, *Translating Life* (1999), pp. 297–313.

overpowering joy' on finding him alive. In 1843 such bravura acting left 'a deep and indelible impression',[1] though it would probably seem very contrived today. Certainly Faucit's essay on the role is highly sentimental. She describes Innogen's brothers as welcoming her like their lost mother returned or the playfellow they never had, and speculates that the reunion with Posthumus is shadowed by premonitions of loss. Her experiences are more than she can sustain: she ends the play exhausted and perhaps had not much longer to live.[2] Faucit's view of Innogen as too pure for the coarse world suggests that her performance mined into a deep vein of nostalgia for fleeting childhood innocence. This Innogen belonged in the nursery, and contact with adult sexuality effectively killed her.

After the 1860s *Cymbeline* began to fall out of the repertoire. Swinburne concluded his *Study of Shakespeare* (1880) with a hymn to Innogen, 'the woman best beloved in all the world of song and all the tide of time', and Tennyson died with the play at his side, opened at the lovers' reunion,[3] but the only notable late Victorian production was Henry Irving's 1896 revival, by which time the play was starting to seem remote from reality. Irving cut the text drastically and built up Iachimo, especially in the last scene, where his long confession became the play's culminating event. He radically redrew the plot, bowdlerizing the wager by removing its sexual content and making Iachimo's motivation intellectual pride rather than desire. He became a man of exquisitely fastidious sensibilities who wished to show that, for all their love, husband and wife did not really understand each other, and he ended the play wearing a 'strange but sad expression of nobility', implying that while his schemes had failed, his superior insight was vindicated.[4] Playgoers were perplexed by this villain who seemed more moral than the moralists, and by Posthumus, who, with his sexual insecurity removed, came out looking merely credulous. But Ellen Terry's Innogen was universally praised. Although well past her youth, she was exquisitely high-spirited and unaffected, unselfconsciously delighting in her own allure (see figure 7). All reports mention her grace and instinctive beauty: Henry James admired her 'immense naturalness', and Shaw praised her 'innocent rapture and frank gladness', 'infinite charm and delicacy of appeal'.[5] This suggests that her Innogen was not just more expressive than Faucit's but had a more energized sexuality. Terry had been a Pre-Raphaelite icon, and her desirability unsettled the role's conjugal emphases: her Innogen was hauntingly beautiful but had a

---

[1] T. Martin, *Helena Faucit, Lady Martin* (1900), p. 103. See also H. Morley, *The Journal of a London Playgoer* (1866), pp. 346–8; Fletcher, *Studies in Shakespeare*, pp. 95–108; and the stage directions in Phelps's text.

[2] Faucit, *On Some of Shakespeare's Female Characters*, pp. 225–6. This idea is partially anticipated in the 1829 acting edition, which notes Innogen's melancholy, the 'too frequent accompaniment of the o'er-informed mind' (p. 5).

[3] Tennyson also wrote an imitation of the dirge, and copied *Cymbeline*'s diction in his *Dualisms* (*Poems*, 146). 'Golden lads and girls' also left its mark on Housman (see his poems 'With rue my heart is laden' and 'As I gird on for fighting').

[4] '*Cymbeline*', *The Theatre*, n.s. 28 (1 October 1896), p. 214. See also A. Hughes, *Henry Irving, Shakespearean* (1981), pp. 205–23; L. Irving, *Henry Irving: The Actor and his World* (1951); and *Cymbeline, A Comedy in Five Acts* (1896).

[5] H. James, *The Scenic Art* (1949), p. 285; Shaw, *Plays and Players*, pp. 122–3. Clement Scott reported that Terry freely interpolated her own impromptu asides into the text: 'It may be heresy . . . [but] everyone loves her for doing it' (*Daily Telegraph*, 23 September 1896).

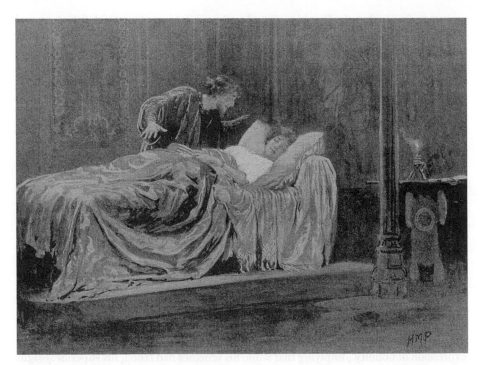

Figure 7. Iachimo (Henry Irving) and Innogen (Ellen Terry) at the Lyceum Theatre, 1896, the bedchamber scene (drawing by H. M. Paget in *The Graphic*)

capacity for passion that implied more complex perspectives on female desire. William Archer thought she lacked tenderness towards Posthumus,[1] and Terry's notes suggest discomfort with the role, a feeling that its sweetness concealed inner disappointments. Although Innogen loves her husband, Terry wrote, she is dissatisfied with him: 'I care for somebody that isn't *worthy* of me, because nobody that's *worth* me *cares* for me.'[2] This comment measures her against the New Woman of the 1890s, and shows how out of touch the play must have seemed to a generation freshly assimilating Ibsen. To Henry James it was a 'florid fairytale'; to Shaw 'stagey trash'.[3]

In the early twentieth century, expectations about the play were at their lowest. Although a trickle of performances took place and a full text was gradually restored (Jupiter and the ghosts returned at Stratford-upon-Avon in 1949), most directors still treated it as a romantic extravaganza that offered the pleasures of fantasy untrammelled by much contact with reality. The problem was exemplified by Peter Hall's 1957 Stratford revival – perhaps the culminating example of this mode and not at all an unreflective production, so its shortcomings were all the more remarkable. Drawing on the myth-criticism of mid-century, Hall saw *Cymbeline* as rooted in folklore and

[1] Archer, *The Theatrical World of 1896*, p. 275.
[2] Her italics; quoted in N. Auerbach, *Ellen Terry: Player in her Time* (1987), pp. 213–14.
[3] James, *The Scenic Art*, p. 282; Shaw, *Plays and Players*, p. 114.

wanted his staging to seem archetypal and marvellous: Kenneth Tynan admired its gothic effect, a 'sinister veil of faery' like 'a Grimm fable transmuted by Cocteau'.[1] As Innogen, Peggy Ashcroft (in her first RSC role) was universally praised: she had ardour, radiance and 'frail delicacy'.[2] However, the play was dominated by an overloaded design, a gauzed and cobwebbed confection that mixed cave and wood, battlements, bedroom and palace in a single composite set, which attempted to offer a visual equivalent for *Cymbeline*'s generic complexity. For many spectators such opulence overwhelmed the play, reducing it to a Victorian 'tissue of nonsense', a 'blithely romantic exercise in theatricality'. And the problem of mood remained unsolved, for reviewers frequently noticed an 'uneasy embarrassing laughter spreading through the house', especially at sensitive moments such as Innogen's lament over the corpse.[3] Little wonder that the play seemed to deserve its neglect: it worked neither as serious drama nor as decorative entertainment.

All this changed with William Gaskill's 1962 Stratford revival, a landmark production that for the first time managed to harness rather than efface *Cymbeline*'s contradictions. In contrast to Hall's overwrought design, Gaskill adopted a stripped-down Brechtian staging that left the play's inconsistencies in place instead of attempting to impose an alien unity upon them. This design enabled events to move with clarity and pace but gave full weight to the spectacle when it finally arrived. Reviewers were astonished by the last act: the battle a vigorous and stylized 'strip cartoon',[4] the ghosts walking somnambulistically against the movement of a turning revolve, and Jupiter descending thunderously on a massive copper eagle (see figure 8). Even more revolutionary was the combination of detachment and involvement in the playing. Gaskill achieved a cool, light-hearted and ironic tone, and audiences were surprised to find their laughter being encouraged. Anomalies and absurdities were presented as normal, and the mood constantly shifted between artifice and reality, grave and gay; this meant that in the scene with the corpse, 'the whole horrible joke' could be taken as read.[5] Eric Porter's Iachimo was not a monstrous incarnation of evil but a sly trickster, whose mocking banter had no more serious aim than deflating and humiliating his rival, but the human cost of his actions was measured in Vanessa Redgrave's Innogen, whom all reviewers found deeply affecting. Redgrave was remarkable for her passion, spirit and intensity, and for the mercurial quality that she brought to the role: she encompassed 'peaks of love, joy, shock and anguish', and was 'utterly satisfying in her truthfulness'.[6] Her special achievement was to confront the corpse scene head on (figure 9), with the body presented semi-realistically, and Innogen going 'full out for horror'.[7] T. C. Worsley wrote that although spectators smiled at her grief, it nonetheless moved them: the

---

[1] Tynan, *A View of the English Stage* (1976), p. 267.
[2] *Daily Mail*, 3 July 1957. Newspaper citations to RSC productions are from the files in the Shakespeare Centre Library at Stratford-upon-Avon. See also Roger Warren's *Cymbeline: Plays in Performance* (1989) for full accounts of the productions by Hall, Gaskill and Alexander.
[3] *Financial Times*, 3 July 1957; *Birmingham Mail*, 3 July 1957.
[4] *Sunday Telegraph*, 12 July 1962.
[5] *Stratford Herald*, 18 July 1962.
[6] *Daily Mail*; *The Times*, 18 July 1962.
[7] *Birmingham Mail*, 18 July 1962.

Figure 8. Jupiter on his eagle in William Gaskill's 1962 production at Stratford-upon-Avon

direction permitted laughter and tears, and embodied 'heroic simplicities . . . in human shapes'.[1] Gaskell's production broke the tradition of sentimental staging by giving full scope to the play's complexity of vision. It initiated the now-prevailing reading of *Cymbeline*, as a modernistic play dominated by irony.

The issue for directors today is to find a style which does justice to the play's ironies without losing touch with the humanizing emotion that made Redgrave's performance so acclaimed. Three remarkable revivals from the 1980s tried sharply opposed solutions. One was Bill Alexander's 1987 chamber *Cymbeline*, staged in the RSC's studio space, The Other Place. Performed in a bare room with the audience in close proximity, this version eschewed large-scale scenic effects and used rough Scandinavian costumes, wind chimes and an evocative musical score to conjure an atmosphere of timeless and magical folktale. It relied for its effect on the spectator's imagination: the opening dialogue was whispered between the Two Gentlemen, sitting in the front row, and much of the verse sounded like urgent prose, accidentally overheard. The result was spellbinding and engrossing – most of all in the bedroom scene, as the audience's intimate perspective on events coopted them into conspiracy with Iachimo. This created almost unbearable tension, making the scene 'an ugly act conducted with the utmost beauty'.[2]

[1] *Financial Times*, 18 July 1962.
[2] *The Times*, 14 November 1987.

Figure 9. Innogen (Vanessa Redgrave) with Cloten's corpse in William Gaskill's production

All the roles emerged strongly individualized, and personal relationships were drawn with great clarity. As Innogen and Posthumus Harriet Walter and Nicholas Farrell were hot-blooded lovers whose mutual desire was never in doubt, but, interestingly, Innogen's relationship with her father was central. Her first encounter with David Bradley's abrasive, beady-eyed king was an explosive argument, in the wake of which their reunion was correspondingly emotional; Walter herself wrote that for the last scene to work, the opening had to be played for all it was worth (see figure 10).[1] Iachimo, too, played differently in a small space, as a cool, thoughtful antagonist who was provoked into deceit by Posthumus's outrageous boasting and who came sincerely to regret his actions. With star performances discouraged in favour of a more 'company' style, the play revolved around a core of high-voltage private relationships, though the cost was uncertainty in the handling of more political or literary material such as the Romans or the Welsh scenes. The play's public conflicts hardly came into view, and the spectacle of the battle, the ghosts and Jupiter was scanted. Such scaling-down was perhaps inevitable in a studio staging – Michael Billington called it a 'whale in an aquarium' – though it fitted Alexander's 'chamber-melodramatic' view of the play.[2] Significantly, when in 1989 this production transferred with a new cast to the main

---

[1] R. Jackson and R. Smallwood, eds., *Players of Shakespeare 3* (1993), p. 205.
[2] *Guardian*, 14 November 1987; *The Listener*, 19 November 1987.

Figure 11. Posthumus (Peter Woodward), dressed as a British peasant, stands under the 'heavens' in Peter Hall's 1988 production at the National Theatre, London

of Celtic ruins – a Romantic fantasy in Victorian England',[1] and she mounted it in correspondingly complex form, as a multilayered theatrical event. The designer, George Tsypin, created a moody mise-en-scène, a shifting, fluid world with scenery on revolving columns, drifting smoke and projected images, backed by a cyclorama with changing collages of gardens, trees, ruins and landscapes (see figure 12). All this was framed by footlights and thick velvet curtains that alluded to the conventions of nineteenth-century theatre but was overlaid aurally by a modernistic electronic score from Philip Glass.

The relationships of the actors were similarly problematized. Colour-blind casting undercut traditional groupings of parts – Innogen was white but had black and Hispanic brothers, while a white Posthumus and black Cloten unsettled the body-doubling of the corpse scene. The costumes evoked both Victorian imperialism and a still more remote past. The British army wore kilts and pith helmets, and the Romans had Italian tunics and plumes à l'antique, making them look like 'toy soldiers',[2] while the princes appeared as North American natives in loincloths and warpaint. Other disorienting effects included fleeting glimpses of a group of fugitives who turned out to be the ghosts of Posthumus's family, and Pisanio's use of a motor scooter for transport into Wales. The critics were shocked that by intensifying the incongruities Akalaitis had violated the wistful 'autumnal mood' they expected the play to have, but her eclecticism challenged the expectation that unity was the only aesthetic value that counted. By filtering an already fractured Renaissance romance through allusions to Victorian stagecraft and its modern appropriations, Akalaitis historicized the meanings accumulated by *Cymbeline* over time, while finding qualities in the play that pre-echoed the rootless post-modernism of her own cultural moment.

The absence of a clear structural centre to *Cymbeline*, and the play's ironic perspective on its own epiphanies, make it uniquely open to radical and unpredictable revision in the theatre. We can end with four recent productions that nicely exemplify the opportunities and risks that it presents to directors today. In Adrian Noble's 1997 RSC main-house revival, style was everything. Noble Japanned the play, setting it in a bare blue box with an orange moon above, and a great sail-like sheet that filled the stage at scene changes. A walkway extended into the auditorium, down which entrances were made Kabuki-fashion, and the battle was spiritedly staged, with waving flags, precisely drilled movement, and furious Kodo drumming. The Queen was followed everywhere by a nervous parasol-bearer and tripping maids, the men were dressed as samurai, and the wager was made over a tea ceremony. This design imposed an Oriental unity on the play, though events were in fact doubly distanced, for the story began as a fable told by the Soothsayer as if to a nomadic tribe around a camp fire. As his tale named them, the players stood up and assumed their characters, and in the unfolding action they stayed partially detached from their parts, always aware of them as performances – most

---

[1] Elinor Fuchs, James Leverett et al., '*Cymbeline* and its critics: a case study', *American Theatre*, 6:9 (December 1989), p. 27. See also Amy S. Green, *The Revisionist Stage* (1994), pp. 90–103; and D. Kennedy, *Looking at Shakespeare* (1993), pp. 300–2.
[2] Green, *The Revisionist Stage*, p. 95.

Figure 12. The battle scene in JoAnne Akalaitis's 1989 production for the New York Shakespeare Festival

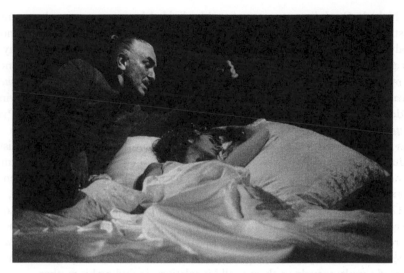

Figure 13. Iachimo (Paul Freeman) approaches the sleeping Innogen (Joanne Pearce) in Adrian Noble's 1997 Stratford-upon-Avon production

notably Guy Henry's hilarious Cloten, a 'long thin prawn who thinks he's a shark',[1] endlessly trying to ensure his embarrassing name was pronounced not 'Clotten' but 'Cloaten'.

As spectacle this was exhilarating and colourful. A strong ensemble style and heavy cuts kept the pace fast, while the ending was funny and touching in equal measure, emotionally charged – not least because Cymbeline genuinely cared about his daughter – but manifestly wish-fulfilment. Yet once again the politics barely registered. Samurai dress obliterated the Roman/British polarity and the Welsh accents conflicted bizarrely with it, while the exotic setting seemed imposed, for it had no meaningful connection with the play's concerns. To many reviewers the wicked Queen was merely Disneyfied, and Iachimo was tainted by melodrama (figure 13). In fact, Paul Freeman's Iachimo was interestingly complex. A middle-aged roué, not sexually confident but dissolute and embittered, he hated Posthumus's idealism and had no regret for his actions, but he was so obviously wicked that it was impossible to suppose that Innogen could be deceived by him.[2] Joanne Pearce's Innogen was vulnerable, warm and unrestrained, but by putting her into a theatrical never-never land driven by exciting production values, Noble made it difficult to feel that her dangers really mattered. Although the emotional stakes were intensified, by jollying up the play with archness, self-parody and imposed effects, this production signalled a lack of confidence in the text's ability to speak for itself. Or perhaps it indicated that scepticism about romance and a controlling providential intelligence is now so ingrained that the play's mythical roots no longer have any real purchase.

---

[1] *The Times*, 28 February 1997.
[2] R. Smallwood, 'Shakespeare performances in England', *S. Sur.*, 51 (1998), p. 230.

If Noble's *Cymbeline* was uncomfortably divided between emotional content and stylistic flippancy, Danny Scheie's production at Santa Cruz in 2000 took post-modern parody to its limit, creating a deliberately camp version that surrounded the play with gags and slapstick, and turned the collision of styles into the main point.[1] Framed by TV monitors and punctuated by musical and visual quotations, this *Cymbeline* was mediated through a blizzard of images and retro allusions that crossed 1960s Swinging London pop culture with *The Sound of Music*, *The Wizard of Oz*, *Monty Python*, *Bewitched* (the nose-wiggling freeze-frame joke, used to signal asides) and much more. In its mad bricolage anything was possible: the two lords became a ventriloquist and his dummy; the Jailer was a beefeater; Belarius and the princes were a Scout master and his troop who had set up tent in Wales; travelling to Rome Posthumus entered a mafioso Italy that owed more to *The Sopranos* and *Goodfellas* than Boccaccio, while the TV monitors played the news in Italian but switched to Latin when the Romans arrived in Britain. The monitors came into their own again in the dream sequence, for they relayed the vision, presenting Jupiter like an animated head out of *South Park* (to music from Mozart's Jupiter symphony), while Hans Altwies, who played Posthumus, appeared simultaneously on them as all his relatives, including his mother.

The core of Scheic's reading was a very contemporary treatment of the central roles. With Iachimo as a 'tough, smoulderingly sexy thug',[2] Posthumus naked for much of the last act, and Susannah Schulman a glamorous, vivacious and emotionally winning princess, the staging rested on strong romantic performances and a frank embrace of physical desire. Against this, the sight gags and campy setting insisted on the story's improbability and registered the tangle of intersections that is Shakespeare in the modern world, between Elizabethan and twentieth-century, literary and theatrical, UK and US. Cloten wore a Union flag waistcoat and the Queen was a deranged hybrid of Elizabeth I and Margaret Thatcher (see figure 15), while a sing-along version of the patriotic hymn 'I vow to thee, my country' competed for space with the Sex Pistols's snarling counter-culture anthem 'God save the Queen'. The production thus staged the modern collapse of distinctions between high culture and low, and it highlighted the contradiction of reviving a play about a British imperial identity that no longer existed for spectators in a country that was now the global superpower which the Soothsayer had predicted that Cymbeline's nation would be. As for the author, he was jokily present in the *Riverside* Shakespeare stamped 'Ovid' that Innogen read in bed, and in the Arden edition from which the soothsayer read his prophecy. Scheie's production celebrated Shakespeare while using the play to ask what, four centuries on and halfway round the globe, his legacy might now be thought to be.

The most recent production by the Royal Shakespeare Company, in the Swan Theatre in 2003, also returned to stylistic eclecticism but used it to develop a markedly post-colonial approach to the play. Directed by Dominic Cooke, this staging made a strong cultural contrast between Britain and Rome. Although in Britain the

---

[1] For reviews, see Orgel, '*Cymbeline* at Santa Cruz', 277–85; and <www.shakespeare.com/reviews/santacruz>.
[2] Orgel, '*Cymbeline* at Santa Cruz', 278.

Figure 14. Amy Thone as the Queen and Gary Armagnac as Cymbeline in Danny Scheie's Santa Cruz production, 2000

Romans wore antique armour, at home they lived *la dolce vita*, lunching on pasta and red wine, and dressed in white suits, sandals, sunglasses and the occasional earring. In this hyper-sophisticated and self-consciously refined world, Iachimo (Anton Lesser) was less envious of Posthumus than amused at his naivety. Sly, cool and arrogant, he enjoyed invading Innogen's bedroom, though his lustful inspection of her body was complicated by admiration of her beauty and by hints of bad conscience. On the other side, the Britons were a primitive but ethnically complex people. Their costumes combined disorderly Victorian wear (open shirts, braces, black trousers, top hats and bowlers) with tribal accessories (tattoos and painted faces, horsehair tails, fly-whisks, lots of plumes, and a ceremonial coat of peacock feathers for the Queen). Cymbeline was supported by a parasol-bearer and courtiers carrying boat-club oars that they banged at moments of excitement; the ghosts were voodoo dolls, and an image of the British god – half-bird, half-human – was lit above the audience, facing the stage for the whole action. In battle the Britons were terrifying: when preparing to fight they performed a haka, the Maori dance associated with the All Blacks rugby team, and after killing Cloten Guiderius returned with his head impaled on a spear (which he then allowed mutely to react to the conversation).

This Britain seemed like a 'minor African dictatorship', giving 'a hint of Conrad's *Heart of Darkness* [to] the Roman outpost of Ancient Britain'.[1] Its association with the imperial power would clearly bring canals, railways and administrators, though

---

[1] Michael Billington, *Guardian*, 8 August 2003; Kate Bassett, *Independent on Sunday*, 31 August 2003.

Rome would learn things from its colony, too. At Jupiter's descent a huge electrical surge extinguished all the theatre lights, including those on the Britons' god, but Jupiter was oddly effeminized and doll-like, and seemed likely to benefit from his new connection with the manly vigour of Belarius and the princes. This political reading allowed Innogen's speech on the swan's nest to resonate, but overall it displaced the lovers from the centre of things. Emma Fielding signalled Innogen's stubbornness by wearing hiking boots under her golden gown, but there was little sexual chemistry with Posthumus (Daniel Evans), and the ending left it uncertain whether their domestic problems really were settled. It seemed unlikely that this very youthful couple would make much difference to Britain, and a general shout of 'Laud we the gods' indicated that larger changes were afoot. Innogen's happiness would be a useful but minor footnote to the future history of nations.

Finally, the most interesting recent British production was that staged by the Kneehigh Theatre Company in 2006–7, seen at Stratford as part of the 'Complete Works' season and subsequently on tour. A much-loved group with a devoted following, Kneehigh are based in Cornwall, far from the centre of the British theatre scene, and they produce devised work with a strong ensemble feel. Led by their artistic director, Emma Rice, their shows arc typically adaptations of well-known stories with a strong mythic element (such as *Don John*, *The Bacchae*, *Tristan and Iseult*), and they are renowned for their experimental, anarchic, and often irreverent style, creating powerful theatrical magic through devices such as naïve staging, puppetry, and live music. Kneehigh's adapted version of *Cymbeline* worked within the play's basic outline but used only a scattering of the original dialogue, metamorphosing Shakespeare's language into rough verse in a modern colloquial idiom, interspersed with original songs performed on stage by a pulsing rock band. Occasionally knockabout in style – as when Innogen misread Posthumus's letter to Pisanio as saying 'Thy mistress hath played the trumpet in my bed – I can't even PLAY the trumpet!' (p. 43)[1] – it nonetheless managed to convey an emotional tug between realism and sentiment that gave full play to each. So the Kneehigh version foregrounded but also booby-trapped Innogen's impulsiveness: 'He's in Milford Haven! He's in Milford Haven! [*puzzled*] Where is Milford Haven?! (*She runs upstairs and checks her globe*) . . . [*delighted*] AH! IT'S IN WALES!' (p. 39). Heading off to Wales, she adopted the less than romantic pseudonym Ian, and here found the lost princes living in a squat. The princes wore parkas which evoked current social debates about 'hoodies', Britain's supposedly thuggish and disenfranchised youth. In the first scene Cymbeline's Queen bought her drugs from a hoodie, and Cloten poisoned Innogen with the notorious date-rape drug, Rohypnol.

In Kneehigh's hands, the story opened out into a fantasy psycho-drama, with several of Shakespeare's narrative gaps and emotional condensations filled in. For example, we learned what Posthumus did in Rome before returning to Britain: apparently he bonded with Iachimo, and passed his time driving around in, and eventually crashing,

---

[1] *Cymbeline*, adapted by Emma Rice, written by Carl Grose (Oberon Books, 2007). There is an excellent account of the production by Valerie Wayne, 'Kneehigh's dream of *Cymbeline*', *Shakespeare Quarterly*, 58 (2007), 228–37. The bracketed additions to quotations here are based on my viewing of it.

Figure 15. Cymbeline (Mike Shepherd) destroying the shrine to the memory of the lost princes, in the Kneehigh production of *Cymbeline*, 2006.

his Ferrari. More seriously, Cymbeline's back-story was amplified, and the Queen's part extended. Formerly the nurse to Cymbeline's lost boys, the Queen had become a predatory drug-abuser, using her narcotics to keep control over her husband, and projecting onto him a hatred that was rooted in her own hatred of herself (and there was a strong hint of incest between her and Cloten). Cymbeline himself had been pole-axed by his sons' disappearance and wife's death, and had never quite recovered from the shock. Here one felt as in no other production that his trauma was real and he was living his life in the shadow of loss: the whole evening opened with him pulling down a shrine to the boys' memory maintained by Innogen. The characters' problems were rooted in the damage caused by family dysfunction. Cymbeline had become a neglectful king and father, and this dispossession was echoed in Posthumus's status as orphan, and even in Iachimo, who narrated to Posthumus his own back-story of parental abandonment. The Queen's suicide and the children's recovery meant a return to emotional wholeness, which was aided here by an invented character, a pantomime drag-queen called Joan Puttock, who introduced each half of the play, held the key to Posthumus's mysterious box, and eventually ran off with Iachimo. All this was tongue-in-cheek, of course, but its bold and sympathetic humour drew out the story's mythical resonances and reasserted the meta-drama of emotional reconciliation. Posthumus's box turned out to be full of memories, in the form of childhood photographs and family pictures, and the play's final image was Cymbeline happily tucking his four returned children into bed. Of all recent productions, this one most effectively mined through to the story's roots in folktale and myth. What its characters needed to recover was their love and respect for each other as a family.

TEXTUAL NOTE

Cymbeline presents relatively few textual problems. The only early printing was in the First Folio (1623), where it stands as the last play. The text is generally clean, and was probably set from a manuscript prepared by the scribe Ralph Crane, who provided copy for several other Folio plays. (The evidence, discussed in the Textual Analysis, is idiosyncrasies such as habits of punctuation which can be paralleled in Crane's other transcripts.) The text shows no sign of preparation for playhouse use, though, given its length, it must have been shortened for performance. Crane's transcript is 'literary', designed for reading, and may have been made from Shakespeare's foul papers or a partially revised manuscript. Cruces at 3.4.85–91, 4.2.288 and 5.3.94 suggest Crane had occasional difficulty in interpreting his copy, perhaps because it contained authorial second thoughts: particularly, there are signs of expansion in Cloten's part. Crane also added presentational flourishes which misrepresented some details of the text, such as new scene divisions in 1.1 and 3.6, garbled stage business in Act 5, and the heading 'SONG' for the spoken dirge at 4.2.256. Once his copy reached the printing house, it was set up by Jaggard's experienced compositor B, but with some help from the apprentice Compositor E, who was prone to make errors.

The text for this edition follows series principles. Spelling is modernized, with archaic forms rendered in modern equivalents where this can be done without losing substantive meaning. Punctuation follows modern conventions (the Folio's punctuation is very dense and probably derives from Crane rather than Shakespeare). Some stage directions are added in square brackets, and speech-headings are expanded and made consistent. The Collation records all substantive emendations, and occasionally mentions changes made by other editors which have not been adopted here.

This edition makes two unusual textual choices. Many scholars believe the name 'Imogen' – which is not recorded before the 1623 Folio – is a misprint and that 'Innogen' is the name intended by Shakespeare (the rationale for this is explained on pp. 36–7, 79). I have adopted 'Innogen' on the basis that this is the name as it appears in the pseudo-history that was Shakespeare's source. Secondly, the ghosts' speeches in 5.3 are printed as fourteeners. In the Folio they appear as short tetrameters and trimeters, probably because the compositor could not fit fourteeners into the book's narrow columns. Returning them to fourteeners allows us to acknowledge the pastiche of mid-Tudor verse that they are.

Cymbeline

LIST OF CHARACTERS

CYMBELINE, King of Britain
INNOGEN, his daughter
GUIDERIUS, known as POLYDORE ⎫ his sons, stolen
ARVIRAGUS, known as CADWAL ⎭ by Belarius
QUEEN, wife to Cymbeline
CLOTEN, her son

POSTHUMUS LEONATUS, a British gentleman, husband to Innogen
BELARIUS, a banished British nobleman, known as Morgan
PISANIO, servant to Posthumus
CORNELIUS, a court physician
Two LADIES attending on Innogen
Two LORDS attending on Cloten
Two GENTLEMEN
Two British CAPTAINS
Two JAILERS

PHILARIO, an Italian gentleman, friend of Posthumus's
IACHIMO, an italian gentleman ⎫
A FRENCHMAN   ⎪ Friends of Philario's
A DUTCHMAN   ⎬ at Rome
A SPANIARD   ⎭

CAIUS LUCIUS, ambassador from Rome to Britain
Two Roman SENATORS
Roman TRIBUNES
A Roman CAPTAIN
A SOOTHSAYER

JUPITER
Ghost of Posthumus's father, SICILIUS LEONATUS
Ghost of Posthumus's MOTHER
Ghosts of Posthumus's TWO BROTHERS

Lords attending on Cymbeline, ladies attending on the Queen, musicians, messengers, British and Roman soldiers

Notes
LIST OF CHARACTERS First given, imperfectly, by Rowe.
CYMBELINE The historical Cymbeline, Cunobelinus, was a king of the powerful Catuvellauni tribe that dominated south-eastern England. He ruled *c*. AD 5–42 and appears in Suetonius, *Caligula*, 44, and Dio Cassius's *Roman History*, 60.19–20 (Matthews). In Shakespeare's

source, Raphael Holinshed's *History of England* (1577), the reign of 'Kymbeline' runs from 23 BC to AD 12 and is depicted as uneventful. Holinshed mentions traditions that Augustus intended to reimpose the lapsed tribute set in 54 BC by Caesar, but he describes no invasion and implies that Kymbeline was always a good friend to Rome.

INNOGEN In the British pseudo-histories deriving from Geoffrey of Monmouth, Innogen is the wife of Brute (great-grandson of Aeneas, first settler of Britain and founder of the British race as well as Rome). Shakespeare's character is called Imogen in F, but the name is not known in this form before 1623, and is cognate with Old French Enygeus, variants of which are widely disseminated in the romance languages (see Nitze, 40–2). Innogen's name appears as Ignogen in Robert Fabyan's *Chronicles* (1516); Innogen in Holinshed's *History* and Drayton's *Poly-Olbion* (1610); and Inogene in Spenser's *The Faerie Queene* (2.10.13). Simon Forman's eyewitness account of *Cym.* (1611) also refers to Innogen. A ghost character Innogen, the wife of Leonato, appears in F in the opening direction of *Ado*: she never speaks, but her husband's name helps to reinforce the Leonatus-Innogen doublet in *Cym*. Probably *Cym.*'s compositor could not disentangle the minims in his copy and made a guess at an unfamiliar name. Given the name's prominence in British myth (and its suitability to a character whose *inn*ocence is so much emphasized), it seems appropriate to return to the form that Shakespeare wrote. This has been done without strain in some recent stage productions.

GUIDERIUS, ARVIRAGUS In Holinshed Guiderius is Cymbeline's successor, refuses tribute to Rome and is killed in battle, AD 45; his brother Arviragus continues to resist the Romans but eventually makes peace. These events have no basis in fact, though a historical Arviragus may have existed, since Juvenal mentions a British prince of this name (*Satires*, IV, 127). A 'tragedy' of Guiderius was added to *The Mirror for Magistrates* in 1587.

POLYDORE This name probably derives from Polydore Vergil, the early Tudor historian. Other Polydores include a character in Montemayor's romance *Diana* (a source for *AYLI*), and, in classical myth, the youngest son of Priam of Troy; his story is told in Ovid's *Metamorphoses*, XIII.

CADWAL Name formed from Cadwallo, king of the Britons AD 635–83, whose wars with the Angles and Saxons are described by Geoffrey of Monmouth; or from Cadwallader (Welsh Cadwaladr), the last British king in the line of descent from Brut, d. 689.

CLOTEN In the British pseudo-history reproduced by Holinshed, 'Cloton' is a Cornish king ruling in the fifth century BC, the most important of the five competing kings left in Britain after the failure of the direct line from Brute. He appears in Sackville and Norton's *Gorboduc* (1562) as 'Clotyn, Duke of Cornwall', and in Harrison's *Description of England* (appended to Holinshed) as 'Cloten'; Simon Forman called him both 'Cloten' and 'Clotan'. F spells him as 'Clotten' down to SD, and 'Cloten' thereafter (save for SD). As the '-tt-' spelling indicates, the name associates him with *clot* (= clod).

POSTHUMUS Posthumus was possible as a given name in Shakespeare's day and was carried by the younger son of Sir Thomas Hoby, among others. See also the autobiography of Lord Herbert of Cherbury: 'My brother Thomas was a Posthumus as being born some weeks after his father's death' (Herbert, 9); and Jonson's description of himself to William Drummond: 'he himself was Posthumus born a month after his father's decease' (*Ben Jonson*, I, 139). In Holinshed Posthumus is a son born to Aeneas after his death, and who was either the father or grandfather of Brute. A character Posthumus appears in Jonson's *Sejanus*, 1603, a play in which Shakespeare acted.

The name LEONATUS (literally, 'lion-born') appears in Philip Sidney's *The Arcadia* (1590), where its holder is the prototype of Edgar in *Lear*. Shakespeare used versions of this name in two plays closely related to *Cym.*, *Ado* (Leonato) and *WT* (Leontes).

BELARIUS The name was probably taken from Bellario in Beaumont and Fletcher's *Philaster*, or from Bellaria in Robert Greene's *Pandosto* (1588; the source for *WT*).

MORGAN Marganus is one of Holinshed's pre-Roman kings: the son of Goneril, he rules Britain jointly after Cordelia's death. In *King Leir*, 1605 (the source play for *Lear*), Ragan's husband is Morgan, Prince of Cambria. He is mentioned in Spenser's *The Faerie Queene*, 2.10.33.

CORNELIUS The cornelian stone supposedly had medicinal properties (G. W. Knight, *The Sovereign Flower*, 1958, p. 197).

IACHIMO An anglicized version of the Italian name Giacomo, comparable to Friar Jacomo in Marlowe's *The Jew of Malta* (1589), or to the steward Jacomo in James Shirley's *The Grateful Servant* (1629). The name is spelled 'Iachimo' in F1, F2 and F3. It was changed to 'Jachimo' by Durfey (1682) and F4 (1685), but Posthumus's alliterating reference to 'the yellow Iachimo' (2.5.14) suggests that the 'I-' form is correct. Following the principles of the Oxford edition, Taylor prints 'Giacomo', but modern Italian delivers the wrong stress. Brian Gibbons suggests that F's form of the name preserves an echo of Iago, and perhaps of Spenser's Archimago.

CAIUS LUCIUS In Geoffrey of Monmouth's *History of the Kings of Britain*, Lucius is a Roman general who is defied by King Arthur, an episode that left its mark on *Cym*. 3.1 (see Introduction, p. 42). More remotely, Britain's first Christian king was supposed to have been called Lucius (second century AD).

SICILIUS In Holinshed this is the name of a minor British king, ruling 430–23 BC.

CYMBELINE

1.1 *Enter two* GENTLEMEN

FIRST GENTLEMAN You do not meet a man but frowns. Our bloods
       No more obey the heavens than our courtiers
       Still seem as does the King.
SECOND GENTLEMAN   But what's the matter?
FIRST GENTLEMAN His daughter, and the heir of's kingdom, whom
       He purposed to his wife's sole son – a widow   5
       That late he married – hath referred herself

Title THE TRAGEDIE OF CYMBELINE F; Cymbeline, King of Britain *Taylor, after* F *(table of contents)* Act 1, Scene 1 1.1 *Actus Primus. Scoena Prima.* F 1–3 *Rowe;* YOu . . . Frownes. / Our . . . Heauens / Then . . . Courtiers: / Still F 2 courtiers] *Boswell (conj. Tyrwhitt);* Courtiers: F; courtiers'; *Hanmer* 3 King] *Knight (conj. Tyrwhitt);* Kings F 4,10 FIRST GENTLEMAN, SECOND GENTLEMAN] *Rowe;* 1, 2 F *throughout scene*

TITLE CYMBELINE In F *Cymbeline* is grouped with the Tragedies and is called 'THE TRAGEDIE [TRAGEDY] OF CYMBELINE' in its head- and running-titles. F's table of contents lists it as 'Cymbeline, King of Britain': Simon Forman echoes this formula, referring to 'Cimbalin king of England'. There is an analogous title in *Pericles, Prince of Tyre*.

Act 1, Scene 1

1 As in many comparable instances on Shakespeare's stage, the location of this scene is not precisely defined, other than as a semi-public space in Cymbeline's court. The reference to the garden (81) is sometimes taken to imply that the scene is laid outside, though it might well be imagined as a room giving on to a garden.

0 SD *Enter two* GENTLEMEN This conversation closely resembles the opening scenes of *WT* and Beaumont and Fletcher's *Philaster*, with two anonymous Gentlemen supplying the background to the plot and introducing a linguistic style that is strangely compressed and hyperbolical. Some productions have dressed the Second Gentleman to indicate that he is a stranger, or a traveller newly returned to Britain.

1 **but frowns** who does not frown.

1–3 **Our bloods . . . king** 'Our moods are not more rigorously dictated by heavenly influence than our courtiers (in their frowning) take their looks from the king.' A terse comparison between the body and the court which uses analogies fostered by the Aristotelian physiology of Shakespeare's day: just as blood was supposed to be controlled by the heavens, so the courtiers (the 'blood' supplying the court's veins) are subject to the king. Hudson 2 compares Chapman's *Tragedy of Byron* (1608): 'They keep all to cast in admiration on the King; for from his face are all their faces moulded' (*Tragedies*, 360).

1 **bloods** bodily dispositions, moods: at this time thought to be rooted in the blood.

3 **King** Some editors preserve F's *King[']s*, assuming 'looks' is implied after *King's* and *courtiers* is possessive, a less complex sense which eventually arrives at 12–15. F's error could have been caught from the plurals ending 1–2.

4 **of's** of his.

5 **purposed to** intended for.

6 **referred** assigned, bestowed. Elsewhere in Shakespeare *refer* means *entrust*: compare *MM* 3.1.245, 'refer yourself to this advantage', and *WT* 3.2.116, 'I do refer me to the oracle'. Perhaps the evasive verb acknowledges Posthumus's social inferiority, in comparison with the equal whom Innogen was expected to wed.

> Unto a poor but worthy gentleman. She's wedded,
> Her husband banished, she imprisoned. All
> Is outward sorrow, though I think the King
> Be touched at very heart.

SECOND GENTLEMAN   None but the King?   10

FIRST GENTLEMAN He that hath lost her too; so is the Queen,
> That most desired the match. But not a courtier,
> Although they wear their faces to the bent
> Of the King's looks, hath a heart that is not
> Glad of the thing they scowl at.

SECOND GENTLEMAN   And why so?   15

FIRST GENTLEMAN He that hath missed the Princess is a thing
> Too bad for bad report; and he that hath her –
> I mean, that married her (alack, good man,
> And therefore banished!) – is a creature such
> As to seek through the regions of the earth   20
> For one his like, there would be something failing
> In him that should compare. I do not think
> So fair an outward and such stuff within
> Endows a man but he.

SECOND GENTLEMAN   You speak him far.

FIRST GENTLEMAN I do extend him, sir, within himself,   25

---

15 of] *Maxwell (conj. Staunton);* at F

7 **She's wedded** There is some doubt about the
legal status of Innogen's marriage, which would
not have been valid in English canon law without
her father's consent. Anne Barton has argued that
although Innogen and Posthumus have exchanged
trothplights (a private espousal which would be recognized in civil law as binding for the transfer of
property), their marriage has not been publicly ratified and is, on the basis of Posthumus's remarks
at 2.5.17, as yet unconsummated. However, the
gentleman's unambiguous reference to Posthumus
as Innogen's 'husband' is supported by Jupiter's
forthright statement that 'in / Our temple was he
married' (5.3.169–70). See Barton, pp. 19–30, and
Introduction, p. 26.

9 **outward** external.

10 **touched . . . heart** deeply hurt (unlike the
courtiers' merely 'outward sorrow').

13 **wear their faces** set their expressions.

13 **bent** inclination.

16 **thing** an abusive term: Cymbeline calls
Posthumus a 'thing' once (1.1.125) and Innogen
twice (1.1.131, 150).

17 **Too . . . report** Even worse than an ill
description would be capable of expressing: one of
several paradoxical hyperboles to which this Gen-

tleman is given.

18 **I mean . . . her** The Gentleman corrects
himself, recognizing, with excessive nicety, that
although Posthumus has married Innogen he cannot be said to 'have' her, being forcibly separated.
The confused syntax of 18–19 additionally permits
a passing suggestion that Posthumus is banished for
being a 'good man'.

20 **to seek** i.e., even if one sought.

21 **failing** lacking.

22 **In . . . compare** In the man eventually
chosen for comparison with Posthumus.

23 **outward** exterior.

23 **stuff** substance.

24 **a** any (Abbott, #81).

24 **speak him far** go far in what you say about
him. Maxwell compares *H8* 1.1.38 (in a similar context): 'you go far'. In fact, subsequent events will
severely qualify this glowing account of Posthumus.

25 **I do . . . himself** 'My praise, however extensive, is within his merit' (Johnson). The momentary
paradox depends on *extend* meaning both 'exagger-
ate' (*OED* extend *v* 7) and 'lay out at full length'
(*OED* 2). Compare 1.4.15: 'wonderfully to extend
him'.

Crush him together, rather than unfold
His measure duly.
SECOND GENTLEMAN   What's his name and birth?
FIRST GENTLEMAN I cannot delve him to the root. His father
    Was called Sicilius, who did join his honour
    Against the Romans with Cassibelan,   30
    But had his titles by Tenantius, whom
    He served with glory and admired success,
    So gained the sur-addition Leonatus;
    And had, besides this gentleman in question,
    Two other sons, who in the wars o'th'time   35
    Died with their swords in hand; for which their father,
    Then old and fond of issue, took such sorrow
    That he quit being, and his gentle lady,
    Big of this gentleman, our theme, deceased
    As he was born. The King he takes the babe   40
    To his protection, calls him Posthumus Leonatus,
    Breeds him, and makes him of his Bedchamber,

---

30 Cassibelan] F *(Cassibulan)*

26–7 **Crush . . . duly** Compress his qualities rather than expound them at the length they deserve.

28 **delve** trace (literally, dig). The obscurity of Posthumus's ancestors allows Cymbeline to accuse him of 'baseness' (1.1.125, 142) even though he claims genteel status on the basis of his father's military achievements. Perhaps the gentleman is trying to steer tactfully around the fact that Posthumus's family has only recently been promoted and lacks a longstanding bloodline.

29 **Sicilius** See note to List of Characters, p. 80.

29–30 **did . . . Cassibelan** 'brought his renowned soldiership to the service of Cassibelan' (Herford). *Honour* here seems to mean 'military renown', though *OED* has no definition that precisely fits, and the distinction between *honour* and *titles* is perplexing. Some editors emend *join* to *gain*.

30 **Cassibelan** The British king who was attacked by Julius Caesar in 55–54 BC, and made tributary to Rome. Holinshed puts his death in 45 BC.

31 **by** from.

31 **Tenantius** In Holinshed Tenantius (Theomantius) is Cassibelan's nephew and successor, and father to Cymbeline. Holinshed puts his death in 23 BC.

33 **sur-addition** As in 'Coriolanus', an agnomen or special title, awarded for a particular service. See *Cor.* 1.9.65: 'Bear th'addition nobly

ever.'

33 **Leonatus** Literally, 'lion-born': the family name that Posthumus must earn for himself.

35 **the wars** After 54 BC there were in fact no further engagements between Britain and Rome until the Claudian conquest (AD 43). Holinshed's *History of England* fills in the gap with reports (some of which Holinshed himself discounts) of tensions between the two nations.

37 **fond of issue** doting on his children; or, perhaps, despairing of having further children.

39 **Big of** Pregnant with.

40–1 **The . . . protection** Such arrangements were occasionally adopted at the Stuart court: for example, in 1582 James took the sons of the Earl of Moray into his care when their father was killed in a feud.

42 **Breeds him** Brings him up.

42 **Bedchamber** As so often in this play, the practices of Cymbeline's court reflect seventeenth-century Whitehall rather than first-century Camulodunum. At the Stuart court the Gentlemen of the Bedchamber were the king's most personal attendants, serving in his private lodgings and sleeping by his bed: a prestigious and intimate office. Under James the Bedchamber was the focus for a group of elite courtiers, who notoriously received the richest favours and rewards. Compare 5.4.21n.

Puts to him all the learnings that his time
Could make him the receiver of, which he took
As we do air, fast as 'twas ministered,   45
And in's spring became a harvest; lived in court –
Which rare it is to do – most praised, most loved;
A sample to the youngest, to th'more mature
A glass that feated them, and to the graver
A child that guided dotards. To his mistress,   50
For whom he now is banished, her own price
Proclaims how she esteemed him; and his virtue
By her election may be truly read,
What kind of man he is.

SECOND GENTLEMAN   I honour him,
Even out of your report. But pray you tell me,   55
Is she sole child to th'King?

FIRST GENTLEMAN   His only child.
He had two sons – if this be worth your hearing,
Mark it – the eld'st of them at three years old,
I'th'swathing clothes the other, from their nursery
Were stol'n, and to this hour, no guess in knowledge   60
Which way they went.

SECOND GENTLEMAN   How long is this ago?

FIRST GENTLEMAN Some twenty years.

53–4 By . . . is] *Rowe; one line in* F   54–6 I . . . King] *Johnson;* I . . . report. / But . . . King? F   58 eld'st] *Singer 2;* eldest F

43 Puts to him Sets before him. Compare *Temp.*
1.1.69: 'to him put / The manage of my state'.
43 learnings education.
43 time time of life.
45 As . . . air i.e., as easily as breathing.
46 in's . . . harvest became prodigiously mature
even in his early youth.
48 sample example; model of excellence.
49 glass mirror.
49 feated them *OED* glosses this unusual
phrase as 'constrained them to propriety' (feat *v* 3,
conjecturally). As an adjective *feat* means 'proper,
neat, apt', so *feated* probably means that Posthumus presented the image of good living by which
the other courtiers adjusted their own behaviour. In
48–50 he sets the standard for the youthful, fully
adult and aged alike.
50 dotards old men, in their dotage.
50 To As for (continuing the construction of the
preceding passage, but varying the meaning).
51 her own price i.e., the punishment that she
is willing to suffer, rather than her value as heir-
apparent. Maxwell compares *MV* 3.2.314: 'Since
you are dear bought, I will love you dear.' Gibbons

finds an echo of Lear on Cordelia: 'When she was
dear to us, we did hold her so, / But now her price
is fallen' (*Lear* 1.1.196).
52–4 and his . . . is Maxwell explains this construction as 'a typically "licentious" piece of late-
Shakespearean syntax': the last six words are an
afterthought expanding on *his virtue*. Some editors
place a stop after *virtue* so that Innogen's *price* (51)
is weighed against *him and his virtue*, but this forfeits the link between *virtue* and *election*. Innogen's
price proclaims her esteem for Posthumus, and her
election testifies to his virtue and *what kind of man he
is*.
53 election choice. In the seventeenth century
the word often bears a strong theological charge,
given the importance in Calvinist thought of the
doctrine of unconditional election (God's providential discrimination between saints and reprobates,
irrespective of the individual's disposition).
55 Even out of Simply on the testimony of.
60 no . . . knowledge perhaps, 'no guess
resulting in any knowledge'.

SECOND GENTLEMAN That a king's children should be so conveyed,
        So slackly guarded, and the search so slow
        That could not trace them!
FIRST GENTLEMAN   Howsoe'er 'tis strange,   65
        Or that the negligence may well be laughed at,
        Yet is it true, sir.
SECOND GENTLEMAN   I do well believe you.

      Enter the QUEEN, POSTHUMUS, *and* INNOGEN

FIRST GENTLEMAN We must forbear. Here comes the gentleman,
        The Queen, and Princess.
                      Exeunt [the two Gentlemen]
QUEEN   No, be assured you shall not find me, daughter,   70
        After the slander of most stepmothers,
        Evil-eyed unto you. You're my prisoner, but
        Your jailer shall deliver you the keys
        That lock up your restraint. For you, Posthumus,
        So soon as I can win th'offended King,   75
        I will be known your advocate: marry, yet
        The fire of rage is in him, and 'twere good
        You leaned unto his sentence with what patience
        Your wisdom may inform you.
POSTHUMUS   Please your highness,
        I will from hence today.
QUEEN   You know the peril.   80
        I'll fetch a turn about the garden, pitying
        The pangs of barred affections, though the King
        Hath charged you should not speak together.   *Exit*

---

68 SD] Sisson; *after 69 in* F   69 SD] *Exeunt / Scena Secunda.* F

63 **conveyed** stolen.
65–7 Howsoe'er . . . sir A strategic disavowal of the story's implausibility very similar to that made by the Gentleman in *WT* 5.2.27–9.
67.0 INNOGEN For this spelling of the name ('Imogen' in F), see the note to the List of Characters, p. 79 above.
69 **forbear** withdraw.
69 SD F begins a new scene at this point, but the division is scribal, the Gentleman's last words clearly indicating that the setting is continuous in the theatre. However, the arrival of royalty does change scenic decorum, and the Gentlemen have to move away since new rules of protocol obtain.

71 **slander** evil repute. The Queen, who bears the hallmarks of fairytale, begins by denying that she is a fairytale villain.
74 That . . . restraint 'That lock you up and confine you' (Maxwell).
75 **win** prevail upon.
76 **marry** a mild oath: by the Virgin Mary.
78 **leaned** deferred (*OED* lean *vb* 6c).
79 **inform** imbue. A second 'with' is implied at the end of the sentence (Maxwell, citing Abbott, #394).
79 **Please** If it please.
80 **peril** danger; the threat of death that hangs over Posthumus.

INNOGEN Oh dissembling courtesy! How fine this tyrant
        Can tickle where she wounds! My dearest husband,   85
        I something fear my father's wrath, but nothing –
        Always reserved my holy duty – what
        His rage can do on me. You must be gone,
        And I shall here abide the hourly shot
        Of angry eyes, not comforted to live,   90
        But that there is this jewel in the world
        That I may see again.
POSTHUMUS   My queen, my mistress!
        O lady, weep no more, lest I give cause
        To be suspected of more tenderness
        Than doth become a man. I will remain   95
        The loyal'st husband that did e'er plight troth.
        My residence in Rome at one Philario's,
        Who to my father was a friend, to me
        Known but by letter, thither write, my queen,
        And with mine eyes I'll drink the words you send,   100
        Though ink be made of gall.

Enter QUEEN

QUEEN   Be brief, I pray you:
        If the King come, I shall incur I know not
        How much of his displeasure. [*Aside*] Yet I'll move him
        To walk this way. I never do him wrong
        But he does buy my injuries to be friends,   105

97 Philario's] *Rowe; Filorio's* F   103 *Aside*] *Rowe; not in* F

84 **courtesy** good manners, in tactfully leaving them alone together.

85 **tickle** soothe. The Queen's manipulativeness resembles that of the beautiful but despotic queen Cecropia in Philip Sidney's *The Arcadia*: see Introduction, p. 10 above.

87 **reserved . . . duty** except for the respect I owe him as his child. A typically contradictory remark from Innogen, whose destiny is to be a dutiful daughter, despite the apparently heroic defiance that she here presents to her father. Some editors take 'duty' to mean 'obligation to my husband', so that Innogen means 'I fear nothing that Cymbeline can do to me, except the possibility of being divorced', but the formula seems very oblique.

89 **hourly** continual.

89–90 **shot . . . eyes** hostile glances.

90 **not . . . live** finding no comfort in living.

91 **this jewel** i.e., Posthumus himself.

95 **become** befit. Posthumus urges Innogen to cease crying lest he, too, starts to weep.

96 **plight troth** exchange promises. See 1.1.7n.

97 **Rome** Some editors emend to *Rome's*, but Posthumus's syntax is compressed under the pressure of the moment.

101 **gall** Oak-gall, an intensely bitter fluid used in ink manufacture (Warren).

103 **move** prompt.

104 **he . . . friends** probably, he mistakes my harms for favours (*friends* = benefits, acts of friendship). Some editors take the Queen to mean 'he repays the injuries I do him with kindness, for the sake of retaining our friendship', but at the end Cymbeline will insist that he never suspected her love to him (5.4.40, 65). The Queen's remark underlines her machiavellian cunning, and the relish with which she pursues it.

Pays dear for my offences.   [*Exit*]

POSTHUMUS   Should we be taking leave
As long a term as yet we have to live,
The loathness to depart would grow. Adieu!

INNOGEN Nay, stay a little;
Were you but riding forth to air yourself   110
Such parting were too petty. Look here, love,
This diamond was my mother's. Take it, heart,
                    [*She gives him a ring*]
But keep it till you woo another wife,
When Innogen is dead.

POSTHUMUS   How, how? Another?
You gentle gods, give me but this I have,   115
And cere up my embracements from a next
With bonds of death.
                    [*He puts on the ring*]
                          Remain, remain thou here,
While sense can keep it on; and sweetest, fairest,
As I my poor self did exchange for you
To your so infinite loss, so in our trifles   120
I still win of you. For my sake wear this:
It is a manacle of love, I'll place it
Upon this fairest prisoner.
                    [*Putting a bracelet on her arm*]

INNOGEN   Oh the gods!
When shall we see again?

---

106 SD] *Rowe; not in* F   112 SD] *Taylor; not in* F   116 cere] F (*seare*)   117 SD] *Rowe (subst.); not in* F   123 SD] *Rowe; not in* F

106–8 Should . . . grow i.e., the longer our parting, the more difficult our separation will be.

110 to air yourself to take the air.

111 petty brief.

111–123 The exchange of gifts is necessary as the plot requires evidence of supposed betrayal, but its emotional weight comes from its repetition of the marriage promises which the lovers made before the play began, effectively presenting a kind of on-stage wedding. Barton, p. 20, notes that rings were sometimes produced in Church courts as testimony to a pre-contract.

112 my mother's One of only four references to Cymbeline's first wife: the others come at 1.6.126, 3.4.2 and 5.4.362. The ring betokens female bonds across two generations.

113 But Only.

116 cere wrap in a cerecloth (= waxed linen used for winding a corpse).

117, 118 thou, it Both pronouns refer to the ring, as performance will readily make clear. Compare the similar change of pronoun at 3.3.104–5.

118 While . . . on For as long as feeling remains.

120 loss disadvantage: Posthumus's status being inferior to Innogen's, he calculates that the 'exchange' benefits him more than her.

121 still always.

121 win of you 'That is, my bracelet is not as valuable as your ring' (Furness). Posthumus's willingness to weigh up the costs of his marriage unsettles the sentimental tone of the parting, as does his description of the bracelet as a 'manacle' (122), which makes it sound as though Innogen needs restraining.

124 see meet. Innogen exactly echoes Cressida's parting from Troilus (*Tro.* 4.5.56).

Enter CYMBELINE *and* LORDS

POSTHUMUS   Alack, the king!

CYMBELINE Thou basest thing, avoid hence, from my sight!   125
    If after this command thou fraught the court
    With thy unworthiness, thou diest. Away,
    Thou'rt poison to my blood.

POSTHUMUS   The gods protect you,
    And bless the good remainders of the court!
    I am gone.   *Exit*

INNOGEN   There cannot be a pinch in death   130
    More sharp than this is.

CYMBELINE   O disloyal thing,
    That shouldst repair my youth, thou heap'st
    A year's age on me.

INNOGEN   I beseech you, sir,
    Harm not yourself with your vexation;
    I am senseless of your wrath. A touch more rare   135
    Subdues all pangs, all fears.

CYMBELINE   Past grace? Obedience?

INNOGEN Past hope and in despair, that way past grace.

CYMBELINE That mightst have had the sole son of my Queen!

INNOGEN Oh blest that I might not! I chose an eagle,
    And did avoid a puttock.   140

CYMBELINE Thou took'st a beggar, wouldst have made my throne

---

126 fraught] F; freight *Warren*   132 heap'st] F; heap'st many *Hanmer;* heap'st instead *Capell*   138 *Rowe;* That . . . had / The . . . Queene. F   141–2 *Rowe;* Thou . . . my / Throne . . . basenesse. F

126 fraught burden.

128 good . . . court courtiers left behind who are virtuous.

130 pinch pain.

132 repair . . . youth restore me to youthfulness: as in the lament of Lucrece's father at her death, 'Poor broken glass, I often did behold / In thy sweet semblance my old age new born' (*Luc.* 1758–9). The line lacks two syllables and something may have dropped out: an adjective or adverbial phrase at the end might improve Cymbeline's slightly cryptic remark. The most convincing emendation is Capell's *thou heap'st instead*, though elsewhere Shakespeare only uses *instead* in conjunction with *of* or *whereof*.

135 senseless of insensible to.

135 A touch . . . rare 'A higher feeling' (Staunton): presumably, the pain of parting from

Posthumus. Compare Belarius at 4.2.243: 'Great griefs, I see, med'cine the less.'

136 Past grace 'Devoid of duty?': a rhetorical question. Innogen's reply deepens Cymbeline's words by quibbling on the theological meanings of 'grace'. A soul is technically in 'despair' (137) when it is convinced that it cannot deserve forgiveness and is beyond the reach of God's grace.

139 might not i.e., 'was able not to', in answer to Cymbeline's *mightst* (138).

139 eagle the king of birds, and a symbol of Roman imperialism, since the eagle figured on legionary standards. The eagle reappears in the soothsayer's dream (4.2.348), and materializes in the vision of Jupiter. See also 1.4.9.

140 puttock kite; a common scavenger and bird of prey.

                    A seat for baseness.

INNOGEN   No, I rather added
          A lustre to it.

CYMBELINE   Oh thou vile one!

INNOGEN   Sir,
          It is your fault that I have loved Posthumus.
          You bred him as my playfellow, and he is   145
          A man worth any woman, over-buys me
          Almost the sum he pays.

CYMBELINE   What, art thou mad?

INNOGEN Almost, sir. Heaven restore me! Would I were
          A neatherd's daughter, and my Leonatus
          Our neighbour shepherd's son.

                    Enter QUEEN

CYMBELINE   Thou foolish thing!   150
          [*To the Queen*] They were again together; you have done
          Not after our command. [*To the Lords*] Away with her,
          And pen her up.

QUEEN   Beseech you, patience. Peace,
          Dear lady daughter, peace! Sweet sovereign,
          Leave us to ourselves, and make yourself some comfort   155
          Out of your best advice.

CYMBELINE   Nay, let her languish
          A drop of blood a day, and being aged
          Die of this folly.

                              [*Exeunt Cymbeline and Lords*]

QUEEN   Fie, you must give way!

142–3 No . . . it.] *Rowe 2; one line in* F   151 SD] *Theobald; not in* F   152 SD] *Taylor; not in* F   153 you] *Warburton;* your
F   158 SD] *Dyce; Exit.* F

146–7 over-buys . . . pays 'pays a price for   153 Beseech I beseech.
me that is almost entirely in excess of my value'   156 advice consideration. Warren suggests that
(*Riverside*).   the Queen may mean that Cymbeline should con-
148–50 A familiar topos in courtly romance, reit-   sult with his councillors.
erated elsewhere in Shakespeare's late plays. Sim-   156 languish either 'pine away (at the rate of a
ilar sentiments recur in *WT* 4.4.1–24, 450–51, and   drop of blood a day)', or 'waste' (as at 1.6.71). Cym-
are elaborately developed in *WT*'s source, Robert   beline's curse echoes his complaint against Innogen
Greene's *Pandosto* (see Bullough, VIII, 164–5). In   at 131–3.
the present context Innogen's wish anticipates her   158 Fie . . . way! Probably spoken to Cymbe-
subsequent journey into the wild.   line in a hypocritical display of support for Inno-
149 neatherd's cowherd's.   gen. Conceivably the whole remark, or all but
150 Thou . . . thing! The last words Cymbeline   its first word, is a rebuke to Innogen, but the
speaks to Innogen until 5.5.93.   Queen's pretence throughout is that she wishes to
152 after according to.   help her.

Enter PISANIO

Here is your servant. How now, sir? What news?

PISANIO My lord your son drew on my master.

QUEEN   Ha?   160

No harm, I trust, is done?

PISANIO   There might have been,
But that my master rather played than fought,
And had no help of anger. They were parted
By gentlemen at hand.

QUEEN   I am very glad on't.

INNOGEN Your son's my father's friend; he takes his part   165
To draw upon an exile. O brave sir!
I would they were in Afric both together,
Myself by with a needle, that I might prick
The goer-back. Why came you from your master?

PISANIO On his command. He would not suffer me   170
To bring him to the haven; left these notes
Of what commands I should be subject to,
When't pleased you to employ me.

QUEEN   This hath been
Your faithful servant. I dare lay mine honour
He will remain so.

PISANIO   I humbly thank your highness.   175

QUEEN Pray walk awhile.

158.1 SD] *Dyce; after* folly. *in* F

159 **drew** i.e., drew his sword.

163 **had no . . . anger** i.e., Posthumus preserved his self-control. Some editors suppose it means that he fought half-heartedly, but the Second Lord contradicts this in 1.2.

165 **takes . . . part** sides with Cymbeline.

166 **To draw** In drawing.

167 **in Afric** in some desert place. Perhaps this is a residual echo of the geography of the Hellenistic romances on which the Innogen–Posthumus plot is based. But compare *Cor.* 4.2.24: 'I would my son were in Arabia, and thy tribe before him.'

168 **needle** monosyllabic (nee'le).

169 **the goer-back** whichever one shies away from fighting.

169 **Why came . . . master** Innogen is surprised that Pisanio had not accompanied Posthumus further on his journey: the first instance of

a recurrent concern with loyal service. There is some ambiguity about whose service Pisanio was in before the marriage. Cloten calls him 'her old servant' (3.5.54), but Posthumus's instructions to Pisanio (1.1.170–3), Innogen's surprise that he came back, and the Queen's remarks in 1.5.49–60 suggest that he was originally Posthumus's attendant. Compare also Innogen's momentary but striking hesitation at 3.2.26. In Acts 3 and 4 this conflict of allegiance turns out to be the main issue in Pisanio's role.

170 **suffer** permit.

171 **haven** port.

174 **lay** wager.

176–8 The repetition of *Pray*, the lack of a syllable after *hence* (176), and F's lineation suggest that the text has been disturbed by the printer. I follow Capell's lineation, and Maxwell's conjecture for emending the metre.

INNOGEN [*To Pisanio*] About some half hour hence,
         Beseech you speak with me. You shall at least
         Go see my lord aboard. For this time leave me.

                                                          Exeunt

1.2 *Enter* CLOTEN *and two* LORDS

FIRST LORD Sir, I would advise you to shift a shirt; the violence of
    action hath made you reek as a sacrifice. Where air comes out, air
    comes in; there's none abroad so wholesome as that you vent.
CLOTEN If my shirt were bloody, then to shift it. Have I hurt him?
SECOND LORD [*Aside*] No, faith; not so much as his patience.   5
FIRST LORD Hurt him? His body's a passable carcass if he be not hurt.
    It is a thoroughfare for steel if he be not hurt.
SECOND LORD [*Aside*] His steel was in debt, it went o'th'backside the
    town.
CLOTEN The villain would not stand me.   10
SECOND LORD [*Aside*] No, but he fled forward still, toward your face.
FIRST LORD Stand you? You have land enough of your own, but he
    added to your having, gave you some ground.
SECOND LORD [*Aside*] As many inches as you have oceans. Puppies!
CLOTEN I would they had not come between us.   15

---

177 Beseech] *this edn (conj. Maxwell); Pray* F; I pray *Capell* 177–8 *Capell*; Pray . . . me; / You . . . aboord. /
For . . . me. F Act 1, Scene 2 1.2 *Scena Tertia.* F 1, 5 SH FIRST LORD, SECOND LORD] *Rowe;* 1, 2 F *through-
out scene* 4 *as prose, Capell; verse,* F 5, 8, 11 *Aside*] *Theobald; not in* F 7 thoroughfare] F3; through-fare F 7 he] *conj.
Brooks; it* F 12–13 *as prose, Pope; verse* F 14, 16, 19, 24, 28 *Aside*] *Pope; not in* F

Act 1, Scene 2
  1 **shift** change.
  1–2 **violence of action** heat of your contention
with Posthumus: obliquely confirming Pisanio's
account of the duel, that Cloten fought angrily and
Posthumus temperately. Cloten's eagerness to fight
is the first of his many similarities with Posthumus,
who is constitutionally inclined to duelling. For the
sustained structural parallel that develops between
the two competitors for Innogen, see Introduction,
pp. 33–4.
  2 **reek** emit vapours.
  2 a **sacrifice** A submerged anticipation of
Cloten's death: at his first appearance he is already
marked as the scapegoat.
  3 **none abroad** no air outside (outrageously flattering Cloten that the sweat he emits is more
'wholesome' than the air that flows in to replen-
ish it).

  3 **vent** give off.
  4 **then** then I would.
  6 **passable** (1) veritable; (2) penetrable (by a
rapier pass).
  7 **he** Brooks suggests that F's 'it' was mistakenly
carried forward from the beginning of the sentence.
Unemended, the parallel with the previous sentence is lost.
  8 **backside the town** backstreets; used by
debtors to evade their creditors. Far from passing
through the *thoroughfare* (= highway) of Posthumus's body, Cloten's rapier slunk dishonourably
around the side.
  10 **stand me** stand his ground before me.
  13 **gave . . . ground** fell back.
  14 **As . . . oceans** i.e., Posthumus gave no
ground at all.
  14 **Puppies!** Autolycus expresses contempt in
the same way for the shepherds in *WT* 4.4.706.

SECOND LORD [*Aside*] So would I, till you had measured how long a
    fool you were upon the ground.

CLOTEN And that she should love this fellow and refuse me!

SECOND LORD [*Aside*] If it be a sin to make a true election, she is
    damned.   20

FIRST LORD Sir, as I told you always, her beauty and her brain go not
    together. She's a good sign, but I have seen small reflection of her
    wit.

SECOND LORD [*Aside*] She shines not upon fools, lest the reflection
    should hurt her.   25

CLOTEN Come, I'll to my chamber. Would there had been some hurt
    done!

SECOND LORD [*Aside*] I wish not so, unless it had been the fall of an ass,
    which is no great hurt.

CLOTEN You'll go with us?   30

FIRST LORD I'll attend your lordship.

CLOTEN Nay, come, let's go together.

SECOND LORD Well, my lord.

Exeunt

1.3 *Enter* INNOGEN *and* PISANIO

INNOGEN I would thou grew'st unto the shores o'th'haven
            And question'dst every sail. If he should write,
            And I not have it, 'twere a paper lost
            As offered mercy is. What was the last
            That he spake to thee?

24–5 *as prose, Rowe; verse* F Act 1, Scene 3 1.3 *Scena Quarta.* F 2 question'dst] *Johnson;* questioned'st F;
question'st *conj. Taylor*

16–17 measured . . . ground To 'measure out
one's length' is to fall prostrate (*OED* measure *v*
2f, citing *MND* 3.2.429).

19 election i.e., in the theological sense, in
which predestination *elects* (= chooses) between
the saved and the damned.

21–2 her beauty . . . together her judgement does not equal her beauty. Maxwell compares
the proverb 'Beauty and folly are often matched'
(Tilley, B164).

22 She's . . . sign She has a good outward show.

22 reflection (1) indication; (2) shining
(Maxwell). The Second Lord's riposte treats the
first lord's 'reflection' literally, to mean light that
Innogen projects and others reflect back at her.

28–9 fall . . . ass The title of a fable in sixteenth-
century school editions of Aesop (Baldwin, I,
630).

31–3 In this brief exchange Cloten takes notice
of the Second Lord for the first time, and over-
rules his hesitancy about keeping with the group.
In some productions it is used to hint at tensions between the three figures. This exit establishes a pattern of departure which, when repeated
in revised form at the end of 2.1, allows the Second
Lord an opportunity of hanging back.

Act 1, Scene 3

1 grew'st unto were inseparably united with,
like a plant.

4 As . . . is Not satisfactorily explained. The
phrase 'as precious (as offered mercy is)' may be
implied, in which case 'mercy' is probably the
mercy of heaven, or a pardon to a condemned man.
However, the sense is far from clear, and the speech
may be missing something.

PISANIO   It was his queen, his queen!   5
INNOGEN Then waved his handkerchief?
PISANIO   And kissed it, madam.
INNOGEN Senseless linen, happier therein than I!
    And that was all?
PISANIO   No, madam, for so long
    As he could make me with this eye or ear
    Distinguish him from others, he did keep   10
    The deck, with glove or hat or handkerchief
    Still waving, as the fits and stirs of's mind
    Could best express how slow his soul sailed on,
    How swift his ship.
INNOGEN   Thou shouldst have made him
    As little as a crow, or less, ere left   15
    To after-eye him.
PISANIO   Madam, so I did.
INNOGEN I would have broke mine eye-strings, cracked them, but
    To look upon him till the diminution
    Of space had pointed him sharp as my needle;
    Nay, followed him till he had melted from   20
    The smallness of a gnat to air, and then
    Have turned mine eye and wept. But good Pisanio,
    When shall we hear from him?
PISANIO   Be assured, madam,
    With his next vantage.
INNOGEN I did not take my leave of him, but had   25
    Most pretty things to say. Ere I could tell him

9 this] *Theobald (after Warburton);* his F   17–18 *Pope;* I . . . eye-strings; / Crack'd . . . diminution F

7 **Senseless** Insentient.
8–22 An imitation of the famous passage in Ovid's *Metamorphoses*, XI, 537–49, where Alcyone watches from the shore as her husband, Ceyx, departs on the voyage which is to end in shipwreck. Innogen's description of the process of diminution with distance is also reminiscent of Edgar's imaginary view over Dover Cliff (*Lear* 4.6.11–24). The verse's bravura quality is created by the way Innogen embroiders and intensifies Pisanio's workmanlike account: unlike Alcyone she does not see her husband depart but suffers with him in imagination. The allusion is the nearest *Cym.* comes to the literal shipwrecks of *WT* and *Temp.*
10 **keep** remain on.
12 **as** as if.
12 **fits . . . mind** mental disturbance.

14 **How** Howsoever: whatever the speed of his ship, Posthumus's mind travels more slowly from Innogen.
14 **made** observed.
15 **ere** before.
16 **after-eye** follow him with your eye (not recorded in *OED*).
17 **eye-strings** tendons of the eye, thought to be capable of cracking under extreme eye strain. Maxwell quotes Thomas Nashe's *The Unfortunate Traveller*: 'my eyes have broken their strings with staring' (*Works*, II, 324).
18 **diminution** contraction.
19 **pointed . . . needle** i.e., reduced him to a mere dot.
24 **With . . . vantage** At his first opportunity.

How I would think on him at certain hours
Such thoughts and such; or I could make him swear
The shes of Italy should not betray
Mine interest and his honour; or have charged him,   30
At the sixth hour of morn, at noon, at midnight,
T'encounter me with orisons, for then
I am in heaven for him; or ere I could
Give him that parting kiss which I had set
Betwixt two charming words, comes in my father,   35
And like the tyrannous breathing of the north
Shakes all our buds from growing.

Enter a LADY

LADY   The Queen, madam,
Desires your highness' company.
INNOGEN [*To Pisanio*] Those things I bid you do, get them dispatched.
I will attend the Queen.
PISANIO   Madam, I shall.   40

Exeunt

1.4 *Enter* PHILARIO, IACHIMO, *a* FRENCHMAN, *a Dutchman, and a*
Spaniard First time in Italy, verse → prose, change of register
A lot of anachronisms (cracks through the surface)

IACHIMO Believe it, sir, I have seen him in Britain. He was then of a
    crescent note, expected to prove so worthy as since he hath been

---

39 SD] *Taylor; not in* F   Act 1, Scene 4   1.4 *Scena Quinta.* F

29 shes women.
30 interest right (in Posthumus). This is one
of those remarks that critics who idealize Innogen
find uncomfortable: Nosworthy deplores it as 'out
of character'.
31 sixth . . . midnight In the Catholic Church
six, noon and midnight are three of the canonical
hours of worship (fixed times for prayer).
32 orisons prayers. Innogen fantasizes that by
praying simultaneously it will be as if she and
Posthumus meet in heaven. However, there is no
vestige of this plan in the midnight prayer that
Innogen voices at 2.2.8–10.
35 charming carrying a magical charm (to protect Posthumus from evil). Maxwell notes that
'charming' began to mean 'delightful' only in the
later seventeenth century.
36 north north wind, which damages spring
flowers. Warren compares *Son.* 18: 'Rough winds
do shake the darling buds of May.'
39 bid i.e., bade.

Act 1, Scene 4
    0 SD *a Dutchman . . . Spaniard* These charac-
ters remain mute, and, like 'ghost' parts in other
plays, must be fossils from an authorial change of
plan. Probably Shakespeare listed them as characters he expected to use in the dialogue, but, having
completed the scene without giving them speeches,
omitted to turn back and delete them from the
opening direction. Their presence demonstrates
that *Frederick of Jennen* was one of the sources that
Shakespeare used for the wager plot. Unlike the
equivalent episode in Boccaccio's *Decameron*, which
sets the dialogue in a company of Italian merchants,
Frederick describes them as a mixed group of Italians, Spanish and French. However, Shakespeare
does upgrade the group socially, changing them
from merchants to gentlemen, and makes Iachimo's
Italy feel more contemporary and cosmopolitan
than either Cymbeline's Britain or Lucius's classical Rome (as is shown by the use of 'signor' as
the term of address, 82, 140).
    2 crescent note growing reputation.

allowed the name of. But I could then have looked on him without
the help of admiration, though the catalogue of his endowments
had been tabled by his side, and I to peruse him by items.   5

PHILARIO You speak of him when he was less furnished than now he
    is with that which makes him both without and within.

FRENCHMAN I have seen him in France. We had very many there
    could behold the sun with as firm eyes as he. — *Posthumus / eagle comparison.*

IACHIMO This matter of marrying his king's daughter, wherein he   10
    must be weighed rather by her value than his own, words him, I
    doubt not, a great deal from the matter.

FRENCHMAN And then his banishment –

IACHIMO Ay, and the approbation of those that weep this lamentable
    divorce under her colours are wonderfully to extend him, be it but   15
    to fortify her judgment, which else an easy battery might lay flat
    for taking a beggar without less quality. But how comes it he is to
    sojourn with you? How creeps acquaintance?

---

13 banishment–] *Pope;* banishment. F

---

3 **allowed . . . of** said to have become. Characteristically Iachimo's faint praise holds back from
attesting that Posthumus has indeed acquired the
worth that his early life promised.

4 **admiration** wonder; reverence and amazement mixed.

4 **though** even if.

5 **tabled** set down in a list. Posthumus is imagined in mercantile terms, as a commodity whose
attributes are catalogued for scrutiny by potential
purchasers.

5 **I** i.e., I were.

6 **furnished** equipped.

7 **which makes him** i.e., which is the making
of him.

7 **without and within** in outward appearance
and inner quality.

9 **behold the sun** An implied comparison
between Posthumus and the eagle, continuing the
train of association begun at 1.1.139, though the
Frenchman uses the comparison to deny that
Posthumus really is different from anyone else. One
sign of the eagle's nobility was its supposed ability
to look directly at the sun. Compare *LLL* 4.3.222:
'What peremptory eagle-sighted eye / Dares look
upon the heaven of her brow, / That is not blinded
by her majesty?'

11–12 **words . . . matter** ascribes a character to
him that is far from the truth. The verb 'words' (=
represents in words) is a nonce-use (see *OED* word
v 4c): Iachimo's sceptical view turns on an underlying distinction drawn from rhetoric, between style

and content.

14 **approbation** approval.

15 **under her colours** on her side: literally, following her ensign. Military terminology continues
in *fortify* and *battery* (16).

15 **are** 'are of a nature' seems to be implied
(Dowden). The verb is plural, being governed by
banishment (13) and *approbation.*

15 **extend** magnify (his reputation): compare
1.1.25.

15 **be it but** if only.

16 **lay flat** demolish. The sense is: Innogen's
poor judgement in choosing Posthumus would
expose her to easy attack, were it not 'fortified'
(16) by her friends' approval.

17 **without less quality** Iachimo means 'without *more* quality', 'someone with no higher rank
than this'. Shakespeare often confuses the grammar of 'less' and 'more', especially in negative
constructions. Compare *Cor.* 1.4.13–14: '*Martius.*
Tullus Aufidius, is he within your walls? *1. Senator.* No, nor a man that fears you less than
he.'

18 **How creeps** How have you stolen into. The
verb seems to suggest condescension and hostility.
Compare Ben Jonson, *Every Man in his Humour*
(1598), 1.3.60–4: 'now doth he creep and wrig-
gle into acquaintance with all the brave gallants
about the town . . . and they flout him invincibly';
and Robert Greene's *Quip for an Upstart Courtier*
(1592): 'not as your worship good master Velvet
Breeches . . . to creep into acquaintance'.

PHILARIO His father and I were soldiers together, to whom I have
  been often bound for no less than my life.   20

Almost chivalrous   *Enter* POSTHUMUS

  Here comes the Briton. Let him be so entertained amongst you as
  suits with gentlemen of your knowing to a stranger of his quality.
  I beseech you all, be better known to this gentleman, whom I
  commend to you as a noble friend of mine. How worthy he is I
  will leave to appear hereafter, rather than story him in his own   25
  hearing.
FRENCHMAN Sir, we have known together in Orleans.
POSTHUMUS Since when I have been debtor to you for courtesies
  which I will be ever to pay, and yet pay still.
FRENCHMAN Sir, you o'errate my poor kindness; I was glad I did   30
  atone my countryman and you. It had been pity you should have
  been put together with so mortal a purpose as then each bore,
  upon importance of so slight and trivial a nature.
POSTHUMUS By your pardon, sir, I was then a young traveller, rather
  shunned to go even with what I heard than in my every action to be   35
  guided by others' experiences; but upon my mended judgment –
  if I offend not to say it is mended – my quarrel was not altogether
  slight.
FRENCHMAN Faith, yes, to be put to the arbitrement of swords, and
  by such two that would by all likelihood have confounded one the   40
  other, or have fallen both.

---

21 Briton] F *(Britaine)*   37 offend not] *Rowe (Durfey);* offend F

20.0 SD Posthumus enters at the rear of the
stage, and a few seconds pass before he encounters
the conversation at the front. This allows time for
Philario's lines, spoken anxiously and *sotto voce*,
to signal an alteration in the social temperature.
Posthumus does not join the group until 'I beseech
you all'.
  22 **suits with** befits.
  22 **knowing** experience in society (compare
2.3.92). A plea for the others to treat Posthumus
with respect; but they have already decided on his
'quality' (17).
  25 **story** give an account of. Philario declines to
embarrass Posthumus by praising him to his face:
an awkwardly tactful gesture typical of this scene's
brittle civility.
  27 **known together** been acquainted.

  29 **which I . . . still** 'for which I will always
be in your debt, though I go on repaying for ever'
(Maxwell, comparing *Son.* 30, 'Which I new pay as
if not paid before').
  30 **o'errate** *OED*'s earliest example of this word.
  31 **atone** reconcile.
  32 **put together** opposed (in combat).
  33 **importance** an affair of (so little) consequence (*OED* importance *sb* 2).
  34–5 **rather . . . with** who rather avoided going
along with. Posthumus admits that, in some limited
ways, his youthful behaviour was wilful.
  35 **than** 'than appear' seems to be implied.
  37 **if . . . not** a token apology: since although his
judgement is *mended* (= improved), on this point
it remains the same.
  40 **confounded** destroyed.

Psychologising → more about his own masculinity than Imogen

IACHIMO Can we with manners ask what was the difference?

FRENCHMAN Safely, I think; 'twas a contention in public, which may
without contradiction suffer the report. It was much like an argument that fell out last night, where each of us fell in praise of our   45
country mistresses, this gentleman at that time vouching – and
upon warrant of bloody affirmation – his to be more fair, virtuous,
wise, chaste, constant, qualified, and less attemptable than any the
rarest of our ladies in France.

IACHIMO That lady is not now living, or this gentleman's opinion by   50
this worn out.

POSTHUMUS She holds her virtue still, and I my mind.

IACHIMO You must not so far prefer her 'fore ours of Italy.

POSTHUMUS Being so far provoked as I was in France, I would abate
her nothing, though I profess myself her adorer, not her friend.   55

IACHIMO As fair and as good, a kind of hand-in-hand comparison, had
been something too fair and too good for any lady in Britain. If
she went before others I have seen as that diamond of yours

is Iachimo the instigator?

---

57 Britain] *Johnson;* Britanie F   58 others] *Pope; others.* F

42 **difference** quarrel.

44 **without contradiction** without any objection.

44 **suffer** admit of.

45–6 **our country mistresses** the lady each of
us loves in his own country. 'Country mistresses'
is hyphenated in F, but this probably comes from
the hand of the scribe, Ralph Crane: see Textual
Analysis, p. 262.

47 **warrant . . . affirmation** a pledge that he
would maintain it with his blood.

48 **qualified** accomplished; endowed with good
qualities.

48 **attemptable** open to attempts (on her honour). *OED*'s sole instance of this word.

48 **any the** any of the.

50–1 **by this** by this time.

52 **mind** opinion.

53 **prefer her** advance her claims.

54–5 **abate her nothing** decrease no part of her
value.

55 **her adorer . . . friend** her worshipper,
not her lover: Posthumus is keen to avoid the
imputation that his praise of Innogen is coloured
by his sexual involvement with her. At this time
'friend' could mean 'lover, sexual partner' in a positive sense (as in *Rom.* 3.5.43, *MM*, 1.4.29) but it

often carried the negative connotation of 'paramour
or concubine', as in Middleton's *Women Beware
Women*, 2.2.347–8: '*Bianca.* I have a husband. *Duke.*
That's a single comfort; take a friend to him';
Chapman's *Bussy D'Ambois*, 2.2.69: 'A husband and
a friend all wise wives have' (*Tragedies*, 72); and
AWW 1.3.37, *Oth.* 3.4.174, *WT* 1.2.109.

56 **As fair** i.e., 'As fair as any lady in your
country.'

56 **hand . . . comparison** a claim for equality,
not superiority.

57 **something** somewhat.

57 **Britain** F's 'Britanie' is probably a transposition error: F has 'Britaine' only fifty lines
earlier (1). However, 'Britany' was a possible variant form for the island's name. It is used, for
example, in Marlowe's *Edward II* (1594), 2.2.42,
and in two plays set in ancient Britain: Fletcher's
Bonduca (*B&F*, 5.1.6) and W. Rowley's *A Shoemaker a Gentleman* (2.1.141, 2.2.101, 2.3.194). In
the 1604 debates over how to name James's new
kingdom, MPs had hesitated between 'Britain'
and 'Britany': see *Commons Journals*, I, 180;
Gordon, *Enotikon;* and Galloway and Levack,
p. 61. There is a full discussion of the name in
Bindoff.

58 **went before** excelled.

outlustres many I have beheld, I could not but believe she excelled
many; but I have not seen the most precious diamond that is, nor   60
you the lady.

POSTHUMUS I praised her as I rated her; so do I my stone.

IACHIMO What do you esteem it at?

POSTHUMUS More than the world enjoys.

IACHIMO Either your unparagoned mistress is dead, or she's outprized   65
by a trifle.

POSTHUMUS You are mistaken. The one may be sold or given, or if
there were wealth enough for the purchase, or merit for the gift.
The other is not a thing for sale, and only the gift of the gods.

IACHIMO Which the gods have given you?   70

POSTHUMUS Which, by their graces, I will keep.

IACHIMO You may wear her in title yours; but, you know, strange fowl
light upon neighbouring ponds. Your ring may be stolen too, so
your brace of unprizable estimations, the one is but frail and the
other casual. A cunning thief or a that way accomplished courtier   75
would hazard the winning both of first and last.

POSTHUMUS Your Italy contains none so accomplished a courtier to
convince the honour of my mistress, if in the holding or loss of that
you term her frail. I do nothing doubt you have store of thieves;
notwithstanding, I fear not my ring.   80

PHILARIO Let us leave here, gentlemen.

---

59 could not but] *Malone;* could not F; could *Warburton*   68 purchase] *Rowe;* purchases F

59 outlustres outshines; exceeds in beauty. A
coinage: *OED*'s earliest example.

59 could not but could not choose but. Malone's insertion of 'but' has been generally accepted:
this whole passage (15–123) was set by Compositor
E and contains many obvious errors. The twist in
Iachimo's argument at this point is to equate Innogen with a commodity, the diamond: once Posthumus accepts this, it is only a short step to supposing
that her value can be weighed and marketed.

62 rated valued; estimated.

64 More . . . enjoys Beyond the value of everything in the world.

65 unparagoned matchless.

65 outprized exceeded in value (because she is
in 'the world', and so worth less than the ring).
OED's earliest example.

67 or if either if.

69 only . . . gods the gift of the gods alone.

72 wear . . . yours enjoy her nominally as your
own. 'Wear her' is used as in the proverbial phrase
'win her and wear her' (*OED* wear v^1 8b), and 'in

title' plays ironically on the legal sense of 'having a right to [some object]': Iachimo is implying
that for all Posthumus's marital possession of Innogen, his ownership is no securer than any other
man's.

73 neighbouring ponds Leontes describes how
wives can be seduced in similar terms: 'many a man
. . . [has] his pond fish'd by his next neighbour, by
Sir Smile, his neighbour' (*WT* 1.2.192–6).

73–4 so your i.e., so as to your.

74 brace . . . estimations pair of objects that
you esteem beyond all price.

74 frail weak (referring to Innogen).

75 casual subject to mischance (referring to the
ring).

76 first and last one and the other.

77 none . . . courtier no courtier so expert.

78 convince overcome.

79 store of thieves plenty of thieves (referring
back to 75). Posthumus is provoked into a sharp
insult against Iachimo's countrymen.

81 leave end.

POSTHUMUS Sir, with all my heart. This worthy signor, I thank him,
  makes no stranger of me; we are familiar at first.

IACHIMO With five times so much conversation I should get ground
  of your fair mistress, make her go back even to the yielding, had   85
  I admittance and opportunity to friend.

POSTHUMUS No, no.

IACHIMO I dare thereupon pawn the moiety of my estate to your ring,
  which in my opinion o'ervalues it something. But I make my wager
  rather against your confidence than her reputation; and to bar your   90
  offence herein, too, I durst attempt it against any lady in the world.

POSTHUMUS You are a great deal abused in too bold a persuasion, and
  I doubt not you sustain what you're worthy of by your attempt.

IACHIMO What's that?

POSTHUMUS A repulse, though your attempt, as you call it, deserve   95
  more – a punishment too.

PHILARIO Gentlemen, enough of this. It came in too suddenly; let it
  die as it was born, and I pray you be better acquainted.

IACHIMO Would I had put my estate and my neighbour's on
  th'approbation of what I have spoke!   100

POSTHUMUS What lady would you choose to assail?

IACHIMO Yours, whom in constancy you think stands so safe. I will
  lay you ten thousand ducats to your ring that, commend me to
  the court where your lady is, with no more advantage than the
  opportunity of a second conference, and I will bring from thence   105
  that honour of hers which you imagine so reserved.

POSTHUMUS I will wage against your gold, gold to it. My ring I hold
  dear as my finger, 'tis part of it.

91 herein, too] *Ingleby;* heerein to F   93 you] F; you'd *Rowe;* you'll *Ingleby*   103 thousand] F3; thousands F

83 **at first** at once.

84 **so much conversation** i.e., as we have just had.

84 **get ground** gain advantage. A duelling phrase that links the wager with Posthumus's fight with Cloten: compare 1.2.13.

85 **go back, yielding** (with bawdy quibbles).

86 **to** as a.

88 **moiety** half.

90–1 **bar your offence** prevent you taking it as an affront. Iachimo makes Posthumus's acceptance of the wager easier by claiming he has nothing against Innogen but wishes only to prove an intellectual point about Posthumus's exaggerated 'confidence' (90) in female fidelity.

92 **abused** deceived.

92 **bold a persuasion** confident an opinion.

93 **you sustain** you will receive (Abbott, #368).

100 **approbation** proof.

103 **lay** wager.

103 **ducats** An anachronism: ducats were the coinage of contemporary Italy, not ancient Rome. The implied sum is huge: in *MV* 1.3 the amount Shylock lends to Antonio is only three thousand ducats.

103 **commend me** give me a letter of introduction.

104–5 **the opportunity . . . conference** (probably), a pretext to address myself to her a second time.

106 **reserved** safe.

IACHIMO You are afraid, and therein the wiser. If you buy ladies' flesh
at a million a dram, you cannot preserve it from tainting. But I   110
see you have some religion in you, that you fear.

POSTHUMUS This is but a custom in your tongue; you bear a graver
purpose, I hope.

IACHIMO I am the master of my speeches, and would undergo what's
spoken, I swear.   115

POSTHUMUS Will you? I shall but lend my diamond till your return.
Let there be covenants drawn between's. My mistress exceeds in
goodness the hugeness of your unworthy thinking. I dare you to
this match: here's my ring.

PHILARIO I will have it no lay.   120

IACHIMO By the gods, it is one. If I bring you no sufficient testimony
that I have enjoyed the dearest bodily part of your mistress, my
ten thousand ducats are yours, so is your diamond too. If I come
off, and leave her in such honour as you have trust in, she your
jewel, this your jewel, and my gold are yours – provided I have   125
your commendation for my more free entertainment.

POSTHUMUS I embrace these conditions; let us have articles betwixt
us. Only, thus far you shall answer: if you make your voyage upon
her, and give me directly to understand you have prevailed, I am
no further your enemy; she is not worth our debate. If she remain   130
unseduced, you not making it appear otherwise, for your ill opinion
and th'assault you have made to her chastity, you shall answer me
with your sword.

---

109 afraid] *Theobald;* a Friend F   109 ladies'] F; lady's *Maxwell*

109 **afraid** Theobald's emendation for F's 'a
Friend' gives clear sense, especially in view of 'fear'
at 111. Given the sexual meaning of 'friend' (see
note to 55), F's reading might be correct: 'as someone with sexual knowledge of women, you are wise
to be reluctant to bet'. But the sense is very oblique,
and as Compositor E set this speech, it seems justified to emend it.
  110 **at . . . dram** at however exorbitant a price.
  111 **you . . . fear** i.e., your fear shows that
you believe in something beyond yourself: a gibe
at Posthumus's blustering self-confidence. Dowden
compares Psalm 3.10: 'The fear of the Lord is the
beginning of wisdom.'
  111 **that** since.
  112 **but a . . . tongue** merely a habit of your
speech.
  114 **I am . . . speeches** 'I know what I have
said; I said no more than I meant' (Steevens).
  114 **undergo** undertake.

117 **covenants** agreements.
  119 **here's my ring** As Posthumus still has his
ring at 2.4.40, his gesture cannot be to give it to
Iachimo but to present it in token of the wager (if,
say, a table was brought on for this scene, it would
be a natural gesture to lay it down). Nosworthy
suggests that he gives it to Philario to hold.
  120 **I . . . lay** I will not allow the bet.
  121–6 Iachimo runs over the wager twice, but
he details only the conditions in which Posthumus
will win: if his proof is unconvincing or he is unable
to undermine Innogen's honour.
  126 **commendation** introduction.
  126 **free entertainment** ready reception.
  127 **have articles** procure a legal agreement.
  128 **make . . . voyage** seduce. Dyce compares
Wiv. 2.1.181: 'If he should intend this voyage
toward my wife, I would turn her loose to him.'
  129 **directly** unambiguously.

IACHIMO Your hand, a covenant. We will have these things set down
　　　by lawful counsel, and straight away for Britain, lest the bargain   135
　　　should catch cold and starve. I will fetch my gold, and have our
　　　two wagers recorded.
POSTHUMUS Agreed.   [*Exeunt Posthumus and Iachimo*]
FRENCHMAN Will this hold, think you?
PHILARIO Signor Iachimo will not from it. Pray, let us follow 'em.   140
　　　　　　　　　　　　　　　　　　　　　　　　　　　　Exeunt

1.5 *Enter* QUEEN, LADIES, *and* CORNELIUS

QUEEN　　Whiles yet the dew's on ground, gather those flowers;
　　　　　Make haste. Who has the note of them?
LADY　　　　　　　　　　　　　　　　　　　I, madam.
QUEEN　　Dispatch.   *Exeunt Ladies*
　　　　　Now, master doctor, have you brought those drugs?
CORNELIUS Pleaseth your highness, ay. Here they are, madam.   5
　　　　　　　　　　　[*Presenting a box*]
　　　　　But I beseech your grace, without offence –
　　　　　My conscience bids me ask – wherefore you have
　　　　　Commanded of me these most poisonous compounds,
　　　　　Which are the movers of a languishing death,
　　　　　But though slow, deadly.
QUEEN　　　　　　　　　　　I wonder, doctor,   10
　　　　　Thou ask'st me such a question. Have I not been
　　　　　Thy pupil long? Hast thou not learned me how
　　　　　To make perfumes, distil, preserve – yea, so

---

138 SD] *Theobald; not in* F　140 *Rowe*; Signior . . . it./Pray . . . 'em. F　**Act 1, Scene 5**　1.5 *Scena Sexta.* F　1 *Rowe;*
Whiles . . . ground, / Gather . . . Flowers, F　3 SD *Exeunt*] F2; *Exit* F　5 SD] *Malone (subst.); not in* F

136 **catch . . . starve** collapse on maturer
consideration.
　140 **from** depart from.

Act 1, Scene 5
　1.5 This scene establishes the circumstances by
which the double mistake over the magic cordial
in 4.2 comes about and is needed to supply a
gap of time in the wager plot. It also gives more
space to the Queen, whose role would otherwise
lack weight.
　0 SD CORNELIUS Always 'doctor' in the dialogue,
and never referred to by name.
　1 **Whiles . . . ground** While the dew is still on
the ground. The Queen's gathering of flowers for

evil purposes anticipates, and is reversed by, the
herbal strewings in 4.2.
　2 **note** list.
　3 **Dispatch** Get on with it.
　6 **without offence** i.e., without wishing to give
offence.
　8 **compounds** compounded drugs, as opposed
to 'simples' (*OED* compound *sb* 2, citing this passage).
　10 **But . . . slow** i.e., But which, though slow,
are (Abbott, #385).
　12 **learned** taught.
　13 **distil, preserve** extract and preserve
essences (from the flowers).

That our great King himself doth woo me oft
For my confections? Having thus far proceeded –   15
Unless thou think'st me devilish – is't not meet
That I did amplify my judgment in
Other conclusions? I will try the forces
Of these thy compounds on such creatures as
We count not worth the hanging, but none human,   20
To try the vigour of them, and apply
Allayments to their act, and by them gather
Their several virtues and effects.

CORNELIUS   Your highness
Shall from this practice but make hard your heart.
Besides, the seeing these effects will be   25
Both noisome and infectious.

QUEEN   Oh, content thee.

                        Enter PISANIO

[*Aside*] Here comes a flattering rascal, upon him
Will I first work. He's factor for his master,
And enemy to my son. – How now, Pisanio?
Doctor, your service for this time is ended;   30
Take your own way.

CORNELIUS [*Aside*]   I do suspect you, madam,

---

27 *Aside*] Rowe; not in F   28 factor] Hudson 2 (after Walker); not in F   31 *Aside*] Rowe; not in F

---

15 **confections** mixtures (of drugs).

15 **proceeded** 'gone forward', but perhaps also with the academic resonance of 'graduated'.

17 **amplify my judgment** enlarge my knowledge. The phrase perhaps suggests the title of Francis Bacon's recently published treatise *The Advancement of Learning* (1605; *De Augmentis Scientiarum* in the Latin version); especially since the subsequent term 'conclusions' (18) means 'experiments' and suggests a Baconian model of scientific inquiry conducted as controlled investigation into the material causes of things. The Queen's activities may be fairytale magic, but they are linked to emergent currents of rationalism. Innogen takes a similarly Baconian view in 'Experience, O, thou disprov'st report!' (4.2.34); and see Hill, 28–9.

22 **Allayments** Diluting agents. *Riverside* glosses 'antidotes', though the yoking of 'vigour' (21) and 'allayments' suggests that the Queen is experimenting with different levels of strength

in her drugs. Compare *Tro.* 4.4.6–8: 'If I could temporize with my affection, / Or brew it to a weak and colder palate, / The like allayment I would give myself.' These are the only two usages of the word recorded by *OED*.

22 **them** presumably, the 'conclusions' (18). The syntax of this sentence is very loose, with both 'try' and 'them' awkwardly repeated.

23 **several virtues** individual properties.

26 **infectious** (1) unhealthy; (2) morally corrupting (*OED* infectious *a* 4).

28 A word seems to be lost from this line in F (see collation). I have followed the usual emendation: an inattentive compositor could easily have set up *for* in place of *factor for*. In a parallel construction at 76, the Queen calls Pisanio 'agent for his master'; see also 1.6.187. Taylor compares *Ant.* 2.6.8–10: 'To you all three, / The senators alone of this great world, / Chief factors for the gods.'

But you shall do no harm.
QUEEN [*to Pisanio, drawing him aside*] Hark thee, a word.
CORNELIUS I do not like her. She doth think she has
    Strange ling'ring poisons. I do know her spirit,
    And will not trust one of her malice with   35
    A drug of such damned nature. Those she has
    Will stupefy and dull the sense a while,
    Which first, perchance, she'll prove on cats and dogs,
    Then afterward up higher; but there is
    No danger in what show of death it makes,   40
    More than the locking up the spirits a time,
    To be more fresh, reviving. She is fooled
    With a most false effect, and I the truer
    So to be false with her.
QUEEN   No further service, doctor,
    Until I send for thee.
CORNELIUS   I humbly take my leave.   *Exit* 45
QUEEN Weeps she still, sayst thou? Dost thou think in time
    She will not quench, and let instructions enter
    Where folly now possesses? Do thou work.
    When thou shalt bring me word she loves my son,
    I'll tell thee on the instant thou art then   50
    As great as is thy master – greater, for
    His fortunes all lie speechless, and his name
    Is at last gasp. Return he cannot, nor
    Continue where he is. To shift his being,
    Is to exchange one misery with another,   55

---

32 SD] *Capell; not in* F   46 *Rowe;* Weepes . . . thou?) / Dost . . . time F

31–44 Cornelius's small debate about how to square his obedience to the Queen with his personal integrity rehearses the ground for the Queen's testing of Pisanio, and Pisanio's later dilemmas over obedience to Posthumus and Cloten (3.5.149–51, 4.3.42).
  36 **damned** damnable.
  38 **prove** test.
  39 **up higher** i.e., on higher creatures.
  40 **show** appearance.
  42 **reviving** on reviving.
  43–4 **I . . . her** A favourite Shakespearean paradox: Maxwell compares *LLL* 4.3.359–60 ('Let

us once lose our oaths to find ourselves, / Or else we lose ourselves to keep our oaths') and *John* 3.1.63–87.
  43 **false** deceptive.
  43 **truer** more honest.
  46–75 The Queen pressures Pisanio by harping on the word *thou*, which makes her promises seem at once solicitous and coercive.
  47 **quench** cool down (*OED* quench *v* 6c: the only instance of this meaning used of a person).
  52–3 **His . . . gasp** The image is a deathbed, on which Posthumus's fortunes and name are expiring.
  54 **shift his being** change his place of abode.

And every day that comes comes to decay
A day's work in him. What shalt thou expect
To be depender on a thing that leans,
Who cannot be new-built, nor has no friends
So much as but to prop him?
[*She drops the box. Pisanio takes it up*]
                  Thou tak'st up   60
Thou know'st not what; but take it for thy labour.
It is a thing I made, which hath the King
Five times redeemed from death. I do not know
What is more cordial. Nay, I prithee take it;
It is an earnest of a farther good   65
That I mean to thee. Tell thy mistress how
The case stands with her; do't as from thy self.
Think what a chance thou changest on, but think
Thou hast thy mistress still; to boot, my son,
Who shall take notice of thee. I'll move the King   70
To any shape of thy preferment, such
As thou'lt desire; and then myself, I chiefly,
That set thee on to this desert, am bound
To load thy merit richly. Call my women.
Think on my words.
                      Exit PISANIO

---

57 work] F; worth *conj. Wilson* 60 SD] *Malone (subst.); not in* F 68 chance thou changest] F; chance thou chancest *Rowe;* change thou chancest *Theobald;* chance thou hangest *(conj. Daniel)* 75 SD] F *(after 74)*

56–7 every . . . him probably, every day that Posthumus now lives destroys what an earlier day had achieved. Two grammatical constructions seem to be overlaid here, involving alternative meanings of 'decay'. In one, *decay* is a transitive verb ('each day comes [in order] to make Posthumus's fortunes deteriorate'); in the other, it is a noun governed by *a day's work:* 'each day, yet one more day's work comes to ruin'.

58 depender dependant; hanger-on.

58 a thing that leans Posthumus is imaged as a rickety building on the point of collapse (a metaphor that develops from the underlying spatial meaning in referring to Pisanio as a 'depender' on Posthumus).

60 So much . . . to Who can even.

64 cordial restorative.

65 earnest token.

68 chance fortuitous opportunity. This line is often emended (see collation), but it makes sense as it stands: 'Think with what a fair prospect of mending your fortunes you now change your present service' (Steevens). For *chance*, compare Posthumus's unexpected 'golden chance' at 5.3.196. Shakespeare often associates *chance* and *change*, e.g., *2H4* 3.1.50–2: 'how chance's mocks / And changes fill up the cup of alteration / With divers liquors!'

69 Thou . . . still i.e., because in serving Cloten, Pisanio will ultimately be serving her.

71 To . . . preferment To preferment of any kind.

73 set . . . desert started you on the path to this reward (Warren).

A sly and constant knave,   75
Not to be shaked; the agent for his master,
And the remembrancer of her to hold
The handfast to her lord. I have given him that
Which, if he take, shall quite unpeople her
Of liegers for her sweet; and which she after,   80
Except she bend her humour, shall be assured
To taste of too.

Enter PISANIO, *and* LADIES

So, so; well done, well done.
The violets, cowslips, and the primroses
Bear to my closet. Fare thee well, Pisanio.
Think on my words, Pisanio.

Exeunt Queen and Ladies

PISANIO   And shall do.   85
But when to my good lord I prove untrue,
I'll choke myself – there's all I'll do for you.   *Exit*

---

78 handfast] F (hand-fast)   85 Think on my words, Pisanio.] *Taylor (after Dowden);* Thinke on my words. F   85 SD
Exeunt] F *(Exit); between lines 85 and 86 in Taylor*

75–8 For all her pretended encouragement, the
Queen perceives that her words have no effect on
Pisanio. Indeed, he is silent through the whole
speech, which, on stage, makes his reluctance to
be drawn all the more evident.

77 **remembrancer of her** person who reminds
her. The term alludes to the administration of city
corporations or royal households: a *remembrancer*
was an official appointed to oversee certain affairs,
especially the collection of debts.

77–8 **hold . . . handfast** maintain the trothplight. By calling Pisanio Innogen's 'remembrancer', the Queen seems to imply that he had
acted as the witness at her betrothal or marriage
with Posthumus (see Lawrence, 251n).

79 **unpeople her** lay her bare (of servants), as in
Ant. 1.5.78.

80 **liegers** literally, resident ambassadors: repre-
sentatives for her husband at court.

81 **bend her humour** change her attitude.

84 **closet** private chamber.

85 This line is several syllables short in F,
and I follow Dowden's conjecture that the Queen
repeated 'Pisanio' as she left the stage. A compositor could easily have skipped the name, given that
a speech-heading for Pisanio immediately follows.
It would be in keeping with the Queen's style of
address to him, which has been deliberately ingra-
tiating throughout the scene (see note to 46–75
above).

85 SD So placed in F. Some editors move the
exit to the end of the line, so that Pisanio's first
three words are spoken directly to the Queen, but
an early exit is supported by his stubborn silence
towards her. However, the placing of the exit is
only a matter of compositorial preference, since in
the copy it would have been written in the margin
and the compositor would have inserted it where
he saw fit.

1.6 *Enter* INNOGEN

INNOGEN A father cruel and a stepdame false,
    A foolish suitor to a wedded lady
    That hath her husband banished – oh, that husband,
    My supreme crown of grief, and those repeated
    Vexations of it! Had I been thief-stol'n,   5
    As my two brothers, happy; but most miserable
    Is the desire that's glorious. Blest be those,
    How mean soe'er, that have their honest wills,
    Which seasons comfort.

Enter PISANIO *and* IACHIMO

                Who may this be? Fie!

PISANIO Madam, a noble gentleman of Rome   10
    Comes from my lord with letters.

IACHIMO   Change you, madam.
    The worthy Leonatus is in safety,
    And greets your highness dearly.
              [He gives her the letters]

Act 1, Scene 6   1.6 *Scena Septima.* F   0 SD *Enter* INNOGEN] F *(Enter Imogen alone)*   7 desire] F2; desires F   9 SD] *Sisson;*
after l.9 in F   13 SD] *Johnson (subst.); not in* F

Act 1, Scene 6

0 SD The setting is a private room in Innogen's personal apartments, though the space is less
intimate than the bedchamber of 2.2: Innogen is
attended here by a male servant, Pisanio, whereas
the bedchamber is wholly feminized. Pisanio's
presence in this scene gives him a significant early
involvement in Innogen's affairs and helps to bind
Iachimo's attack on Innogen to the Queen's attack on
Posthumus (1.5).

1–9 Innogen's speech is compressed and elliptical, and editors have frequently tinkered with it:
this is, indeed, another passage set by the unreliable
Compositor E. However, disconnectedness may be
part of the point, as Innogen reviews her circumstances in rapid, exclamatory fashion.

4 **repeated** related: referring to her enumera-
tion of Cymbeline, the Queen and Cloten (1–2) as
the 'Vexations' or irritants to her grief over Posthumus. Alternatively, it could be their vexing of her,
by their continual enmity, that is 'repeated'.

6 **happy** i.e., then had I been happy.

6–7 **most . . . glorious** probably, 'ungratified

longings are most painful when experienced by
great persons (like myself)'. Innogen's sentiment
resembles her remarks at 1.1.148–50 and 3.6.80–5:
the great are often unsatisfied despite their glory,
whereas you can be poor and happy. F's 'desires'
for 'desire' is a typical Compositor E error, a slip
repeated at 27.

8 **How . . . soe'er** However humble they be.

8 **wills** desires.

9 **seasons** gives relish to. It is unclear where
lies the antecedent for 'Which': probably Innogen
means the general satisfaction that the humble get
when they achieve their desires, despite their lack
of wealth.

11 **Change you, madam** I take Iachimo's greeting to be a reassurance to Innogen that he brings
good news, and that she can put melancholy or vex-
ation out of her looks. Some editors print 'Change
you, madam?' as if it were a rhetorical question
responding to Innogen blushing with excitement
or anxiety. But would Iachimo introduce himself
so familiarly? And how would he know what was
her natural colour?

INNOGEN   Thanks, good sir,
    You're kindly welcome.
IACHIMO [*Aside*] All of her that is out of door most rich!   15
    If she be furnished with a mind so rare
    She is alone th'Arabian bird, and I
    Have lost the wager. Boldness be my friend;
    Arm me, audacity, from head to foot,
    Or like the Parthian I shall flying fight –   20
    Rather, directly fly.
INNOGEN (*Reads*) 'He is one of the noblest note, to whose kindnesses
    I am most infinitely tied. Reflect upon him accordingly,
    as you value
                Your truest Leonatus.'   25
    So far I read aloud;
    But even the very middle of my heart
    Is warmed by th'rest, and takes it thankfully.
    You are as welcome, worthy sir, as I
    Have words to bid you, and shall find it so   30
    In all that I can do.

---

15 *Aside*] Pope; not in F . 22 SD] F *(centred)* 24–25 value / Your] *undivided prose in* F 25 truest] *Hanmer; trust.* F 28 takes] *Pope; take* F

15 **out of door** visible, exterior. Compare 1.1.23.
16 **a mind so rare** inner quality as exceptional (as is her outward appearance).
17 **She is alone** She above all is (Abbott, #18). Compare *AYLI* 2.7.136: 'Thou seest, we are not all alone unhappy'; *TN* 1.1.15: 'So full of shapes is fancy / That it alone is high fantastical'; and *Ant.* 4.6.30: 'I am alone the villain of the earth.'
17 **th'Arabian bird** the phoenix: a symbol of matchless perfection, since only one existed at any one time. The phoenix was also symbolically linked to virginity, since it reproduced itself asexually, immolating itself and being reborn from its own ashes. It often appeared in Elizabeth I's iconography: Shakespeare calls her 'the maiden phoenix' in *H8* 5.4.40. All his other references to the phoenix apply it only to men.
19 **Arm me, audacity** May audacity arm me.
20 **the Parthian** The Parthians (inhabitants of an ancient kingdom in present-day Iraq) were renowned for their mounted archers, whose battle manoeuvre was to shoot arrows backwards while rapidly retreating. Compare *Ant.* 3.1.1: 'darting Parthia'.
21 **directly fly** fly away at once.
22 **note** reputation.
23 **Reflect** Bestow attention (*OED* reflect *v* 11b). Compare 1.2.00–0.
24–5 **as you . . . Leonatus** F's 'as you value your trust' gives adequate sense but seems inappropriately admonitory. I have preferred Hanmer's attractive emendation, which interprets the message as ending with a precious epistolary flourish. Posthumus's signing-off makes the encounter a test of his and Iachimo's relative worth, and puts Innogen in a double bind: it enjoins her to welcome Iachimo, but does not make it apparent that by welcoming him too much she will demonstrate how little she esteems her husband.
26 **So far** So much. '*So far* need not imply that what Innogen suppresses . . . follows what she has read aloud' (Warren).

IACHIMO   Thanks, fairest lady.
          What, are men mad? Hath nature given them eyes
          To see this vaulted arch and the rich crop
          Of sea and land, which can distinguish 'twixt
          The fiery orbs above and the twinned stones   35
          Upon th'unnumbered beach, and can we not
          Partition make with spectacles so precious
          'Twixt fair and foul?
INNOGEN   What makes your admiration?
IACHIMO It cannot be i'th'eye – for apes and monkeys
          'Twixt two such shes would chatter this way, and   40

---

36 th'unnumbered] *Theobald;* the number'd F

32–50 Iachimo exploits the conventions of address on the Jacobean stage by speaking in front of Innogen almost as if he were in soliloquy, an effect which is doubly disconcerting since his preceding speech was an 'authentic' aside. His plan is to unsettle Innogen by insinuating that Posthumus has been unfaithful to her, and to bewilder her by pretending a shock and moral revulsion at Posthumus's behaviour which, for reasons of tact, he can only obliquely express. To this end he adopts a deliberately riddling language and syntax quite unlike his normal conversational manner as established two scenes earlier (see Freer, p. 103). Most spectators eventually perceive that his broad objective is to entrap Innogen in a false tale, but his speeches are so dense and elliptical that they present the audience with a version of her dilemma, over how to disentangle and interpret his real meaning. See the discussion in the Introduction, p. 21.
33 **vaulted arch** i.e., the sky, which arches over the earth. Compare 'the azur'd vault', *Temp.* 5.1.43.
33 **crop** harvest: probably in the metaphorical sense of the 'harvest which the eye gathers in, consisting of sea and land' (Vaughan), rather than the material and agricultural sense. Iachimo images the sky as an arch framing the lower elements in a great picture.
35 **fiery orbs** stars.
35 **twinned** identical.
36 **unnumbered** numberless; referring to the infinity of stones between which the eye can distinguish even though they all look so similar. Theobald's emendation (of another Compositor E error) is strongly supported by *Lear* 4.6.20–1: 'the murmuring surge, / That on the unnumbered idle pebbles chafes'. Editors who retain F's *numbered* have to interpret it as 'numerous, abounding in numbers of stones', but this contradicts Iachimo's

paradox, in which the stones are countless yet still distinct. Abbott (#375) notes that Shakespeare often used the passive participle *-ed* as if it were *-able*: hence in *R3* 1.4.27 'inestimable stones, *unvalued* [= invaluable] jewels'; and in *MV* 3.4.52 'With all *imagined* [= imaginable] haste'.
37 **Partition** Distinction.
37 **spectacles so precious** such keenly sensitive organs of sight.
38 **fair and foul** i.e., objects with totally opposed qualities. A favourite Shakespearean doublet (as in *Mac.* 1.1.11), but here looking ahead to the *two such shes* (40) that Iachimo is about to invent.
38 **admiration** amazement. This is an implied stage direction for the actor playing Iachimo. Compare *Lear* 1.4.237: 'This admiration, sir, is much o'th'savour / Of other your new pranks'; and *WT* 5.2.9: 'I make a broken delivery of the business; but the changes I perceived in the King and Camillo were very notes of admiration.'
39–46 A series of parallels between the response of the eye, the judgement and the appetite to 'two such shes' (40) = two women, one fair and one foul. Iachimo implies that Posthumus has acquired an Italian mistress, and feigns astonishment at his poor choice: in any other comparison between Innogen and another woman, monkeys, idiots and even the appetite itself would testify to her superiority. The speech's difficulty arises from its excessively compressed syntax, here at its most elliptical, and close in manner to Leontes's speeches of almost incoherent jealousy (*WT* 1.2.108–207).
39 **th'eye** Since vision was the sense which carried exterior impressions into the mind, it was regarded as the most vulnerable to being seduced by appearances.
40 **chatter this way** indicate their preference for the *she* who looks like Innogen.

Contemn with mows the other; nor i'th'judgment –
For idiots in this case of favour would
Be wisely definite; nor i'th'appetite –
Sluttery, to such neat excellence opposed,
Should make desire vomit emptiness,   45
Not so allured to feed.

INNOGEN What is the matter, trow?

IACHIMO   The cloyèd will –
That satiate yet unsatisfied desire, that tub
Both filled and running – ravening first the lamb,
Longs after for the garbage.

INNOGEN   What, dear sir,   50
Thus raps you? Are you well?

IACHIMO   Thanks, madam, well.
[*To Pisanio*] Beseech you sir,
Desire my man's abode where I did leave him:
He's strange and peevish.

51–2 Thanks . . . sir,] *Cambridge; one line in* F   52 SD] *Rowe; not in* F

41 **mows** grimaces
42 **case of favour** question about beauty. 'Case' is used in a judicial sense, as a question being propounded for solution by a court or casuist.
42–3 **would . . . definite** would decide wisely (despite their intellectual weakness).
43 **appetite** hunger; sexual desire.
43–6 **nor . . . feed** The general sense is: even sexual desire ('appetite'), when comparing the sluttish Italian mistress with Innogen's beauty, would throw up all it has – which is nothing – in disgust, rather than satisfy itself by 'feeding' (= possessing the available woman sexually). Desire 'vomit[s] emptiness' because, being the condition of lack, its emptiness is all it has; there is a verbal link to *Luc.* 703–4 ('Drunken Desire must vomit his receipt / Ere he can see his own abomination'). This language of sexual disgust seems at the opposite pole to Posthumus's idealism, but is its inevitable counterpart and is adopted by Posthumus himself in 2.5. Iachimo similarly dwells on the physical details of Posthumus's 'disloyalty' at 99–112 below.
44 **neat** elegant.
46 **so** thus, this way.
47 **What . . . will** Like other editors, I print this exchange as two halves of a single line, though it is notable that Iachimo's three words complete the hanging half-line that ends his previous speech. In effect, 40–51 are one continuous speech, to which Innogen's words are an interjection seemingly unheard by him.

47 **cloyèd will** lust overfed to the point of surfeit, yet still desiring further physical satisfaction. Warren compares *Ant.* 2.2.242–4: 'Other women cloy / The appetites they feed, but she makes hungry / Where most she satisfies'. The paradoxes of lustful desire, unsatisfied even when sated, are most famously explored in *Son.* 129.
48 **satiate** glutted.
48 **tub** A passing allusion to the Danaides, the fifty daughters of Danaus who, having murdered their husbands, were condemned in Hades to fill a constantly leaking tub with water (Ovid, *Metamorphoses*, IV, 574). Renaissance commentators moralized this as an emblem of insatiable appetite: like their tub, lust constantly wastes that with which it is replenished.
49 **running** emptying.
49 **ravening** devouring voraciously.
50 **garbage** offal; as opposed to the lamb, a symbol of purity. Innogen thinks of herself as the lamb at 3.4.95.
50–7 **What . . . madam** In F this passage has several half-lines, and is very hard to order satisfactorily. My arrangement marks off Pisanio's contribution with short lines at 52 and 55, and leaves 57 very short, to register Iachimo's deliberately cryptic response to Innogen's question and the ensuing pause.
51 **raps** transports. Another implied stage direction, similar to *Mac.* 1.3.142.
53 **Desire . . . abode** Ask my man to wait.
54 **strange** a foreigner (and so easily fretted).

PISANIO   I was going, sir,
          To give him welcome.   *Exit*   55
INNOGEN Continues well my lord? His health, beseech you?
IACHIMO Well, madam.
INNOGEN Is he disposed to mirth? I hope he is.
IACHIMO Exceeding pleasant; none a stranger there
          So merry and so gamesome. He is called   60
          The Briton reveller.
INNOGEN   When he was here
          He did incline to sadness, and oft-times
          Not knowing why.
IACHIMO   I never saw him sad.
          There is a Frenchman his companion, one
          An eminent monsieur, that it seems much loves   65
          A Gallian girl at home. He furnaces
          The thick sighs from him, whiles the jolly Briton –
          Your lord, I mean – laughs from's free lungs, cries 'Oh,
          Can my sides hold, to think that man who knows
          By history, report, or his own proof   70
          What woman is, yea, what she cannot choose
          But must be, will's free hours languish for
          Assurèd bondage?'
INNOGEN   Will my lord say so?
IACHIMO Ay, madam, with his eyes in flood with laughter.
          It is a recreation to be by   75
          And hear him mock the Frenchman: but heavens know
          Some men are much to blame.
INNOGEN   Not he I hope.

---

56 *Rowe;* Continues . . . Lord? / His . . . you? F 61 Briton] F *(Britaine)* 72–3 *Steevens-Reed 2;* But . . . languish / For .
. . bondage? F 76–7 *Pope;* And . . . Frenchman: / But . . . blame. F

59 **none a stranger** no other foreigner (adjective used adverbially for emphasis: see Abbott,
#53, 85). Compare 1.4.77: 'none so accomplished
a courtier'.
60 **gamesome** merry.
62 **sadness** seriousness. The phrasing harks
back to the inexplicable melancholy afflicting Antonio in *MV.* 1.1.1 ('In sooth, I know not why I am so
sad'), but the implied meaning seems to be more
ethical, as 'sobriety' or 'gravity'. In Peter Hall's
1988 production, Posthumus was set apart from the
other gentlemen by his rich but sombre clothing, a
Puritan ill at ease with the worldly-wise Cavaliers.

66 **Gallian** French.
66 **furnaces** (compare *AYLI* 2.7.147–8: 'the
lover, / Sighing like furnace').
67 **thick** frequent; following thick upon one
another.
68 **free** unrestrained, open.
70 **proof** experience.
72 **will's . . . languish** waste his time in pining.
72 **hours** (pronounced as a disyllable).
73 **Assurèd** Certain: and glancing at the cognate meaning 'betrothed', to which Innogen would
be especially sensitized (Nosworthy).

IACHIMO Not he; but yet heaven's bounty towards him might
　　　　　Be used more thankfully. In himself 'tis much;
　　　　　In you, which I account his, beyond all talents.　　　　　　　80
　　　　　Whilst I am bound to wonder, I am bound
　　　　　To pity too.
INNOGEN　　　　　　　What do you pity, sir?
IACHIMO Two creatures heartily.
INNOGEN　　　　　　　　　　　　Am I one, sir?
　　　　　You look on me; what wreck discern you in me
　　　　　Deserves your pity?
IACHIMO　　　　　　　　　　Lamentable! What,　　　　　　　85
　　　　　To hide me from the radiant sun, and solace
　　　　　I'th'dungeon by a snuff?
INNOGEN　　　　　　　　　　　I pray you, sir,
　　　　　Deliver with more openness your answers
　　　　　To my demands. Why do you pity me?
IACHIMO That others do –　　　　　　　　　　　　　　　　　90
　　　　　I was about to say, enjoy your – but
　　　　　It is an office of the gods to venge it,
　　　　　Not mine to speak on't.
INNOGEN　　　　　　　　　You do seem to know
　　　　　Something of me, or what concerns me. Pray you,
　　　　　Since doubting things go ill often hurts more　　　　　95
　　　　　Than to be sure they do – for certainties
　　　　　Either are past remedies, or, timely knowing,

---

78 *Rowe;* Not he: / But . . . might F 96, 98 do – . . . born –] *Dowden;* do . . . borne. F

79–80 **In . . . talents** 'Heaven's bounty has been great in the personal endowments it has given Posthumus; in what it has given him indirectly by giving him you, its bounty is incalculable.' *Talents* here seems to mean both 'riches' and 'natural endowments'. In conjunction with *account*, it activates a submerged allusion to the parable of the talents (Matthew 25.14–29), which lays out the expectation that individual souls will be judged according to the way they have used whatever gifts they have been given. Such concerns are on Posthumus's mind in prison, 5.3.109–22. Taylor accepts Pope's *count* for *account*, as an improvement to the metre, but this forfeits the possible wordplay.

83 **Two creatures** Presumably, Innogen and Posthumus.

84 **You look on me** An implied stage direction.

84 **wreck** state of ruin.

87 **snuff** burnt-out candle end (opposed to the 'sun' of Innogen's own presence).

92 **office** function.

92 **venge** avenge.

95 **doubting** fearing. Innogen's phrase resembles Othello's parallel avowal: 'I swear 'tis better to be much abused / Than but to know't a little' (*Oth.* 3.3.336).

97 **timely knowing** if one knows in time. The parenthesis opposes evil *certainties* for which nothing can be done (*past remedies*) to those for which, if caught in time, some solution may be *born*. Although bad, both are preferable to suspected ills, which leave one in a state of nagging uncertainty.

The remedy then born – discover to me
What both you spur and stop.

IACHIMO   Had I this cheek
To bathe my lips upon; this hand, whose touch,   100
Whose every touch, would force the feeler's soul
To th'oath of loyalty; this object which
Takes prisoner the wild motion of mine eye,
Fixing it only here: should I, damned then,
Slaver with lips as common as the stairs   105
That mount the Capitol; join grips with hands
Made hard with hourly falsehood – falsehood as
With labour; then by-peeping in an eye
Base and illustrous as the smoky light
That's fed with stinking tallow – it were fit   110
That all the plagues of hell should at one time
Encounter such revolt.

INNOGEN   My lord, I fear,
Has forgot Britain.

---

104 Fixing] F2; Fiering F   108 by-peeping] *Knight;* bypeeping F   109 illustrous] *Collier 1;* illustrious F

99 **What . . . stop** What you seem at once to urge forward and to rein in. An image from horsemanship.

99–112 Had I . . . revolt Iachimo imagines himself in Posthumus's position, protesting that if he had Innogen's cheek, hand and person to love, he would not want the lips, hand or eye of any other person; but this betrayal (he implies) Posthumus has committed, and with a Roman prostitute.

101–2 **force . . . loyalty** compel the person who is touching to be loyal (Warren). An Oath of Allegiance was in fact issued on 2 June 1610, as part of the scare that followed the assassination of Henri IV of France. See the discussion of the play's date in the Introduction, p. 6.

102 **this object** (probably) Innogen herself; though Iachimo perhaps means her eye, given the contrast he makes with the 'illustrous' eye of the Roman mistress (108–9).

103 **wild motion** unconfined action.

104 **Fixing** Some editors retain F's reading *Fiering* (firing = setting it afire), but F2's emendation of an x/r misreading by Compositor E makes good sense after *wild motion*.

104 **damned then** damned by doing so.

105 **Slaver** Slobber.

105 **common** open to all, prostituted: alluding to the proverb 'as common as the highway' (Tilley,

H457). The lips belong to the imagined Italian mistress, not to the speaker.

105–6 **stairs . . . Capitol** the public way to the Temple of Jupiter in Rome.

106 **join grips** clasp.

106–8 **hands . . . labour** i.e., her hands have been hardened by false embraces with different men every hour, and as much by the falseness as by the labour of doing it.

108 **by-peeping** peeping sidelong, gazing covertly (?). This compound verb is not otherwise known. Although the emendation gives reasonable sense, it is by no means clear that it corresponds to the original meaning of this corrupt passage, as the construction seems to require a verb inflected in parallel to 'Slaver' (105) and 'join grips' (106). The comparison with 103–5 suggests that Iachimo intends a contrast between his response to Innogen's eye and to the prostitute's: his vision is 'fixed' (104) on Innogen, but only 'peeps' pruriently at the prostitute.

109 **illustrous** lacking lustre, radiating no light. This is *OED*'s only example of the word, but F's *illustrious* gives quite the wrong sense and is probably a minim misreading by the compositor.

110 **tallow** i.e., from a tallow candle (harking back to the image at 87).

112 **Encounter** Attack; punish.

112 **revolt** apostacy.

IACHIMO   And himself. Not I
    Inclined to this intelligence pronounce
    The beggary of his change, but 'tis your graces   115
    That from my mutest conscience to my tongue
    Charms this report out.
INNOGEN   Let me hear no more.
IACHIMO O dearest soul, your cause doth strike my heart
    With pity that doth make me sick! A lady
    So fair, and fastened to an empery   120
    Would make the great'st king double, to be partnered
    With tomboys hired with that self exhibition
    Which your own coffers yield; with diseased ventures
    That play with all infirmities for gold
    Which rottenness can lend nature; such boiled stuff   125
    As well might poison poison! Be revenged,
    Or she that bore you was no queen, and you
    Recoil from your great stock.
INNOGEN   Revenged?
    How should I be revenged? If this be true –

113–14 **Not I . . . pronounce** It is not through any inclination to tell this news that I report.

115 **beggary** vileness.

116 **mutest** most silent and secretive. The silent 'conscience' is contrasted with the noisy tongue that reports Posthumus's betrayal: Innogen's 'graces' (115) have 'charm[ed]' (117) Iachimo into revealing what he would otherwise have kept secret.

118 **Charms** The verb is governed by *graces* (115), but takes a singular form through proximity to *tongue*.

120 **an empery** an empire; Britain, a territory so great as to *double* (121) the power of the greatest king. Maxwell finds this comment hyperbolical and inappropriately patriotic for the heat of the moment. But the debate over the Jacobean union had made such language automatic: James I, though a single individual, was indeed a *double* king (as ruler of England and Scotland), whose territories were an 'empery'. The remark also reinforces the association between Innogen and the British state: like Cloten, Iachimo's attempted seduction hurts the nation.

121 **partnered** equated. *OED*'s earliest example of 'partner' as a verb.

122 **tomboys** strumpets. Compare L. Tomson, transl., *Calvin's Sermons on the Epistles to Timothy*

and Titus (1579), 203: 'St Paul meaneth that women must not be impudent, they must not be tomboys, to be short, they must not be unchaste.'

122 **self exhibition** self-same allowance: Posthumus pays his prostitutes with Innogen's money.

123 **ventures** risk-takers, gamblers. In a commercial context a *venture* is a speculative enterprise in which money is staked: here the word applies to the persons who run the risk. 'Venturer' is used to mean 'prostitute' in Dekker and Webster's *Westward Ho*, 1605: 'Had thy Circean magic me transformed . . . [and] I were turned common venturer, I could not love this old man' (Dekker, II, 341).

124 **play** gamble: the prostitutes wager their health against the gold they hope to win. Compare the gambling phrase 'play against all comers'.

124 **infirmities** diseases.

125 **Which** i.e., the 'infirmities' (124), not 'gold' (as it first seems).

125 **boiled stuff** women who have undergone the sweating treatment used to cure venereal disease. In her retort to Iachimo, Innogen unflinchingly picks up this pun with 'Romish stew' (152).

126 **As . . . poison** i.e., They are so diseased that even poison would be poisoned by them.

128 **Recoil** Degenerate (*OED* recoil *sb* 3b).

128 **stock** ancestry.

As I have such a heart that both mine ears   130
Must not in haste abuse – if it be true,
How should I be revenged?

IACHIMO   Should he make me
Live like Diana's priest betwixt cold sheets
Whiles he is vaulting variable ramps
In your despite, upon your purse – revenge it.   135
I dedicate myself to your sweet pleasure,
More noble than that runagate to your bed,
And will continue fast to your affection,
Still close as sure.

INNOGEN   What ho, Pisanio!

IACHIMO Let me my service tender on your lips.   140

INNOGEN Away, I do condemn mine ears that have
So long attended thee. If thou wert honourable
Thou wouldst have told this tale for virtue, not
For such an end thou seek'st, as base as strange.
Thou wrong'st a gentleman who is as far   145
From thy report as thou from honour, and
Solicits here a lady that disdains
Thee and the devil alike. What ho, Pisanio!
The King my father shall be made acquainted
Of thy assault. If he shall think it fit   150
A saucy stranger in his court to mart
As in a Romish stew, and to expound

---

133 Live] F; Lie *Walker*   147 Solicits] F; Solicit'st F2 *(subst.)*

---

130 **As** Inasmuch as. Innogen means that she
must not let her ears mislead her heart.

132 **Should . . . me** Not literally true, but advice
to Innogen: 'If I were in your shoes.'

133 **Live** It is tempting to adopt Walker's conjecture *Lie*, though it creates an awkward assonance
with *like* immediately after.

133 **Diana** Goddess of chastity, whose priests
were all virgins.

134 **vaulting** leaping (in a sexual sense).

134 **variable ramps** a range of trollops. For
ramps, compare *Bartholomew Fair* (1614): 'Yonder
is your punk of Turnbull, ramping Alice' (*Ben
Jonson*, VI, 105).

135 **In . . . purse** In scorn of you, and with your
own money.

137 **runagate** renegade.

138 **fast** constant.

139 **close** secret.

140 **tender** present.

142 **attended** listened to.

142 **thee** Innogen switches from the polite *you*
to a more distant form of address (and adopts the
regal *us* at 154).

147 **Solicits** i.e., solicit'st. The verb's ending is
compressed for the sake of euphony (compare *refts*
at 3.3.103).

151 **saucy** impudent.

151 **to mart** should do his business.

152 **stew** brothel: compare 'boiled stuff' (125).
The literal sense is clear, though Innogen's adjective 'Romish' for 'Roman' is contemporary rather
than first-century usage and gives the phrase a
political colouring. A Jacobean audience would
almost certainly have associated 'Romish stew' with
anti-Catholic polemic, in which the Pope was often
called the Whore of Babylon, and the Roman
Catholic Church colourfully depicted as morally
corrupt. It was also claimed that the Roman broth-
els paid rent to the Pope: see Donne, 119.

His beastly mind to us, he hath a court
He little cares for, and a daughter who
He not respects at all. What ho, Pisanio!   155
IACHIMO O happy Leonatus! I may say;
The credit that thy lady hath of thee
Deserves thy trust, and thy most perfect goodness
Her assured credit. Blessed live you long,
A lady to the worthiest sir that ever   160
Country called his; and you his mistress, only
For the most worthiest fit. Give me your pardon.
I have spoke this to know if your affiance
Were deeply rooted, and shall make your lord
That which he is new o'er; and he is one   165
The truest mannered, such a holy witch
That he enchants societies into him;
Half all men's hearts are his.
INNOGEN   You make amends.
IACHIMO He sits 'mongst men like a descended god;
He hath a kind of honour sets him off   170
More than a mortal seeming. Be not angry,
Most mighty princess, that I have adventured
To try your taking of a false report, which hath
Honoured with confirmation your great judgment
In the election of a sir so rare,   175
Which you know cannot err. The love I bear him
Made me to fan you thus, but the gods made you,

---

156 Leonatus!] *Leonatus* F 168 men's] F2 *(subst.);* men F 168 descended] F2; defended F

157–9 **The credit . . . credit** The confidence that Innogen has in you deserves your trust, and your perfect goodness justifies her confident belief in you.
161 **called his** called its own.
163 **affiance** marriage promise; trothplight.
164 **shall** i.e., it shall.
165 **new o'er** all over again.
165 **one** above all others (an emphatic use: see Abbott, #18).
166 **truest mannered** most honestly disposed.
166 **witch** wizard: at this time 'witch' was used indifferently for male and female sorcerers. Posthumus's witchcraft is 'holy' because it is 'white' magic, used to good ends.
167 **societies** crowds of people.
167 **into** unto.

168 **Half . . . his** Every man has given him half his affection.
169 **a descended god** a comparison that anticipates the spectacular events of Act 5.
170 **sets him off** distinguishes him.
171 **More . . . seeming** Giving him a more than mortal presence.
173 **try** test.
176 **Which** i.e., Innogen's 'judgment' (174). Nosworthy and Maxwell think 'Which' refers back to 'sir' (175) and so is hyperbolical praise of Posthumus. This is possible, but it would be more idiomatic to speak of an 'unerring judgment' than an unerring individual.
177 **fan** winnow, separate chaff from grain by blowing on it: (figuratively) test.

Unlike all others, chaffless. Pray, your pardon.

INNOGEN All's well, sir. Take my power i'th'court for yours.

IACHIMO My humble thanks. I had almost forgot   180
    T'entreat your grace but in a small request,
    And yet of moment too, for it concerns
    Your lord. Myself and other noble friends
    Are partners in the business.

INNOGEN   Pray, what is't?

IACHIMO Some dozen Romans of us and your lord –   185
    Best feather of our wing – have mingled sums
    To buy a present for the Emperor,
    Which I, the factor for the rest, have done
    In France. 'Tis plate of rare device, and jewels
    Of rich and exquisite form; their value's great,   190
    And I am something curious, being strange,
    To have them in safe stowage. May it please you
    To take them in protection?

INNOGEN   Willingly,
    And pawn mine honour for their safety, since
    My lord hath interest in them. I will keep them   195
    In my bedchamber.

IACHIMO   They are in a trunk,
    Attended by my men. I will make bold
    To send them to you, only for this night.
    I must aboard tomorrow.

---

179 *Rowe;* All's . . . Sir: / Take . . . yours. F   182 concerns] *Rowe (D'Urfey);* concernes: F   183 lord.] *after Rowe;* Lord,
F   186 Best] *Pope;* The best F   190 value's] *Collier 2;* valewes F

178 **chaffless** without chaff, pure grain: a Shakespearean coinage.

181 **but** only.

182 **of moment** important.

186 **Best** This emendation greatly improves the metre. As Taylor notes, *The* is a word that could easily have been interpolated by scribe or compositor.

188 **factor** agent.

189 **plate** a dish or vessel made of precious metal.

189 **of rare device** ingeniously designed or engraved.

189 **jewels** jewellery. Iachimo's circumstantial explanation gives his plot a realistic grounding within the context of contemporary courtly manners, his gifts being tokens of the kind that passed regularly between European princes and their servants. For example, at Jacobean Whitehall every New Year's Day saw elaborate gift-giving ceremonies, in which James exchanged plate and money with his courtiers, symbolically reaffirming the social and political ties between them.

191 **something curious** somewhat anxious.

191 **strange** a stranger.

192 **safe stowage** This device seems far-fetched today, but in an age before banks, the protection of valuables was a recurrent problem. Compare Richard Brome's *A Jovial Crew* (1641), 1.1, in which the steward Springlove tries to persuade his master to take the estate valuables into his own closet, where they will be safer than in Springlove's.

194 **pawn . . . safety** with an irony obvious to the audience, since it is indeed her honour that is under threat.

INNOGEN   Oh no, no.

IACHIMO Yes, I beseech, or I shall short my word   200
    By length'ning my return. From Gallia
    I crossed the seas on purpose and on promise
    To see your grace.

INNOGEN   I thank you for your pains;
    But not away tomorrow!

IACHIMO   Oh, I must madam,
    Therefore I shall beseech you, if you please   205
    To greet your lord with writing, do't tonight.
    I have outstood my time, which is material
    To th'tender of our present.

INNOGEN   I will write.
    Send your trunk to me, it shall safe be kept,
    And truly yielded you. You're very welcome.   210

Exeunt

2.1 *Enter* CLOTEN *and the* two LORDS

CLOTEN Was there ever man had such luck? When I kissed the jack upon an upcast, to be hit away! I had a hundred pound on't; and then a whoreson jackanapes must take me up for swearing, as if I borrowed mine oaths of him, and might not spend them at my pleasure.   5

2.1 *Actus Secundus. Scena Prima.* F

200 **short my word** fall short of my promise.
202 **on promise** (to Posthumus).
207 **outstood** outstayed.
207 **material** crucial.
208 **tender** giving.
210 **yielded** returned.

Act 2, Scene 1
This scene develops the structural parallel between Cloten and Posthumus, whose likeness now extends to a shared taste for game-playing and wagering. Cloten's bowling-green bets reiterate Posthumus's gambling with Innogen's honour, and he, too, sees Iachimo as a personal adversary. Inevitably, his lack of luck augurs ill for Posthumus's future.

1 **jack** in bowls, the small ball which is the target at which the larger bowls are rolled. Cloten's bowl 'kissed' the jack (i.e., came to rest touching it) but was eventually knocked away, so he lost the game. Bowling was a favourite aristocratic pastime in early modern England, and Jacobean London was well stocked with bowling greens.

2 **upon an upcast** with my best throw: not necessarily the last throw, but the best in the game until it is beaten. 'Upcast' is cognate with 'upshot' in archery; compare T. Middleton, *The Family of Love*, 5.3.313, 'an arrow that sticks for the upshot against all comers'. OED's definition of *upcast* as a 'chance or accident' seems to be a misapprehension.

2 **had** had wagered.

2 **a hundred pound** The gambling debts incurred by Jacobean courtiers were often astronomical: for example, Sir Robert Cecil lost more than £800 in a single night in 1603, and a further £1,000 in 1605 (Stone, p. 570). Extravagant gambling was pursued by aristocrats as part of the public display of spending power, and it provoked anxious comment from contemporary moralists.

3 **jackanapes** impertinent fellow; literally, a tame monkey.

3 **take me up** rebuke me.

FIRST LORD What got he by that? You have broke his pate with your
bowl.

SECOND LORD [*Aside*] If his wit had been like his that broke it, it
would have run all out.

CLOTEN When a gentleman is disposed to swear, it is not for any   10
standers-by to curtail his oaths, ha?

SECOND LORD No, my lord – [*aside*] nor crop the ears of them.

CLOTEN Whoreson dog! I give him satisfaction? Would he had been
one of my rank!

SECOND LORD [*Aside*] To have smelled like a fool.   15

CLOTEN I am not vexed more at anything in th'earth. A pox on't,
I had rather not be so noble as I am! They dare not fight with
me because of the Queen my mother. Every jack-slave hath his
bellyfull of fighting, and I must go up and down like a cock that
nobody can match.   20

SECOND LORD [*Aside*] You are cock and capon too, and you crow , cock,
with your comb on.

CLOTEN Sayst thou?

SECOND LORD It is not fit your lordship should undertake every
companion that you give offence to.   25

6 SH FIRST LORD] *Rowe*; 1. F *(throughout scene)*   8 SH SECOND LORD] *Rowe*; 2. F *(throughout scene)*   8, 13, 32 SD]
Theobald; not in F   8 his] *Hanmer*; him F   13 give] F2; gaue F   21, 41 SD] *Pope; not in* F   21 SD] *Rowe; not in* F
21 crow,] *Theobald*; crow F   24 your] F3; you F

6 **pate** head.

8–9 **it . . . out** presumably, because it was weak
and watery. Maxwell retains F's reading 'him' for
'his' and argues that the Second Lord's aside is a
jibe at Cloten's cowardice. But though a braggart
and a bully, Cloten is not a coward, being only
too ready to prove himself physically: the joke is
against his stupidity, the thinness of his wit.

11 **curtail** (F: *curtall*) crop, as might be done
to the tail of an animal. This literal meaning
is exploited in the Second Lord's next scornful
aside.

13 **I . . . satisfaction** A rhetorical question:
Cloten has been challenged to a duel by the man
he struck, but he refuses to give him 'satisfaction'
because of the social disparity between them. This
snobbery continues in his discussion of Iachimo
(30–43), and perhaps subversively echoes Posthumus's pompous moral superiority in 1.4. In F
(where the text reads *gaue* for *give*) the meaning
is slightly different: Cloten congratulates himself
for striking the man who offended him.

14 **rank** (1) status; (2) smell, a latent meaning on
which the second lord plays in his retort. In *AYLI*

1.2.101–2 Rosalind mocks Le Beau's conversation
with the same poor pun.

18 **jack-slave** low-born fellow, as opposed to
Cloten's preeminent status. The escalation of private quarrels into full-scale duels was so common
a feature of aristocratic behaviour under James I
that in 1613 and 1614 proclamations were issued
against duelling.

19 **cock** a fighting cock; the leader of the barn-
yard.

21 **capon** a castrated cock fattened up for eating;
metaphorically, an idiot (compare *Err.* 3.1.32:
'Mome, malthorse, capon, coxcomb, idiot, patch').

21 **and** if.

21 **crow, cock,** This seems the likeliest interpretation of F's 'crow Cock,'. Or one could read 'crow
cock': 'crow like a cock' (Maxwell) or 'brag as if
you were proud as a cockerel' (Warren).

22 **comb** (1) crest, of which the cockerel is
proud; (2) coxcomb, such as would be worn by a
fool.

23 **Sayst thou?** What are you saying?

24 **undertake** engage with.

25 **companion** low fellow (contemptuous).

CLOTEN No, I know that, but it is fit I should commit offence to my
    inferiors.
SECOND LORD Ay, it is fit for your lordship only.
CLOTEN Why, so I say.
FIRST LORD Did you hear of a stranger that's come to court tonight?   30
CLOTEN A stranger, and I not know on't?
SECOND LORD [*Aside*] He's a strange fellow himself, and knows it not.
FIRST LORD There's an Italian come, and, 'tis thought, one of Leona-
    tus'friends.
CLOTEN Leonatus? A banished rascal; and he's another, whatsoever he   35
    be. Who told you of this stranger?
FIRST LORD One of your lordship's pages.
CLOTEN Is it fit I went to look upon him? Is there no derogation in't?
SECOND LORD You cannot derogate, my lord.
CLOTEN Not easily, I think.   40
SECOND LORD [*Aside*] You are a fool granted, therefore your issues,
    being foolish, do not derogate.
CLOTEN Come, I'll go see this Italian. What I have lost today at bowls
    I'll win tonight of him. Come, go.
SECOND LORD I'll attend your lordship.   45

                            [*Exeunt Cloten and First Lord*]
        That such a crafty devil as is his mother
        Should yield the world this ass! A woman that
        Bears all down with her brain, and this her son
        Cannot take two from twenty, for his heart,
        And leave eighteen. Alas, poor princess,   50
        Thou divine Innogen, what thou endur'st
        Betwixt a father by thy stepdame governed,

---

30 tonight] F2; night F   45 SD] *Capell; Exit.* F   51 endur'st] *Ingleby;* endur'st, F

26 commit offence to (1) take on in combat;
(2) be impolite towards (OED offence *sb* 7) – which
would show Cloten's true lack of breeding.
32 strange outlandish.
35 whatsoever whoever.
38 derogation loss of dignity.
39 derogate impair your dignity (with the
implication, because you have none).
41 a fool granted 'admitted on all hands to be
a fool' (Deighton).
41 issues (1) deeds; (2) offspring: the foolish-
ness of Cloten's 'issue' will confirm that stupidity
is the family trait.

43-4 Come . . . him This remark sets up false
expectations before Iachimo's appearance in Innogen's bedroom: since he is assumed to be gambling
with Cloten, his emergence from the trunk is all the
more startling.
46-59 This monologue makes no material contribution to the plot but is needed to create a
buffer between Cloten's comedy and Innogen's
bedchamber. It raises the dramatic temperature,
hinting at the oncoming attack and its likely
seriousness.
48 Bears all down Sweeps all before her.
49 for his heart to save his life.

A mother hourly coining plots, a wooer
More hateful than the foul expulsion is
Of thy dear husband, than that horrid act   55
Of the divorce he'd make! The heavens hold firm
The walls of thy dear honour, keep unshaked
That temple, thy fair mind, that thou may'st stand
T'enjoy thy banished lord and this great land!   [*Exit*]

2.2 [*A trunk is brought on, and*] INNOGEN [*thrust forth in her bed, reading.
Enter to her*] A LADY

INNOGEN Who's there? My woman Helen?
LADY   Please you, madam.
INNOGEN What hour is it?
LADY   Almost midnight, madam.
INNOGEN I have read three hours then. Mine eyes are weak;
    Fold down the leaf where I have left. To bed.
    Take not away the taper, leave it burning;   5
    And if thou canst awake by four o'th'clock,
    I prithee call me. Sleep hath seized me wholly.

                                                        [*Exit Lady*]

---

55 husband, than] F4; Husband. Then F   56 make! The] *Theobald;* make the F   59 SD] *Exeunt.* F   Act 2, Scene 2   2.2
Scena Secunda. F   0 SD] *This edn; Enter Imogen, in her Bed, and a Lady.* F   1, 2 SH LADY] F; HELEN *Taylor*   3 *Rowe;* I
. . . then: / Mine . . . weake, F   7 SD] *after Rowe; not in* F

53 **coining** devising.
55 **than** looking back to 'than' in 54. Cloten's hatefulness is doubled: he is more hateful than Posthumus's exile, and than the intended divorce.
55–6 **than . . . he'd make** In F this passage is garbled by a double error. As Brooks explains, Compositor E mistakenly set 'make the' for 'make. The' (56). This was marked for correction, but the change was erroneously applied to 'then' (55).
57 **honour, keep** F's punctuation (*Honour. Keepe*) makes this second clause a separate imperative addressed to Innogen, but the subject of *keep* is probably *The heavens*. The full sentence presents Innogen as pure citadel: her honour is the outer wall and her mind the temple within, while the whole image emblematizes the integrity of the nation (*this great land*). This is the first hint that the domestic plot centring on Innogen and Posthumus might also be read on a level of political symbolism.

Act 2, Scene 2
0 SD The location is identified as Innogen's bed-chamber by the presence of the bed, a large symbolic property that could have been thrust forward through one of the stage doors; the Lady would have entered through the opposite door. Alternatively, Innogen might have been discovered in her bed in a central space at the rear of the stage, if one were available. The trunk would either have been carried on, or lifted up through a trap. Maximum dramatic effect dictates that the trunk be positioned downstage rather than discovered behind.
1 **Helen** An ominous name, linked in the Troy story with sexual guilt, marital betrayal and political disaster. In this perspective Iachimo's ploy for gaining entrance is a variation on the Trojan horse: see Miola, *Rome*, 214.
2 **hour** a disyllable.
2 **midnight** The most dangerous part of the night: compare *Mac.* 4.1.48, 'you secret, black, and midnight hags'.
5 **Take . . . taper** The candle has to be left so that Iachimo can observe the room, but Innogen's command intensifies the hints of foreboding.

> To your protection I commend me, gods.
> From fairies and the tempters of the night
> Guard me, beseech ye.   *Sleeps*   10
>   IACHIMO [*comes*] *from the trunk*
> IACHIMO The crickets sing, and man's o'er-laboured sense
> Repairs itself by rest. Our Tarquin thus
> Did softly press the rushes, ere he wakened
> The chastity he wounded. Cytherea,
> How bravely thou becom'st thy bed! Fresh lily,   15
> And whiter than the sheets! That I might touch,
> But kiss, one kiss! Rubies unparagoned,

[handwritten marginal note: 'Rape of Lucrece' / Macbeth also likens himself to him]

10.1 SD *comes*] *Collier 1; not in* F

9 fairies malign spirits. *MND* notwithstanding, fairies were most commonly believed to be malevolent beings who threaten and terrify mortals: in Reginald Scot's *Discovery of Witchcraft* (1584), p. 85, they are listed alongside witches, urchins and hags. Nosworthy notes that both Holinshed and Simon Forman described the witches who met Macbeth as 'fairies'.

11–51 Iachimo's nightmarish emergence from the trunk is the first of the play's three 'dream sequences', episodes that happen while characters are asleep or half-awake, the other two being Innogen's 'resurrection' in 4.2, and Posthumus's vision in 5.3. All three are characterized by their intense poetic and theatrical power. This scene, and its later recapitulation, 2.4.66f, is densely tissued with literary and mythical reference, especially to Shakespeare's reading of Ovid: such allusions testify to Innogen's beauty and value, but also to the problematically conflicting sensations of reverence and desire which she arouses. Mythologically alert audiences would have recognized situational parallels with the story of Actaeon spying on the naked Diana: see 2.4.82.

11 o'er-laboured exhausted.

12 Our 'The speaker is an Italian' (Johnson).

12 Tarquin Sextus Tarquinius (sixth century BC), son of Lucius Tarquinius Superbus, the last of the semi-mythical early kings of Rome. He ravished Lucretia, who killed herself; in revenge the Roman people overthrew the Tarquins and established a new state under the consuls. The story is told in Livy's *History*, I, 57–9, and Ovid's *Fasti*, II, 721–852. Shakespeare treated the myth at length in *The Rape of Lucrece*, which poem this scene several times echoes: particularly, in *Luc.* 365–435 Tarquin stealthily enters Lucrece's chamber and

gazes at her as she sleeps. Compare also *Mac.* 2.1.54–6, where the Murderer's approach to his victim is outlined in similar terms: '[Murder,] with his stealthy pace, / With Tarquin's ravishing strides, towards his design / Moves like a ghost.' The allusion identifies Iachimo's invasion of Innogen's space as a kind of rape, and although she is not physically touched, it leaves her seeming obscurely tainted.

12 thus in this manner.

13 rushes that would have been strewn on the floor of the bedroom, and on the stage.

14 Cytherea Venus, the goddess of sexual love: identified by her birthplace, the island of Cythera. By invoking Innogen as Venus, Iachimo foregrounds her beauty and her sexual provocativeness. For the opposite association, with Diana, see 2.3.64 and 2.4.82.

15 bravely admirably.

15 lily An emblem of purity, especially through its association with the Virgin Mary: see *H8* 5.3.61, 'A most unspotted lily shall she pass.' But lilies were also sacred to Juno, the goddess of marriage and motherhood, and were associated with her in Jonson's masque *Hymenaei*, 1606 (*Ben Jonson*, VII, 217). See Barton, 4.

16 whiter than the sheets Recalling the description in *Venus and Adonis* of the desire aroused by seeing one's lover in bed: 'Teaching the sheets a whiter hue than white' (*Ven.* 398). And for white skin and sheets, compare *Luc.* 472 and *Oth.* 5.2.4, 273.

17 Rubies i.e., Innogen's lips. Iachimo isolates the conventional colours of beauty, red and white.

17 unparagoned matchless: an exact reversal of Iachimo's words at 1.4.65.

How dearly they do't! 'Tis her breathing that
Perfumes the chamber thus. The flame o'th'taper
Bows toward her, and would underpeep her lids   20
To see th'enclosèd lights, now canopied
Under these windows, white and azure laced
With blue of heaven's own tinct. But my design –
To note the chamber. I will write all down.

[*Takes out his notebook*]

Such and such pictures; there the window; such   25
Th'adornment of her bed; the arras, figures,
Why, such and such; and the contents o'th'story.
Ah, but some natural notes about her body
Above ten thousand meaner movables
Would testify, t'enrich mine inventory.   30

20 lids] *Cambridge (Rowe:* lids,)*;* lids. F   22 azure laced] F*;* azure-laced *Maxwell (after Nicholson, conj. in Cambridge)*   24
SD] *Collier 2 (subst.); not in* F

18 **dearly** exquisitely.

18 **do't** presumably, kiss one another. In Shakespeare *do* often carries an underlying sexual connotation: see *Ham.* 4.5.60, 'Young men will do't if they come to't.' Warren supposes that Iachimo means he has just kissed Innogen, and in some productions he has done this (though not always at this point: in Noble's 1998 production he kissed the mole on her breast, 38). But for the argument that the scene tantalizes Iachimo with a desire that he feels but knows he dare not satisfy, see Introduction, 32: with her lips caressing each other, Innogen's sexuality seems provocatively self-sufficient and free from male interference. Ingleby compares Venus on Adonis's lips: 'Long may they kiss each other, for this cure' (*Ven.* 505).

19 **Perfumes** A mistress's breath was often conventionally called sweet-smelling (see *Ven.* 443–4), but at the Blackfriars Innogen's chamber might literally have been perfumed, for synaesthetic effects with vapours were sometimes used in court masques (e.g., in *Ben Jonson*, VII, 232–3).

20 **underpeep** (OED's first recorded use).

21 **lights** eyes.

21 **canopied** covered: echoing *Luc.* 397–8: 'Her eyes like marigolds had sheathed their light, / And canopied in darkness sweetly lay.'

22 **windows** shutters (not apertures, but the wooden doors that enclose and protect them: compare *JC* 3.2.259, 'Pluck down forms, windows, any thing').

22 **laced** fretted. Iachimo is describing the appearance of Innogen's eyelids, the whiteness of which is mingled with delicate blue veins: Tarquin similarly admires Lucrece's 'azure veins'

(*Luc.* 419). Many editors print 'azure-laced', feeling that Iachimo's description of Innogen's eyelids as azure *and* laced with blue is awkwardly repetitive. However, the compound would be hard to convey in performance, and it is not redundant for Iachimo to expand on his description, by explaining that Innogen's azure veins take their blue from the heavens themselves. For a possible echo in a similar situation, compare Porphyro admiring Madeline's 'azure-lidded sleep' in Keats's *The Eve of St Agnes*, 630.

23 **tinct** colour.

25–7 Iachimo's notes do not correspond point by point with his report in 2.4, but since the room's furnishings only exist as his words summon them up, an exact equivalence is not dramatically necessary. What counts is the evocation of a richly decked bedchamber – and one broadly seventeenth-century in its furnishings.

26 **arras** tapestry; hanging on the wall, or possibly around the bed.

26 **figures** perhaps figures in the tapestry, though at 2.4.82 Iachimo also describes elaborate sculptures on the chimney-piece,

27 **contents o'th'story** narrative depicted on the tapestry, called 'the story' at 2.4.69. 'Story' was a technical term in fine art for a historical painting or sculpture (OED story *sb* 8): in *MWW* 4.5.7 Falstaff's chamber is 'painted about with the story of the Prodigal', and 'the story of the Prodigal' in *2H4* 2.1.146 refers to a wall painting.

28 **notes** marks.

29 **meaner movables** ordinary items of furniture.

O sleep, thou ape of death, lie dull upon her,
And be her sense but as a monument,
Thus in a chapel lying. Come off, come off –
                [*Taking off her bracelet*]
As slippery as the Gordian knot was hard!
'Tis mine, and this will witness outwardly,   35
As strongly as the conscience does within,
To th'madding of her lord. On her left breast   *microscopic*
A mole cinque-spotted, like the crimson drops   *detail*
I'th'bottom of a cowslip. Here's a voucher,
Stronger than ever law could make; this secret   40
Will force him think I have picked the lock and ta'en
The treasure of her honour. No more. To what end?
Why should I write this down that's riveted,
Screwed to my memory? She hath been reading late
The tale of Tereus; here the leaf's turned down   45
Where Philomel gave up. I have enough;
To th'trunk again, and shut the spring of it.
Swift, swift, you dragons of the night, that dawning

→ *Ovid's 'Metamorphoses'*
  → *a lot of allusions*

33 SD] *Rowe; not in* F

31 **sleep ... death** proverbial: see Tilley, S527.
31 **ape** imitator.
32 **sense** feeling, sensation.
32 **but as** merely like.
32 **a monument** a recumbent marble effigy, on a tomb. In *Luc.* 391 Lucrece sleeps 'like a virtuous monument'.
34 **Gordian knot** An intricate knot tied by King Gordias of Phrygia and which, according to an oracle, would only be untied by the future ruler of Asia; Alexander the Great cut it with his sword. The Gordian knot was often used as an emblem of the inextricable ties of marriage: Barton, p. 4, compares *The Duchess of Malfi* (1614): 'Bless, heaven, this sacred Gordian, which let violence / Never untwine' (Webster, I, 489); and see Marston and Barksted, *The Insatiate Countess*, 2.1.5–8.
36 **conscience** inner knowledge or conviction.
38 **cinque-spotted** made of five spots: a detail taken directly from Boccaccio's *Decameron*.
39 **voucher** piece of evidence.
42 **treasure** along with 'jewel', a recurrent euphemism for maidenhead. Compare *Ham.* 1.3.31–2: 'your chaste treasure open / To his unmastered importunity'; and *Luc.* 1191–2: 'Dear lord of that dear jewel I have lost, / What legacy

shall I bequeath to thee.'
45 **Tereus** Ovid's *Metamorphoses*, VI, tells the legend of Tereus and Philomel. Tereus, a Thracian king, raped his sister-in-law Philomel and cut out her tongue to prevent discovery. She revealed the truth by weaving it into a tapestry; eventually she was turned into a nightingale. Like Tarquin and Lucretia, this is another tale of violent rape to which Shakespeare repeatedly returned: Philomel reappears in *Tit.* 2.4.38, 4.1.47, and *Luc.* 1079, 1128.
46 **gave up** succumbed, surrendered. But Iachimo is wrong, for in Ovid Philomel does not 'give up'.
47 **spring** catch.
48 **dragons of the night** A chariot of the night, drawn by dragons, is summoned by the witch Medea in Ovid's *Metamorphoses*, VII, 217–23. See also *MND* 3.2.379: 'night's swift dragons cut the clouds full fast'; Marlowe's *Hero and Leander*, I, 108–9, where Night's 'yawning dragons draw her thirling car / From Latmus' mount up to the gloomy sky' (*Poems*, 20); and the dragon chariot in which Marlowe's *Faustus* rides.
48 **dawning** Possibly a scribal or compositorial error for 'dawn'?

May bare the raven's eye! I lodge in fear;
Though this a heavenly angel, hell is here.   50
Clock strikes
One, two, three: time, time!   *Exit* [*into the trunk*]
[*The trunk is carried off, and the bed withdrawn*]

(↳ how close to comedy?)

2.3 *Enter* CLOTEN *and* [*the two*] LORDS

FIRST LORD Your lordship is the most patient man in loss, the most
    coldest that ever turned up ace.
CLOTEN It would make any man cold to lose.
FIRST LORD But not every man patient after the noble temper of your
    lordship. You are most hot and furious when you win.   5
CLOTEN Winning will put any man into courage. If I could get this
    foolish Innogen, I should have gold enough. It's almost morning,
    is't not?
FIRST LORD Day, my lord.
CLOTEN I would this music would come. I am advised to give her   10
    music o'mornings; they say it will penetrate.

---

49 bare] *Steevens (after Theobald);* beare F   51 SD] *Rowe (subst.); Exit.* F   51.1 SD] *this edn; not in* F   Act 2, Scene
3   2.3 *Scena Tertia.* F   0 SD *the two] Taylor; not in* F   1, 4, 9 SH FIRST LORD] *Rowe;* 1. F   6 SH CLOTEN] F4; *not in*
F *(catchword at foot of preceding page is* Clot.*)*   11 o'] F *(a)*

49 bare ... eye As Dowden explains, the raven
always wakes early; more generally, it is a bird of ill
omen. See *Tit.* 2.3.96–7: 'the nightly owl, or fatal
raven'.
50 here around me, or inside me. In *Son.* 129
lust is expressed as a heaven/hell conjunction:
'All this the world well knows, yet none knows
well, / To shun the heaven that leads men to this
hell.'
51 time Innogen had asked to be woken at four.
The striking clock is anachronistic in first-century
Britain; here it seems to be a projection of Iachimo's
guilt (Nevo, p. 77).

Act 2, Scene 3
1–2 most coldest (the double superlative was an
acceptable construction at this time: Abbott, #11).
2 ace a single pip, the lowest score on the dice
with which Cloten has been gambling; his hopeless
losing streak continues. There may be an aural pun
on ace/ass, as in *MND* 5.1.312–17.
3 cold gloomy.

4 patient By ascribing to Cloten a 'cold' (2)
and 'patient' bearing, the First Lord is trying to
praise him for his stoicism and calmness in adver-
sity, though Cloten only half-grasps his meaning. In
the following scene Posthumus will likewise exhibit
a lack of patience.
4 temper temperament.
5 furious passionate.
6–7 If ... enough Perhaps, success in love will
boost my 'courage' and rescue my fortunes as a gam-
bler. Alternatively, Cloten may be referring to the
inheritance he stands to gain with Innogen.
10 music band of musicians. Compare *MV*
5.1.98: 'it is your music, madam'.
11 penetrate touch the feelings, but with a
bawdy quibble carried forward in *fingering* (12) and
tongue (13). Shakespeare has arranged events so
that the exquisitely refined song that follows is
framed by Cloten's obscene punning: this underlines Cloten's boorish insensitivity, but also activates a layer of erotic suggestion latent in the song
itself. See Introduction, p. 22.

Enter MUSICIANS

Come on, tune. If you can penetrate her with your fingering, so;
we'll try with tongue too. If none will do, let her remain; but I'll
never give o'er. First, a very excellent good-conceited thing; after,
a wonderful sweet air, with admirable rich words to it; and then   15
let her consider.   [*Music*]
MUSICIAN (*Sings*) Hark, hark, the lark at heaven's gate sings,
            And Phoebus 'gins arise,
        His steeds to water at those springs
            On chaliced flowers that lies,   20
        And winking Mary-buds begin to ope their golden eyes;
        With everything that pretty is, my lady sweet, arise;
                    Arise, arise!

14 good-conceited] *Capell*; good conceited F   16 SD *Music*] *Taylor; not in* F   17 MUSICIAN (*Sings*)] *Taylor*; SONG
F   22 is] F; bin *Hanmer*

12 **so** that's well.

13 **tongue** i.e., vocal music.

13 **remain** stay as she is.

14–15 **First . . . it** Cloten calls for two characteristic musical items: an instrumental fantasia or
'fancy', played by a consort of three or four viols
('horsehairs and calves' guts', 25–6), then an 'air'
(15) or accompanied song for single voice. This is
very similar to the arrangement adopted for the
aubade 'Who is Sylvia' in *TGV* 4.2. As Granville-
Barker noted, the instrumental introduction gives
Innogen longer to dress before her reappearance.
For a full analysis, see Long, pp. 50–65.

14 **good-conceited** (F: good conceyted) fanciful, full of pleasant conceit.

16 **consider** reflect on it.

17 MUSICIAN, 24 CLOTEN These speech-
prefixes are missing in F, and Warren speculates
that Cloten himself could have been the singer. But
the dialogue strongly implies that Cloten pays for
both the fantasia and the song, and that the singer
is a boy (see 26 and note). It is more likely that
the textual arrangement, with the song embedded
into Cloten's speech, reflects the 'literary' presentational habits of the scribe, Ralph Crane: see Textual
Analysis, pp. 259–63 below.

17–23 **Hark . . . arise** This famous aubade survives in an early musical setting probably, though
not certainly, by Robert Johnson, a composer
closely associated with the King's Men. For a transcript and full discussion of the textual problems
arising from it, see 'Hark, hark, the lark', pp. 253–5
below.

17 **lark . . . gate** Compare *Son*. 29: 'Like to the
lark at break of day arising / From sullen earth

sings hymns at heaven's gate.'

18 **Phoebus** the sun; here imagined as the god
Apollo embarking across the sky in his chariot.

18 **'gins** begins to.

19 **His . . . at** To give his horses water from

20 **chaliced flowers** cup-like blossoms, possibly daffodils (from their shape: Warren notes
that 'chalice-flower' was an old name for the daf-
fodil, though 'chaliced' is a Shakespearean coinage,
OED's earliest example). These cups hold the early
morning dew, the evaporation of which is poeti-
cally ascribed to its being drunk up by the horses
of the sun. The image presents a striking reminiscence of the spotted cowslip to which the mole on
Innogen's breast was compared (2.2.39), thereby
aligning Iachimo's overt voyeurism with Cloten's
aestheticized but no less erotic persuasions.

20 **lies** single verb with plural relative pronoun, acceptable grammar at this time (Abbott,
#247).

21 **winking** sleeping, with closed eyes: the flowers open their petals with the warmth of the rising
sun.

21 **Mary-buds** marigolds. Compare *WT*
4.4.105–6: 'The marigold that goes to bed with
the sun, / And with him rises weeping.'

22 **is** As a way of 'improving' the rhyme-scheme,
Hanmer changed 'is' to 'bin', and some modern editors, such as Alexander and Maxwell, are
tempted to follow him. But the change is unwar-
ranted, as well as ungrammatical, since 'bin' is a
plural participle of 'to be'. The manuscript preserving Robert Johnson's setting of the song supports
the reading 'is'. See Thompson, p. 81, and Hunt,
pp. 460–1.

CLOTEN   So, get you gone. If this penetrate, I will consider your music
the better; if it do not, it is a vice in her ears which horsehairs   25
and calves' guts, nor the voice of unpaved eunuch to boot,
can never amend.

                                                    [*Exeunt Musicians*]

                    Enter CYMBELINE *and* QUEEN

SECOND LORD   Here comes the King.
CLOTEN   I am glad I was up so late, for that's the reason I was up so
early. He cannot choose but take this service I have done   30
fatherly. – Good morrow to your majesty, and to my gracious
mother.
CYMBELINE   Attend you here the door of our stern daughter?
            Will she not forth?
CLOTEN   I have assailed her with musics, but she vouchsafes no notice.   35
CYMBELINE   The exile of her minion is too new;
            She hath not yet forgot him. Some more time
            Must wear the print of his remembrance out,
            And then she's yours.
QUEEN   You are most bound to th'King,
            Who lets go by no vantages that may   40

---

24 SH CLOTEN] *Dyce; not in* F   25 vice] *Rowe;* voyce F   27 amend] F2; amed F   27 SD] *Theobald; not in* F   28 SH
SECOND LORD] *Rowe;* 2. F   38 out] *Rowe (*F2: ou't*);* on't F

24 **consider** (probably) remunerate. The verb
is twice used in this sense in *WT* 4.2.17–20 and
4.4.794. However, this usage is rare, and Cloten
may simply mean 'appreciate'.
   25 **vice** flaw. F's *voyce* (a Compositor E error)
was picked up from *voyce* in the following line; presumably the copy read *vyce*.
   25–6 **horsehairs . . . guts** bowstrings and fiddle-
strings; the consort's instruments.
   26 **unpaved** without stones (i.e., testicles); castrated. Presumably the singer was a boy or a
counter-tenor, though Cloten's word 'eunuch' suggests some knowledge of modern Italianate culture.
Castrati existed in Italy from the late sixteenth
century, and although not imported into England
until 1667 the practice was known and understood.
Compare *Cor.* 3.2.112–15, and two plays with
Italianate settings: *TN* 1.2.54–9, and Jonson's first
version of *Every Man in his Humour*, 1.2.58–9 (*Ben
Jonson*, III, 204).
   26 **to boot** in addition.
   29–30 **I am . . . early** A joke linking Cloten to
another clownish night-owl, Sir Toby Belch (*TN*
2.3.1).

31 **fatherly** in fatherly manner.
   33 **Attend you** Are you waiting on. Note that
Cymbeline's arrival shifts the dialogue into verse.
   35 **musics** Possibly a compositorial error (of
which this passage has several), but the plural is supported by *AWW* 3.7.39–40 ('Every night he comes /
With musics of all sorts') and Sidney's *New Arcadia*,
334: 'Musics at her window'.
   36 **minion** darling; sexual favourite.
   38 **print** memory: in Aristotelian psychology
believed to be imprinted on the brain. Compare
Ham. 1.5.103.
   38 **wear . . . out** erase the impress of his memory. F reads 'on't' for 'out', and some editors retain
this, pointing out that the presence of an apostrophe indicates that the 'n' is not merely a turned
letter. For some similar (and disputed) cases, see
TN 3.4.205 and *WT* 4.4.160. Sisson, reading 'on't',
glosses 37–8 as 'more time must elapse which will
still bear the impress of his memory'. However,
Warren emends and finds a parallel idiom at 4.4.22–
4: 'many years . . . not wore him/From my remembrance'.
   40 **vantages** opportunities.

Prefer you to his daughter. Frame yourself
To orderly solicits, and be friended
With aptness of the season; make denials
Increase your services; so seem as if
You were inspired to do those duties which   45
You tender to her; that you in all obey her,
Save when command to your dismission tends,
And therein you are senseless.

CLOTEN   Senseless? Not so.

[Enter a MESSENGER*]*

MESSENGER So like you, sir, ambassadors from Rome;
The one is Caius Lucius.

CYMBELINE   A worthy fellow,   50
Albeit he comes on angry purpose now;
But that's no fault of his. We must receive him
According to the honour of his sender,
And towards himself, his goodness forespent on us,
We must extend our notice. Our dear son,   55
When you have given good morning to your mistress,
Attend the Queen and us; we shall have need
T'employ you towards this Roman. Come, our Queen.

                              Exeunt [all but Cloten]

CLOTEN If she be up, I'll speak with her; if not
Let her lie still and dream. By your leave ho!   60

                                        [Knocks]

42 solicits] F2; *solicity* F   48 SD] *Rowe; not in* F   58 *Rowe;* T'employ . . . Romane. / Come . . . Queene. F   58 SD *all but Cloten]* Globe; *not in* F   60 SD] *Theobald; not in* F

41 **Prefer** Recommend.

42 **orderly solicits** well-regulated solicitations. 'Solicits' is OED's first recorded use. F's 'solicity' is probably a compositorial slip caught from the preceding word, or a foulcase error. Walker compares J. Shirley, *The Arcadia*, pr. 1640: 'tired with his solicits I had no time to perfect my desires'.

42–3 **be . . . season** take assistance from the appropriateness of the moment. The Queen means Cloten's wooing should be ardent but tactful.

46 **that** referring back to 'so seem as if' (44).

47 **command** (Innogen's command).

47 **dismission** rejection (rather than 'dismissal', which, as Maxwell notes, is a nineteenth-century coinage).

48 **senseless** insensible, i.e., deaf. Cloten stupidly takes her to mean 'stupid'.

50 **The one** i.e., The principal one (Warren).

51 **Albeit** Although.

53 **his sender** (Augustus Caesar).

54 **his . . . us** because of kindnesses he previously bestowed on us (a parenthesis). Cymbeline's courtesy towards Lucius (here and at 3.1.66–9) implies a community of outlook between international elites that reflects the seventeenth-century culture of aristocratic honour and the emergent professionalism of Europe's diplomatic cadres.

58 **T'employ you** Presumably, as leader of Lucius's welcoming party. Ambassadors to Stuart Whitehall were always escorted into London from the coast by delegations of high-profile courtiers, whose leaders were chosen according to meticulous considerations of rank, reflecting the relative importance of each embassy. For numerous examples, see *Finetti Philoxenus*, 1656, the records of Charles I's Master of Ceremonies, Sir John Finet.

I know her women are about her; what
If I do line one of their hands? 'Tis gold
Which buys admittance – oft it doth – yea, and makes
Diana's rangers false themselves, yield up
Their deer to th'stand o'th'stealer; and 'tis gold   65
Which makes the true man killed and saves the thief,
Nay, sometime hangs both thief and true man. What
Can it not do and undo? I will make
One of her women lawyer to me, for
I yet not understand the case myself. –   70
By your leave!   *Knocks*

Enter a LADY

LADY   Who's there that knocks?
CLOTEN   A gentleman.
LADY   No more?
CLOTEN Yes, and a gentlewoman's son.

61–71 These lines may be an afterthought by Shakespeare, since the dialogue at 60 is continuous with 72, and the repetition of Cloten's knocking and words 'by your leave' (60, 71) is a tell-tale sign of inserted material. The monologue, spoken direct to the audience and full of colloquialisms, proverbial ideas and riddling logic, helps to underline Cloten's status as the play's clown: compare 4.1.1–22.

62 line fill with money.

62–3 'Tis . . . admittance a proverbial sentiment (Tilley, M1050).

64 Diana goddess of chastity, used figuratively for Innogen (in contrast to Iachimo's comparison of her with Venus, 2.2.14).

64 rangers gamekeepers; figuratively, Innogen's women. Diana was often depicted as a queen-like huntress ranging through the forests, and attended by a train of nymphs. However, Cloten's phrase makes Diana herself sound like the deer being hunted, betrayed rather than protected by her 'rangers'. Behind this is an allusion to the story of Actaeon (told in Ovid's *Metamorphoses*, V, 138–252), the huntsman who witnessed Diana bathing and was punished by being turned into a stag.

64 false corrupt.

65 stand fixed station from which a hunter shot at game (see *LLL* 4.1.10: 'A stand where you may

make the fairest shoot'); possibly with a bawdy innuendo (stand = erection).

65 stealer poacher.

66 true honest.

68 do and undo perhaps with a bawdy quibble, as at 2.2.18.

69 lawyer advocate.

70 understand more bawdy punning, reinforced by *case* = (1) lawsuit (2) vagina.

71.0 SD LADY As Innogen eventually calls this woman Dorothy (132), she is presumably a different person from Helen in 2.2 (also called 'Lady' in F). Since Shakespeare is frequently careless with the names of minor parts, this may be a simple slip, though Cloten certainly assumes that she has several 'women' (61: but compare note to 3.2.75). Mahood, p. 45, observes that Dorothy's seemingly pointless exchange with Cloten creates an impression of feminine solidarity in a world of male distrust, Diana's ranger proving more resistant to bribery than Cloten expected. She is also more resilient than Innogen, possessing the darting wit of the shrewd wenches who often appear in Shakespeare's early comedies.

72–80 Although I follow the usual arrangement of these lines, the verse is all but submerged in the repartee, and it could be printed as prose with little loss.

LADY   That's more
            Than some whose tailors are as dear as yours
            Can justly boast of. What's your lordship's pleasure?   75
CLOTEN   Your lady's person. Is she ready?
LADY   Ay,
            To keep her chamber.
CLOTEN   [*giving money*]   There is gold for you,
            Sell me your good report.
LADY   How, my good name? Or to report of you
            What I shall think is good?

                        Enter INNOGEN

                        The Princess.   [*Exit*]   80
CLOTEN   Good morrow, fairest sister. Your sweet hand.
INNOGEN Good morrow, sir. You lay out too much pains
            For purchasing but trouble. The thanks I give
            Is telling you that I am poor of thanks,
            And scarce can spare them.
CLOTEN   Still I swear I love you.   85
INNOGEN If you but said so, 'twere as deep with me.
            If you swear still, your recompense is still
            That I regard it not.
CLOTEN   This is no answer.
INNOGEN But that you shall not say I yield being silent,
            I would not speak. I pray you, spare me. Faith,   90

76–7 Ay . . . chamber] *Hanmer; one line in* F   77 SD] *This edn; not in* F   80 *Enter* innogen] *So placed by Sisson; after*
l.80 in F   80 *Exit*] *Capell; not in* F   81 fairest sister.] *Capell;* fairest, Sister F; fairest. Sister *Johnson*

73–5 That's . . . of i.e., many as expensively
dressed as you are gentlemen only in their clothes.
A joke from the world of Jacobean city comedy,
where fashions and status were the recurrent obsession.
    74–5 Than . . . of; 77 To . . . chamber Tay-
lor marks both these rude remarks as asides, and
certainly Dorothy's backhanded insults resemble
the Second Lord's treatment of Cloten in 1.2 and
2.1. However, Cloten does hear and respond to her
words, the exchange preparing for the more serious
row with Innogen that follows. Dorothy's needling
begins to shift Cloten from a clown to a figure of
potentially serious violence.
    76 ready (1) dressed; (2) prepared (the meaning
played on by Dorothy).

77 keep keep within.
    79 good name reputation.
    80 What . . . good i.e., What I choose to think
of you.
    81 fairest sister The emended punctuation
improves the movement of the line, though F's
pointing (fairest, Sister) also makes adequate sense.
    82 lay out expend.
    83 but only. Innogen is thanking Cloten for the
music, but with purely formal politeness.
    86 but said so merely said it (without swearing).
    86 deep serious.
    87 still . . . still continually . . . always.
    89 But . . . say Except to prevent you claiming.
    89 I . . . silent alluding to the proverb, 'silence
gives consent' (Tilley, S446).

> I shall unfold equal discourtesy
> To your best kindness. One of your great knowing
> Should learn, being taught, forbearance.
>
> CLOTEN   To leave you in your madness, 'twere my sin.
> I will not.
>
> INNOGEN   Fools cure not mad folks.   95
>
> CLOTEN   Do you call me fool?
>
> INNOGEN   As I am mad, I do.
> If you'll be patient, I'll no more be mad;
> That cures us both. I am much sorry, sir,
> You put me to forget a lady's manners
> By being so verbal: and learn now, for all,   100
> That I, which know my heart, do here pronounce
> By th'very truth of it, I care not for you,
> And am so near the lack of charity
> To accuse myself I hate you; which I had rather
> You felt than make't my boast.
>
> CLOTEN   You sin against   105
> Obedience, which you owe your father. For
> The contract you pretend with that base wretch –
> One bred of alms and fostered with cold dishes,

---

95 cure] *Theobald (after Warburton);* are F   104 To . . . myself] *Keightley;* To . . . my selfe, F; (To . . . myself) *Capell*

91 **unfold equal discourtesy** display discourtesy equal.

92 **knowing** social accomplishment (ironical). Compare 'known together' (1.4.27).

93 **forbearance** restraint, sensitivity (compare *R2* 4.1.120: 'Then true noblesse would / Learn him forbearance from so foul a wrong'). Cloten takes her to mean that he should remove himself – which, given her freezing civility, is an understandable mistake.

95 **cure** Warburton's emendation for 'are' makes evident sense; it is supported by 'cures' at 98, and Innogen's subsequent admission that she has been impolite. Editors who defend F's reading assume that she is being self-deprecating rather than insulting, but this makes Cloten's response difficult to explain, and perhaps arises from a Victorian reluctance to believe that Innogen might be anything but perfect. She is exasperated by Cloten's courtship and anxious about her bracelet: an angry admission of her real feelings is not out of place.

99 **put** compel.

100 **verbal** talkative, instead of keeping silent as I wanted (at 89–90). Some editors take 'verbal' to refer to Cloten's pestering of Innogen, but he has said less than she and she subsequently becomes even more verbal. Innogen alludes to the common expectation that women should be of few words, and that excess speech was a sign of immodesty.

100 **for all** for once and all.

103–4 **am so . . . you** 'I am so near to lacking Christian charity as to be forced to accuse myself of hating you' (Maxwell). This paraphrase is tortuous but follows Innogen's thought: she worries about lacking charity both in feeling hatred for Cloten and in condemning herself for it. The alternative, treating 'To accuse myself' as a parenthesis, leaves a contradiction between her being *near* a lack of charity, and actively hating Cloten.

105 **make't my boast** proclaim it openly.

107 **contract** marriage contract.

108 **bred of alms** brought up on charity.

With scraps o'th'court – it is no contract, none.
And though it be allowed in meaner parties –   110
Yet who than he more mean? – to knit their souls,
On whom there is no more dependency
But brats and beggary, in self-figured knot,
Yet you are curbed from that enlargement by
The consequence o'th'crown, and must not foil   115
The precious note of it with a base slave,
A hilding for a livery, a squire's cloth,
A pantler – not so eminent.

INNOGEN   Profane fellow,
Wert thou the son of Jupiter, and no more
But what thou art besides, thou wert too base   120
To be his groom! Thou wert dignified enough,
Even to the point of envy, if 'twere made
Comparative for your virtues to be styled

---

115 foil] F *(foyle)*; soil *Hanmer;* 'file *conj. Ingleby*   122 envy, if] F2; Enuie. If F

109 **scraps** leftovers from meals, given away to the poor or allowed to the servants. In *The Alchemist* 1.1.52 Face keeps back the 'chippings' that his master intended for charitable distribution (*Ben Jonson*, V, 297).

109 **it is no contract** i.e., because it has been entered into without parental consent: hence Innogen sins against 'obedience' (106).

110 **And . . . parties** Cloten shifts the ground of his complaints from parental approval to constitutional objections arising from the fact that Innogen is a princess.

110 **meaner** socially inferior. Cloten's sneer at Posthumus's status underlines that, as an orphan and a royal ward, his honour is not innate but merely imputed.

111 **to knit their souls** This phrase is completed by 'in self-figured knot' (113), 'On whom . . . beggary' (112–13) being an intrusive parenthesis: Cloten's outrage complicates his syntax.

112–13 **On . . . beggary** 'In the case of whose marriage no other result is depending except the rearing of brats in beggary' (Deighton).

113 **self-figured** formed by themselves, instead of chosen by their parents. There may be a suggestion that Innogen's and Posthumus's marriage, being clandestine, was not adequately ratified by ceremony (see Barton, pp. 6–11); however, the primary sense is that royalty are less free to love where they will than are the poor.

113 **knot** bond.

114 **curbed** restricted.

114 **enlargement** freedom of action.

115 **consequence . . . crown** significance of the crown, to which you are heir. The question of the crown prince's lack of marital choice was a burning issue in 1610. James was looking for a wife for Prince Henry, and for reasons of diplomacy and dowry wanted a Catholic princess, a choice to which Henry was bitterly opposed; this problem remained unresolved at Henry's death in 1612 (see Strong, pp. 80–4). For a female heir the freedom of manoeuvre would have been even less.

115 **foil** dishonour. Some editors emend to *soil* or *'file* (= defile, pollute), but Cloten is talking about the social consequences of Innogen marrying below her status, rather than propounding a sacramental view of monarchy.

116 **note** renown.

117 **hilding** good-for-nothing (also at *2H4* 1.1.57, *AWW* 3.6.3); usually applied to a horse.

117 **for a livery** fit only to be a servant: 'livery' is the household uniform worn by one master's group of servants.

117 **squire's cloth** retainer wearing distinctive dress.

118 **pantler** servant in the pantry.

122 **Even . . . envy** And even this would make people envy you.

122–3 **if . . . virtues** if the offices each of you held corresponded to your respective virtues. 'Your' is plural, referring to both Cloten and Posthumus.

123 **to be styled** for you to be called.

> The under-hangman of his kingdom, and hated
> For being preferred so well.

CLOTEN   The south-fog rot him!   125

INNOGEN He never can meet more mischance than come
> To be but named of thee. His meanest garment,
> That ever hath but clipped his body, is dearer
> In my respect than all the hairs above thee,
> Were they all made such men. How now, Pisanio!   130

Enter PISANIO

CLOTEN His garment? Now the devil –
INNOGEN To Dorothy my woman hie thee presently.
CLOTEN His garment?
INNOGEN   I am sprited with a fool,
> Frighted, and angered worse. Go bid my woman
> Search for a jewel that too casually   135
> Hath left mine arm. It was thy master's. 'Shrew me
> If I would lose it for a revenue
> Of any king's in Europe! I do think
> I saw't this morning; confident I am
> Last night 'twas on mine arm; I kissed it.   140
> I hope it be not gone to tell my lord
> That I kiss aught but he.
PISANIO   'Twill not be lost.
INNOGEN I hope so; go and search.

> [*Exit Pisanio*]

---

127 meanest] F2; mean'st F   131 garment] F2; Garments F   139 am] *Knight;* am. F   141 SD] *Hanmer; not in* F

124 **under-hangman** assistant executioner: the same miserable office undertaken by Pompey Bum in *MM* 4.2. Innogen means that, were Posthumus to rule a kingdom, this would be the highest occupation for which Cloten's virtue would qualify him.
125 **preferred** promoted.
125 **south-fog** fog blown in by the south wind (the south wind was thought to be especially unwholesome, and to carry plague and pestilence). Compare 4.2.349, 'the spongy south', and *Cor.* 1.4.30.
127, 150 **meanest** F prints 'mean'st', but 'meanest' appears at 144 and is required by the metre. F2 has 'meanest'.
127 **meanest garment** most lowly clothing. Presumably Innogen means Posthumus's underwear – which explains Cloten's exaggerated sense of outrage, and his subsequent fixation on Posthumus's clothes.

128 **clipped** embraced.
129 **respect** esteem.
129 **hairs above thee** hairs on your head.
131 **garment** F's *Garments* is a characteristic compositorial error: see 1.4.68 (purchase/purchases), and Textual Analysis, p. 267.
132 **presently** immediately.
133 **sprited with** haunted by. *OED*'s earliest example.
135 **casually** accidentally.
136 **'Shrew me** Beshrew me.
140 **kissed** monosyllabic; the metre allows an emphatic pause between 'arm' and 'I' (Abbott, #508).
141–2 I . . . **he** A remark suggesting that Innogen is afraid lest she seem unfaithful?
143 **I hope so** I hope you are right (the modern idiom is 'I hope not').

CLOTEN   You have abused me.
    His meanest garment?
INNOGEN   Ay, I said so, sir.
    If you will make't an action, call witness to't.   145
CLOTEN   I will inform your father.
INNOGEN   Your mother too;
    She's my good lady, and will conceive, I hope,
    But the worst of me. So I leave you, sir,
    To th'worst of discontent.   *Exit*
CLOTEN   I'll be revenged.
    His meanest garment? Well!   *Exit*   150

2.4 *Enter* POSTHUMUS *and* PHILARIO

POSTHUMUS   Fear it not, sir. I would I were so sure
    To win the King as I am bold her honour
    Will remain hers.
PHILARIO   What means do you make to him?
POSTHUMUS   Not any; but abide the change of time,
    Quake in the present winter's state, and wish   5
    That warmer days would come. In these seared hopes
    I barely gratify your love; they failing,
    I must die much your debtor.
PHILARIO   Your very goodness and your company
    O'erpays all I can do. By this, your king   10
    Hath heard of great Augustus. Caius Lucius

---

149 you,] F3; your F   Act 2, Scene 4   2.4 *Scena Quarta.* F   6 seared] *Knight 2 (conj. Tyrwhitt);* fear'd F   6 hopes] F2; hope F

145 **action** law case.
147 **my good lady** ironical.
147 **I hope** I expect: more neutral than it sounds to modern ears. Maxwell compares *Ant.* 2.1.38: 'I cannot hope / Caesar and Antony shall well greet together.'

Act 2, Scene 4
  This second Roman scene is in verse, indicating the increase in emotional temperature since 1.4.
2 **win** win over. This comparison deftly joins the domestic and political plots, making the test of Innogen's chastity seem a part of Posthumus's public fortunes.
2 **bold** confident.

3 **means** overtures.
4 **abide** wait for.
6 **seared** withered. Many editors accept F (*fear'd hopes*), explaining it as 'hopes mixed with fears'. However, Posthumus means not that his hopes and fears are equally mixed but that his hopes are shrivelled up and need 'warmer days' to revive them. The implied image, carried forward from 4–5, is a tree in winter: compare *Mac.* 5.3.24–5, 'My way of life is fallen into the sear, the yellow leaf.' It would be a simple foulcase error for the compositor to substitute 'f' for a long 's'.
7 **gratify** requite.
8 **much your debtor** considerably in your debt.
11 **of** from.

Will do's commission throughly. And I think
He'll grant the tribute, send th'arrerages,
Or look upon our Romans, whose remembrance
Is yet fresh in their grief.

POSTHUMUS   I do believe –   15
Statist though I am none, nor like to be –
That this will prove a war, and you shall hear
The legions now in Gallia sooner landed
In our not-fearing Britain than have tidings
Of any penny tribute paid. Our countrymen   20
Are men more ordered than when Julius Caesar
Smiled at their lack of skill, but found their courage
Worthy his frowning at. Their discipline,
Now mingled with their courage, will make known
To their approvers they are people such   25
That mend upon the world.

Enter IACHIMO

PHILARIO   See, Iachimo!
POSTHUMUS The swiftest harts have posted you by land,
And winds of all the corners kissed your sails
To make your vessel nimble.

---

18 legions] *Theobald;* Legion F   24 mingled] F2; wing-led F; winged *conj. Cambridge*   24 courage] *Dyce;* courages F

12 **throughly** thoroughly.
13 **arrerages** arrears.
14 **Or** Probably 'ere, rather than': Cymbeline will send the tribute in preference to reencountering the Romans, whose force he knows too well. As Posthumus's reply indicates, Philario has not just spelled out the obvious, but called British honour into question. 'Or' and 'ere' often appeared in close combination: see Abbott, #131.
14 **look upon** face.
15 **fresh** It was in fact fifty-four years since the previous Roman invasion; but see notes to 1.1.35 and 3.1.0.
15 **their** (the British).
16 **Statist** Politician.
18 **legions** (F: Legion). For Compositor B's inconsistency over terminal '-s', see Textual Analysis, p. 267 (and other examples at 24, 60 below).
19 **not-fearing** fearless.
20 **penny** (a minor anachronism).
21 **more ordered** better disciplined.
21 **Julius Caesar** In *The Gallic War*, 4.20–38, 5.1–23, Caesar recounted two expeditions against Britain, one (55 BC) repulsed by Cassibelan, the

other (54 BC) a decisive victory, after which tribute was imposed. Caesar's narrative does in fact acknowledge the Britons' tactical skill. See 3.1.26 and note.
23–4 **Their . . . courage** F's otherwise unknown phrase *wing-led* can be made to yield sense if some ingenuity is applied: Dowden takes 'wing' to refer to a division of the army, and glosses it 'led in disciplined formation'. But this is still quite a stretch, and it reverses Posthumus's point, which seems to be that British courage has been improved with a new discipline, not vice versa. It is, of course, true that scribes or compositors do not usually replace common words with rare ones. However, hyphenated compound forms are characteristic of the hand of the scribe Ralph Crane, and most likely he is responsible for this crux.
25 **approvers** those who put them to the test.
25–6 **such . . . world** whose reputation is on the increase.
27 **posted** conveyed. The remark is comparative: Iachimo's horses were as speedy as the 'swiftest harts'.
28 **of . . . corners** from all corners of the earth.

PHILARIO   Welcome, sir.
POSTHUMUS I hope the briefness of your answer made   30
         The speediness of your return.
IACHIMO   Your lady
         Is one the fairest that I have looked upon.
POSTHUMUS And therewithal the best, or let her beauty
         Look through a casement to allure false hearts,
         And be false with them.
IACHIMO   Here are letters for you.   35
POSTHUMUS Their tenor good, I trust.
IACHIMO   'Tis very like.
                  [*Posthumus reads the letters*]
PHILARIO Was Caius Lucius in the Briton court
         When you were there?
IACHIMO   He was expected then,
         But not approached.
POSTHUMUS   All is well yet.
         Sparkles this stone as it was wont, or is't not   40
         Too dull for your good wearing?
IACHIMO   If I had lost it,
         I should have lost the worth of it in gold.
         I'll make a journey twice as far t'enjoy
         A second night of such sweet shortness which
         Was mine in Britain – for the ring is won.   45
POSTHUMUS The stone's too hard to come by.

---

32 one the] *Steevens-Reed;* one of the F   34 through] *Rowe²;* thorough F   36 SD] *Collier³ (subst.); not in* F   37
PHILARIO] *Capell; Post.* F   41 had] *Singer (Durfey);* haue F

---

30 **answer** (answer given by Innogen).
32 **one the fairest** Omission of F's *of* satisfies the metre and explains Posthumus's reply,
since Iachimo's emphatic phrase situates Innogen as 'fairest above all' (Abbott, #18: compare
1.6.164–5, 'one / The truest mannered', and the
related form at 1.6.17). Posthumus follows up
'the fairest' with 'the best' (33), but Iachimo's
intention will evidently be 'fairest but *not* most
virtuous'.
34 **casement** window: if Innogen is less virtuous than beautiful, she is no better than a prostitute, who would attract her customers from a window. Compare *Tim.* 4.3.116–17: 'those milk paps, /
That through the window bars bore at men's eyes';
and, in Jonson's *Volpone*, Corvino's insane jealousy
when his wife shows herself at a window. The sit-

uation also recalls *Ado*, and Claudio's repudiation
of Hero on similar grounds. Posthumus's comment
suggests how predisposed he is to attribute whore-
dom to Innogen.
37–8 This speech must be Philario's, since
Posthumus needs time to glance at the letter, and
the question better fits Philario, as it is an enquiry
that a Roman might readily make about a fellow-
countryman.
39 **not approached** not yet arrived: see 2.3.58
and note.
41 **had** F's 'have' has been accepted by many
editors, but the idiom is very difficult to explain
satisfactorily. Most probably the compositor set it
in anticipation of 'have' in 42.
42 **I . . . gold** (Because those were the terms of
the wager in 1.4.)

IACHIMO   Not a whit,
    Your lady being so easy.

POSTHUMUS   Make not, sir,
    Your loss your sport. I hope you know that we
    Must not continue friends.

IACHIMO   Good sir, we must
    If you keep covenant. Had I not brought   50
    The knowledge of your mistress home, I grant
    We were to question further; but I now
    Profess myself the winner of her honour,
    Together with your ring, and not the wronger
    Of her or you, having proceeded but   55
    By both your wills.

POSTHUMUS   If you can make't apparent
    That you have tasted her in bed, my hand
    And ring is yours. If not, the foul opinion
    You had of her pure honour gains or loses
    Your sword or mine, or masterless leaves both   60
    To who shall find them.

IACHIMO   Sir, my circumstances
    Being so near the truth as I will make them,
    Must first induce you to believe; whose strength
    I will confirm with oath, which I doubt not
    You'll give me leave to spare when you shall find   65
    You need it not.

POSTHUMUS   Proceed.

IACHIMO   First, her bedchamber —

---

47 not] F2; note F   57 you] F2; yon F   60 leaves] *Rowe;* leaue F

47 **easy** liberal of herself. Iachimo quibbles on Posthumus's *hard* (46), hence the retort about not making 'Your loss your sport' (48).
  50 **keep covenant** keep to the agreement.
  51 **knowledge** carnal knowledge.
  52 **question** dispute, go to swords over (see 1.4.132–3).
  56 **wills** perhaps with a bold pun on *will* = sexual organ (as in *Son.* 135: 'Wilt thou, whose will is large and spacious, / Not once vouchsafe to hide my will in thine').
  57 **tasted** had experience of.
  58 **is** single verb with two single subjects: see Abbott, #336.
  59–60 **gains . . . mine** gains one of us the other's sword (which the other forfeits by death).

60 **masterless** i.e., because we will both be dead.
  61 **circumstances** particulars.
  65 **spare** omit.
  66–91 Iachimo's description of the bedchamber continues the contradictory signals of purity and desirability begun in 2.2, emphasizing the eroticism of Innogen's closet. It is underpinned by allusions to Ovid, and situates Innogen in a visual frame out of which the observer 'reads' her violation (rather like *Luc.*, with its *ekphrasis* of a tapestry depicting the fall of Troy, implicitly a commentary on Lucrece's rape). The furnishings are made to seem as if in the richest and most up-to-date Renaissance style. For some examples of similar contemporary decoration, see Simonds, pp. 95–135.

Where I confess I slept not, but profess
Had that was well worth watching – it was hanged
With tapestry of silk and silver; the story
Proud Cleopatra when she met her Roman,
And Cydnus swelled above the banks, or for   70
The press of boats or pride – a piece of work
So bravely done, so rich, that it did strive
In workmanship and value, which I wondered
Could be so rarely and exactly wrought,
Such the true life on't was.   75

POSTHUMUS   This is true;
And this you might have heard of here by me,
Or by some other.

IACHIMO   More particulars
Must justify my knowledge.

POSTHUMUS   So they must,
Or do your honour injury.

IACHIMO   The chimney   80
Is south the chamber, and the chimney-piece
Chaste Dian bathing. Never saw I figures
So likely to report themselves. The cutter

76 Such] *Singer² (Mason);* Since F   76 on't was.] *Hanmer;* on't was– F; was out on't. *conj. Cambridge*

68 watching staying awake for.
69 silver silver thread; a very expensive cloth.
70 Cleopatra A reminiscence of Shakespeare's description of the meeting between Cleopatra and Antony at the River Cydnus (*Ant.* 2.2.190–226). It associates Innogen with a famous sensual female, a parallel all the more forceful for coming from Rome's recent past. It allows Iachimo to imply that both Innogen and Cleopatra are dangerous and seductive foreigners who undermine Roman masculinity. Cleopatra was a popular subject on seventeenth-century tapestries (Simonds, p. 97).
71 or for either because of.
72 pride i.e., Cydnus swelled with pride at bearing Cleopatra's person.
73 bravely excellently.
73–4 it . . . value it was doubtful whether the workmanship or cost was greater. Thiselton compares the Palace of the Sun in Ovid's *Metamorphoses*, II: 'the cunning workmanship of things therein far passed / The stuff whereof the doors were made'.
76 Such . . . was It was so lifelike. I follow other

editors in assuming that the compositor garbled the speech by misreading 'Since' for 'Such', then added a dash to imply that Posthumus interrupted and prevented Iachimo from completing his remark. However, this emendation still leaves the line a syllable short (see collation).
79 justify confirm.
81 the chimney-piece the carving on the mantel (most comparable English mantels were in fact plasterwork). This is *OED*'s earliest example of this phrase.
82 Dian bathing Presumably a depiction of Diana being discovered by Actaeon, naked in her bath. Ovid tells how, for his voyeurism, Actaeon was turned into a stag and hunted by his own hounds (*Metamorphoses*, III, 138–252). This allusion to the goddess of chastity paradoxically underlines Innogen's position as an object of desire: see 2.3.64 and Introduction, p. 32.
83 So . . . themselves so lifelike that they seemed almost capable of describing their own artistry: a confounding of art and nature very similar to *WT* 5.3.23–68.
83 cutter sculptor.

Was as another Nature, dumb; outwent her,
Motion and breath left out.

POSTHUMUS   This is a thing   85
Which you might from relation likewise reap,
Being, as it is, much spoke of.

IACHIMO   The roof o'th'chamber
With golden cherubins is fretted. Her andirons –
I had forgot them – were two winking Cupids
Of silver, each on one foot standing, nicely   90
Depending on their brands.

POSTHUMUS   This is her honour!
Let it be granted you have seen all this – and praise
Be given to your remembrance – the description
Of what is in her chamber nothing saves
The wager you have laid.

IACHIMO   Then, if you can   95
Be pale, I beg but leave to air this jewel. See!
                    [*Showing the bracelet*]
And now 'tis up again. It must be married
To that your diamond; I'll keep them.

POSTHUMUS   Jove!
Once more let me behold it. Is it that
Which I left with her?

IACHIMO   Sir, I thank her, that.   100

96 SD] *Globe; not in* F   100 that.] *Johnson; that* F

84 as . . . dumb i.e., seemed like another
Nature, albeit a speechless one. Iachimo poses as
an aesthetic connoisseur reflecting in a sophisticated way on the limits of art: the sculptor might
be said to have surpassed Nature herself, except
that he could not carve speech and movement.
  86 relation hearsay.
  88 cherubins cherubs (appropriate decoration
for a ceiling).
  88 fretted carved: presumably in geometric patterns.
  88 andirons fire-dogs.
  89 winking Cupids blind Cupids, with closed
eyes. Eros and his younger brother Anteros can
be found in Plato (*Phaedrus* 255D) and the Greek
Anthology. They were interpreted in the Renaissance as Love and Love-in-Return, figuring the
reciprocal nature of desire: see Merrill, pp. 265–

84, and *Ben Jonson*, VII, 192, 394–5. The fact that
Innogen's Cupids are placed in the fire, and have
their eyes shut, identifies their eroticism as burning
and indiscriminate.
  91 Depending . . . brands Leaning on their
torches. Torches are associated with marriage and
the flames of desire, and so are symbolically apt
for Cupids (as often in court masques: *Ben Jonson*, VII, 188, 254). Compare John Lyly's *Euphues*
(1578): 'the brands of Cupid' (Lyly, 99).
  93 remembrance memory.
  94 nothing not at all.
  95–6 if . . . pale to see if you can be made to turn
pale (I will show my real evidence). Alternatively,
Maxwell thinks Iachimo is challenging Posthumus
to 'be pale', i.e., keep his colour unflushed in the
face of his shocking evidence.
  97 up away.

She stripped it from her arm. I see her yet:
Her pretty action did outsell her gift,
And yet enriched it too. She gave it me,
And said she prized it once.
POSTHUMUS   Maybe she plucked it off
To send it me.
IACHIMO   She writes so to you, doth she?   105
POSTHUMUS Oh no, no, no, 'tis true! Here, take this too.
                        [*Gives the ring*]
It is a basilisk unto mine eye,
Kills me to look on't. Let there be no honour
Where there is beauty, truth where semblance, love
Where there's another man. The vows of women   110
Of no more bondage be to where they are made
Than they are to their virtues, which is nothing.
Oh, above measure false!
PHILARIO   Have patience, sir,
And take your ring again; 'tis not yet won.
It may be probable she lost it, or   115
Who knows if one her women, being corrupted,
Hath stol'n it from her?
POSTHUMUS   Very true,
And so I hope he came by't. Back my ring!
                        [*Taking back the ring*]
Render to me some corporal sign about her
More evident than this, for this was stolen.   120
IACHIMO By Jupiter, I had it from her arm.
POSTHUMUS Hark you, he swears; by Jupiter he swears.
    'Tis true – nay, keep the ring, 'tis true – I am sure

---

106 SD] *Johnson; not in* F   116 one her women] F; one of her women F2; one her woman *Collier²*

102 **outsell** surpass in value (literally, sell for more than). *OED*'s earliest example.

107 **basilisk** a fabulous reptile, supposed to kill merely by looking at its prey. Also in *WT* 1.2.388, 'Make me not sighted like the basilisk.'

109 **semblance** seeming.

110–12 **The vows . . . nothing** '(Let) women's vows be no more binding to those to whom they are made than women are bound to their own virtues – which is not at all.'

113 **patience** An echo of Cloten's more temperate response to his gambling losses: compare

2.3.1–5, and 2.4.150.

115 **probable** capable of proof.

116 **one her** one of her. For the idiom, compare 32.

116 **corrupted** bribed.

118 **Back** Give back.

119 **corporal** bodily; material.

120 **evident** conclusive. This debate about the credibility of remote testimony harks back to the Queen's concern with material proof at 1.5.18.

121 **By Jupiter** Iachimo provides the oath that he had claimed would not be needed (64).

She would not lose it. Her attendants are
All sworn and honourable. They induced to steal it?   125
And by a stranger? No, he hath enjoyed her.
The cognizance of her incontinency
Is this. She hath bought the name of whore thus dearly.

                    [*Gives Iachimo the ring*]

There, take thy hire, and all the fiends of hell
Divide themselves between you!

PHILARIO   Sir, be patient.   130
This is not strong enough to be believed
Of one persuaded well of.

POSTHUMUS   Never talk on't;
She hath been colted by him.

IACHIMO   If you seek
For further satisfying, under her breast –
Worthy the pressing – lies a mole, right proud   135
Of that most delicate lodging. By my life,
I kissed it, and it gave me present hunger
To feed again, though full. You do remember
This stain upon her?

POSTHUMUS   Ay, and it doth confirm
Another stain, as big as hell can hold,   140
Were there no more but it.

IACHIMO   Will you hear more?

POSTHUMUS Spare your arithmetic; never count the turns.
Once, and a million!

IACHIMO   I'll be sworn –

128 SD] *Taylor (subst.); not in* F   132 of.] F; *of* – *Rowe*   135 the] *Rowe;* her F   142–3 *Hanmer;* Spare . . . Arethmaticke, / Neuer . . . Million. F

125 **sworn** i.e., have taken oaths of fidelity.

127 **cognizance** badge (heraldic term).

128 **this** the ring, as performance will clarify. In F's pointing (*this: she*), 'this' might refer forwards to the ensuing phrase, but the colon probably marks an emphatic pause, and 'thus dearly' is the jewel's literal cost.

129 **hire** fee.

130 **you** Iachimo and Innogen (Warren).

132 **Of . . . of** About one who is thought well of. Some editors think the phrase seems cryptic and unfinished: possibly Posthumus interrupts Philario and one should print 'of–'.

133 **colted** mounted.

135 **Worthy . . . pressing** An Ovidian echo:

'How apt her breasts were to be pressed by me' (*Amores*, 1.5.20).

135 **the** F's error was probably contracted from 'her' in 134.

136–7 **By . . . it** Since everything Iachimo says in this dialogue is technically true, though not quite in the sense that Posthumus takes it, perhaps this remark indicates that at 2.2.39 he had kissed the mole.

139 **stain** (1) mark; (2) blot.

141 **no . . . it** nothing more (in hell) than that single stain.

142 **turns** number of bouts. Compare *Ant.* 2.5.59: 'the best turn i'th'bed'.

POSTHUMUS   No swearing.
     If you will swear you have not done't, you lie,
     And I will kill thee if thou dost deny   145
     Thou'st made me cuckold.
IACHIMO   I'll deny nothing.
POSTHUMUS Oh that I had her here, to tear her limb-meal!
     I will go there and do't i'th'court, before
     Her father. I'll do something.   *Exit*
PHILARIO   Quite besides
     The government of patience! You have won.   150
     Let's follow him, and pervert the present wrath
     He hath against himself.
IACHIMO   With all my heart.
                                                      Exeunt

2.5 *Enter* POSTHUMUS

POSTHUMUS Is there no way for men to be, but women
     Must be half-workers? We are all bastards,

---

151 follow him] F; follow *Taylor*   Act 2, Scene 5   2.5 *new scene Pope; scene continues in* F

147 limb-meal limb from limb.
149 I'll . . . something Reminiscent of the derangement of tragic heroes in states of extreme anguish, such as *Lear* 2.4.279–82 and *Oth.* 4.1.200. There is a passing similarity to Atreus in Seneca's *Thyestes*, 267–70, formulating his horrible plan to kill Thyestes' children and feed them to their father: see Miola, *Tragedy*, p. 200.
149 besides out of. Compare *TN* 4.2.86: 'How fell you besides your five wits?'
151 follow him Taylor reads 'follow', conjecturing that the pronoun was interpolated into an otherwise regular line.
151 pervert turn aside.

Act 2, Scene 5
2.5 Posthumus, Iachimo and Philario having left the stage by one of the two doors at the back of the stage, Posthumus immediately reenters by the other. F does not mark a new scene at this point, and Posthumus's reentry indicates that his monologue continues the action. But although the general locale is unchanged, a new area seems to be implied, so I follow other editors in beginning another scene. Compare Middleton's *Changeling* (1622), 3.1.10, where De Flores hangs some swords by one door, then leaves and reenters at the other

as if in a nearby spot. In Kyd's *Spanish Tragedy*, 1587, 3.11.8, the SD '*He goeth in at one door and comes out at another*' is a device that signals mental distraction.
1 be exist.
2 half-workers collaborators. A standard misogynist trope, found widely in seventeenth century literature: for example, Milton's *Paradise Lost*, X, 888–95. The ultimate source is Euripides' *Hippolytus* (transl. P. Vellacott, 1953), 616–00: 'O Zeus! Why have you established in the sunlit world this counterfeit coin, woman, to curse the human race? If you desired to plant a mortal stock, why must the means for this be woman? A better plan would be for men to come to your temples and put down a price in bronze, or iron, or weight of gold, and buy their sons in embryo, for a sum befitting each man's wealth. Then they could live at home like free men – without women.' The misogyny of Hippolytus in Seneca's *Phaedra* is very similar, though the idea is not precisely repeated.
2 bastards because the chastity of even the saintliest woman cannot be trusted. Posthumus's misogyny calls in question his genetic connection with his father, since if his mother was unfaithful – like all women – his father could have been anyone.

And that most venerable man which I
Did call my father was I know not where
When I was stamped. Some coiner with his tools   5
Made me a counterfeit; yet my mother seemed
The Dian of that time; so doth my wife
The nonpareil of this. Oh vengeance, vengeance!

Othello comp. Me of my lawful pleasure she restrained,
And prayed me oft forbearance; did it with   10
A pudency so rosy, the sweet view on't
Might well have warmed old Saturn – that I thought her
As chaste as unsunned snow. Oh, all the devils!
This yellow Iachimo in an hour – was't not? –
Or less – at first? Perchance he spoke not, but   15
Like a full-acorned boar, a German one,

---

12 *Pope;* Might . . . Saturne; / That . . . her F   16 a German one] *Rowe;* a Iarmen on F

5 stamped (1) engendered; (2) impressed, like a coin: hence the imagery of false stamping that follows.

5 coiner counterfeiter.

5 tools (1) equipment for coin-making; (2) sexual organs.

7 Dian most chaste woman, as if she were the goddess Diana.

8 nonpareil person without equal.

8 vengeance Posthumus slips into tragic mode, a tormented Senecan hero seeking relief in revenge.

9 lawful pleasure sexual pleasure allowed within marriage (see *OED* lawful *a* 2c).

10 prayed . . . forbearance entreated me to refrain.

11 pudency bashfulness (*OED*'s earliest cited instance).

11 rosy i.e., from her blushes.

12 Saturn The most ancient Roman deity, hence a type of unimaginable old age, associated with melancholy and coldness.

13 chaste . . . snow proverbial: Tilley, I1, 'as chaste as ice (snow)'. Posthumus appears confused about whether Innogen is hot ('rosy') or cold, and

seems to find her 'pudency' arousing: the contradictions in his language suggest the conflicting emotions he is struggling with. Compare 5.4.180:–1: 'He spake of her as Dian had hot dreams, / And she alone were cold.'

14 yellow sallow(?); a simple insult, or perhaps alluding to Iachimo's more Mediterranean complexion. Yellow is the colour of jealousy, as at *WT* 2.3.104–7.

15 at first at once; as soon as he met her.

16 full-acorned well-fed, hence sexually aroused; perhaps also carrying the suggestion 'with huge testicles'(?). This is *OED*'s earliest example of this word. The boar and violent sexual arousal are associated in *Ven.* 1111–16.

16 German Rowe's emendation has been generally accepted, and is supported by *2H4* 2.1.145 (where in the 1600 quarto 'German' is printed as 'Iarman'), and by 'Iarman' in Hand D of *Sir Thomas More*, 128. Presumably Posthumus has in mind the size and fierceness of German wild boar, and the comparison further insults Iachimo, to whom, as a Roman, Germany was home to barbarians. There may be a remote pun on 'germen' = seed, sperm.

Cried 'Oh!' and mounted; found no opposition
But what he looked for should oppose, and she
Should from encounter guard. Could I find out
The woman's part in me – for there's no motion   20
That tends to vice in man, but I affirm
It is the woman's part: be it lying, note it,
The woman's; flattering, hers; deceiving, hers;
Lust and rank thoughts, hers, hers; revenges, hers;
Ambitions, covetings, change of prides, disdain,   25
Nice longing, slanders, mutability,
All faults that earth can name, nay, that hell knows,
Why hers, in part, or all, but rather all;
For even to vice
They are not constant, but are changing still   30
One vice but of a minute old for one
Not half so old as that. I'll write against them,
Detest them, curse them; yet 'tis greater skill
In a true hate, to pray they have their will:
The very devils cannot plague them better.   *Exit*   35

---

27 earth can name] *this edn (conj. Taylor)*; name F; may be nam'd F2; have a name *conj. Dyce;* man may name *Walker;* name may name *Vaughan*   **28–9** *Capell;* one line in F   **30 still**] *Johnson;* still; F

18 what . . . oppose what he expected to find placed against him. Barton (00) takes this to mean that the newly married Innogen was still a virgin, though this leaves a problem with the suggestion at 9–10 that Posthumus already had sexual knowledge of her.

19 encounter A word with specific sexual connotations, as in *Tro.* 3.2.205: 'which bed, because it shall not speak of your pretty encounters, press it to death'.

20 motion impulse.

20–8 Posthumus modulates from specific accusations about Innogen to a tirade against 'women' in general.

21 to towards.

24 rank licentious.

25 change of prides continually varying extravagances (*prides* = gorgeous finery: *OED* pride *sb* 7). Compare *Son.* 76: 'Why is my verse so barren of new pride, / So far from variation or quick change?'

26 Nice longing pernicketiness; or perhaps, wanton appetites (as in *LLL* 3.1.19–21: 'These are compliments, these are humours, these betray nice wenches, that would be betrayed without these').

26 mutability fickleness.

27–32 F's text is clearly disturbed at this point, possibly because of some imperfectly assimilated revisions. For full discussion, see Longer Notes, p. 250.

30 still continuously.

33 Detest Denounce (*OED* detest *v* 1). Posthumus's response to betrayal resembles that of Claudio in *Ado* 4.1.56 ('Out on thee seeming! I will write against it'), a parallel that reinforces the impression of posturing and of collapse from tragic anguish into bombast. The soliloquy *has* to tail off, since Posthumus has no role for the next two acts, and his descent into fustian links him once more with Cloten, who ended 2.3 speechless with outrage.

33 skill expertness (*OED* skill *sb* 6); artistry (in hate).

35 The rhyme at 33–4 shows the scene has finished, but Posthumus's anger overflows the measure.

3.1 *Enter in state* CYMBELINE, QUEEN, CLOTEN, *and* LORDS *at one door, and at another,* CAIUS LUCIUS *and attendants*

CYMBELINE Now, say, what would Augustus Caesar with us?
LUCIUS When Julius Caesar – whose remembrance yet
        Lives in men's eyes, and will to ears and tongues
        Be theme and hearing ever – was in this Britain
        And conquered it, Cassibelan thine uncle,   5
        Famous in Caesar's praises no whit less
        Than in his feats deserving it, for him
        And his succession granted Rome a tribute,
        Yearly three thousand pounds, which by thee lately
        Is left untendered.
QUEEN   And, to kill the marvel,   10
        Shall be so ever.
CLOTEN   There be many Caesars

Act 3, Scene 1   3.1 *Actus Tertius, Scena Prima.* F   12 There] F; There will *(Taylor, after Warburton)*

Act 3, Scene 1

3.1 The invasion is entirely unhistorical and is developed from some slight hints in Holinshed's *History of England*. Holinshed reports that after Caesar's death the Britons declined to pay the tribute he had imposed on them, and that Augustus three times planned to invade Britain so as to levy it, but each time was diverted by more pressing affairs elsewhere. Holinshed gives these testimonies no great weight, and reports that other sources describe Cymbeline's reign as a time of friendship with Rome. See Bullough, VIII, 43–4.

0 SD *in state* The direction indicates that this would have been a grand ceremonial scene, reflected in fine costumes and as many supernumeraries as could be mustered. Presumably Lucius's 'attendants' would be other Romans in his party, though they could be British lords since a welcoming delegation has been sent to him (2.3.52–8). The text does not specifically provide any Roman attendants until the 'Captains' of 4.2.332.

2 Julius Caesar who invaded Britain in 55 and 54 BC: see note to 2.4.21 above.

2 remembrance memory.

3 Lives . . . eyes Because of the works he left behind him(?).

4 theme topic.

5 Cassibelan the British chieftain in 54BC: see 1.1.30.

5 uncle great uncle: Cassibelan was brother to Lud, Cymbeline's grandfather. Shakespeare may have been confused by a passing speculation in Holinshed that Cassibelan was Lud's son and so brother to Tenantius, Cymbeline's father.

6 Famous . . . it i.e., his fame came from Caesar's praises of him, and was deserved by his own achievements.

8 succession successors.

9 three thousand pounds i.e., pounds weight of gold, though Elizabethan ears might have heard pounds sterling. The figure is taken from Holinshed (Bullough, VIII, 42).

10 untendered unpaid.

10 to . . . marvel to put an end to wonder (by making nonpayment the normal state of affairs).

11–14 The metre of this speech is very rough, and it is tempting to believe, with Nosworthy, that it is really prose: later in the scene Cloten speaks only prose. In lineating I assume a hefty pause after 'Julius', and that 'A world . . . pay' is one line (Pope's lineation, expanding 'Britain's' to 'Britain is'). Taylor's suggestion that 'will' has dropped out of 11 is also attractive.

11 be will be.

       Ere such another Julius. Britain's
       A world by itself, and we will nothing pay
       For wearing our own noses.
QUEEN   That opportunity
       Which then they had to take from's, to resume   15
       We have again. Remember, sir, my liege,
       The kings your ancestors, together with
       The natural bravery of your isle, which stands
       As Neptune's park, ribbed and paled in
       With oaks unscalable and roaring waters,   20
       With sands that will not bear your enemies' boats,
       But suck them up to th'topmast. A kind of conquest

12–13 Britain's / A world by] *Pope (subst.);* Britaine's a world / By F   20 oaks] F *(Oakes); rocks Hanmer (conj. Theobald); banks Taylor, conj. Wells (bākes)*

12–13 **Britain's . . . itself** A tag expressing the completeness and separateness of the British Isles, which derives from Virgil's first *Eclogue*, 66, 'et penitus toto divisus orbe Britannos' (the Britons quite cut off from the world). Supposedly expressing the surprise of Roman travellers at discovering another land beyond Europe's northern edge, it was often used in Stuart royal panegyric to underwrite the British Union and, incidentally, to voice an attitude of noninvolvement in Europe. Jonson alluded to it in the 1604 royal entry ('Orbis Britannicus, Divisus ab orbe . . . to show that this empire is a world divided from the world') and frequently in his court masques (*Ben Jonson*, VII, 84, 364, 368). Such isolationism will be pointedly rejected by Innogen (3.4.134–9). See Bennett, pp. 114–40, and Introduction, pp. 40, 44.

14 **for . . . noses** for being ourselves. A jibe at the Roman nose (also at 36).

15 **resume** take back.

16 **my liege** The Queen slips into a chivalric form of address that fits her pose of patriotic defiance, harking back as it does to the rhetoric of Shakespeare's Histories. Her account of Britain's natural separateness strongly recollects John of Gaunt's praise of the 'sceptred isle' (*R2* 2.1.40–68): see Introduction, p. 43.

17 **ancestors** At this time very little factual information was known about pre-Caesarian Britain, but in his *History of the Kings of Britain*, the medieval chronicler Geoffrey of Monmouth had invented a complete genealogy of mythical rulers between Brute, the first king, and Cassibelan. The Queen voices the Galfridian view that Britain existed as an independent state long before the Romans arrived, but by 1610 this idea was start-

ing to look like bad history.

18 **bravery** state of defiance.

19 **Neptune** In Stuart iconography Neptune, god of the sea, often represented the patron deity of the island: compare Jonson's masque *Neptune's Triumph for the Return of Albion* (1624). According to Geoffrey of Monmouth, Albion, the original ruler before Brute, was Neptune's son. Note that this allusion reverses *R2* 2.1.62–3, which describes the island as threatened by 'the envious siege / Of watery Neptune': here Neptune's defences protect Britain from foreign attack.

19 **ribbed . . . in** enclosed (like ribs around a body) and fenced in (like a *park* or protected enclosure).

20 **oaks unscalable** i.e., the densely afforested British coastline, resembling the perimeter of a deer park, with its high wooden paling, perhaps echoing Cloten's image of Innogen as a hunted deer (2.3.64–5). Many editors, thinking that Britain's cliffs are meant, emend F's 'Oakes' to 'rocks'. However, this is to anticipate the 'rocks' of line 29, and no alteration is necessary, for the image follows on logically from 'Neptune's park' (19) and is comprehensible as it stands. Caesar's *The Gallic War* (V, 1) details the difficulties he had in finding a place to land. Compare also Ben Jonson's masque *Love Restored* (1610), 75–6, in which the spirit Robin Goodfellow, attempting to climb over various walls and fences in order to gain access to the court, likens the tall yeomen of the guard to 'oaks . . . upon whose arm I hung' and past whom he cannot make way.

22 **topmast** upper section of the mast: all that is left of the ships once they are sucked into Britain's quicksands.

Caesar made here, but made not here his brag
Of 'Came, and saw, and overcame'. With shame –
The first that ever touched him – he was carried   25
From off our coast, twice beaten; and his shipping,
Poor ignorant baubles, on our terrible seas
Like eggshells moved upon their surges, cracked
As easily 'gainst our rocks. For joy whereof
The famed Cassibelan, who was once at point –   30
O giglot Fortune! – to master Caesar's sword,
Made Lud's Town with rejoicing fires bright,
And Britons strut with courage.

CLOTEN Come, there's no more tribute to be paid. Our kingdom is
stronger than it was at that time, and, as I said, there is no moe   35
such Caesars. Other of them may have crook'd noses, but to owe
such straight arms, none.

CYMBELINE Son, let your mother end.

CLOTEN We have yet many among us can gripe as hard as Cassibelan.
I do not say I am one, but I have a hand. Why tribute? Why should   40
we pay tribute? If Caesar can hide the sun from us with a blanket,
or put the moon in his pocket, we will pay him tribute for light;
else, sir, no more tribute, pray you now.

---

35 moe] F *(mo)*; more F2

24 **Came . . . overcame** Caesar's boast at the battle of Zela (in Asia Minor), 47 BC; reported in Plutarch's *Life of Caesar*, 1.1.21, 2.2.97.

26 **twice beaten** The Queen is following the account of Caesar's invasions popularized by Geoffrey of Monmouth, whose *History* is very hostile to Caesar. Geoffrey describes Caesar as suffering two humiliating defeats and flying shamefully from Cassibelan: he eventually conquers only through the treachery of a disaffected British noble (*History of the Kings of Britain*, IV, 3–8). This story does not correspond with Caesar's own narrative but it was widely known to medieval and Renaissance historians: see Nearing, 889–929, and the full discussion in the Introduction, p. 42.

27 **ignorant** uninformed (applied figuratively to the ships' unawareness of the tides: *OED* ignorant *sb* 1b).

27 **baubles** toys.

28–9 **cracked . . . rocks** Caesar writes that both his invasions were hit by violent storms: *Gallic War*, V, 1–2.

30–1 **once . . . sword** Geoffrey's claim that Caesar lost his sword in hand-to-hand combat with the Britons (*History of the Kings of Britain*, IV, 3) is repeated in Holinshed (Bullough, VIII, 42), though

in this fanciful episode the Briton responsible is Cassibelan's brother, Nennius.

31 **giglot** fickle; whorish. Fortune is called a 'giglot' in Ben Jonson's *Sejanus* (1603), 5.206; a play in which Shakespeare acted.

32 **Lud's Town** Supposedly the old name of London, deriving from Cymbeline's grandfather King Lud, and surviving in such names as Ludgate.

32 **rejoicing fires** Geoffrey describes elaborate British celebrations after Caesar's first defeat (*History of the Kings of Britain*, IV, 8).

34–43 Cloten's speeches deliberately interrupt the decorum of the scene, but are they an afterthought by Shakespeare? Without them the half-lines at 33 and 44 would dovetail perfectly, and it is tempting to suppose that Shakespeare inserted them belatedly, after he had drafted the verse passages. Given the roughness of 11–14, perhaps the whole of Cloten's contribution to this confrontation was added in later.

35 **moe** more.
36 **owe** own.
37 **straight** strong.
39 **gripe** grapple (looking back to 30–1).
43 **else** otherwise.
43 **sir** i.e., Cymbeline.

CYMBELINE You must know,
    Till the injurious Romans did extort   45
    This tribute from us, we were free. Caesar's ambition,
    Which swelled so much that it did almost stretch
    The sides o'th'world, against all colour here
    Did put the yoke upon's, which to shake off
    Becomes a warlike people, whom we reckon   50
    Ourselves to be. We do say then to Caesar,
    Our ancestor was that Mulmutius which
    Ordained our laws, whose use the sword of Caesar
    Hath too much mangled, whose repair and franchise
    Shall, by the power we hold, be our good deed,   55
    Though Rome be therefore angry. Mulmutius made our laws,
    Who was the first of Britain which did put
    His brows within a golden crown and called
    Himself a king.
LUCIUS   I am sorry, Cymbeline,
    That I am to pronounce Augustus Caesar –   60
    Caesar, that hath moe kings his servants than
    Thyself domestic officers – thine enemy.
    Receive it from me, then: war and confusion
    In Caesar's name pronounce I 'gainst thee. Look
    For fury not to be resisted. Thus defied,   65

---

51 be. We do say] *Malone;* be, we do. Say F

45 **injurious** hurtful; or perhaps, insulting.
46 **free** Cymbeline picks up the Queen's Galfridian rhetoric: Geoffrey strongly emphasizes the status of the Britons as a free people, menaced by greedy and self-serving Roman imperialism.
48 **sides . . . world** *Ant.* 1.2.192 uses the same phrase to express limitless geographical parameters; and compare the account of Antony as a colossus at *Ant.* 5.2.79–86.
48 **against all colour** without any pretence of right.
51 **We do** F awkwardly attaches 'we do' to the preceding sentence (see collation); the easiest solution is Malone's simple change to the punctuation. For the emphatic idiom see *H8* 5.1.97–9: 'I have . . . Heard many grievous – I do say, / Grievous – complaints of you'; and Fletcher and Massinger's *Beggar's Bush*: 'Sir, I do say, she is no merchandize' (*B&F*, III, 272). Cymbeline's royal 'We' looks forward to 'Our' (52). The suggestion by the Globe editors that 'We do' was interjected by Cloten and

the British Lords comes straight out of Victorian melodrama.
52 **Mulmutius** Dunwallo Mulmutius: in Geoffrey and Holinshed a British king from the fourth century BC, and son to Cloten, King of Cornwall. He pacified the realm after the civil war between Ferrex and Porrex, established weights and measures, and invented laws that (Geoffrey claimed) survived in the Anglo-Saxon legal code.
54 **franchise** free exercise.
56 The repetition of 'Mulmutius made our laws' (53), and the line's awkwardness and excessive length, may be further signs of Shakespeare's second thoughts in this scene.
57–9 **the first . . . king** Geoffrey says Mulmutius was the first king of the whole island.
60 **pronounce** proclaim.
61 **moe . . . servants** Compare *Ant.* 3.12.5: 'Which had superfluous kings for messengers' (Maxwell).
65 **Thus defied** Having issued this declaration.

I thank thee for myself.

CYMBELINE   Thou art welcome, Caius.
Thy Caesar knighted me; my youth I spent
Much under him; of him I gathered honour,
Which he to seek of me again, perforce,
Behoves me keep at utterance. I am perfect   70
That the Pannonians and Dalmatians for
Their liberties are now in arms, a precedent
Which not to read would show the Britons cold;
So Caesar shall not find them.

LUCIUS   Let proof speak.

CLOTEN His majesty bids you welcome. Make pastime with us a day   75
or two, or longer. If you seek us afterwards in other terms, you
shall find us in our salt-water girdle. If you beat us out of it, it is
yours; if you fall in the adventure, our crows shall fare the better
for you, and there's an end.

LUCIUS So, sir.   80

CYMBELINE I know your master's pleasure, and he mine.
All the remain is 'Welcome'.

Exeunt

3.2 *Enter* PISANIO, *reading of a letter*

PISANIO How? Of adultery? Wherefore write you not
What monster's her accuser? Leonatus,
O master, what a strange infection

Act 3, Scene 2   3.2 *Scena Secunda.* F   2 accuser] *Capell;* accuse F

68 **Thy ... me** Holinshed reports that Cymbeline was educated at Rome, knighted by Augustus,
and served in his wars (Bullough, VIII, 43). Such
an upbringing in aristocratic service resembles the
career pattern of many a gentleman in Renaissance
Europe.

69 **he ... again** (now) he intends to reclaim it
from me. For the pronoun + infinitive construction, see Abbott, #356, #216.

70 **keep at utterance** defend (it) to the death.
From the French, *à l'outrance*, with a hint of chivalric defiance: compare *Mac.* 3.170–1, 'come fate into
the list, / And champion me to th'utterance'.

70 **perfect** well informed.

71 **Pannonians, Dalmatians** inhabitants of
Roman provinces, in modern Hungary and the
Adriatic. Holinshed says that these rebellions
diverted Augustus from his design of invad-

ing Britain, but dates them to Tenantius's reign
(Bullough, VIII, 44).

73 **read** interpret.

73 **cold** without spirit.

77 **salt-water girdle** i.e., the sea, as Britain's
protective barrier. Compare Jonson's masque
Hymenaei, 1606: 'No less . . . bound within his
realms / Than they are with the Ocean's streams'
(*Ben Jonson*, VII, 225).

78 **adventure** attempt.

82 **the remain** that remains.

Act 3, Scene 2

1 How? What?

2 **monster's her accuser** monster accuses her.
F prints 'Monsters her accuse', but the inversion
is inappropriately poetic at this moment, and the
'false Italian' (4) shows that the compositor has
incorrectly read the possessive noun as a plural.

Is fall'n into thy ear? What false Italian,
As poisonous tongued as handed, hath prevailed   5
On thy too ready hearing? Disloyal? No.
She's punished for her truth, and undergoes,
More goddess-like than wife-like, such assaults
As would take in some virtue. O my master,
Thy mind to hers is now as low as were   10
Thy fortunes. How? That I should murder her,
Upon the love and truth and vows which I
Have made to thy command? I, her? Her blood?
If it be so to do good service, never
Let me be counted serviceable. How look I,   15
That I should seem to lack humanity
So much as this fact comes to? [*Reads*] 'Do't: the letter
That I have sent her, by her own command
Shall give thee opportunity'. O damned paper,
Black as the ink that's on thee! Senseless bauble,   20
Art thou a fedary for this act, and look'st
So virgin-like without? Lo, here she comes.

Enter INNOGEN

I am ignorant in what I am commanded.
INNOGEN How now, Pisanio?
PISANIO Madam, here is a letter from my lord.   25

---

10 hers] *Hanmer;* her F   17 SD] *Rowe (subst.); not in* F

---

4 into thy ear As in *Oth.* 2.3.323: 'I'll pour this pestilence into his ear' (Maxwell).

4 Italian supposed to be experts in poisoning. One of the play's shifts between ancient and modern: Lucius's 'Rome' is replaced with Iachimo's more contemporary 'Italy'.

5 As . . . tongued As poisonous in his tongue (as he is capable of poisoning by hand).

7 truth loyalty.

7 undergoes endures.

9 take in conquer: picking up the military metaphor of 'assaults' (8).

10–11 Thy . . . fortunes Your mind is now as much below her mind, as your fortunes were beneath hers.

11 How? Another exclamation, like that at line 1. Pisanio works through the letter, and reacts to each astonishing statement.

12 Upon As a consequence of. Maxwell glosses 'On top of', but Pisanio paraphrases as he reads.

14–15 If . . . serviceable A radical sentiment:

the idea that there may be circumstances in which servants are justified in disobeying their masters strikes at the root of many Renaissance assumptions about political obligation. Compare 5.1.5–7, and the behaviour of the servant in *Lear* 3.7.

17 fact crime; deed.

17–19 Do't . . . opportunity Beginning with 'That', F italicizes these words, as a quotation from the letter. They do not appear in the letter as Innogen reads it in 3.4, but the inconsistency is not noticeable in performance.

20 Senseless bauble Insensible trifle.

21 fedary accomplice; confederate. The word is a variant of *foedary* (= a feudal tenant), but Shakespeare, uniquely and through mistaken association with Latin 'foedus' (= covenant), uses it this way. See *OED* fedarie; and instances at *MM* 2.4.122 and *WT* 2.1.90.

23 I am . . . commanded I must give no hint of what I have been told to do.

INNOGEN Who, thy lord that is my lord, Leonatus?
　　　　　Oh, learned indeed were that astronomer
　　　　　That knew the stars as I his characters;
　　　　　He'd lay the future open. You good gods,
　　　　　Let what is here contained relish of love,   30
　　　　　Of my lord's health, of his content – yet not
　　　　　That we two are asunder; let that grieve him.
　　　　　Some griefs are med'cinable; that is one of them,
　　　　　For it doth physic love – of his content
　　　　　All but in that. Good wax, thy leave. Blest be   35
　　　　　You bees that make these locks of counsel! Lovers
　　　　　And men in dangerous bonds pray not alike;
　　　　　Though forfeiters you cast in prison, yet
　　　　　You clasp young Cupid's tables. Good news, gods!

[*Reads*] 'Justice, and your father's wrath, should he take me in   40
his dominion, could not be so cruel to me as you, O the
dearest of creatures, would even renew me with your eyes.
Take notice that I am in Cambria, at Milford Haven.
What your own love will out of this advise you, follow. So
he wishes you all happiness, that remains loyal to his   45
vow, and
　　　　　　　　Your increasing in love
　　　　　　　　Leonatus Posthumus.'

47–8 and / Your . . . love / Leonatus] *this edn; and your . . . Loue.* Leonatus F

26–30 Even before she reads the letter, Innogen's verbal style is effusive and unpredictable, marked by sudden changes of direction and precious comparisons. The Victorian Innogenolators admired her raptures, but Jacobean audiences may have taken such emotional tendencies to be a sign of danger.
　27 **astronomer** astrologer.
　28 **characters** handwriting.
　30 **relish** taste.
　31 **not** i.e., not content.
　33 **are med'cinable** have medicinal value.
　34 **physic** make healthy. Compare *WT* 1.1.20: 'it is a gallant child; one that, indeed, physics the subject, keeps old hearts fresh'.
　35 **but** except.
　35 **thy leave** by thy leave (addressed to the 'wax' sealing the letter).
　36 **locks of counsel** seals on confidential documents.

36–7 **Lovers . . . alike** A sentiment exactly the reverse of Posthumus's views at 5.3.97–8.
　37 **dangerous bonds** risky contracts (which are also protected with waxen seals).
　38 **forfeiters** men who have broken their bonds.
　39 **Cupid's tables** love letters ('tables' are literally writing tablets).
　41 **as** i.e., but that.
　42 **even** completely (Warren): an intensifier.
　43 **Cambria** the ancient Latin name for Wales; supposedly named after Camber, the second son of Brute.
　43–4 **Milford Haven** a seaport in Pembrokeshire, remembered for having been the landing-place of Henry Tudor in 1485. For its historiographical associations, see Introduction, p. 41.
　44 **advise you** i.e., advise you to do.
　46–7 **Your . . . Posthumus** Another of Posthumus's disingenuous epistolary flourishes: compare 1.6.23–4.

O for a horse with wings! Hear'st thou, Pisanio?
He is at Milford Haven. Read, and tell me   50
How far 'tis thither. If one of mean affairs
May plod it in a week, why may not I
Glide thither in a day? Then, true Pisanio,
Who long'st like me to see thy lord, who long'st –
O let me bate! – but not like me – yet long'st   55
But in a fainter kind – O, not like me,
For mine's beyond beyond; say, and speak thick –
Love's counsellor should fill the bores of hearing,
To th'smothering of the sense – how far it is
To this same blessèd Milford. And by th'way   60
Tell me how Wales was made so happy as
T'inherit such a haven. But first of all,
How we may steal from hence; and for the gap
That we shall make in time from our hence-going
And our return, to excuse; but first, how get hence.   65
Why should excuse be born or ere begot?
We'll talk of that hereafter. Prithee speak,
How many score of miles may we well ride
'Twixt hour and hour?
PISANIO   One score 'twixt sun and sun,
Madam, 's enough for you, and too much too.   70
INNOGEN Why, one that rode to's execution, man,
Could never go so slow. I have heard of riding wagers
Where horses have been nimbler than the sands
That run i'th'clock's behalf. But this is fool'ry.

---

57 beyond beyond] *Steevens-Reed 2 (conj. Ritson);* beyond, beyond F   65 And] F; Till *Pope*   65 get] F2; ger F
68 score] F2; store F   68 ride] F2; rid F

51 **mean affairs** ordinary business.
55 **bate** abate; qualify (what I have just said).
56 **fainter** less forceful.
57 **thick** rapidly; one word on top of another.
58 **Love's counsellor** A lover's adviser.
58 **bores of hearing** ears.
59 **sense** i.e., sense of hearing. Pisanio's information is so important that it must crowd out all other sensation.
60 **by** on.

65 **And** The expected construction would be 'from . . . till': 'And' might be a substitution by Compositor E, carried forward from 62. Some editors emend accordingly.
66 **or ere begot** before the need for it arises.
69 **'Twixt . . . hour** From one hour to the next.
71 **execution** (with an obvious irony).
72 **riding wagers** races with bets on them.
74 **i'th'clock's behalf** in place of a clock (in an hourglass).

Go, bid my woman feign a sickness, say   75
She'll home to her father; and provide me presently
A riding-suit, no costlier than would fit
A franklin's housewife.

PISANIO   Madam, you're best consider.

INNOGEN I see before me, man. Not here, nor here,
Nor what ensues, but have a fog in them   80
That I cannot look through. Away, I prithee,
Do as I bid thee. There's no more to say.
Accessible is none but Milford way.

Exeunt

3.3 [*A cave discovered. From it*] *enter* BELARIUS, GUIDERIUS, *and*
ARVIRAGUS

BELARIUS A goodly day not to keep house with such
Whose roof's as low as ours! Stoop, boys; this gate

---

79 Not . . . nor] *Chambers;* nor . . . not F   Act 3, Scene 3   3.3 *Scena Tertia.* F   0 SD *A . . . it*] *this edn; not in* F   2 Stoop]
Hanmer; Sleepe F

---

75 **my woman** Possibly this is the vestige of an
earlier plan for Act 3, as if Shakespeare had first
intended Innogen to travel accompanied by a Lady.
Alternatively, Innogen has to command her woman
to be sent away so that Cymbeline can find her
apartments locked and empty at 3.5.43; but if that
is the case, what has happened to the larger retinue
of ladies that seems to be implied at 2.3.61 and
2.4.116, 124? These off-stage inconsistencies are
knots in the plotting that are never quite resolved
but pass unnoticed in performance.

76 **presently** immediately after.

77 **riding-suit** overcoat, to protect against cold
and rain.

78 **franklin** a small landowner of yeoman status.

78 **you're best** you were best. Maxwell compares *Temp.* 1.2.366, 'thou'rt best', and Abbott,
#230.

79 **I see before me** I see only what is immediately before me – whereas I am ignorant of
things whatever is on either side ('Not here, nor
here'), or beyond the immediate future ('what
ensues').

79 **Not, nor** Many editors emend to 'Nor . . .
nor', but the likeliest mistake is that the compositor
reversed the two words, or that he set up both as
'Not' (or 'nor') and corrected the wrong one. The
same idiom occurs at *MM* 2.2.60–1.

83 **none** no path.

Act 3, Scene 3

0 SD **A cave** Given the command to 'stoop'
(2) and references to the 'rock' (8, 70), it seems
likely that the exiles' cave was represented by a
substantial stage property, probably thrust through
one of the stage's rear openings. Simon Forman's
eyewitness report says that Innogen met her brothers at 'the cave in the woods' (see Introduction,
p. 3). Jacobean stage resources could have matched
this: the Rose Theatre props list of 1598 included
a 'rock', as well as several trees (Henslowe, p. 319).
In Ben Jonson's *Oberon* (1611; performed at Whitehall with elaborate perspective scenery, though not
of the kind available on the noncourt stage),
the masquers entered from a palace hidden inside a
great rock. At the National Theatre in 1988, the
exiles climbed out of a trapdoor that rose in the
centre of the stage.

1–2 **A . . . ours** The first of Belarius's many
homely apophthegms on the theme 'Humble without but great within'. The topos is conventional,
but since the princes are destined for empire, there
may be a pointed reminiscence of Aeneas's visit to
the house of King Evander, which, though on the
future site of Rome, was a simple dwelling. 'Arrived
at the palace, the king said, "Hercules stooped to
enter this door; this humble palace received the
conquering hero"' (*Aeneid*, VIII, 362–3: see Parker,
p. 202).

2 **gate** entrance.

Instructs you how t'adore the heavens, and bows you
To a morning's holy office. The gates of monarchs
Are arched so high that giants may jet through   5
And keep their impious turbans on, without
Good morrow to the sun. Hail, thou fair heaven!
We house i'th'rock, yet use thee not so hardly
As prouder livers do.

GUIDERIUS   Hail, heaven!

ARVIRAGUS   Hail, heaven!

BELARIUS Now for our mountain sport. Up to yon hill,   10
Your legs are young; I'll tread these flats. Consider,
When you above perceive me like a crow,
That it is place which lessens and sets off,
And you may then revolve what tales I have told you
Of courts, of princes, of the tricks in war: 15
This service is not service, so being done,
But being so allowed. To apprehend thus
Draws us a profit from all things we see,
And often to our comfort shall we find

3 **Instructs . . . heavens** i.e., by forcing you to bow. Unlike Cymbeline's court, where Jove is worshipped, the exiles observe a theologically nonspecific religion, in which reasons for piety are imbibed from the natural world. This culminates with the pagan materialism of the dirge in 4.2; and compare also 4.4.41.

4 **office** ceremony.

5 **giants** Often thought of as Saracen, hence the 'turbans' (6), a detail that intensifies the scene's romance coloration: in Spenser's *The Faerie Queene*, the giant Disdain wears 'on his head a roll of linnen plight, / Like to the Mores of Malaber' (6.7.43). Holinshed and Geoffrey of Monmouth say that Britain's first inhabitants were giants, who were expelled by Brute, and gigantic ancestral figures sometimes appeared in civic pageants (Venezky, p. 176). As descendants of the Titans, giants were enemies to Jove, the deity of this play: see *The Faerie Queene* 2.7.41, 3.7.47.

5 **jet** strut.

8 **thee** i.e., heaven.

8 **so hardly** with such callousness: the rock's literal hardness contrasts with the hard hearts of 'prouder livers' who inhabit luxurious surroundings.

11–26 For the relationship between Belarius's views on the superiority of country over court and hermit figures in romance, see Introduction, p. 12.

11 **these flats** this plain.

12 **like a** as small as.

13 **place** (1) physical position (2) status.

13 **sets off** enhances.

14 **revolve** consider.

15 **tricks** accidents.

16 **This service** Any particular act of service: in public life services are measured not by their intrinsic value but by how they are 'allowed' (= acknowledged). For the idiom compare *Mac.* 1.7.10: 'this even-handed justice'. Taylor suspects an error and emends 'This' to 'That', but the line is explicable as it stands: Belarius offers the proposition as fact, and does not expect the boys to 'revolve' it any further.

17 **apprehend thus** view things in this way.

The sharded beetle in a safer hold   20
Than is the full-winged eagle. O, this life
Is nobler than attending for a check,
Richer than doing nothing for a bribe,
Prouder than rustling in unpaid-for silk;
Such gain the cap of him that makes them fine,   25
Yet keeps his book uncrossed. No life to ours.

GUIDERIUS Out of your proof you speak. We, poor unfledged,
Have never winged from view o'th'nest, nor know not
What air's from home. Haply this life is best,
If quiet life be best; sweeter to you   30
That have a sharper known, well corresponding
With your stiff age; but unto us it is
A cell of ignorance, travelling abed,
A prison for a debtor that not dares
To stride a limit.

ARVIRAGUS   What should we speak of   35
When we are old as you? When we shall hear

---

23 bribe] *Hanmer;* Babe F; bauble *Rowe*   25 them] *Rowe;* him F   26 keeps] F; keep *Hudson*   28 know] F2; knowes F   33
travelling] F *(trauailing)*   34 for] *Pope;* or F

20 The . . . eagle This commendation of the
humble life derives from Aesop's *The Scarab and
the Eagle*, a fable elaborately discussed in Erasmus's
Adages (Baldwin, I, 634–5).

20 sharded encased in dung: hence, most lowly.
The shard beetle (so called because often found
in dung) was anciently thought to be born from
dung: see Stephanus's Greek dictionary as cited by
Baldwin, I, 635. The modern view that 'shards'
means 'wing-cases' apparently derives from Dr
Johnson's gloss on 'the shard-born [F: borne]
beetle' in *Mac.* 3.3.42, which euphemized the
phrase to mean 'borne aloft on wings'. *Shards* are
commonly taken as *wings* after Johnson's edition,
but not before. Compare *OED* shard; and David
Bevington's excellent note on *Ant.* 3.2.20 (New
Cambridge Shakespeare).

22 attending . . . check waiting (at court), only
to receive a rebuke.

23 bribe F's 'babe' is clearly wrong, and
Hanmer's emendation gives best sense. An ri/a
misreading would be easy, and 'bribe' fits with
Belarius's bitter reflections on court life. Many editors emend to 'bauble' (supposing that the copy
read 'bable'). This is possible but is metrically less
satisfactory, and involves a complicated metaphorical shift: bauble = worthless trifle = badge of
empty honour. And in the two preceding scenes,
'bauble' appears without any hint of compositorial

misreading (3.1.27, 3.2.20).

25–6 Such . . . uncrossed 'Such people are rev-
erenced by [*gain the cap of*] the tailor who has set
them out, yet their debts remain uncancelled in his
ledger.' In F this passage seems manifestly corrupt,
but it is difficult to know where to stop emending.
Rowe's 'them' assumes that 'him' in 'makes him'
was carried forward from earlier in the line, yet 26
still feels ungrammatical and possibly Hudson is
correct in changing 'keepes' to 'keep' (which supposes that 'keepes' was picked up from 'makes').

27 proof experience.

27 unfledged (harking back to the eagle, 21).

29 What . . . home What other places are like.

29 Haply Perhaps.

33 travelling abed travel in the mind only; day-
dreaming.

34–5 that . . . limit i.e., because he will be
arrested if he steps beyond the threshold. Many
editors defend F's 'or', as a turn of speech no bolder
than other instances in this play, but a simpler
explanation is that Compositor E dropped a letter.

35–44 Though romanticized, the exiles' country retreat is a 'hard' pastoral, lacking the comforts of civilized life and felt by the boys to be
barbaric. For its relationship to ideas of Britain
before the arrival of the Romans, see Introduction,
pp. 45–9.

The rain and wind beat dark December, how,
In this our pinching cave, shall we discourse
The freezing hours away? We have seen nothing.
We are beastly: subtle as the fox for prey,   40
Like warlike as the wolf for what we eat.
Our valour is to chase what flies; our cage
We make a choir, as doth the prisoned bird,
And sing our bondage freely.

BELARIUS   How you speak!
Did you but know the city's usuries,   45
And felt them knowingly; the art o'th'court,
As hard to leave as keep, whose top to climb
Is certain falling, or so slipp'ry that
The fear's as bad as falling; the toil o'th'war,
A pain that only seems to seek out danger   50
I'th'name of fame and honour, which dies i'th'search
And hath as oft a sland'rous epitaph,
As record of fair act – nay, many times
Doth ill deserve by doing well; what's worse,
Must curtsy at the censure. O boys, this story   55
The world may read in me: my body's marked
With Roman swords, and my report was once
First with the best of note. Cymbeline loved me,

---

40 beastly: subtle] *after* F; beastly-subtle *Maxwell*

38 **pinching** narrow; or possibly, cold.
40 **beastly** no better than beasts.
41 **Like warlike as** No more warlike than.
42 **Our . . . flies** i.e., It is no valour, because wasted on a fearful adversary.
44 **sing . . . freely** i.e., we voluntarily praise our condition, blind to the fact that it is imprisonment.
45–55 A poetic set-piece contrasting the happiness of the country life with the disadvantages of the city, court and camp. The classic models for such a comparison are Virgil's second *Georgic* and Horace's second *Epode*.
45 **usuries** corrupt business practices.
46 **felt** Cambridge's conjecture 'feel' is tempting, and would clarify the confusion between past and present tenses. However, the syntax of 45–55 is loose and is in fact incomplete: although Belarius initiates a series of subordinate clauses, the main clause proposition to which they seem to lead ('then

you would understand that . . .') never quite arrives.
46 **felt . . . knowingly** compare *Lear* 4.6.152: 'I see it feelingly.'
47 **As hard . . . keep** A paradox glossed in the following lines: political office is painful both to achieve and to lose, and its loss is always inevitable. Dover Wilson compares Francis Bacon's 'Of Great Place': 'The standing is slippery, and the regress is either a downfall, or at least an eclipse' (*Essays*, p. 24).
50 **pain** labour.
50 **only** modifying 'seek' rather than 'seems' (Furness).
51 **which** i.e., 'pain' (50), here lightly personified: 'Labour seeks fame and honour, but, perishing, has slanders for its epitaph.'
54 **deserve** earn.
55 **curtsy . . . censure** bow to the judgement.
57 **report** reputation.

And when a soldier was the theme, my name
Was not far off. Then was I as a tree   60
Whose boughs did bend with fruit; but in one night,
A storm or robbery, call it what you will,
Shook down my mellow hangings, nay, my leaves,
And left me bare to weather.

GUIDERIUS   Uncertain favour!

BELARIUS My fault being nothing, as I have told you oft,   65
But that two villains, whose false oaths prevailed
Before my perfect honour, swore to Cymbeline
I was confederate with the Romans. So
Followed my banishment, and this twenty years
This rock and these demesnes have been my world,   70
Where I have lived at honest freedom, paid
More pious debts to heaven than in all
The fore-end of my time. But up to th'mountains!
This is not hunters' language. He that strikes
The venison first shall be the lord o'th'feast;   75
To him the other two shall minister,
And we will fear no poison, which attends
In place of greater state. I'll meet you in the valleys.

                                   Exeunt [*Guiderius and Arviragus*]

How hard it is to hide the sparks of nature!
These boys know little they are sons to th'King,   80
Nor Cymbeline dreams that they are alive.
They think they are mine, and though trained up thus meanly

---

78 *Hanmer;* In . . . State: / Ile . . . Valleyes. F   78 SD] *Theobald; Exeunt.* F   82 *Rowe;* They . . . mine, / And . . .
meanely F

60–1 tree . . . fruit a stock image for court
favour. Compare *The Duchess of Malfi*: 'He and his
brother are like plum trees . . . rich and o'erladen
with fruit, but none but crows, pies and caterpillars
feed on them' (Webster, I, 474).

63 mellow hangings ripe fruit.

67 perfect unsullied.

69 this possibly a compositorial error for 'these',
substituted by anticipation of 'This rock' (70).
Compare 'these twenty years' (5.4.337).

70 demesnes regions. Warren modernizes to
'domains'.

71 at in.

73 fore-end . . . time earlier part of my life.

76 minister act as servant.

77 attends is present.

78 place . . . state any more elevated world (i.e.,
in courts).

79–107 Like Cornelius's aside at 1.5.33–44, this
speech adopts the simplest possible narrative style,
resembling the naive expository devices of Elizabethan stage romance. Its language is at the furthest
possible remove from Iachimo's artful sophistication.

82 trained up educated.

82 meanly humbly.

I'th'cave wherein they bow, their thoughts do hit
The roofs of palaces, and nature prompts them
In simple and low things to prince it much   85
Beyond the trick of others. This Polydore,
The heir of Cymbeline and Britain, who
The King his father called Guiderius – Jove!
When on my three-foot stool I sit and tell
The warlike feats I have done, his spirits fly out   90
Into my story; say 'Thus mine enemy fell,
And thus I set my foot on's neck', even then
The princely blood flows in his cheek, he sweats,
Strains his young nerves, and puts himself in posture
That acts my words. The younger brother, Cadwal,   95
Once Arviragus, in as like a figure
Strikes life into my speech, and shows much more
His own conceiving.
                    [*A hunting-horn sounds*]
                    Hark, the game is roused!
O Cymbeline, heaven and my conscience knows
Thou didst unjustly banish me, whereon   100
At three and two years old I stole these babes,
Thinking to bar thee of succession as

---

83 wherein they bow] *Warburton;* whereon the Bowe F   86 Polydore] *Rowe (subst.); Paladour* F   98, 107 SD] *Collier 2*
(subst.); not in F

83 **wherein they bow** The usual emendation
for F's very opaque phrase. Belarius is reiterating
his views on the value of pastoral humility (1–26),
the low surroundings within which the boys' innate
princeliness is confined. Compare the account of
Caesar's ambition, which 'stretch[ed] / The sides
o'th'world' (3.1.47–8).
    83–4 **hit . . . palaces** Possibly echoing Ben Jon-
son's *Sejanus* (1603), 5.1.7–9: 'My roof receives me
not . . . / And at each step I feel my advanced
head/Knock out a star in heaven.'
    84 **nature . . . them** Characters whose seem-
ingly 'wild' state conceals an underlying civility
often recur in pastoral and romance contexts: for
example, Sir Satyrane and the 'savage man' in
Spenser's *The Faerie Queene* 1.6 and 6.4 (see Introduction, p. 12). But as the boys are aristocrats by
lineage, their 'nature' is a sign of their hidden status, and so is very like that of Perdita in *WT*.
    85 **prince it** behave like princes: compare *WT*

4.4.449: 'I'll queen it no inch further.'
    86 **trick** knack.
    94 **nerves** sinews.
    96 **in . . . figure** in a similar pose.
    98 **His own conceiving** His own conception (of
my story): his response is even more eager than
Guiderius's.
    98 **roused** alerted.
    99–107 Taylor conjectures that these lines were
interpolated at a late stage of composition. He suggests that the repetition of 'the game is roused
/ The game is up' and the off-stage sound, and
the huddled way in which narrative detail is supplied, are telltale signs of revision. This is possible,
though the passage does not seem as unintegrated
as Taylor claims (this is all information that Belarius needs to give), and 'roused / up' is not a simple
repetition but a sequence suggesting a hunt getting
under way.
    102 **succession** successors.

Thou refts me of my lands. Euriphile,
Thou wast their nurse; they took thee for their mother,
And every day do honour to her grave.   105
Myself, Belarius, that am Morgan called,
They take for natural father.
             [*A hunting-horn sounds*]
                        The game is up.   *Exit*

3.4 *Enter* PISANIO *and* INNOGEN [*in a riding-suit*]

INNOGEN Thou told'st me, when we came from horse, the place
              Was near at hand. Ne'er longed my mother so
              To see me first as I have now. Pisanio, man,
              Where is Posthumus? What is in thy mind
              That makes thee stare thus? Wherefore breaks that sigh   5
              From th'inward of thee? One but painted thus
              Would be interpreted a thing perplexed
              Beyond self-explication. Put thyself
              Into a haviour of less fear, ere wildness
              Vanquish my staider senses. What's the matter?   10
                    [PISANIO *gives her a letter*]
              Why tender'st thou that paper to me with
              A look untender? If't be summer news,
              Smile to't before; if winterly, thou need'st

---

106 Morgan] *Rowe; Morgan* F   Act 3, Scene 4   3.4 *Scena Quarta.* F   0 SD *in a riding-suit*] *Taylor; not in* F
11 SD] *Capell (subst.); not in* F

103 refts deprived. Compressed from 'reft'st', for the sake of euphony: the same elision as with 'solicits' at 1.6.147.
103 Euriphile Literally, 'Lover of Europe'.
104 nurse i.e., wet-nurse. It was customary in aristocratic families for infants to be suckled by a servant, so Euriphile was a substitute mother even before the princes were stolen. The boys were thus not altogether cut off from family.
105 her sometimes emended to 'your', but such changes of pronoun are not unusual. Compare *Tim.* 1.2.122–3: 'Hail to thee, worthy Timon, and to all / That of his bounties taste.'

Act 3, Scene 4
0 SD The riding-suit is called for at 3.2.76: it is the first of the play's many symbolic shifts of clothing.
1 **came from horse** dismounted. The pretence that the characters have left their horses off-stage is a common device to get round the limitations of the stage: for example, *Mac.* 3.3.11, and P. Massinger,

A New Way to Pay Old Debts, 2.3.60, 3.1.1.
3 **have** i.e., have such a longing to see Posthumus (*Riverside*). Innogen's recollection of her mother just after Belarius's talk of Euriphile creates a momentary link to her brothers even before she has met them.
6 **painted thus** so represented in a painting.
7 **perplexed** distressed.
8 **Beyond self-explication** i.e., incapable of explaining his perplexity even to himself.
9 **haviour . . . fear** less frightening bearing.
10 **staider** more settled.
11–12 **tender'st . . . untender** Innogen puns on *tender* as a verb (*offer*) and an adjective (*kind*), but combines this with the rhetorical figures of epanalepsis (word at beginning of sentence repeated at end) and polyptoton (repetition of word with implied change in meaning) to create a moment of conspicuous linguistic playfulness. A very similar pun is developed by Polonius in *Ham.* 1.3.103–9.
12 **summer** i.e., happy.

But keep that count'nance still. My husband's hand?
That drug-damned Italy hath outcraftied him,   15
And he's at some hard point. Speak, man. Thy tongue
May take off some extremity which to read
Would be even mortal to me.

PISANIO   Please you read,
And you shall find me, wretched man, a thing
The most disdained of fortune.   20

INNOGEN (*reads*) 'Thy mistress, Pisanio, hath played the strumpet in
my bed, the testimonies whereof lies bleeding in me. I speak not
out of weak surmises, but from proof as strong as my grief and
as certain as I expect my revenge. That part thou, Pisanio, must
act for me, if thy faith be not tainted with the breach of hers. Let   25
thine own hands take away her life. I shall give thee opportunity
at Milford Haven – she hath my letter for the purpose – where, if
thou fear to strike and to make me certain it is done, thou art the
pander to her dishonour and equally to me disloyal.'

PISANIO [*Aside*] What shall I need to draw my sword? The paper   30
Hath cut her throat already. No, 'tis slander,
Whose edge is sharper than the sword, whose tongue
Outvenoms all the worms of Nile, whose breath
Rides on the posting winds and doth belie
All corners of the world. Kings, queens, and states,   35

---

22 lies] F; lie *Rowe*   30 SD] *Taylor; not in* F

14 But Merely.
15 drug-damned (the same reaction as Pisanio's, 3.2.4).
15 outcraftied outwitted: *OED*'s only example. Possibly a misprint for 'outcrafted', though Dyce notes 'muddied' appears twice in *AWW* 5.2.4, 22.
16 hard point crisis.
17 take ... extremity lessen some of the shock.
17–18 to read ... me if I read it, would kill me.
22 testimonies evidence.
22 lies F's 'lyes' could be caught from the ending of 'testimonies', but a plural subject with a single verb is possible grammar at this time (Abbott, #247).
22 lies bleeding a reminiscence of the subtitle of Beaumont and Fletcher's *Philaster, or Love Lies A-Bleeding*. Adelman, 213, notes that this assertion reverses the expected gender-codes, since the blood staining Posthumus's marital bed should have been Innogen's.

23 grief wrong, injury.
27–9 where ... disloyal In requiring Pisanio to obey him unquestioningly, Posthumus is behaving like Cloten, who will voice this attitude in extreme form in 3.5.108–13.
29 pander procurer
30 What ... need What need will it be.
31–2 slander ... sword Echoing *WT* 2.3.86–7: 'slander, / Whose sting is sharper than the sword's'.
33 Outvenoms Is more poisonous than.
33 worms serpents (as in *Ant.* 5.2.241, 'the pretty worm of Nilus'). In Geoffrey Whitney's *A Choice of Emblems*, 1586, Envy is depicted with a snake for a tongue (see Simonds, pp. 18–19).
34 posting travelling post-haste.
34 belie fill with lies (*OED* belie *v*² 8: *OED*'s only example of this sense).
35 states great dignitaries (*OED* state *sb* 24). As in Middleton, *Women Beware Women*, 1.3.97: 'all our chief states of Florence'.

Maids, matrons, nay, the secrets of the grave
This viperous slander enters. – What cheer, madam?
INNOGEN False to his bed? What is it to be false?
To lie in watch there, and to think on him?
To weep 'twixt clock and clock? If sleep charge nature,   40
To break it with a fearful dream of him,
And cry myself awake? That's false to's bed, is it?
PISANIO Alas, good lady!
INNOGEN I false? Thy conscience witness! Iachimo,
Thou didst accuse him of incontinency.   45
Thou then look'dst like a villain; now, methinks,
Thy favour's good enough. Some jay of Italy,
Whose mother was her painting, hath betrayed him.
Poor I am stale, a garment out of fashion,
And for I am richer than to hang by th'walls,   50
I must be ripped. To pieces with me! Oh,
Men's vows are women's traitors! All good seeming,
By thy revolt, O husband, shall be thought
Put on for villainy; not born where't grows,
But worn a bait for ladies.
PISANIO   Good madam, hear me.   55
INNOGEN True honest men being heard like false Aeneas
Were in his time thought false, and Sinon's weeping

---

39 **in watch** awake.

40 **'twixt . . . clock** from hour to hour.

40 **charge** weigh down.

41 **fearful** anxious.

44 **Thy conscience witness** Probably addressed to the absent Posthumus, to whom Innogen speaks at 53 and 59. Warren thinks the addressee is Pisanio, but Innogen does not turn to him until 62, and his brief interjections suggest that at this point she is oblivious to his presence. It is not clear how Pisanio's 'conscience' could 'witness' to her truthfulness, though she might expect Posthumus's to do so.

45 **incontinency** sexual indulgence.

47 **favour** countenance.

47 **jay** strumpet; a flashy, chattering bird (see *MWW* 3.3.44: 'We'll teach him to know turtles from jays').

48 **Whose . . . painting** Who's created by her cosmetics, not by nature.

50 **richer** too valuable.

50 **than to** i.e., than that which is fit to. For the idiom compare *John* 4.2.256–9: 'My form . . . Is

yet the cover of a fairer mind / Than to be butcher of an innocent child' (Abbott, #390).

50 **hang . . . walls** like discarded clothing, or the rusty armour in *MM* 1.2.171, *Tro.* 3.3.151–3.

51 **ripped** so as to be reused (as an old but expensive fabric would be recycled).

52 **seeming** appearance.

53 **revolt** faithlessness.

54 **not . . . grows** not natural but assumed (Nosworthy).

55 **a bait** as a temptation.

56 **being . . . Aeneas** when they were heard to speak like Aeneas (since his false promises made all truths come under suspicion).

56 **Aeneas** who abandoned Dido and sailed to Rome despite professing love for her (Virgil, *Aeneid*, IV).

57 **Sinon** who betrayed Troy to the Greeks by persuading the Trojans to accept the horse. Virgil describes the crocodile tears he wept while trying to convince them of his sincerity (*Aeneid*, II); they are mentioned in *Luc.* 1549.

Did scandal many a holy tear, took pity
From most true wretchedness. So thou, Posthumus,
Wilt lay the leaven on all proper men;   60
Goodly and gallant shall be false and perjured
From thy great fail. [*To Pisanio*] Come, fellow, be thou honest,
Do thou thy master's bidding. When thou seest him,
A little witness my obedience. Look,
I draw the sword myself. Take it, and hit   65
The innocent mansion of my love, my heart.
Fear not, 'tis empty of all things but grief.
Thy master is not there, who was indeed
The riches of it. Do his bidding, strike.
Thou mayst be valiant in a better cause,   70
But now thou seem'st a coward.

PISANIO   Hence, vile instrument,
Thou shalt not damn my hand! [*Throws away his sword*]

INNOGEN   Why, I must die,
And if I do not by thy hand thou art
No servant of thy master's. Against self-slaughter
There is a prohibition so divine   75
That cravens my weak hand. Come, here's my heart.
Something's afore't – soft, soft, we'll no defence,
Obedient as the scabbard. What is here?
                    [*Pulling letters from her bosom*]
The scriptures of the loyal Leonatus,
All turned to heresy? Away, away,   80
Corrupters of my faith, you shall no more

---

72 SD] *this edn; not in* F   77 afore't–] *Rowe;* a-foot: F   78 SD] *Steevens; not in* F

58 scandal bring into disrepute.
58–9 took . . . wretchedness robbed genuine
misery of sympathy (Warren).
60 lay the leaven infect, like sour dough. Echoing 1 Corinthians 5.6: 'Know ye not that a little leaven leaveneth the whole lump' (a warning
against fornication).
60 proper honest.
62 fail failure; lapse.
64 A little witness Testify somewhat to.
66 mansion . . . heart Innogen compares her
heart to a house once, but no longer, inhabited by
Posthumus.
75 prohibition The Bible does not specifically
forbid suicide, but from earliest times the Church

understood it to come within the sixth command-
ment. See Augustine, *The City of God*, I, 20; and
(inevitably) *Ham.* 1.2.131–2. Here and in *Hamlet*,
'self-slaughter' is a Shakespearean coinage. Note
that, in this Romanized play, Innogen pointedly
refuses the Roman way of death.
76 cravens renders cowardly. This is *OED*'s earliest example of 'craven' as a verb.
77 afore't in front of it.
78 Obedient As ready to receive the sword (as
is the scabbard itself): expressing total submission
to Posthumus's will.
79 scriptures (1) writings, (2) sacred texts:
hence Innogen's ensuing complaint that Posthumus
has taught 'heresy' (80) and corrupted her faith.

Be stomachers to my heart! Thus may poor fools
Believe false teachers; though those that are betrayed
Do feel the treason sharply, yet the traitor
Stands in worse case of woe. And thou Posthumus,   85
That didst set up
My disobedience 'gainst the King my father,
And make me put into contempt the suits
Of princely fellows, shalt hereafter find
It is no act of common passage but   90
A strain of rareness; and I grieve myself
To think, when thou shalt be disedged by her
That now thou tirest on, how thy memory
Will then be panged by me. [*To Pisanio*] Prithee, dispatch;
The lamb entreats the butcher. Where's thy knife?   95
Thou art too slow to do thy master's bidding
When I desire it too.

PISANIO   O gracious lady,
Since I received command to do this business
I have not slept one wink.

INNOGEN   Do't, and to bed then.

PISANIO I'll wake mine eyeballs out first.

INNOGEN   Wherefore then   100
Didst undertake it? Why hast thou abused

86–8 *Ingleby;* That . . . King / My . . . suites F   88 make] *Malone;* makes F; mad'st *conj. Gibbons*   94 SD] not in F
100 out first] *Ingleby (conj. Johnson);* first F; blind first *Hanmer*

82 stomachers ornamental coverings worn in the opening of the bodice.

83 false teachers who promote 'heresy' (80).

83–5 though . . . woe Probably Innogen tears up the letters as she speaks these lines: she 'feels the treason', but the letters suffer the more woeful consequences of their treachery. Without some such action, her remarks make little sense.

86–9 This passage carries signs of disturbance in F and may contain imperfectly assimilated revisions. See Longer Notes, pp. 250–1.

86 set up incite, instigate.

89 princely fellows suitors of royal rank.

90 It Referring to Innogen's disobedience to her father, her rejection of high-born suitors, or her resolution to submit as Posthumus's sacrificial victim. See Longer Notes, p. 250.

90 act . . . passage no ordinary occurrence.

91 strain of rareness impulse befitting an extraordinary individual.

92 disedged blunted; with the (sexual) appetite taken away. A Shakespearean coinage: *OED*'s earliest example.

93 tirest on consume, like a ravenous bird of prey. Another of the play's eagle images, but with the bird's violence foregrounded.

94 panged tormented.

94 dispatch do it quickly.

100 out first F's reading is clearly wrong. The usual emendation gives good sense, though the idiom 'wake . . . out' is otherwise unknown. Steevens finds analogues in *The Bugbears* (1565?), 2.4.37: 'for lack of my sleep I shall watch my eyes out'; and Middleton and Dekker's *The Roaring Girl*, 4.2.172–3: 'I'll . . . watch out mine eyes'. Ingleby compares P. Woodhouse, *Democritus his Dream*, 1605: 'Thou'lt laugh no more, but weep thine eyeballs out.' Collier emends 'wake' to 'crack': compare 1.3.17.

So many miles with a pretence? This place,
Mine action, and thine own? Our horses' labour?
The time inviting thee? The perturbed court
For my being absent, whereunto I never   105
Purpose return? Why hast thou gone so far,
To be unbent when thou hast ta'en thy stand,
Th'elected deer before thee?
PISANIO   But to win time
To lose so bad employment, in the which
I have considered of a course. Good lady,   110
Hear me with patience.
INNOGEN   Talk thy tongue weary; speak.
I have heard I am a strumpet, and mine ear,
Therein false struck, can take no greater wound,
Nor tent to bottom that. But speak.
PISANIO   Then, madam,
I thought you would not back again.
INNOGEN   Most like,   115
Bringing me here to kill me.
PISANIO   Not so, neither;
But if I were as wise as honest, then
My purpose would prove well. It cannot be
But that my master is abused. Some villain,
Ay, and singular in his art, hath done you both   120
This cursèd injury.
INNOGEN Some Roman courtesan.
PISANIO   No, on my life.
I'll give but notice you are dead, and send him
Some bloody sign of it, for 'tis commanded
I should do so. You shall be missed at court,   125
And that will well confirm it.
INNOGEN   Why, good fellow,

104 **inviting thee** giving you such a good opportunity.
107 **To be unbent** 'Only to unbend your bow again' (Maxwell); a metaphor from hunting. For the 'stand', see 2.3.65.
108 **elected** chosen.
108–9 **to win . . . lose** Verbal antithesis and syntactic repetition (anaphora) combined.

113 **false struck** slanderously abused.
114 **tent** (in surgery) a roll of lint, used to cleanse a wound or 'bottom' it (= probe its depth).
115 **back** go back.
117 **But . . . were** i.e., I thought that if I were.
118 **prove** turn out.
119 **abused** deceived.
120 **singular** unmatched.

What shall I do the while? Where bide, how live,
Or in my life what comfort, when I am
Dead to my husband?

PISANIO   If you'll back to th'court –

INNOGEN No court, no father, nor no more ado   130
With that harsh, noble, simple nothing,
That Cloten, whose love-suit hath been to me
As fearful as a siege.

PISANIO   If not at court,
Then not in Britain must you bide.

INNOGEN   Where then?
Hath Britain all the sun that shines? Day, night,   135
Are they not but in Britain? I'th'world's volume
Our Britain seems as of it, but not in't;
In a great pool a swan's nest. Prithee, think
There's livers out of Britain.

PISANIO   I am most glad
You think of other place. Th'ambassador,   140
Lucius the Roman, comes to Milford Haven
Tomorrow. Now if you could wear a mind
Dark as your fortune is, and but disguise
That which t'appear itself must not yet be
But by self-danger, you should tread a course   145

---

129 court–] *Pope;* Court. F   131 harsh, noble] F; harsh, nothing noble *Ingleby;* harsh Queen, that noble *Nosworthy;*
harsh, churlish noble *Taylor*

---

127 bide abide.

131 This line lacks two syllables, and most editors assume a fourth adjective, or a name, has dropped out: the best guesses are in the collation. However, the line is forceful as it is and can stand without emendation. In performance its thumping stresses will slow it down, or there will be a hefty pause before Innogen names the man she detests.

135 Hath . . . shines A question eventually answered in the Soothsayer's dream, 4.2.351, 5.4.470.

136–8 I'th'world's . . . nest A remark that contributes to the debate over British identity: Innogen invokes the proud British separateness proclaimed by Cloten (3.1.12–13), but she reverses his emphasis by stressing that Britain's isolation diminishes her importance. See Introduction, p. 44.

136 world's volume book of the world (from which Britain is a detached page).

138 swan's nest which would be built in the

middle of the pool and high above the water, in 'rickety isolation' (Edwards, p. 88). A similar image appears in Giles Fletcher's poem *Christ's Victory* (1610), which compares Britain to a halcyon's nest built 'in the mid'st of Neptune's angry tide'. This 'on the waves doth ride, / And softly sailing, scornes the waters pride; / While all the rest, drown'd on the continent, / And toss'd in bloody waves, their wounds lament, / And stand to see our peace, as struck with wonderment' (quoted in Harris, p. 218). Fletcher voices the common Stuart view that Britain's isolation from Europe is protective, but Innogen's image makes it seem much more a shortcoming: see Introduction, p. 44.

139 livers people who live.

143 Dark Shadowed: = (1) impenetrable to other people, (2) ill-fortuned.

144 That Implicitly, Innogen's sex. The 'self-danger' (145) is danger of rape, which Innogen immediately intuits (151).

Pretty and full of view; yea, haply, near
The residence of Posthumus; so nigh, at least,
That though his actions were not visible, yet
Report should render him hourly to your ear
As truly as he moves.

INNOGEN   O, for such means,   150
Though peril to my modesty, not death on't,
I would adventure.

PISANIO   Well then, here's the point:
You must forget to be a woman; change
Command into obedience; fear and niceness –
The handmaids of all women, or, more truly,   155
Woman it pretty self – into a waggish courage,
Ready in gibes, quick-answered, saucy, and
As quarrelous as the weasel. Nay, you must
Forget that rarest treasure of your cheek,
Exposing it – but O, the harder heart!   160
Alack, no remedy – to the greedy touch
Of common-kissing Titan, and forget
Your laboursome and dainty trims, wherein
You made great Juno angry.

---

146 haply] F (*happily*)

146 **full** . . . **view** with good prospects of turning out well (Capell): reversing 'Dark' (143). Alternatively, Pisanio may mean 'having many opportunities of observing Posthumus' (Onions).

146 **haply** maybe.

149 **render** describe.

151 **Though** . . . **on't** Although it put my chastity in danger, but did not destroy it.

152 **adventure** take the risk.

154 **Command** Authority (as a princess).

154 **niceness** coyness: echoing Posthumus's satire of women (2.5.26). Despite his sympathy for Innogen, Pisanio's assumptions about typical female behaviour are much the same as Posthumus's: compare 162–3.

156 **it** its (Abbott, #228).

156 **waggish** roguish.

158 **weasel** Proverbially quarrelsome: see Dent, W211.1, and *1H4* 2.3.78–9: 'A weasel hath not such a deal of spleen / As you are toss'd with.'

159 **rarest** . . . **cheek** Innogen's complexion, which will suffer if she leaves off her mask (or her cosmetics?). This suggests that Jacobean Innogens wore contemporary costume rather than ancient British dress.

160 **O** . . . **heart** 'O, the more than cruelty of it' (Dowden). Probably a generalized expression of pity by Pisanio rather than (as some editors suppose) an accusation addressed to Posthumus or a reflection that Innogen's heart will now be hardened. Given the circumstances, there is a self-conscious artifice in having Pisanio pause to bewail the damage male disguise will do to Innogen's skin tones.

162 **Titan** The sun, whose beams touch all people alike, here seen as a promiscuous lover. A striking reminiscence of Posthumus's anxieties about Innogen (2.5.12–13).

163 **laboursome** effortful.

163 **trims** adornments. Perhaps echoing 2.5.25.

164 **You** . . . **angry** Presumably out of envy at her beauty: Innogen provokes desire in male deities and envy in female. Juno is the female counterpart to the male god who ultimately presides over events.

INNOGEN   Nay, be brief.
I see into thy end, and am almost   165
A man already.
PISANIO   First make yourself but like one.
Forethinking this, I have already fit –
'Tis in my cloakbag – doublet, hat, hose, all
That answer to them. Would you in their serving,
And with what imitation you can borrow   170
From youth of such a season, 'fore noble Lucius
Present yourself, desire his service, tell him
Wherein you're happy – which will make him know
If that his head have ear in music – doubtless
With joy he will embrace you, for he's honourable,   175
And, doubling that, most holy. Your means abroad:
You have me, rich, and I will never fail
Beginning nor supplyment.
INNOGEN   Thou art all the comfort
The gods will diet me with. Prithee away.
There's more to be considered, but we'll even   180
All that good time will give us. This attempt
I am soldier to, and will abide it with
A prince's courage. Away, I prithee.
PISANIO Well, madam, we must take a short farewell,
Lest, being missed, I be suspected of   185
Your carriage from the court. My noble mistress,
Here is a box – I had it from the Queen –
What's in't is precious. If you are sick at sea

173 will] F; you'll *Hanmer;* we'll *conj. Malone*

165 **into thy end** where you are heading.
167 **Forethinking** Anticipating.
167 **fit** ready.
168 **hose** breeches.
169 **answer to** go with.
169 **in their serving** with their aid.
171 **season** age.
172 **his service** service under him.
173 **happy** accomplished.
173–4 **which . . . music** 'which he will quickly discover if he has the smallest ear for music' (Deighton): Arviragus endorses Innogen's musical accomplishments, 4.2.48. The parenthesis is elliptical and perhaps corrupt: alternatively, 'make him

know' could be equivalent to 'convince him' (*Riverside*).
175 **embrace** welcome.
176 **holy** virtuous.
176 **Your means abroad** As for your financial needs.
178 **supplyment** continuance of supply.
179 **diet** feed.
180 **even** keep pace with.
182 **soldier to** courageously prepared for.
183 **prince** used at this time for both male and female rulers.
184 **short** hurried.
186 **Your carriage** Carrying you away.

Or stomach-qualmed at land, a dram of this
Will drive away distemper. To some shade,   190
And fit you to your manhood. May the gods
Direct you to the best!

INNOGEN   Amen. I thank thee.

Exeunt [opposite ways]

3.5 *Enter* CYMBELINE, QUEEN, CLOTEN, LUCIUS, and
lords [and attendants]

CYMBELINE Thus far, and so farewell.
LUCIUS   Thanks, royal sir.
   My emperor hath wrote I must from hence;
   And am right sorry that I must report ye
   My master's enemy.
CYMBELINE   Our subjects, sir,
   Will not endure his yoke, and for ourself   5
   To show less sovereignty than they must needs
   Appear unkinglike.
LUCIUS   So, sir. I desire of you
   A conduct over land to Milford Haven.
   Madam, all joy befall your grace, and you.
CYMBELINE My lords, you are appointed for that office;   10
   The due of honour in no point omit.
   So farewell, noble Lucius.
LUCIUS   [*To Cloten*]   Your hand, my lord.
CLOTEN Receive it friendly, but from this time forth
   I wear it as your enemy.
LUCIUS   Sir, the event
   Is yet to name the winner. Fare you well.   15

---

192 SD] *after Theobald; Exeunt.* F   Act 3, Scene 5   3.5 *Scena Quinta.* F   0 SD LORDS *and attendants*] *Hanmer; and*
Lords F

190 shade covert.
191 fit adjust.

Act 3, Scene 5
1 Thus far Words which locate the scene on
the threshold that divides the court's private and
public spaces.
2 wrote written. Compare 21, and *Lear* (quarto
text) 1.2.86 (Abbott, #343).
3 am I am.

6 sovereignty royal dignity.
7 So Very well. An evasion: Lucius declines to
pursue the subject but concedes no ground.
8 conduct escort.
9 and you probably a parting politeness to Cymbeline. Not addressed to Cloten, of whom a more
barbed leave is taken at 12–15.
11 due of honour ceremonies owing to Lucius's
status as ambassador.
14 event outcome.

CYMBELINE Leave not the worthy Lucius, good my lords,
　　　　　Till he have crossed the Severn. Happiness!

　　　　　　　　　　　　　　　Exeunt Lucius [and Lords]

QUEEN He goes hence frowning, but it honours us
　　　　That we have given him cause.

CLOTEN 　　　　　　　　　　　　'Tis all the better;
　　　　Your valiant Britons have their wishes in it.   20

CYMBELINE Lucius hath wrote already to the emperor
　　　　How it goes here. It fits us therefore ripely
　　　　Our chariots and our horsemen be in readiness.
　　　　The powers that he already hath in Gallia
　　　　Will soon be drawn to head, from whence he moves   25
　　　　His war for Britain.

QUEEN 　　　　　　　　　　'Tis not sleepy business,
　　　　But must be looked to speedily and strongly.

CYMBELINE Our expectation that it would be thus
　　　　Hath made us forward. But, my gentle Queen,
　　　　Where is our daughter? She hath not appeared   30
　　　　Before the Roman, nor to us hath tendered
　　　　The duty of the day. She looks us like
　　　　A thing more made of malice than of duty;
　　　　We have noted it. Call her before us, for
　　　　We have been too slight in sufferance.

　　　　　　　　　　　　　　　　[Exit a Messenger]

QUEEN 　　　　　　　　　　　　　Royal sir,   35
　　　　Since the exile of Posthumus most retired
　　　　Hath her life been, the cure whereof, my lord,
　　　　'Tis time must do. Beseech your majesty,
　　　　Forbear sharp speeches to her. She's a lady
　　　　So tender of rebukes that words are strokes,   40
　　　　And strokes death to her.

---

17 SD] *Malone; Exit Lucius, &c* F   32 looks us] *Johnson;* looke vs F   35 SD] *after Hanmer; not in* F   40 strokes,] F2; stroke;, F

17 **Severn** the boundary between England and Wales, whither Innogen has gone.

18 **honours** does us credit.

22 **It . . . ripely** It is high time (Maxwell).

24 **Gallia** France; conquered by Caesar 58–51 BC.

25 **head** full strength.

29 **forward** prompt.

32 **duty of the day** daily greeting.

32 **looks us** probably, 'seems to us', though 'looks at' might be meant. Abbott (#220) compares Jonson's *The Sad Shepherd* 2.1.30–1, '[a river] in which . . . I look myself' (*Ben Jonson*, VII, 29).

35 **too . . . sufferance** too lax in allowing her behaviour.

37–8 **the cure . . . do** proverbial: see Tilley T322, 'Time tames the strongest grief.'

40 **tender** of sensitive to.

Enter a MESSENGER

CYMBELINE   Where is she, sir? How
Can her contempt be answered?
MESSENGER   Please you, sir,
Her chambers are all locked, and there's no answer
That will be given to th'loud'st of noise we make.
QUEEN   My lord, when last I went to visit her   45
She prayed me to excuse her keeping close,
Whereto, constrained by her infirmity,
She should that duty leave unpaid to you
Which daily she was bound to proffer. This
She wished me to make known, but our great court   50
Made me too blame in memory.
CYMBELINE   Her doors locked?
Not seen of late? Grant, heavens, that which I fear
Prove false!   [*Exit Cymbeline and attendants*]
QUEEN   Son, I say, follow the King.
CLOTEN   That man of hers, Pisanio, her old servant
I have not seen these two days.
QUEEN   Go, look after.   55
                                        [*Exit Cloten*]
Pisanio, thou that stand'st so for Posthumus!
He hath a drug of mine; I pray his absence
Proceed by swallowing that, for he believes
It is a thing most precious. But for her,
Where is she gone? Haply despair hath seized her,   60
Or, winged with fervour of her love, she's flown

44 loud'st of] *Capell;* lowd of F; loudest *Rowe*   52–3 *Rowe;* Not . . . I / Feare . . . false. F   53 SD] *this edn; Exit.* F
56 SD] *Capell; after* days. *in* F

42 **answered** justified.
44 **loud'st of** The usual emendation for F's 'loud of', though Rowe's 'loudest' is possible. F may be correct, given that Elizabethan English allowed adjectives to be used as abstract nouns: compare *Ven.* 389–91 ('A sudden pale . . . usurps her cheek'); *MM* 2.4.170 ('my false o'erweighs your true'); and *Son.* 68 ('Before these bastard signs of fair were born'). Some emendation seems necessary, however, as a superlative sense is demanded.
46 **close** shut up.
47 **infirmity** sickness. Innogen is indeed sick in 4.2.
49 **bound** required.
50 **our . . . court** i.e., our court being enlarged

with crowds of visitors during Lucius's reception.
51 **too . . . memory** reprehensibly forgetful (Warren). For the adjectival usage 'too blame' (= culpable), see *R3* 2.2.13 (Q1), 'The King mine Vnckle is too blame for it'; and *OED* blame *v* 6.
55 **these two days** an indication of the time telescoped between 3.2 and 3.5. In the theatre such bold adjustments can be assimilated with little strain.
56 **stand'st so** so much stands up for. In repunctuating the line (F prints 'Posthumus,'), most editors take it as an exclamation of satisfaction by the Queen.
58 **Proceed by** Results from.
60 **Haply** It may be.

To her desired Posthumus. Gone she is
To death or to dishonour, and my end
Can make good use of either. She being down,
I have the placing of the British crown.   65

Enter CLOTEN

How now, my son?

CLOTEN   'Tis certain she is fled.
Go in and cheer the King. He rages, none
Dare come about him.

QUEEN   [*Aside*]   All the better. May
This night forestall him of the coming day.   *Exit*

CLOTEN   I love and hate her. For she's fair and royal,   70
And that she hath all courtly parts more exquisite
Than lady, ladies, woman – from every one
The best she hath, and she, of all compounded,
Outsells them all – I love her therefore; but
Disdaining me, and throwing favours on   75
The low Posthumus, slanders so her judgment
That what's else rare is choked; and in that point
I will conclude to hate her, nay, indeed,
To be revenged upon her. For when fools
Shall –

---

68 SD] *Globe (conj. Walker); not in* F   69 SD] F *(Exit Qu.)*   79–80] *Rowe;* To . . . shall– / Who . . . sirrah? F

63 **end** objective.

65 **I have . . . crown** The Queen spells out the
political implications of Innogen's disappearance.
Without Innogen, Cymbeline's lineage comes to
an end, and Britain falls under the control of the
Queen's succession.

69 **forestall . . . day** prevent him from seeing
another day (by making his rage fatal). With this
emphatic rhyme the Queen imposes her will on this
part of the action; but these are her last words in
the play.

70 **I . . . her** A common sentiment in the literature of courtly love, the ultimate source for which
is Catullus, *Carmina* 85: 'Odi et amo.'

70 **For** Because. This speech is confusingly
pointed in F, but it all unfolds from Cloten's first
five words. Lines 70–5 expand on 'I love her', and
75–9 on 'I hate her.'

71 **that** i.e., for that.

72 **lady . . . woman** 'than any lady, than all

ladies, than all woman kind' (Johnson). There is an
exactly parallel construction in *AWW* 2.3.201–2.

72–4 **from . . . all** A compliment echoing Pliny's
story of the artist Zeuxis, who created a picture of
Juno by synthesizing the best parts of the five most
beautiful women he could find (*Natural History*,
35.61–6); see also Catullus, 86. Widely imitated
in the Renaissance, the topos was a favourite with
Shakespeare: see *AYLI* 3.2.141–52, *WT* 5.1.13–5
and *Temp.* 3.1.46–8.

73 **compounded** composed.

74 **Outsells** Exceeds in value: see 2.4.102.

75 **Disdaining** The fact that she disdains.

76 **slanders** discredits.

77 **what's else rare** what else is exceptional
about her.

79 **revenged** a parodic echo of Posthumus at
2.5.8. This whole speech, with its absurdly clear-
cut self-contradictions, is a boiled-down version of
Posthumus's venomous monologue.

Enter PISANIO

Who is here? What, are you packing, sirrah?   80
Come hither. Ah, you precious pander! Villain,
Where is thy lady? In a word, or else
Thou art straightway with the fiends.

PISANIO   O good my lord!

CLOTEN Where is thy lady? or, by Jupiter,
I will not ask again. Close villain,   85
I'll have this secret from thy heart, or rip
Thy heart to find it. Is she with Posthumus,
From whose so many weights of baseness cannot
A dram of worth be drawn?

PISANIO   Alas, my lord,
How can she be with him? When was she missed?   90
He is in Rome.

CLOTEN   Where is she, sir? Come nearer,
No further halting. Satisfy me home,
What is become of her?

PISANIO O my all-worthy lord!

CLOTEN   All-worthy villain,
Discover where thy mistress is at once,   95
At the next word. No more of 'worthy lord'!
Speak, or thy silence on the instant is
Thy condemnation and thy death.

PISANIO   Then, sir,
This paper is the history of my knowledge
Touching her flight.
                [Presenting Posthumus's letter]

---

86 heart] F; tongue *Taylor*   100 SD] *Malone (subst.); not in* F

80–98 In his recollection of this encounter, Pisanio says Cloten 'foamed at the mouth' (5.4.276).
80 **packing** scheming.
80 **sirrah** a form of address to an inferior, often contemptuous.
81 **pander** go-between.
85 **Close** Secretive.
86 **heart** This is comprehensible as it stands, but Nosworthy speculates that the repetition of 'heart' (87) is due to compositorial eyeskip. Taylor emends 'heart' in 86 to 'tongue' on the basis of Shakespeare's frequent use of this antithesis elsewhere.

89 **dram** (in apothecaries' *weights*) a tiny quantity, a fraction of an ounce.
89 **drawn** extracted.
91 **Come nearer** Be more direct.
92 **halting** hesitation.
92 **home** completely.
99 **This paper** Presumably the same letter (or a version of it) which was given to Innogen in 3.2, though the phrase quoted at 127 does not appear in the text as read by Innogen. Compare 5.4.279, 'a feignèd letter of my master's'. Such details are too widely separated for the inconsistency to be noticed in performance.

CLOTEN   Let's see't. I will pursue her   100
     Even to Augustus' throne.
PISANIO [*Aside*]   Or this or perish.
     She's far enough, and what he learns by this
     May prove his travel, not her danger.
CLOTEN [*Reads*]   Hum!
PISANIO [*Aside*] I'll write to my lord she's dead. O Innogen,
     Safe mayst thou wander, safe return again!   105
CLOTEN Sirrah, is this letter true?
PISANIO Sir, as I think.
CLOTEN It is Posthumus' hand; I know't. Sirrah, if thou wouldst not
     be a villain but do me true service, undergo those employments
     wherein I should have cause to use thee with a serious industry –   110
     that is, what villainy soe'er I bid thee do, to perform it directly and
     truly – I would think thee an honest man. Thou shouldst neither
     want my means for thy relief, nor my voice for thy preferment.
PISANIO Well, my good lord.
CLOTEN Wilt thou serve me? For since patiently and constantly thou   115
     hast stuck to the bare fortune of that beggar Posthumus, thou canst
     not in the course of gratitude but be a diligent follower of mine.
     Wilt thou serve me?
PISANIO Sir, I will.
CLOTEN Give me thy hand; here's my purse. Hast any of thy late   120
     master's garments in thy possession?
PISANIO I have, my lord, at my lodging the same suit he wore when
     he took leave of my lady and mistress.
CLOTEN The first service thou dost me, fetch that suit hither. Let it
     be thy first service, go.   125
PISANIO I shall, my lord.   *Exit*

101 SD] *Rowe; not in* F   103 SD] *this edn; not in* F   104 SD] *Theobald; not in* F   104 write to] F; write *Walker*

101 Or Either.
103 prove . . . danger cause him to travel, but not put Innogen in peril.
104 write to perhaps (as Walker conjectures) this should be 'write': compare *1H4* 4.1.31, 'He writes me here.' This would improve the metre, though the unstressed syllables can easily be elided.
109 undergo undertake.
110 serious industry careful diligence.

111–12 villainy . . . truly a parody of Posthumus's outrageous commands to Pisanio at 3.4.27–9. These riddling paradoxes also bear comparison with those at 5.3.215–60 by the play's other clown, the Jailer (a role sometimes doubled with Cloten).
113 relief sustenance.
113 voice support.
113 preferment promotion.
116–17 thou . . . but you cannot avoid being.

CLOTEN [*Reads*] 'Meet thee at Milford Haven!' – I forgot to ask him
one thing; I'll remember't anon. – Even there, thou villain Posthumus, will I kill thee. I would these garments were come. She said
upon a time – the bitterness of it I now belch from my heart –   130
that she held the very garment of Posthumus in more respect than
my noble and natural person, together with the adornment of my
qualities. With that suit upon my back will I ravish her; first kill
him, and in her eyes; there shall she see my valour, which will then
be a torment to her contempt. He on the ground, my speech of   135
insultment ended on his dead body, and when my lust hath dined –
which, as I say, to vex her I will execute in the clothes that she so
praised – to the court I'll knock her back, foot her home again.
She hath despised me rejoicingly, and I'll be merry in my revenge.

Enter PISANIO [*with a suit of clothes*]

Be those the garments?   140
PISANIO Ay, my noble lord.
CLOTEN How long is't since she went to Milford Haven?
PISANIO She can scarce be there yet.
CLOTEN Bring this apparel to my chamber. That is the second thing
that I have commanded thee. The third is that thou wilt be a   145
voluntary mute to my design. Be but duteous, and true preferment
shall tender itself to thee. My revenge is now at Milford; would I
had wings to follow it! Come, and be true.   *Exit*

---

127 SD] *this edn; not in* F   127 'Meet . . . Haven'] *Hanmer;* Meet . . . Hauen F   136 insultment] F2; insulment F
139 SD] *Rowe; Enter Pisanio.* F   146 duteous, and true] F; duteous and true, *Dyce 2 (after Walker)*

127–8 I forgot . . . thing i.e., what time Innogen
left (142).
132–3 adornment of my qualities enhance-
ment of my natural gifts.
133–8 With . . . again Planning to assault
Innogen in her husband's clothes, Cloten not only
plays out a material version of Iachimo's symbolic rape but becomes a dramatic duplicate of
Posthumus's long-distance violence. His intention
of raping her on Posthumus's dead body also harks
back to Chiron's proposals for Lavinia in *Tit.*
2.3.128–30; and perhaps to a sensational episode
in Thomas Nashe's *The Unfortunate Traveller*
(1594).
136 insultment contemptuous triumph (*OED*'s
only example). Baldwin (II, 160) compares the

Latin term *insultatio*, defined in T. Cooper's
Thesaurus, 1565, as 'a bragging or triumphing
against one'.
138 foot kick.
146 mute silent servant: in Oriental courts a
'mute' was a servant whose tongue had been cut
out, and hence not at all 'voluntary'. Compare *TN*
1.2.62.
146 true preferment i.e., substantial preferment, in contrast to the beggarly rewards brought
by service to Posthumus. But perhaps F's punctuation should be 'duteous and true,': Pisanio takes
'true' to refer to his duty (149–50), and 'true service' is the issue at 108–12.
148 wings recalling Innogen's 'O for a horse
with wings' (3.2.49).

PISANIO Thou bid'st me to my loss; for true to thee
     Were to prove false, which I will never be   150
     To him that is most true. To Milford go,
     And find not her whom thou pursuest. Flow, flow,
     You heavenly blessings on her. This fool's speed
     Be crossed with slowness; labour be his meed.   *Exit*

3.6 [*A cave discovered.*] Enter INNOGEN [*in boy's clothes*]

INNOGEN I see a man's life is a tedious one.
     I have tired myself, and for two nights together
     Have made the ground my bed. I should be sick,
     But that my resolution helps me. Milford,
     When from the mountain-top Pisanio showed thee,   5
     Thou wast within a ken. O Jove, I think
     Foundations fly the wretched – such, I mean,
     Where they should be relieved. Two beggars told me
     I could not miss my way. Will poor folks lie,
     That have afflictions on them, knowing 'tis   10
     A punishment or trial? Yes; no wonder,
     When rich ones scarce tell true. To lapse in fulness
     Is sorer than to lie for need, and falsehood
     Is worse in kings than beggars. My dear lord,
     Thou art one o'th'false ones. Now I think on thee,   15
     My hunger's gone, but even before I was

Act 3, Scene 6   3.6 *Scena Sexta.* F   0 SD] *This edn; Enter Imogen alone.* F

151 him . . . true probably this refers to Posthumus, though given what Pisanio knows about him, the phrase is hyperbolical. Alternatively, one could tinker with the pronouns, and print 'thy' for 'my' (149) or 'her' for 'him' (151), but these interpretations are inferior. Presumably Pisanio still thinks Posthumus is 'abused' by 'some villain' (3.4.119), and so believes he must still be good despite all that has happened. His faith in Posthumus is important for keeping this part of the play on the side of comedy.
  153–4 This . . . meed Combining two proverbs: see Tilley F518, 'Fool's haste is no speed'; and L1, 'He has his labour for his pains'.
  154 crossed with hampered by.
  154 meed reward.

Act 3, Scene 6
  0 SD *A cave* This scenic property, first seen at 3.3.0, is required for the stage business at 24ff.

1 tedious remotely echoing Rosalind in a similar situation (*AYLI* 2.4.1–8).
  3 sick A signal which prepares for Innogen's sudden illness in 4.2.
  4 helps cures (a common Shakespearean usage).
  6 within a ken in sight.
  7 Foundations (1) Security; (2) charitable institutions: a quibbling meaning that emerges as the speech proceeds.
  8–9 Two . . . way This little anecdote is highlighted by Innogen choosing to moralize sentimentally on it. It seems a redundant detail, but it is strategically embedded here in order that it can be recollected three scenes later: see note to 4.2.291–3.
  11 trial test of their virtue.
  12 scarce rarely.
  12 lapse in fulness do wrong when in prosperity.
  13 sorer a greater crime.
  13 for need out of necessity.
  16 even before a moment ago.

At point to sink for food. But what is this?
Here is a path to't. 'Tis some savage hold.
I were best not call; I dare not call; yet famine,
Ere clean it o'erthrow nature, makes it valiant.   20
Plenty and peace breeds cowards, hardness ever
Of hardiness is mother. Ho! Who's here?
If anything that's civil, speak; if savage,
Take or lend. Ho! No answer? Then I'll enter.
Best draw my sword, and if mine enemy   25
But fear the sword like me, he'll scarcely look on't.
Such a foe, good heavens!   *Exit [into the cave]*

Enter BELARIUS, GUIDERIUS, *and* ARVIRAGUS

BELARIUS You, Polydore, have proved best woodman and
Are master of the feast. Cadwal and I
Will play the cook and servant, 'tis our match.   30
The sweat of industry would dry and die
But for the end it works to. Come, our stomachs
Will make what's homely savory; weariness
Can snore upon the flint, when resty sloth
Finds the down pillow hard. Now peace be here,   35
Poor house, that keep'st thyself!   *[Exit into the cave]*
GUIDERIUS   I am throughly weary.
ARVIRAGUS I am weak with toil, yet strong in appetite.

---

27 SD] *after Rowe; Exit.* F   27.0 *Scena Septima.* F   36 SD] *this edn; not in* F

17 **At point** Just about.
18 **savage hold** stronghold of uncivilized creatures.
20 **clean** completely.
22 **hardiness** fortitude (quibbling on 'hardness' = hardship).
24 **Take or lend** i.e., Take my money, or give me food (reading 'lend' as 'give', as in 'lend aid'). Shakespeare draws here a linguistic line between 'civil' and 'savage', since Innogen expects civil creatures will respond verbally, but the savage only with signs. The same assumptions obtain in *Temp.* 1.1.355–8, 429–31, and express common Renaissance ideas about the nature of civility. However, the exiles have not only language, but also sophisticated manners and rituals that make their hard life seem ceremonious (e.g., 29–36).
25–7 Innogen's timidity in male attire links her with Viola, who similarly suffers in *TN* 4.1.
26 **But** Only.
27.0 SD F begins a new scene at this point, but this division is scribal, since the action is clearly

continuous.
28 **woodman** hunter.
30 **match** agreement: looking back to 3.3.74–6, as if the action were all within the same day. But Pisanio's return to court in 3.5 suggests that in his scenes the clock is moving much faster.
31 **The . . . die** i.e., 'Men would no longer labour' (Maxwell, understanding 'sweat' figuratively as 'toil'): the promise of the feast to follow motivates them to work. A dystopian sentiment in keeping with the Welsh scenes' 'hard' pastoralism.
33 **homely** plain.   34 **flint** flinty ground.
34 **resty** lazy.   36 **keep'st** looks after.
36 **throughly** thoroughly.
36, 39 SDs F does not indicate an exit for Belarius, but he has to enter the cave to see Innogen, and the boys' dialogue fills stage time while this action is performed. His words at 35–6 are a benediction suitable for crossing a threshold: compare Ananias in *The Alchemist*, 4.7.42: 'Peace to the household' (*Ben Jonson*, V, 383).

GUIDERIUS There is cold meat i'th'cave. We'll browse on that
    Whilst what we have killed be cooked.

[*Enter* BELARIUS]

BELARIUS   Stay, come not in!
    But that it eats our victuals, I should think   40
    Here were a fairy.
GUIDERIUS   What's the matter, sir?
BELARIUS By Jupiter, an angel – or, if not,
    An earthly paragon. Behold divineness
    No elder than a boy!

Enter INNOGEN

INNOGEN   Good masters, harm me not.
    Before I entered here I called, and thought   45
    To have begged or bought what I have took. Good troth,
    I have stol'n naught, nor would not, though I had found
    Gold strewed i'th'floor. Here's money for my meat.
    I would have left it on the board so soon
    As I had made my meal, and parted   50
    With prayers for the provider.
GUIDERIUS   Money, youth?
ARVIRAGUS All gold and silver rather turn to dirt,
    As 'tis no better reckoned but of those
    Who worship dirty gods.
INNOGEN   I see you're angry.
    Know, if you kill me for my fault, I should   55
    Have died had I not made it.
BELARIUS   Whither bound?
INNOGEN To Milford Haven.
BELARIUS   What's your name?

---

39 SD] *Rowe (subst.); not in* F

  38 browse nibble.
  40 victuals food; vittels.
  41 fairy a misapprehension by Belarius, since in folklore fairies often eat food left out for them. His neuter pronoun 'it' implies an uncertainty about the 'fairy's' sex.
  43 earthly paragon the same phrase is used of Silvia in *TGV* 2.4.146.
  44 elder older.

  49 board table.
  49 so as.
  50, 57 These lines are short, perhaps suggesting tentativeness on Innogen's part.
  50 made completed.
  50 parted left.
  53 of by.
  56 made committed.

INNOGEN Fidele, sir. I have a kinsman who
       Is bound for Italy. He embarked at Milford,
       To whom being going, almost spent with hunger,   60
       I am fall'n in this offence.
BELARIUS   Prithee, fair youth,
       Think us no churls, nor measure our good minds
       By this rude place we live in. Well encountered!
       'Tis almost night; you shall have better cheer
       Ere you depart, and thanks to stay and eat it.   65
       Boys, bid him welcome.
GUIDERIUS   Were you a woman, youth,
       I should woo hard but be your groom in honesty;
       Ay, bid for you as I'd buy.
ARVIRAGUS   I'll make't my comfort
       He is a man, I'll love him as my brother;
       [*To Innogen*] And such a welcome as I'd give to him   70
       After long absence, such is yours. Most welcome!
       Be sprightly, for you fall 'mongst friends.
INNOGEN   'Mongst friends,
       If brothers! [*Aside*] Would it had been so that they
       Had been my father's sons. Then had my price

---

68 Ay,] *Taylor;* I F   68 I'd] *Johnson (after Tyrwhitt);* I do F   70 SD *after Hanmer; not in* F   73 SD] *Theobald; not in* F;
placed before If *by Rowe*   74 price] F (*prize*); peize *conj. Vaughan*

58 **Fidele** 'the faithful one': opposing Innogen's loyalty to Posthumus's inconstancy (as in
many tragicomedies deriving from Guarini's *Pastor Fido*, which frequently revolve around questions
of female fidelity). The name is Italian, and therefore anachronistic in Cymbeline's Britain: there is
a Princess Fidelia in one of the play's sources, *The
Rare Triumphs of Love and Fortune*. In John Florio's
Italian-English dictionary, 1611, the word 'fedele' is
glossed as 'faithful, trusty, honest, loyal, of credit,
religious. Also a trusty friend' (Pitcher).
    59 **embarked** i.e., was to embark (Thiselton).
    60 **spent** exhausted.
    61 **in** into.
    62 **churls** peasants.
    63 **rude** uncivilized.
    65 **and thanks** i.e., we will thank you.
    67 **hard** vigorously.
    67 **but be** 'before I should fail to be' (Dowden).
    67 **groom** bridegroom; partner.
    67 **in honesty** 'in an honourable way' (Wyatt).
    68 **Ay . . . buy** yes, offer (honourable love) for
you as I'd obtain you. This line is obscure and
hypermetrical in F, but two simple modernizations
resolve it: (1) the initial 'I' is equivalent to 'Ay',

as so often (see the comparable cases at 3.7.11 and
4.2.207); (2) 'I do' is probably a compositorial misreading of 'Ide' (= 'I'd').
    68–9 **I'll . . . brother** 'I'll console myself for
his being a man by loving him as my brother'
(Maxwell). This is *Cymbeline*'s nearest approach
to the 'incest averted' motif which modern psy-
choanalytical criticism sees as central to romance:
Innogen must reunite with her brothers, but avoid
the dangers of getting too close to them.
    72 **sprightly** cheerful.
    72–3 **'Mongst . . . brothers** 'You must be
friends, being so brother-like.' F prints "Mongst
Friends? / If brothers:', which some editors take
as rhetorical question and answer; but in early modern punctuation '?' frequently meant '!', and Innogen's words are more naturally a single exclamation
taking up the boys' play with notions of brotherhood and friendship. Some editors mark the whole
speech as an aside.
    74 **price** value; because I would not then have
been heir to the throne. Innogen intuits the solution
that will eventually allow Cymbeline to approve
her union with Posthumus: see Introduction, p. 34.

Been less, and so more equal ballasting   75
To thee, Posthumus.
BELARIUS   He wrings at some distress.
GUIDERIUS Would I could free't.
ARVIRAGUS   Or I, whate'er it be,
What pain it cost, what danger. Gods!
BELARIUS   Hark, boys.
                    [*They talk apart*]
INNOGEN Great men
That had a court no bigger than this cave,   80
That did attend themselves and had the virtue
Which their own conscience sealed them, laying by
That nothing-gift of differing multitudes,
Could not outpeer these twain. Pardon me, gods,
I'd change my sex to be companion with them,   85
Since Leonatus' false.
BELARIUS   It shall be so.
Boys, we'll go dress our hunt. Fair youth, come in.
Discourse is heavy, fasting; when we have supped
We'll mannerly demand thee of thy story,
So far as thou wilt speak it.
GUIDERIUS   Pray, draw near.   90
ARVIRAGUS The night to th'owl and morn to th'lark less welcome.
INNOGEN Thanks, sir.
ARVIRAGUS I pray, draw near.
                              Exeunt [into the cave]

---

78 SD] *after Capell; not in* F   86 Leonatus'] *Singer 2; Leonatus* F   91 *Pope;* The . . . Owle, / And . . . welcome. F
93 SD] *Taylor; Exeunt.* F

F prints 'prize', but, as Taylor points out, this spelling of 'price' was still current in Shakespeare's day (also 'prise': see *OED* price *sb*). Alternatively, given the figurative use of 'ballast' in the next line, there might have been an e/r confusion over the word 'peize' = weight. Shakespeare uses 'peize' to mean 'weigh down' in *R3* 5.3.105 and *MV* 3.2.22.

75 more . . . ballasting of more equal weight. Ballast is heavy material placed in the hold of a ship to provide stability when under way.

76 wrings writhes.

77 free remove.

81 attend themselves wait on themselves, without throngs of courtiers.

82 conscience . . . them self-knowledge confirmed in them.

83 nothing-gift worthless gift; i.e., the servile and variable adulation that monarchs receive from the crowd. Or the 'multitudes' could themselves be the 'nothing-gift', so that Innogen reflects on the difference between busy court and quiet cave.

83 differing variable and unsteady. Theobald compares *2H4* Prol., 19: 'The still discordant wavering multitude'.

84 outpeer surpass (a Shakespearean coinage).

86 Leonatus' i.e., 'Leonatus is', the verb being elided into the preceding s. Furness compares 2.2.50: 'Though this a heavenly angel'.

87 dress our hunt prepare our game for cooking.

88 fasting on an empty stomach.

89 mannerly politely.

3.7 *Enter two* ROMAN SENATORS, *and* TRIBUNES

FIRST SENATOR This is the tenor of the Emperor's writ:
      That since the common men are now in action
      'Gainst the Pannonians and Dalmatians,
      And that the legions now in Gallia are
      Full weak to undertake our wars against   5
      The fall'n-off Britons, that we do incite
      The gentry to this business. He creates
      Lucius proconsul, and to you the tribunes,
      For this immediate levy, he commends
      His absolute commission. Long live Caesar!   10
TRIBUNE Is Lucius general of the forces?
SECOND SENATOR   Ay.
TRIBUNE Remaining now in Gallia?
FIRST SENATOR   With those legions
      Which I have spoke of, whereunto your levy
      Must be supplyant. The words of your commission
      Will tie you to the numbers and the time   15
      Of their dispatch.
TRIBUNE   We will discharge our duty.

                              Exeunt

Act 3, Scene 7 3.7 *Scena Octaua*. F 9 commends] F *(commands – a variant spelling)* 14 supplyant] F *(suppliant)*

Act 3, Scene 7

3.7 In terms of chronology, this scene belongs much earlier, since the clock ruling the play's political events is moving more swiftly than that in Innogen's plot (which takes a few days at most). But Shakespeare foreshortens the political plot so that it seems to develop in parallel with Innogen's journey, absurd though that is were events to be rigorously timetabled. This scene also fills in the time during which Innogen lodges with her brothers. Without it there is no space before Cloten's arrival in the vicinity, which breaks up their household.

0 SD The staging of this scene is an intriguing puzzle since if the cave were represented by a scenic property, it would probably have remained visible during this dialogue. The cave is needed for the whole of 3.6 and 4.2, a 500-line sequence, and would hardly have been shunted on and off for sixteen lines. The situation is similar to *Lear* 2.2, where Kent is asleep in the stocks in one location while Edgar delivers a brief monologue on the same stage but apparently in a different place. The contradiction is all the sharper since the Roman characters are in another country and probably wear different dress. This is, in fact, *Cymbeline*'s only scene to be set in classical Rome, as opposed to the contemporary Italy that Iachimo and Philario seem to inhabit.

0 SD TRIBUNES Roman officials appointed from the citizens (as opposed to the more aristocratic Senators).

2 **common men** ordinary soldiers.

5 **Full** Very.

6 **fall'n-off** revolted.

6 **incite** stir up.

8 **proconsul** governor of a colony or conquered province. Lucius is to be Britain's new ruler, under Caesar: paralleling the Queen's claim that she now rules Britain (3.5.65).

9 **commends** entrusts.

10 **absolute** unrestricted.

14 **supplyant** auxiliary (*OED*'s only instance).

15 **tie you to** specify to you.

4.1 *Enter* CLOTEN *alone* [*in Posthumus' suit*]

CLOTEN I am near to th'place where they should meet, if Pisanio have
mapped it truly. How fit his garments serve me! Why should his
mistress, who was made by him that made the tailor, not be fit too?
The rather – saving reverence of the word – for 'tis said a woman's
fitness comes by fits; therein I must play the workman. I dare   5
speak it to myself – for it is not vainglory for a man and his glass
to confer in his own chamber – I mean, the lines of my body are
as well-drawn as his; no less young, more strong, not beneath him
in fortunes, beyond him in the advantage of the time, above him
in birth, alike conversant in general services, and more remarkable   10
in single oppositions; yet this imperceiverant thing loves him in
my despight. What mortality is! Posthumus, thy head, which now
is growing upon thy shoulders, shall within this hour be off, thy
mistress enforced, thy garments cut to pieces before her face;
and all this done, spurn her home to her father, who may haply be a   15

Act 4, Scene 1   4.1 *Actus Quartus. Scena Prima.* F   0 SD] *after Oxford; Enter Clotten alone.* F   5 workman.] *Johnson;*
Workman, F   11 imperceiverant] F *(imperseuerant)*   14 her] *Hanmer (conj. Warburton); thy* F

Act 4, Scene 1

1–20 The convention of simultaneous location
allows Cloten to speak as if he were still some distance from Innogen, even though the scenic property standing for the cave was probably visible on
stage; see note to 3.7.0 above. Although Cloten talks
to himself, he seems more than half-aware of an
audience: like his shorter monologue at 2.3.60–70,
this is a clown's speech. His boastful self-regard
perhaps recollects Malvolio in the letter scene (*TN*
2.5).

2 fit perfectly. The ensuing remarks pun on further meanings of *fit*: sexually suitable (3); sexual
inclination (= *fitness*, 5); and fits and starts (5).
Cloten's notion, that because Posthumus's clothes
fit him so should his mistress, harks back to Innogen's complaint that to Posthumus she is 'a garment
out of fashion' (3.4.49).

3 him . . . tailor i.e., God.

4 The rather All the more so.

4 saving . . . word An absurd apology to the
word 'fit' for playing with it so bawdily.

5 therein . . . workman my own body, rather
than Posthumus's clothes, must make me desirable.

6 glass looking-glass. Cloten's point-by-point
comparison between himself and Posthumus pre-

pares the ground for Innogen's failure to distinguish between the two bodies at 4.2.308–16.

9 advantage . . . time opportunities for future
advancement; or perhaps 'current reputation'
(Furness).

10 conversant experienced.

10 general services military engagements, performed with others.

11 single oppositions private duels. Compare
1H4 1.3.99: 'In single opposition hand to hand'
(Capell).

11 imperceiverant undiscerning. A unique
usage: this is *OED*'s only instance, though it has
several examples of 'perceiverance' meaning 'perception', the latest from 1618 (Maxwell).

12 mortality human life.

14 enforced violated.

14 her F's 'thy' is probably repeated from 'thy
garments', one of many pronoun substitutions (see
Textual Analysis, p. 267).

15 spurn force. Cloten's plans for punishing
Innogen play out the violence that Posthumus
planned to do to her (see 2.4.147–9), so continuing
the parallels between them.

15 haply perhaps.

little angry for my so rough usage; but my mother, having power
of his testiness, shall turn all into my commendations. My horse is
tied up safe; out, sword, and to a sore purpose! Fortune put them
into my hand. This is the very description of their meeting-place,
and the fellow dares not deceive me.   *Exit*   20

4.2 *Enter* BELARIUS, GUIDERIUS, ARVIRAGUS AND INNOGEN
from the cave

BELARIUS [*To Innogen*] You are not well. Remain here in the cave,
    We'll come to you after hunting.
ARVIRAGUS [*To Innogen*]   Brother, stay here.
    Are we not brothers?
INNOGEN   So man and man should be,
    But clay and clay differs in dignity,
    Whose dust is both alike. I am very sick.   5
GUIDERIUS Go you to hunting, I'll abide with him.
INNOGEN So sick I am not, yet I am not well;
    But not so citizen a wanton as
    To seem to die ere sick. So please you, leave me,
    Stick to your journal course; the breach of custom   10
    Is breach of all. I am ill, but your being by me
    Cannot amend me. Society is no comfort
    To one not sociable. I am not very sick,
    Since I can reason of it. Pray you trust me here,
    I'll rob none but myself, and let me die,   15
    Stealing so poorly.

16–17 power of control over.
18 sore grievous (with a quibble on sword/sore).
18 Fortune May Fortune.

Act 4, Scene 2
4 clay and clay different persons, moulded
from the same dust. Innogen's language is proverbial, deriving ultimately from Ecclesiastes 3.20 ('All
go to one place, and all was of the dust, and all
shall return to the dust': Dent, A119), but her
stress on social distance reverses the idiom's thrust.
Her rejection of the term 'brother' is the first of a
series of teasing ironies that underscore the characters' lack of insight into their circumstances, culminating in Innogen's catastrophic misrecognition

of Cloten's body. The audience can see that Arviragus's intuition is correct, but events have yet to
put the characters into a situation where they can
see the truth of their feelings.
   4 dignity honour; social esteem.
   8 citizen a wanton excessively delicate; one
pampered with the comforts of city life. This is
OED's only instance of 'citizen' = 'citizenish'.
   9 ere sick before I am really sick.
   10 journal daily.
   10 custom habitual order.
   15–16 let . . . Stealing may I die if I steal.
   16 so poorly where there is so little to take. But
Innogen also plays on her own poverty: I must die
if I steal what little I have left.

GUIDERIUS   I love thee; I have spoke it;
      How much the quantity, the weight as much,
      As I do love my father.
BELARIUS   What? How, how?
ARVIRAGUS If it be sin to say so, sir, I yoke me
      In my good brother's fault. I know not why   20
      I love this youth, and I have heard you say
      Love's reason's without reason. The bier at door,
      And a demand who is't shall die, I'd say
      'My father, not this youth.'
BELARIUS [*Aside*]   O noble strain!
      O worthiness of nature, breed of greatness!   25
      Cowards father cowards, and base things sire base;
      Nature hath meal and bran, contempt and grace.
      I'm not their father, yet who this should be
      Doth miracle itself, loved before me. –
      'Tis the ninth hour o'th'morn.
ARVIRAGUS   Brother, farewell.   30
INNOGEN I wish ye sport.
ARVIRAGUS   You health. [*To Belarius*] So please you, sir.
INNOGEN [*Aside*] These are kind creatures. Gods, what lies I have
                                [heard!
      Our courtiers say all's savage but at court.

---

24 SD *Capell; not in* F   26–7 *in quotation marks* F   31 SD] *conj. Capell* (F *inserts long dash*)   32 *Rowe;* These . . . Creatures.
/ Gods . . . heard: F

17 How . . . much Doubled for emphasis: 'as much in quantity, as in weight'. Dowden glosses it as a comparison between time and substance: however superior Guiderius's love for his father is in terms of years, his love for Fidele equals it in intensity.
22 Love's . . . reason proverbial; Dent, L517, 'Love is without reason.'
24 strain disposition, inherited character. Belarius is not praising the boys' display of affection for itself, but because it testifies to their hidden aristocratic status.
25 breed lineage.
26–7 F gives these lines quote marks, signalling that the scribe took them as aphorisms. Walker compares Horace's *Odes* 4.4.29–36: 'It is only from brave parents that brave sons are born; in steers

and horses, the merits of their sires appear; fierce eagles do not breed timid doves.'
27 meal and bran grains and husks; finer and coarser parts.
28–9 who . . . me 'that this boy of whom we know nothing should be loved more than me is miraculous' (Deighton). The passage seems compressed because Belarius conflates speculation about Fidele's identity ('who this should be') with his wonder at the boys' spirit.
29 miracle Treated here as a reflexive verb. Compare the nonce-use of 'monster' in *Lear* 1.1.218–20: 'Sure her offence / Must be of such unnatural degree / That monsters it' (Deighton).
31 So . . . sir The men talk to one side while Innogen reflects privately.

Experience, O, thou disprov'st report!
Th'imperious seas breeds monsters; for the dish,   35
Poor tributary rivers as sweet fish.
I am sick still, heart-sick. Pisanio,
I'll now taste of thy drug.
GUIDERIUS   I could not stir him.
He said he was gentle, but unfortunate;
Dishonestly afflicted, but yet honest.   40
ARVIRAGUS Thus did he answer me, yet said hereafter
I might know more.
BELARIUS   To th'field, to th'field!
We'll leave you for this time. Go in, and rest.
ARVIRAGUS We'll not be long away.
BELARIUS   Pray be not sick,
For you must be our housewife.
INNOGEN   Well or ill,   45
I am bound to you.
BELARIUS   And shalt be ever.

                        [*Exit Innogen, into the cave*]
This youth, howe'er distressed he appears, hath had
Good ancestors.
ARVIRAGUS   How angel-like he sings!

---

35 breeds] F; breed F2   46 SD] *Theobald; Exit. F. So placed by Capell; after* you *in* F   47 distressed he appears,] *Knight;* distrest, appeares he F

34 **Experience . . . report!** Another aphorism: provable knowledge and not mere hearsay is the foundation of truth. This is one of the moments when the play seems to register the impact of Francis Bacon's thought: see also 1.5.17 and note.

35 **breeds** Conceivably an error for *breed* (and so emended in F2), though, as Maxwell notes, 'seas' may be collective and hence a singular noun.

35–6 A comparison that reverses the court's presumed superiority to the country. As the country is to the court, so the 'tributary' rivers (= rivers that pay tribute to the ocean) are to the 'imperious' (= imperial) seas: their fish are just as sweet, but they lack the monsters that lurk at sea. Some editors have been perplexed by Innogen's stiff sententiousness, but it is part of the shifting decorum of this scene, which, with its pastoral lament and grotesque awakening sequence, makes no attempt at naturalism and foregrounds its artifice.

38–42 Possibly these lines provide the space in which Innogen swallows the potion, and some edi-

tors insert a direction to that effect. But she says only that she now resolves to take it, and it might be inappropriate for her to do so in full view of characters who are at that moment discussing her.

38 **stir him** move him (to tell his story).

39 **gentle** well-born.

40 **Dishonestly afflicted** Oppressed by shameful circumstances.

45 **housewife** housekeeper.

47–8 **This . . . ancestors** I follow Knight's emendation of F, which assumes that the words 'he appears' were accidently transposed during composition or correction. There are similar transpositions at 4.4.2 and 5.4.467 ; an error could have arisen from whatever disturbed the text at 49–51. Many editors accept the line as it stands, but the syntax is very unorthodox: Abbott (#411) explains it as conflating two constructions: 'He hath had, [it] appears, good masters' and 'He appears to have had'.

GUIDERIUS   But his neat cookery! He cut our roots in characters,
              And sauced our broths, as Juno had been sick   50
              And he her dieter.
ARVIRAGUS   Nobly he yokes
              A smiling with a sigh, as if the sigh
              Was that it was for not being such a smile;
              The smile mocking the sigh, that it would fly
              From so divine a temple to commix   55
              With winds that sailors rail at.
GUIDERIUS   I do note
              That grief and patience, rooted in him both,
              Mingle their spurs together.
ARVIRAGUS   Grow patience,
              And let the stinking elder, grief, untwine
              His perishing root with the increasing vine.   60
BELARIUS   It is great morning. Come away! Who's there?

                         Enter CLOTEN

CLOTEN   I cannot find those runagates; that villain

---

49 cookery! He] *as Capell;* Cookerie? / *Arui.* He F   57 him] *Pope;* them F   58 patience] *Rowe;* patient F

49, 51 GUIDERIUS ARVIRAGUS In F Arvi-ragus's name appears in two successive speech-headings, suggesting that something has dropped out, probably a remark of Guiderius's. I follow the customary emendation. This creates an irregular line (49), but since text is missing it is hard to find an alternative. Taylor retains F's lineation by reas-signing the first doubled speech to Belarius, but this disrupts the episode's dramatic function, which is to establish the brothers' developing emotional con-nection with their unrecognized sister. To involve Belarius would dilute the family bond: his role, at 61, is to bring the boys' reflections to an abrupt end.

49 characters letters or emblematic shapes; a courtly innovation in the wilds of Wales. Fanci-ful ways of presenting food were part of the art of Renaissance cuisine: for example, J. Murrell's *A Daily Exercise for Ladies*, 1617, includes instruc-tions for preparing food in the shape of letters, knots, beads, chains, gloves, keys, knives, and hooks and eyes.

50 Juno Queen of the gods, who would expect exceptionally fine food.

53 that what.

54 that because.

55 commix mingle.

56 winds . . . at adverse winds.

57 him Another of Compositor B's pronoun transpositions, prompted by proximity to 'both'. F's 'them' has been explained as saying that grief and patience are both apparent in Innogen's sighs and smiles, but this is a sophistication: the whole pas-sage elaborates the notion that she is torn between grief (sighs) and patience (smiles). Shakespeare associates patience with smiles in *TN* 2.4.114–15: 'She sate like Patience on a monument, / Smil-ing at grief'; and *Per.* 5.1.137–9, 'thou didst look / Like Patience gazing on kings' graves, and smiling / Extremity out of act'.

58 spurs lateral roots. The image is two trees which have intertwined their roots, so that each is strangling the other. A happier version of the same idea is used for the embrace of Innogen and Posthumus, 5.4.263–4.

58 patience actually the common name of a plant, the edible dock or monk's rhubarb, known for its medicinal properties. See Simonds, p. 254, and John Gerard's *Herbal*, 1597, p. 314.

59 stinking elder The elder's foul smell was traditionally put down to the belief that Judas hanged himself on this tree.

60 perishing deadly.

60 with from.

61 great morning broad daylight.

62 runagates runaways.

Hath mocked me. I am faint.

BELARIUS   Those runagates?
Means he not us? I partly know him; 'tis
Cloten, the son o'th'Queen. I fear some ambush.   65
I saw him not these many years, and yet
I know 'tis he. We are held as outlaws. Hence!

GUIDERIUS He is but one. You and my brother search
What companies are near. Pray you away,
Let me alone with him.

                            [*Exeunt Belarius and Arviragus*]

CLOTEN   Soft, what are you   70
That fly me thus? Some villain mountaineers?
I have heard of such. What slave art thou?

GUIDERIUS   A thing
More slavish did I ne'er than answering
A slave without a knock.

CLOTEN   Thou art a robber,
A law-breaker, a villain. Yield thee, thief.   75

GUIDERIUS To who? To thee? What art thou? Have not I
An arm as big as thine, a heart as big?
Thy words I grant are bigger, for I wear not
My dagger in my mouth. Say what thou art,
Why I should yield to thee.

CLOTEN   Thou villain base,   80
Know'st me not by my clothes?

GUIDERIUS   No, nor thy tailor, rascal,
Who is thy grandfather. He made those clothes,
Which, as it seems, make thee.

---

70 SD] *Rowe; not in* F   71 mountaineers] F *(Mountainers)*

67 **held** regarded.

69 **companies** followers; the retinue that Cloten is likely to have.

71 **mountaineers** mountain-dwellers; outlaws. The word is Shakespeare's coinage and is repeated in *Temp*. 3.3.44. Cloten assumes that the exiles must be hill-dwelling brigands such as are frequently depicted in literary romances. Compare 120 below: 'traitor, mountaineer'.

73 **slavish** low-spirited.

74 **A slave** Guiderius replies with the same insult: or perhaps 'slave' should be in quote marks, as the specific word to which he reacts. Compare *Rom*. 3.1.125–6, 'Now, Tybalt, take the "villain" back again / That late thou gavest me' (Malone).

78–9 **I wear . . . mouth** i.e., I am not all talk. Also with an echo of *Ham*. 3.2.396: 'I will speak daggers to her, but use none.'

81 **Know'st . . . clothes** Cloten means that his clothes proclaim his rank, not his identity: but this also helps to prepare for Innogen's mistake over his body.

82–3 **He made . . . thee** Proverbial, 'the tailor makes the man' (Dent, T17, citing *Lear* 2.2.54–5, 'You cowardly rascal, Nature disclaims in thee: a tailor made thee'). Guiderius turns Cloten's boast about his courtliness into an insult on his manhood, especially since tailors were proverbially great cowards.

CLOTEN   Thou precious varlet,
　　My tailor made them not.
GUIDERIUS   Hence then, and thank
　　The man that gave them thee. Thou art some fool;   85
　　I am loath to beat thee.
CLOTEN   Thou injurious thief,
　　Hear but my name, and tremble.
GUIDERIUS   What's thy name?
CLOTEN Cloten, thou villain.
GUIDERIUS Cloten, thou double villain, be thy name,
　　I cannot tremble at it. Were it Toad, or Adder, Spider,   90
　　'Twould move me sooner.
CLOTEN   To thy further fear,
　　Nay, to thy mere confusion, thou shalt know
　　I am son to th'Queen.
GUIDERIUS   I am sorry for't, not seeming
　　So worthy as thy birth.
CLOTEN   Art not afeard?
GUIDERIUS Those that I reverence, those I fear, the wise.   95
　　At fools I laugh, not fear them.
CLOTEN   Die the death!
　　When I have slain thee with my proper hand,
　　I'll follow those that even now fled hence,
　　And on the gates of Lud's town set your heads.
　　Yield, rustic mountaineer.

　　　　　　　　　　　　　　　　　　　　　　　Fight and exeunt

　　　　　　　Enter BELARIUS *and* ARVIRAGUS

BELARIUS   No company's abroad?   100
ARVIRAGUS None in the world. You did mistake him, sure.
BELARIUS I cannot tell. Long is it since I saw him,
　　But time hath nothing blurred those lines of favour

---

100 company's] F *(Companie's)*; companies Globe

83 **precious** arrant.
84 **My . . . not** (because the clothes are Posthumus's).
86 **injurious** insulting.
89 **Cloten . . . name** even if your name were 'Cloten, thou double villain' (Delius).
90 **Toad, or Adder, Spider** venomous creatures.
92 **mere confusion** utter ruin.

93 **not seeming** since you do not seem.
97 **proper** own.
99 **on . . . heads** In Shakespeare's day the heads of executed traitors were displayed on the gateway to London Bridge.
103 **lines of favour** facial lineaments. Compare Drayton, *Works*, 2.148: 'Oft in thy face, one favour from the rest / I singled forth.'

Which then he wore. The snatches in his voice,
And burst of speaking were as his. I am absolute   105
'Twas very Cloten.
ARVIRAGUS   In this place we left them.
I wish my brother make good time with him,
You say he is so fell.
BELARIUS   Being scarce made up,
I mean to man, he had not apprehension
Of roaring terrors; for defect of judgment   110
Is oft the cause of fear –

Enter GUIDERIUS [*with Cloten's head*]

                    But see, thy brother.
GUIDERIUS This Cloten was a fool, an empty purse,
There was no money in't. Not Hercules
Could have knocked out his brains, for he had none.
Yet I not doing this, the fool had borne   115
My head as I do his.
BELARIUS   What hast thou done?
GUIDERIUS I am perfect what: cut off one Cloten's head,
Son to the Queen, after his own report,
Who called me traitor, mountaineer, and swore
With his own single hand he'd take us in,   120
Displace our heads where, thank the gods, they grow,
And set them on Lud's town.

---

111 fear–] *after Capell;* Feare. F   111 SD] *Theobald; Enter Guiderius.* F   121 thank] *Steevens;* thanks F

104 **snatches** catches, checks. Combined with 'burst of speaking', this implies that Cloten's verbal mannerism is to speak in fits and starts. This may be an implied stage direction to the actor, analogous to the information in *1H4* that Hotspur stammered.
   105 **absolute** quite certain.
   106 **very Cloten** Cloten himself.
   107 **make good time with** do well against.
   108 **fell** fierce.
   108 **Being . . . up** Probably, while he was still in his youth. Some editors take it to mean that Cloten is mentally deficient, still a child: Ingleby compares *R3* 1.1.20–1, 'sent before my time / Into this breathing world, scarce half made up'. But since Belarius left court before Cloten was fully grown (see 4.4.23), the first meaning seems more likely.
   109 **apprehension** perception.

110–11 **for . . . fear** – In F Belarius's speech ends with a stop, and his last ten words contradict what went before and what we see of Cloten's behaviour. No solution to this crux is wholly satisfactory. My emendation to the punctuation supposes that he is interrupted by the return of Guiderius and does not get to complete his sentence. Other editors think 'cause' is a misprint for 'cease'; or perhaps (as Maxwell suggests), Shakespeare 'merely got into a tangle about opposites'.
   113 **Hercules** classical hero who undertook a series of impossible tasks. Finding Cloten's brain is the apex of impossibility.
   115 **I not doing** had I not done.
   117 **perfect** well aware.
   118 **after** according to
   120 **take us in** overcome us.

BELARIUS   We are all undone.

GUIDERIUS Why, worthy father, what have we to lose,
    But that he swore to take, our lives? The law
    Protects not us; then why should we be tender   125
    To let an arrogant piece of flesh threat us,
    Play judge and executioner all himself,
    For we do fear the law? What company
    Discover you abroad?

BELARIUS   No single soul
    Can we set eye on, but in all safe reason   130
    He must have some attendants. Though his humour
    Was nothing but mutation, ay, and that
    From one bad thing to worse, not frenzy, not
    Absolute madness could so far have raved
    To bring him here alone. Although perhaps   135
    It may be heard at court that such as we
    Cave here, hunt here, are outlaws, and in time
    May make some stronger head, the which he hearing –
    As it is like him – might break out, and swear
    He'd fetch us in; yet is't not probable   140
    To come alone, either he so undertaking,
    Or they so suffering. Then on good ground we fear,
    If we do fear this body hath a tail
    More perilous than the head.

ARVIRAGUS   Let ord'nance
    Come as the gods foresay it; howsoe'er,   145
    My brother hath done well.

BELARIUS   I had no mind
    To hunt this day. The boy Fidele's sickness
    Did make my way long forth.

---

132 humour] *Theobald;* Honor F   133–4 *Capell;* From . . . Frenzie, / Not . . . rau'd F

125 **tender** submissive.
128 **For** Because.
130 **safe** likely.
131 **humour** mental trait. F's 'Honor' could be correct, were Belarius using the title sarcastically. However, this misreading is an easy minim confusion: exactly the same error occurs at *Wiv.* 1.3.83 ('honor' in F, 'humor' in Q).
132 **mutation** changeableness.
137 **Cave** Dwell in caves (not previously recorded in this sense in *OED*).
138 **head** insurrection.
141 **To come** That he would come.
142 **suffering** allowing.
143 **tail** followers: the underlying image is implicitly that of a scorpion.
144 **ord'nance** that which is ordained.
145 **foresay** predict.
145 **howsoe'er** notwithstanding.
148 **my . . . forth** my way forth seem long.

GUIDERIUS   With his own sword,
    Which he did wave against my throat, I have ta'en
    His head from him. I'll throw't into the creek   150
    Behind our rock, and let it to the sea
    And tell the fishes he's the Queen's son, Cloten.
    That's all I reck.   *Exit*
BELARIUS   I fear 'twill be revenged.
    Would, Polydore, thou hadst not done't, though valour
    Becomes thee well enough.
ARVIRAGUS   Would I had done't,   155
    So the revenge alone pursued me. Polydore,
    I love thee brotherly, but envy much
    Thou hast robbed me of this deed. I would revenges
    That possible strength might meet would seek us through
    And put us to our answer.
BELARIUS   Well, 'tis done.   160
    We'll hunt no more today, nor seek for danger
    Where there's no profit. I prithee, to our rock;
    You and Fidele play the cooks. I'll stay
    Till hasty Polydore return, and bring him
    To dinner presently.
ARVIRAGUS   Poor sick Fidele,   165
    I'll willingly to him. To gain his colour
    I'd let a parish of such Clotens blood,
    And praise myself for charity.   *Exit [into the cave]*

---

153 reck] F *(reake)*   168 SD] *Taylor; Exit.* F

148–50 **With . . . him** In *Mucedorus* (1588), one
of the dramatic romances which *Cymbeline* imitates
(see Introduction, p. 13), the wild man Bremo is
killed with his own club. This moment prefigures
5.2, where Posthumus, disguised as a peasant, dis-
arms the more courtly Iachimo, though as befits
the mountain-bred Guiderius, the violence used on
Cloten is more brutal.

149–53 The disposal of Cloten's head alludes
obliquely to the tale of Orpheus, as told in Ovid's
Metamorphoses, XI. The divine poet Orpheus was
dismembered by a mob of Thracian women in a
frenzy; his head was thrown into the River Hebrus
and washed down to the ocean. During the Renaissance this story was interpreted as an allegory of
the destruction of wisdom by barbarism (and its
eventual return in subsequent cultures), though its

roots lie in primitive vegetation myths of sacrifice and rebirth. The allusion helps to shape the
play's upward turn. Cloten has already been called
a 'sacrifice' (1.2.2); his slaughter prefigures Innogen's 'death' and reawakening and makes structurally possible Posthumus's psychological rebirth.
See Simonds, pp. 75–7.

151 **let it** let it go.

153 **reck** care.

156 **So** So that.

156 **alone . . . me** pursued me alone.

159 **That . . . meet** i.e., That it would take all
our power to oppose.

159 **seek us through** search thoroughly for us.

166 **gain** restore.

167 **let . . . blood** draw blood from a whole parish
of Clotens.

BELARIUS   O thou goddess,
Thou divine Nature, how thyself thou blazon'st
In these two princely boys! They are as gentle   170
As zephyrs blowing below the violet,
Not wagging his sweet head; and yet as rough,
Their royal blood enchafed, as the rud'st wind
That by the top doth take the mountain pine,
And make him stoop to th'vale. 'Tis wonder   175
That an invisible instinct should frame them
To royalty unlearned, honour untaught,
Civility not seen from other, valour
That wildly grows in them, but yields a crop
As if it had been sowed. Yet still it's strange   180
What Cloten's being here to us portends,
Or what his death will bring us.

Enter GUIDERIUS

GUIDERIUS   Where's my brother?
I have sent Cloten's clotpoll down the stream,
In embassy to his mother. His body's hostage
For his return.
                        Solemn music
BELARIUS   My ingenious instrument!   185

169 how] *Pope;* thou F   185 ingenious] F *(ingenuous)*

168–80 A series of reflections on the opposition between 'nature' and 'nurture' similar to the
more extended treatment in *The Winter's Tale*. The
goddess Nature (169) is the same deity who presides over *WT* (2.2.58, 4.4.88), and the boys recall
Perdita, whose aristocratic bearing shows that her
status is higher than the humble place where she
lives (*WT* 4.4.1–5, 156–9).
169 thyself . . . blazon'st you display yourself.
The term 'blazon' is heraldic: Nature sets herself
out as in the boys' coat of arms.
171 zephyrs mild winds.
173 enchafed aroused in anger.
178 Civility Civilized behaviour.
178 not . . . other not acquired by imitation of
others.
179 wildly without cultivation.
183 clotpoll blockhead; a 'jingle' on Cloten's
name (Knight, *Crown*, p. 132). King Lear uses the
same contemptuous term for Oswald (*Lear* 1.4.46).
In the theatre the false head which Guiderius holds
really is made of some wooden or inert material.
Cloten is reduced to stage lumber, a mere thing.
185 SD *Solemn music* In all Shakespeare's
late plays, music is used to intensify visionary or

emotional moments, the direction 'solemn music'
reappearing at *Temp.* 5.1.57 and *H8* 4.2.80; see
also *Cym.* 5.3.123 SD. In Jacobean stage practice
this would have meant a consort of recorders:
'Recorders or other solemn music' are called for
in Middleton's *Second Maiden's Tragedy*, 1610 (ed.
W. W. Greg, 1909, i.2454), and 'Still music of
records' accompanies religious ceremonials in
TNK 5.1.136. Recorders provide funeral music in
Middleton's *A Chaste Maid in Cheapside*, 1613,
and in Fletcher and Massinger's *The Fatal Dowry*,
1619.
185 ingenious instrument The music is supposed to be produced by some artificial contrivance,
like a wind organ. Automatic instruments and
mechanical novelties were a source of scientific
curiosity in the Renaissance, however anachronistic
in *Cymbeline*'s time. Examples include the combined organ and carillon sent by Queen Elizabeth to the Sultan of Turkey, the famous perpetual
motion at Eltham, and a 'musical organ with divers
strange and rare motions' shown at Coventry in
1624 (Long, p. 57). Possibly there is a suggestion
of a wind-harp, since harps were part of the iconography of Welshness.

Hark, Polydore, it sounds. But what occasion
Hath Cadwal now to give it motion? Hark!
GUIDERIUS Is he at home?
BELARIUS   He went hence even now.
GUIDERIUS What does he mean? Since death of my dear'st mother
It did not speak before. All solemn things   190
Should answer solemn accidents. The matter?
Triumphs for nothing and lamenting toys
Is jollity for apes and grief for boys.
Is Cadwal mad?

Enter [from the cave] ARVIRAGUS, *with* INNOGEN *dead,*
bearing her in his arms

BELARIUS   Look, here he comes,
And brings the dire occasion in his arms   195
Of what we blame him for.
ARVIRAGUS   The bird is dead
That we have made so much on. I had rather
Have skipped from sixteen years of age to sixty,
To have turned my leaping time into a crutch,
Than have seen this.
GUIDERIUS   O sweetest, fairest lily!   200
My brother wears thee not one half so well
As when thou grew'st thyself.
BELARIUS   O melancholy,
Who ever yet could sound thy bottom, find

188 *Pope;* What . . . meane? / Since . . . Mother F   194.0 *from the cave*] *Taylor; not in* F   201 not] *Rowe 2; not the* F

189 Since . . . before An obsolete simple past
tense with 'since' in place of the complete present
(Abbott, #347). Compare *Ant.* 1.3.1, 'I did not see
him since'.
191 answer correspond to.
191 accidents events.
192 Triumphs Public celebrations.
192 lamenting toys lamentation over trifles.
193 jollity . . . boys superficial joy and shallow
grief (Warren).
193 apes monkeys (who merely imitate human
behaviour); or perhaps fools.
193 boys (whose fidelity cannot be relied on:
Warren helpfully compares 5.4.106–7).
194 SD *dead* F's SD withholds from the reader
the fact that Innogen only appears to be dead, thus
paralleling the effect of Arviragus's entry on stage.
The word 'dead' is missing from the equivalent SD
in *Lear* (5.3.257): '*Enter Lear with Cordelia in his*
arms'.
197 on of.
199 turned . . . crutch turned my youth into

old age. A reversal of Mamillius's effect on old men
in *WT* 1.1.39–41: 'They that went on crutches ere
he was born desire yet their life to see him a man.'
201 not F's extra-metrical 'the'is probably a compositorial interpolation. Taylor suggests that it was
caught from 'thee' earlier in the same line.
202, 207 melancholy This word is repeated
twice within a short space, and Warren takes it
as evidence of revision, 202–8 preserving Shakespeare's first and second thoughts for Belarius's
speech. He suggests that 201–5 was a first attempt
that was marked for deletion, but the copyist
mistakenly transcribed both versions. This is possible, though the repetition is probably inten-
tional. This section of the scene moves into a
self-consciously heightened pastoral lament, and
Belarius's extended apostrophe is in keeping with
the new stylistic decorum.
203 sound thy bottom plumb your depth (a
river-going metaphor, continued in the following
lines).

The ooze to show what coast thy sluggish crare
Might easil'est harbour in? Thou blessed thing,   205
Jove knows what man thou mightst have made; but ay,
Thou diedst a most rare boy, of melancholy.
How found you him?

ARVIRAGUS   Stark, as you see;
Thus smiling, as some fly had tickled slumber,
Not as death's dart being laughed at; his right cheek   210
Reposing on a cushion.

GUIDERIUS   Where?

ARVIRAGUS   O'th'floor,
His arms thus leagued. I thought he slept, and put
My clouted brogues from off my feet, whose rudeness
Answered my steps too loud.

GUIDERIUS   Why, he but sleeps.
If he be gone, he'll make his grave a bed.   215
With female fairies will his tomb be haunted,
And worms will not come to thee.

ARVIRAGUS   With fairest flowers,
Whilst summer lasts and I live here, Fidele,
I'll sweeten thy sad grave. Thou shalt not lack

---

204 crare] *Steevens (conj. Sympson);* care F   205 Might] F2; Might'st F   205 easil'est] F *(easilest)*   206 ay] *Ingleby (after Nicolson conj.);* I F

204 sluggish slow moving.
204 crare a small trading boat. Sympson's conjecture in Steevens (for 'care' in F) has been generally accepted.
205 Might F's 'Might'st' is probably a compositorial anticipation of 'might'st' in 207.
205 easil'est most easily. Taylor compares the word and its elision to 'maidenl'est' in *Lear* 1.2.132. See also 'busil'est' in *Temp.* 3.1.15 (the usual emendation for F's 'busie lest').
206 ay (F: I) Many editors read 'I', and gloss 'what I know is', but this seems very forced. More likely it is a sigh or interjection, the compositor using *I* to indicate *ay*. This is a common convention: there are nearly twenty instances in the Folio text of *Cymbeline* alone. Additionally, the compositor was short of space in this line, and perhaps used *I* for *ay* to save measure.
208 Stark Stiff.
210 Not . . . at Not as if he were laughing at Death's arrow (but only at some troublesome fly): alluding to 1 Corinthians 15.55, 'O death, where is thy sting' (Dover Wilson). Fidele's posture, serenely smiling and lying on a cushion as

if asleep, resembles the modish taste in Jacobean funerary sculpture for representing the dead in naturalistic attitudes. Compare Bosola's remark in *The Duchess of Malfi*, 1614: 'princes' images on their tombs do not lie, as they were wont, seeming to pray up to heaven, but with their hands under their cheeks, as if they died of the tooth-ache' (Webster, I, 543).
212 leagued folded.
213 clouted brogues hobnailed shoes. At this time *brogues* were associated with primitive or 'Irish' attire: see *OED*, brogue n.² 1a.
214 Answered . . . loud Made my steps echo too noisily.
215 he'll . . . bed i.e., his grave will be as peaceful as a bed to him.
217 to thee The sudden change of address and slight metrical irregularity suggests that the line could have been misread by a compositor anticipating the pronouns of the following speech: 'to thee' has been emended to 'there' (Capell) and to 'to him' (Rann). However, performance will make clear the shift in direction.

The flower that's like thy face, pale primrose, nor   220
The azured harebell, like thy veins; no, nor
The leaf of eglantine, whom not to slander,
Outsweetened not thy breath. The ruddock would
With charitable bill – O bill sore shaming
Those rich-left heirs that let their fathers lie   225
Without a monument! – bring thee all this,
Yea, and furred moss besides, when flowers are none,
To winter-ground thy corpse.

GUIDERIUS   Prithee have done,
And do not play in wench-like words with that
Which is so serious. Let us bury him,   230
And not protract with admiration what
Is now due debt to th'grave.

ARVIRAGUS   Say, where shall's lay him?

GUIDERIUS By good Euriphile, our mother.

ARVIRAGUS   Be't so;

---

223 ruddock] F (Raddocke)   227 besides,] Theobald; besides. F   228 corpse.] Capell (subst.); Coarse– F   232 debt to]
this edn; debt. To F

220 pale primrose Also invoked by Perdita, in
WT 4.4.122, as emblematic of maidens who die
before achieving sexual maturity. The whole speech
is reminiscent of WT 4.4.116–27 and Per. 4.1.13–
20: there is a long tradition of flower catalogues
in pastoral elegy, the most notable English example coming in Milton's 'Lycidas'. This passage
underlines the overtly artificial character of the
laments over Innogen, and schematically reverses
the Queen's malicious use of flowers (1.5). Its invo-
cation of a natural cycle also prepares the ground
for Innogen's subsequent resurrection.
   221 azured harebell bluebell. Innogen's azured
eyelids were admired by Iachimo (2.2.22).
   222 eglantine sweet briar (a species of rose).
   222 whom a false relative pronoun: a grammatical error symptomatic of this speech's linguistic
excess (Abbott, #246).
   223 Outsweetened not Was not sweeter than
(hence the apology to the eglantine for this seeming
'slander' on its sweetness). OED's earliest example
of 'outsweeten'.
   223 ruddock robin redbreast: whose supposed
habit of covering the dead was taken as an emblem
of natural charity. Steevens cites Drayton, The Owl,
1604: 'Covering with moss the dead's unclosed
eye, / The little redbreast teacheth charity' (Works,
2: 482); and see Simonds, p. 206.
   224–6 O bill . . . monument A parenthetical observation which voices a complaint about the

decay of contemporary manners more reminiscent
of Jacobean satire than Cymbeline's Britain.
   227–8 The punctuation in F ('besides. . . .
Coarse –') treats this last clause as a new sentence, which Guiderius interrupts. Possibly the
scribe or compositor, puzzled by the obscure term
'winter-ground', attempted to rescue the sense by
treating it as a new and incomplete remark. As
Maxwell notes, this is very like 2.4.76, another
occasion where a dash was apparently intruded into
a difficult reading. However, when the pointing is
adjusted, the clause 'when flowers are none' follows on without difficulty from the robin's moss-
bringing.
   228 winter-ground apparently a neologism; not
otherwise known. As Steevens explains, the implied
meaning is something like 'protect against winter
by providing cover'. Possibly it is a compositorial misreading for 'winter-green': as a noun this
means 'evergreen foliage', though it is not elsewhere recorded as a verb (Douce).
   231 admiration wonder, reverence.
   232 debt to The punctuation in F (debt. To)
leaves Guiderius's last words as an unexpectedly
curt command, and creates some redundancy, since
he has already said 'Let us bury him.' This edition suggests that 'Let . . . grave' is all one sentence, and F's pointing is incorrect. The grave is
a metaphorical debtor in R3 4.4.27: 'Woe's scene,
world's shame, grave's due by life usurped'.

And let us, Polydore, though now our voices
Have got the mannish crack, sing him to th'ground   235
As once our mother; use like note and words,
Save that 'Euriphile' must be 'Fidele'.
GUIDERIUS Cadwal,
I cannot sing. I'll weep, and word it with thee;
For notes of sorrow out of tune are worse   240
Than priests and fanes that lie.
ARVIRAGUS   We'll speak it then.
BELARIUS Great griefs, I see, med'cine the less: for Cloten
Is quite forgot. He was a queen's son, boys,
And though he came our enemy, remember
He was paid for that. Though mean and mighty rotting   245
Together have one dust, yet reverence,
That angel of the world, doth make distinction
Of place 'tween high and low. Our foe was princely,
And though you took his life as being our foe,
Yet bury him as a prince.
GUIDERIUS   Pray you, fetch him hither.   250
Thersites' body is as good as Ajax',
When neither are alive.
ARVIRAGUS   If you'll go fetch him,
We'll say our song the whilst. Brother, begin.
                                        [*Exit Belarius*]

236 once] *Pope;* once to F   253 SD] *Hanmer; not in* F

234–41 This discussion contributes to the seriousness of the moment, and underlines the boys' status as adolescents on the cusp of manhood. For the mistaken supposition that it indicates a change of plan by Shakespeare, faced with actors who could not sing, see Longer Notes, p. 251.

236 once F's 'once to' is extra-metrical and gives the wrong sense (the dirge was not sung to Euriphile but for her burial). Probably 'to' was intruded under the influence of the preceding phrase.

236 note tune.

237 Save ... Fidele Some editors worry that, despite this prediction, the name itself does not occur in the dirge, but the omission passes unnoticed in performance.

239 word speak (*OED* word *v* 2, citing this example).

241 fanes temples.

243 med'cine cure. A proverbial sentiment: see

Dent, G446, 'the greater grief drives out the less'.

245–8 Though . . . low Echoing Innogen's words at 4.2.3–5, though with the point of view reversed.

246 reverence respect; social deference.

247 angel . . . world 'divinely sent messenger' (Deighton); 'power that keeps peace and order in the world' (Johnson).

251 Thersites the most cowardly and cynical of the Greek warriors at the siege of Troy.

251 Ajax Greek hero, second only to Achilles in bravery. In *Troilus and Cressida* Shakespeare depicts Ajax much more sceptically.

253, 256 begin The repetition of 'begin', and the contradiction of Arviragus's first command that they speak, may indicate that these lines are a late insertion, added to allow time for Belarius's exit. In framing the dirge Shakespeare makes it a family event involving only the three siblings.

GUIDERIUS Nay, Cadwal, we must lay his head to th'east.
      My father hath a reason for't.
ARVIRAGUS   'Tis true.   255
GUIDERIUS Come on then, and remove him.
ARVIRAGUS   So. Begin.
GUIDERIUS Fear no more the heat o'th'sun,
      Nor the furious winter's rages.
      Thou thy worldly task hast done,
      Home art gone, and ta'en thy wages.   260
      Golden lads and girls all must,
      As chimney-sweepers, come to dust.

ARVIRAGUS Fear no more the frown o'th'great,
      Thou art past the tyrant's stroke.
      Care no more to clothe and eat,   265
      To thee the reed is as the oak.
      The sceptre, learning, physic, must
      All follow thee and come to dust.

256 So. Begin.] *Capell (subst.);* So, begin. F   256 Begin.] begin. / SONG. F   268 thee] *Hanmer; this* F

254 to th'east As in early Celtic custom, the opposite of Christian practice. This is a nice concession to historical authenticity, but it also prepares for the dirge, which is conspicuously devoid of Christian consolation.

257 F heads the dirge 'SONG', but this is probably an addition by the scribe, Ralph Crane, who was inclined to add presentational flourishes (see Textual Analysis, p. 263). No musical setting survives before that of William Boyce (1746); the dirge is all the sadder for being spoken rather than sung. For its grimly materialist sentiments, compare 5.3.221–33, and see Introduction, p. 23.

257–8 heat, winter Nature as a source of extremes rather than wholeness. Similar polarizations of weather are mentioned at 3.4.161 and 4.4.29–30; the climate of Cymbeline's Britain is harsh and intemperate.

260 Home That is, to the grave, not to heaven: see Corin, 'Dirge'. Compare *Tit.* 1.1.83 (referring to the entombment of Titus's sons): 'These that I bring unto their latest home'.

260 ta'en thy wages proverbial (Dent, W3.1, citing E. Grymestone, *Miscelanea*, 1604, 'Fear not now [at death] to go take thy wages').

261 Golden lads Youths in a condition of perfect wellbeing, as opposed to the 'dust' of the grave (which echoes Genesis 3.19, 'You are dust, and to dust you shall return'). The contrast between golden lads and chimney-sweepers sets life's health, freshness and potential against the grimy dissolution to which all will come. Dr Johnson's magisterial gloss on the couplet was 'All human excellence is equally subject to the stroke of death.'

262 chimney-sweepers Possibly a reference to the ribwort plantain, the seeds of which turn black and scatter. Not in *OED*, but recorded as a Warwickshire word by Joseph Wright, *English Dialect Dictionary* (1898–1905).

266 reed, oak emblematic opposites; as in Aesop's fable, in which the seemingly immovable oak is overthrown by great winds, whereas the reed survives the storm by yielding before it. The fable's concern with greatness and time-serving matches the political theme of this stanza.

267 sceptre, learning, physic power, knowledge, medicine: the three prime areas of man's activity.

268 thee, 274 this I have adopted Dover Wilson's suggestion that these two difficult readings in F were produced by a single printing-house mistake. It is a remarkable coincidence that the only semantic problems in the dirge involve mirror-image pronoun confusions. At 268 F's 'this' does not have a referent (other than, vaguely, 'all the above observations'), whereas 'thee' produces excellent sense. At 274 'Consign to thee' is usually glossed 'submit to the same terms with thee' (Johnson) or 'seal the same contract with thee' (Steevens). However, this construction is strained and cannot be paralleled elsewhere (see *OED* consign *v* 5b), whereas reading 'Consign to this' delivers good sense. Dover Wilson conjectured that in each case the compositor originally set up 'thee', and that when the error was spotted, the wrong 'thee' was corrected, thus leaving the pronouns reversed. This beautifully economical scenario satisfactorily explains the awkward readings in the second and third stanzas.

GUIDERIUS Fear no more the lightning flash,
ARVIRAGUS Nor th'all-dreaded thunder-stone.   270
GUIDERIUS Fear not slander, censure rash,
ARVIRAGUS Thou hast finished joy and moan.
BOTH   All lovers young, all lovers must
                 Consign to this and come to dust.

GUIDERIUS No exorciser harm thee,   275
ARVIRAGUS Nor no witchcraft charm thee.
GUIDERIUS Ghost unlaid forbear thee,
ARVIRAGUS Nothing ill come near thee.
BOTH   Quiet consummation have,
                 And renownèd be thy grave.   280

               Enter BELARIUS *with the body of* CLOTEN

GUIDERIUS We have done our obsequies. Come, lay him down.
BELARIUS Here's a few flowers, but 'bout midnight more;
                 The herbs that have on them cold dew o'th'night
                 Are strewings fitt'st for graves. Upon th'earth's face
                 You were as flowers, now withered; even so   285
                 These herblets shall, which we upon you strow.
                 Come on, away, apart upon our knees –

274 this] *Johnson, conj.;* thee F   281 *Pope;* We . . . obsequies: / Come . . . downe. F   284 graves. Upon th'earth's face]
this edn (conj. Staunton); Graues: vpon their Faces. F; grows upon th'earth's face *Taylor*   287 knees–] *Rowe;* knees: F;
line omitted conj. Keightley

269 Fear . . . flash (But the fearful lightning
flash will materialize at 5.3.157.)
270 thunder-stone thunderbolt: with which
stones were thought to come down. See *Oth.*
5.2.234–5, 'Are there no stones in heaven / But
what serves for the thunder?'; and Chapman,
Bussy D'Ambois, 5.1.16, 'The stony birth of clouds'
(*Tragedies*, p. 147).
274 Consign Submit, deliver themselves.
275–8 This charm against nighttime terrors
recalls Spenser's 'Epithalamion', 334–52 (*Minor
Poems*, 431). Innogen's prayer before sleep (2.2.8–
10) also has a similar petition.
275 exorciser conjurer. One who raises spirits,
not lays them; as in *JC* 2.1.323: 'Thou, like an
exorcist, has conjur'd up / My mortified spirit'.
276 charm bewitch.
279 consummation completion of life. Warren
notes an echo of the 1559 burial service, 'that we .
. . may have our perfect consummation and bliss':
though more immediately there is Hamlet's 'consummation devoutly to be wished' (*Ham.* 3.1.62–3).
284 Upon th'earth's face All editors are
unhappy with F's reading ('vpon their Faces.'). It

could be a command, but it is hard to ascertain the
implied action, and it indelicately draws attention
to Cloten's headlessness. I have adopted Staunton's
emendation, which offers reasonable sense: there
is a similar image in *R3* 5.3.266: 'this cold corpse
on the earth's cold face'. Taylor follows the same
emendation but presents it as a pendant to the
preceding noun 'graves': this is possible, though
'graves upon th'earth's face' seems verbose and
redundant. Perhaps this section of the printer's
copy had imperfect revisions: there is a line missing
at 287, and at 286 the ellipsis after 'shall' (possible
in itself, but rather compressed) could be another
loose end.
286 These herblets shall i.e., these little flowers will also wither. 'Herblets' is a coinage, first
recorded here by *OED*.
287 A line is probably missing after 'knees'. The
sense is incomplete, and the rhyming couplets at
285–6 and 288–89 imply that something has been
lost. In F the whole speech is tightly crammed at
the foot of the page: the pressure under which
the compositor was working may have produced
an error.

The ground that gave them first has them again;
Their pleasures here are past, so is their pain.
                    Exeunt [Belarius, Guiderius and Arviragus]
INNOGEN (*Awakes*) Yes, sir, to Milford Haven, which is the way?   290
I thank you. By yon' bush? Pray, how far thither?
'Od's pitikins, can it be six mile yet?
I have gone all night. Faith, I'll lie down and sleep.
                    [*She sees the body*]
But soft, no bedfellow! O gods and goddesses!
These flowers are like the pleasures of the world,   295
This bloody man, the care on't. I hope I dream;
For so I thought I was a cave-keeper,
And cook to honest creatures. But 'tis not so.
'Twas but a bolt of nothing, shot at nothing,
Which the brain makes of fumes. Our very eyes   300
Are sometimes like our judgments, blind. Good faith,
I tremble still with fear; but if there be
Yet left in heaven as small a drop of pity
As a wren's eye, feared gods, a part of it!

289 is] *Pope; are* F   290 SH] F *lacks the speech prefix but prints 'Imogen awakes.' centred above the speech (head of column)*
293 SD] *after Rowe; not in* F

290–331 Innogen's awakening beside the head-less trunk has numerous precedents in the sensational twists of exemplary romance. The closest parallels occur in the third century Greek romance *Clitophon and Leucippe* and the Elizabethan play *Sir Clyomon and Clamydes*; there are more distant similarities to the *Ephesiaca* (third century) and Sir Philip Sidney's *The Arcadia* (all discussed in the Introduction). Only Shakespeare, though, combines the mistake over the body with the heroine's resurrection from apparent death. Innogen's speech occupies a hinterland between sleep and waking, as she gradually moves from being still in a dream (290–3), to hoping she were dreaming (294–306), to full wakefulness (307f). For most actresses this highly wrought moment is the role's climax, though the audience knows Innogen's grief is not the whole story. The pain of her full-throated tragic lament is mitigated by the complex irony of her misunderstanding the circumstances.

290–2 Yes . . . night These words take us back to 3.6.8, Innogen's conversation with the beggars about travel directions. Effectively, they return her to where she was before meeting her brothers, as if the entire subsequent encounter has been dreamed (compare 297).

292 'Od's pitikins A diminutive form of 'God's pity', i.e., God have mercy, reducing the oath to its mildest possible form. One of the miniaturized turns of phrase which the Victorians so admired in Innogen.

294 But . . . bedfellow Innogen registers the presence of the body, but does not dare look at it again until 305: the intervening lines attempt to deny its reality. Her word 'bedfellow' hints at an erotic, if ironic, undertow: Cloten does share a bed with Innogen, but not in the manner he anticipated.

297 so in that. Innogen hopes the corpse is a dream, as was (she now supposes) her time in the cave.

299 bolt arrow.

300 fumes vapours (which, in contemporary physiology, were thought to produce dreams and irrational behaviour by rising from the body to the brain).

300–1 Our . . . blind This reverses the usual Renaissance hierarchy between the judgement and the eyes: the eyes were the instruments of judgement, but being sensuous organs, could misreport truth.

304 a wren's eye i.e., a minute quantity, the wren being regarded as the smallest bird.

The dream's here still; even when I wake, it is   305
Without me, as within me; not imagined, felt.
A headless man? The garments of Posthumus?
I know the shape of's leg; this is his hand,
His foot Mercurial, his Martial thigh,
The brawns of Hercules; but his Jovial face –   310
Murder in heaven! How? 'Tis gone. Pisanio,
All curses madded Hecuba gave the Greeks,
And mine to boot, be darted on thee! Thou,
Conspired with that irregulous devil, Cloten,
Hath here cut off my lord. To write and read   315
Be henceforth treacherous! Damned Pisanio
Hath with his forgèd letters – damned Pisanio –
From this most bravest vessel of the world
Struck the main-top! O Posthumus, alas,
Where is thy head? Where's that? Ay me, where's that?   320
Pisanio might have killed thee at the heart,
And left thy head on. How should this be? Pisanio?
'Tis he and Cloten. Malice and lucre in them
Have laid this woe here. O 'tis pregnant, pregnant!
The drug he gave me, which he said was precious   325

---

322 thy head] *Hanmer;* this head F   322 be?] *Capell;* be, F

305 **The . . . still** Innogen now finds the courage
to return to the body.
306 **not imagined, felt** not only in my dream,
but physically present.
307–11 The culminating moment in the play's
structural parallellism between Cloten and Posthumus.
309–10 **Mercurial, Martial, Jovial** like Mercury, like Mars, like Jove. Innogen expresses
Posthumus's divine beauty by linking his bodily
parts to suitable deities. As messenger of the gods,
Mercury is the appropriate patron for his foot;
Mars, and Hercules, express strength; Jove is king-
liness.
310 **brawns** muscles.
312 **Hecuba** Queen of Troy, whose husband
Priam was slaughtered by the Greeks. Her fren-
zied grief at the death of her husband and family
is described in Ovid's *Metamorphoses*, XIII. As in
Ham. 2.2.501–18 and *Luc.* 1443–91, she is invoked
as the archetype of the suffering tragic heroine. There may also be an underlying allusion to
Virgil's *Aeneid*, II, in which Priam is remembered
as a headless body lying on the shore (James,

161–2), but it is also part of the delicate irony of
Innogen's situation that she is not in fact the great
tragic victim she assumes herself to be.
313 **to boot** in addition.
314 **irregulous** lawless (a coinage: *OED*'s only
example). The word is created from the Latin *reg-
ula* = law.
314 **Cloten** Innogen's accusations of Cloten and
Pisanio are wide of the mark, but they have symbolic force, as if Cloten's plans in 3.5 had been
carried through and she was suffering the consequences.
315 **Hath** A double irregularity: 'Thou . . . with
. . . Cloten' treated as a plural subject and 'hath'
used for 'have' (Maxwell).
319 **main-top** top of a mainmast.
322 **thy** F's 'this' is defensible but is probably a
pronoun substitution, caught by anticipation from
'How should this be?': a common error throughout
F.
323 **lucre** greed (the malice is Cloten's, the lucre
Pisanio's).
324 **pregnant** obvious.

And cordial to me, have I not found it
Murd'rous to th'senses? That confirms it home.
This is Pisanio's deed, and Cloten. O,
Give colour to my pale cheek with thy blood,
That we the horrider may seem to those   330
Which chance to find us. O, my lord, my lord!
           [*She falls on the body*]

    Enter LUCIUS, CAPTAINS *and a* SOOTHSAYER

CAPTAIN To them, the legions garrisoned in Gallia
      After your will have crossed the sea, attending
      You here at Milford Haven with your ships.
      They are here in readiness.
LUCIUS   But what from Rome?   335
CAPTAIN The senate hath stirred up the confiners
      And gentlemen of Italy, most willing spirits
      That promise noble service, and they come
      Under the conduct of bold Iachimo,
      Siena's brother.
LUCIUS   When expect you them?   340
CAPTAIN With the next benefit o'th'wind.
LUCIUS   This forwardness
      Makes our hopes fair. Command our present numbers
      Be mustered; bid the captains look to't.
                    [*Exit one or more*]
              [*To the Soothsayer*] Now, sir,

---

331 SD] *Globe; not in* F   335 are here] F; are F2   343 SD *Exit . . . more*] *Taylor; not in* F   343 SD *To Soothsayer*] *Hanmer; not in* F

326 **cordial** restorative.

327 **it** i.e., my deduction.

328 **Cloten** Sometimes emended to 'Cloten's', though the possessive is probably implicit. Such ellipses are often found in the reverse formulation: compare 'Until her husband and my lord's return' (*MV* 3.4.30), and Abbott, #397. F often overlooks the terminal '-s': see Textual Analysis, p. 267.

329 **Give . . . blood** Innogen either embraces the body, thus getting blood on her face, or (more dramatically) deliberately smears herself with it. Either way, it unexpectedly fulfils Arviragus's wish at 4.2.166–7, to restore Fidele's paleness with Cloten's blood.

332 **To them** In addition to them (= some other troops): the Captain continues a speech which

began off-stage. For the possible textual problem at this point, see Longer Notes, pp. 251–2.

333 **After** According to.

335 **here** Some editors think 'here' is superfluous, and was mistakenly repeated from 334.

336 **confiners** inhabitants. A rare usage; *OED* confiners *sb* 2 has only one other example, from Daniel's *Civil Wars* (1595).

340 **Siena** A modern Italian state, treated here as if a dukedom ('Siena's brother' = 'the brother of the duke of Siena'), though in fact it was a republic. One of the seeming anachronisms that underlines that Iachimo is a Machiavellian Italian rather than a classical Roman.

341 **benefit** advantage.

What have you dreamed of late of this war's purpose?

SOOTHSAYER Last night the very gods showed me a vision –   345
    I fast and prayed for their intelligence – thus:
    I saw Jove's bird, the Roman eagle, winged
    From the spongy south to this part of the west,
    There vanished in the sunbeams; which portends,
    Unless my sins abuse my divination,   350
    Success to th'Roman host.

LUCIUS   Dream often so,
    And never false. Soft ho, what trunk is here
    Without his top? The ruin speaks that sometime
    It was a worthy building. How, a page,
    Or dead or sleeping on him? But dead rather,   355
    For nature doth abhor to make his bed
    With the defunct, or sleep upon the dead.
    Let's see the boy's face.

CAPTAIN   He's alive, my lord.

LUCIUS He'll then instruct us of this body. Young one,
    Inform us of thy fortunes, for it seems   360
    They crave to be demanded. Who is this
    Thou mak'st thy bloody pillow? Or who was he
    That, otherwise than noble nature did,
    Hath altered that good picture? What's thy interest
    In this sad wreck? How came't? Who is't?   365
    What art thou?

---

365 wreck] F *(wracke)*

344 purpose outcome.

346 fast fasted ('-ed' omitted for the sake of euphony: see Abbott, #341).

346 intelligence information.

347 Jove's bird The appearance of the eagle in the Soothsayer's dream and in Posthumus's helps to bind them together, emphasizing the links between the play's visionary moments.

348 spongy damp. Compare 'spongy April' (*Temp.* 4.1.65). The fertile Roman climate contrasts with Britain's more extreme weather.

350 abuse falsify. The Soothsayer's mistaken interpretation does not in fact arise from his 'sins', or private faults, but from the inherent limits to his pagan wisdom, which the play's transcendent

conclusion will overtake.

352 Soft But wait.

353 speaks indicates.

353 sometime once.

355 Or . . . or Either . . . or.

356 nature doth abhor i.e., it is against nature.

361 crave . . . demanded beg to be asked about.

363 did painted. 'Do' could be used as a technical term signifying creation in painting or sculpture, as in Iachimo's 'a piece of work / So bravely done' (2.4.72–3). There is an informative comparison in *TN* 1.5.233–36: '*Olivia.* We will draw the curtain, and show you the picture . . . Is't not well done? *Viola.* Excellently done, if God did all.'

365 wreck catastrophe.

INNOGEN   I am nothing; or if not,
    Nothing to be were better. This was my master,
    A very valiant Briton and a good,
    That here by mountaineers lies slain. Alas,
    There is no more such masters. I may wander   370
    From east to occident, cry out for service,
    Try many, all good; serve truly; never
    Find such another master.
LUCIUS   'Lack, good youth,
    Thou mov'st no less with thy complaining than
    Thy master in bleeding. Say his name, good friend.   375
INNOGEN Richard du Champ. [*Aside*] If I do lie and do
    No harm by it, though the gods hear, I hope
    They'll pardon it. – Say you, sir?
LUCIUS   Thy name?
INNOGEN   Fidele, sir.
LUCIUS Thou dost approve thyself the very same;
    Thy name well fits thy faith, thy faith thy name.   380
    Wilt take thy chance with me? I will not say
    Thou shalt be so well mastered, but be sure
    No less beloved. The Roman Emperor's letters,
    Sent by a consul to me, should not sooner
    Than thine own worth prefer thee. Go with me.   385
INNOGEN I'll follow, sir. But first, an't please the gods,
    I'll hide my master from the flies as deep
    As these poor pickaxes can dig; and when
    With wildwood leaves and weeds I ha' strewed his grave

---

376 SD] *Rowe; not in* F   389 wildwood leaves] *Neilson-Hill, subst. (conj. Cambridge);* wild wood-leaues F

367 **Nothing . . . better** It were better if I could
be nothing. Innogen's despair pre-echoes Posthumus's in 5.1–3.
371 **occident** west.
376 **Richard du Champ** The name suggests
the kind of knight regularly met with in Elizabethan dramatic romance – a chivalric anachronism
in this context – but it also literally translates the
name of the printer of *Venus and Adonis* (1593)
and *The Rape of Lucrece* (1594), Richard Field
(see Kane, 206). Field was born in Stratford-upon-
Avon, and called himself 'Ricardo del Campo' when
printing Spanish. Perhaps this is a moment of
Shakespearean whimsy.

379 **approve** demonstrate.
380 **Thy . . . faith** Lucius's gloss on Fidele's
name completes Innogen's transformation from
faithful lover to faithful servant (without her dangerous eroticism). Until the final scene, her role is
now effectively over.
385 **prefer** recommend.
388 **pickaxes** her fingers.
389 **wildwood leaves** leaves from (this) unfre-
quented wood. Warren notes that the hyphen
in F's 'wild wood-leaues' reflects one of Ralph
Crane's typical scribal habits; emendation corrects
the metre by restoring the stress on 'wild'.

And on it said a century of prayers,   390
Such as I can, twice o'er, I'll weep and sigh,
And leaving so his service, follow you,
So please you entertain me.

LUCIUS   Ay, good youth,
And rather father thee than master thee.
My friends,   395
The boy hath taught us manly duties. Let us
Find out the prettiest daisied plot we can,
And make him with our pikes and partisans
A grave. Come, arm him. Boy, he is preferred
By thee to us, and he shall be interred   400
As soldiers can. Be cheerful, wipe thine eyes;
Some falls are means the happier to arise.

                                              Exeunt

4.3 *Enter* CYMBELINE, LORDS *and* PISANIO

CYMBELINE [*To a lord*] Again, and bring me word how 'tis with her.
                                          [*Exit Lord*]
A fever with the absence of her son,
A madness of which her life's in danger. Heavens,
How deeply you at once do touch me! Innogen,

394–5 *Pope; one line in* F   399 he is] F2; hee's F   Act 4, Scene 3   4.3 *Scena Tertia.* F   1 SD] *Capell, subst.; not in* F

390 **century** of hundred.
391 **can** am able to.
393 **entertain me** take me into your service.
395–402 The irregularity of 395 (crammed into the end of 394 in F) perhaps indicates that this conclusion was tacked on as a belated afterthought, to cover the removal of Cloten's body. Certainly the scene would end just as effectively were 394 the final line. Compare the parallel change of plan at 3.3.98–106.
397 **daisied** a Shakespearean coinage: *OED*'s earliest example.
398 **partisans** long-handled spears with broad blades.
399 **arm him** take him up in your arms.
401 **can** can be.
402 **Some . . . arise** This line is a compressed

prediction of the personal trajectory which Posthumus is about to undergo, and it anticipates Jupiter's parallel formulation at 5.3.167. All of Shakespeare's late plays foreground the paradox of seeming hurt out of which happiness eventually comes: e.g., *Temp.* 5.1.205–6: 'Was Milan thrust from Milan, that his issue / Should become kings of Naples?'

Act 4, Scene 3
1 **Again** Go back again.
2 **with** caused by. The Queen's off-stage seizure seems unrealistic but, as Adelman notes (p. 205), in killing Cloten, Guiderius also brings about her demise: with no heir, she has no dramatic future. Knight, *Crown*, 132, relates her response to Cloten's death to her 'possessive maternal instinct'.
3 **of** from.
4 **touch** afflict.

The great part of my comfort, gone; my Queen   5
Upon a desperate bed, and in a time
When fearful wars point at me; her son gone,
So needful for this present! It strikes me past
The hope of comfort. [*To Pisanio*] But for thee, fellow,
Who needs must know of her departure and   10
Dost seem so ignorant, we'll enforce it from thee
By a sharp torture.

PISANIO   Sir, my life is yours,
I humbly set it at your will; but for my mistress,
I nothing know where she remains, why gone,
Nor when she purposes return. Beseech your highness,   15
Hold me your loyal servant.

FIRST LORD   Good my liege,
The day that she was missing he was here.
I dare be bound he's true, and shall perform
All parts of his subjection loyally. For Cloten,
There wants no diligence in seeking him,   20
And will no doubt be found.

CYMBELINE   The time is troublesome.
[*To Pisanio*] We'll slip you for a season, but our jealousy
Does yet depend.

SECOND LORD   So please your majesty,
The Roman legions, all from Gallia drawn,
Are landed on your coast, with a supply   25
Of Roman gentlemen by the senate sent.

CYMBELINE Now for the counsel of my son and Queen!
I am amazed with matter.

FIRST LORD   Good my liege,
Your preparation can affront no less

---

9 SD] *Taylor; not in* F   16, 28 FIRST LORD] *Capell; Lord* F   22 SD] *Johnson; not in* F   23 SECOND LORD] *Capell; Lord* F

6 **desperate bed** deathbed.
8 **So needful** So much needed.
9 **comfort** recovery.
11 **seem** pretend to be.
16 **Hold** Consider.
19 **subjection** service as a subject (*OED* subjection 5).
20 **wants** lacks.
21 **will** he will (Abbott, #400).
22 **slip you** let you loose (as a dog is let from a

leash).
22–3 **our . . . depend** our suspicion still hangs over you.
28 **amazed with matter** confounded by the variety of business. Despite Britain's military preparedness, the realm is adrift, and it continues so until the true heirs are recovered.
29 **preparation** force already under arms.
29 **can . . . less** is able to face an army no smaller.

Than what you hear of. Come more, for more you're ready.   30
The want is but to put those powers in motion
That long to move.

CYMBELINE   I thank you. Let's withdraw
And meet the time as it seeks us. We fear not
What can from Italy annoy us, but
We grieve at chances here. Away!   35

Exeunt [Cymbeline and Lords]

PISANIO I heard no letter from my master since
I wrote him Innogen was slain. 'Tis strange.
Nor hear I from my mistress, who did promise
To yield me often tidings. Neither know I
What is betid to Cloten, but remain   40
Perplexed in all. The heavens still must work.
Wherein I am false, I am honest; not true, to be true.
These present wars shall find I love my country,
Even to the note o'th'king, or I'll fall in them.
All other doubts, by time let them be cleared: 45
Fortune brings in some boats that are not steered.   *Exit*

4.4 [*A confused noise of troops is heard.*] *Enter* BELARIUS, GUIDERIUS
and ARVIRAGUS

GUIDERIUS The noise is round about us.
BELARIUS   Let us from it.
ARVIRAGUS What pleasure, sir, find we in life, to lock it
From action and adventure?
GUIDERIUS   Nay, what hope
Have we in hiding us? This way the Romans

---

35 SD] *Hanmer; Exeunt* F   40 betid] F *(betide)*   Act 4, Scene 4   4.4 *Scena Quarta.* F   0 SD *A . . . heard.*] *this edn; not
in* F   2 find we] F2; *we finde* F

31 **want** need.
35 **chances** events.
40 **is betid** has happened.
42 **Wherein . . . true** Pisanio means that the lies
and half-truths he has told (to Posthumus, Cymbeline and Cloten) are justified by the greater good
of his faithfulness to Innogen.
44 **to . . . king** i.e., the king himself will
observe my valour. Pisanio does indeed appear
beside Posthumus and the princes after the battle
(5.3.94 SD), though Shakespeare does not bother
to give him the specific space that this seems to
promise.

45–6 **All . . . steered** Even some drifting boats
come accidentally to harbour. A consolation very
similar to Viola's, *TN* 2.2.40–41.

Act 4, Scene 4
0 SD I have added the off-stage sound which the
dialogue requires. In general, F marks very few cues
for effects.
2 **find we** (F: *we finde*) a simple transposition,
such as might easily occur during compositorial
correction. Compare 5.4.467.
2 **lock** imprison.
4 **This way** i.e., If we follow this course.

         Must or for Britons slay us, or receive us   5
         For barbarous and unnatural revolts
         During their use, and slay us after.
BELARIUS   Sons,
         We'll higher to the mountains; there secure us.
         To the King's party there's no going. Newness
         Of Cloten's death – we being not known, not mustered   10
         Among the bands – may drive us to a render
         Where we have lived, and so extort from's that
         Which we have done, whose answer would be death
         Drawn on with torture.
GUIDERIUS   This is, sir, a doubt
         In such a time nothing becoming you   15
         Nor satisfying us.
ARVIRAGUS   It is not likely
         That when they hear the Roman horses neigh,
         Behold their quartered fires, have both their eyes
         And ears so cloyed importantly as now,
         That they will waste their time upon our note,   20
         To know from whence we are.
BELARIUS   O, I am known
         Of many in the army; many years,
         Though Cloten then but young, you see, not wore him
         From my remembrance. And besides, the King
         Hath not deserved my service nor your loves,   25

---

8 us.] F2; v. F   17 the] *Rowe;* their F   18 fires] F; files *Rann*

5 **or for** either as.
5 **receive** embrace.
6 **revolts** rebels.
7 **During . . . use** While they can make use of us.
9–10 **Newness . . . death** Cloten's death being so recent.
10–11 **mustered . . . bands** listed among the forces.
11 **a render** an account.
13 **answer** reward.
14 **Drawn on with** Brought about by; or brought near by (*OED* draw *v* 86e, citing W. Waterman, *Fardle of Facions*, 1555, 'when any man lieth in drawing on').
17 **the** F's 'their' is possible, but is probably an anticipation of 'their' in 18.
18 **quartered fires** campfires in their quarters. Rann's emendation of 'fires' to 'files' (= military

formations) is tempting, given the easy r/l confusion, and Taylor suggests that 'files' and 'horses' (17) together describe an imminent Roman attack. However, Shakespeare always uses 'quarter(ed)' to mean a camp (e.g., *1H6* 1.2.67–9: 'for myself, most part of all this night, / Within her quarter and mine own precinct / I was employ'd in passing to and fro'). Arviragus is describing the mustering of troops which is the source of the noise, and imagining how the Britons will feel when they hear these sounds.
19 **cloyed importantly** encumbered with important matters; fully occupied (*OED* cloyed cites this passage; and this is the earliest appearance of 'importantly').
20 **upon our note** on observing us.
23 **then** was then.
23 **not wore** did not wear.

Who find in my exile the want of breeding,
The certainty of this hard life; aye hopeless
To have the courtesy your cradle promised,
But to be still hot summer's tanlings and
The shrinking slaves of winter.   30
GUIDERIUS   Than be so,
Better to cease to be. Pray, sir, to th'army.
I and my brother are not known; yourself
So out of thought, and thereto so o'ergrown,
Cannot be questioned.
ARVIRAGUS   By this sun that shines
I'll thither. What thing is't that I never   35
Did see man die, scarce ever looked on blood,
But that of coward hares, hot goats, and venison,
Never bestrid a horse save one that had
A rider like myself, who ne'er wore rowel
Nor iron on his heel! I am ashamed   40
To look upon the holy sun, to have
The benefit of his blest beams, remaining
So long a poor unknown.
GUIDERIUS   By heavens, I'll go.
If you will bless me, sir, and give me leave,
I'll take the better care; but if you will not,   45
The hazard therefore due fall on me by
The hands of Romans.

---

27 hard] F2; heard F

26 **want of breeding** absence of suitable education.

27 **certainty** inescapable continuance (Vaughan). 'The certainty of this hard life' relates to 'exile', not 'want of breeding' (which it parallels rather than follows). The certainty lies in its continuity, not its want of breeding.

28 **courtesy** refined manners. Warren glosses 'courtesy' as 'respect (to a king's children)', but the boys do not yet know they are Cymbeline's sons. They think their 'cradle' (= birth) was courtly, but not that it was royal.

29 **tanlings** persons tanned by the sun (a Shakespearean coinage, and *OED*'s sole early example; subsequent instances are Victorian poeticisms, almost certainly imitations of this same passage). Belarius expresses his anxiety about the boys' future: Guiderius and Arviragus will lose both status and looks by labouring in the open air, unpro-

tected from the extremes of nature. Compare the old shepherd, a 'weather-bitten conduit of many kings' reigns', in *WT* 5.2.55–6, and the 'sunburn'd sicklemen, of August weary' (*Temp.* 4.1.134). This is one prospect which Fidele has escaped by dying (see 4.2.258–9).

30 **shrinking . . . winter** i.e., recoiling from winter's cold like slaves under the lash.

33 **o'ergrown** bearded; or maybe just 'grown old'. Belarius's white beard is mentioned at 5.3.17.

35 **What thing** i.e., What a shameful thing.

37 **hares, goats** traditionally regarded as, respectively, timid and lecherous (*hot*).

39 **rowel** spur (actually the circular disc attached to it).

41 **the holy sun** (recalling the boys' devotion to the heavens at 3.3.1–9).

46 **the hazard . . . due** the risk which I incur by my disobedience.

ARVIRAGUS   So say I, amen.
BELARIUS No reason I, since of your lives you set
          So slight a valuation, should reserve
          My cracked one to more care. Have with you, boys!   50
          If in your country wars you chance to die,
          That is my bed too, lads, and there I'll lie.
          Lead, lead!

                              [*Exeunt Guiderius and Arviragus*]
          The time seems long; their blood thinks scorn,
          Till it fly out and show them princes born.   [*Exit*]

5.1 *Enter* POSTHUMUS [*dressed as a Roman, carrying a bloody handkerchief*]

POSTHUMUS Yea, bloody cloth, I'll keep thee, for I wished
          Thou shouldst be coloured thus. You married ones,
          If each of you should take this course, how many
          Must murder wives much better than themselves
          For wrying but a little! O Pisanio,   5
          Every good servant does not all commands;
          No bond, but to do just ones. Gods, if you

---

53 SD] *this edn; not in* F   54 SD] F *(Exeunt.)*   Act 5, Scene 1   5.1 *Actus Quintus. Scena Prima.* F   o SD] *Enter Posthumus alone.* F   1 wished] *Pope;* am wisht F; once wished *Taylor (conj. Kellner)*

48 of with regard to (Abbott, #174).

51 country country's (as at 1.4.46, though perhaps it is another instance of F's tendency to omit terminal '-s').

53 blood (1) mettle, high temper; (2) family stock.

53 thinks scorn holds itself in contempt. Belarius's prediction is precisely answered by Iachimo's response in defeat, 5.2.7.

Act 5, Scene 1
The principal business of 5.1–5.3 is the reactivation of Posthumus, last seen in 2.5. Although these scenes are packed with incident, they are bound together as a unit by Posthumus's three big speeches, his two soliloquies (5.1.1–33, 5.3.97–123) and the set-piece battle narrative (5.3.3–51).

o SD *bloody handkerchief* The token sent to Posthumus by Pisanio at 3.4.124. Posthumus wears it in place of the ring as a sign of his guilt; being like a knightly favour, it gives his attitude to Innogen a chivalric cast.

1 I wished Pope's reading (for 'I am wisht') has

been widely accepted, though the reason for F's error is obscure. Taylor suggests the manuscript read 'I onc wisht' (for *once*: compare *patienc* at 4.2.58), but this delivers an uncomfortably packed ending to the line. See Textual Essay, p. 264 n. 3.

2 You married ones Posthumus speaks to the audience. This direct address creates a continuity with 2.5, since his departing lines were also generalizations spoken in a monologue half-conscious of the audience. However, his attitudes have now been completely reversed.

3 take this course i.e., revenge for betrayal.

5 wrying deviating from virtue. Posthumus forgives Innogen, even though he still believes her guilty of adultery – a remarkable gesture at a time when sexual infidelity was usually fatal to a woman's moral character. His forgiveness is the single most important change that Shakespeare made to the wager plot. See Introduction, p. 35.

7 bond obligation: a scarcely less unorthodox remark than the preceding one, as it suggests that Posthumus now condones his servant's disobedience. Compare 3.2.14–15 and note.

Should have ta'en vengeance on my faults, I never
Had lived to put on this; so had you saved
The noble Innogen to repent, and struck   10
Me, wretch, more worth your vengeance. But alack,
You snatch some hence for little faults; that's love,
To have them fall no more. You some permit
To second ills with ills, each elder worse,
And make them dread it, to the doer's thrift.   15
But Innogen is your own; do your best wills,
And make me blest to obey. I am brought hither
Among th'Italian gentry, and to fight
Against my lady's kingdom. 'Tis enough
That, Britain, I have killed thy mistress; peace,   20
I'll give no wound to thee. Therefore good heavens,
Hear patiently my purpose. I'll disrobe me
Of these Italian weeds, and suit myself
As does a Briton peasant. So I'll fight

8 **Should have** Had.

9 **put on** instigate, encourage (my own course of vengeance). Compare *Lear* 1.4.208: 'you protect this course, and put it on / By your allowance'. Wayne (p. 16) thinks the phrase refers literally to putting on the handkerchief like a scarf, but 'so' immediately after seems to imply a causally prior action.

12 **little faults** Precisely reversing 2.5.27, where Innogen is accused of 'All faults that earth can name, nay, that hell knows'.

12 **love** i.e., a sign of the gods' mercy, since in striking some down for small sins, they prevent them from falling into worse. Compare Isaiah 57.1: 'Merciful men are taken away, none considering that the righteous is taken away from the evil to come' (Furness).

14 **second** back up.

14 **elder** later. A metaphorical sense: literally elder ills would be the preceding ones. Dowden notes that in *R2* 2.3.43 'elder days' are later days.

15 **thrift** accumulated profit. The general sense is that the gods allow some sinners to become entangled more deeply in sin in order that their eventual repentance will be all the more strongly motivated. The problem is the ambiguity of the antecedents for 'them' and 'it': I take 'them' to be the sinners and 'it' the process of one sin leading to yet worse sins. Possible emendations are 'it' for 'ill' in 15 (Taylor), or 'dreaded' for 'dread it' (Theobald, so that 'them' is the sins themselves). Either way, the subsequent appearance of 'doer's'

superfluously duplicates the sentence's object.

16 **But** i.e., However, I see that. Posthumus ceases questioning the gods and submits to his future. Warren finds an echo of Hebrews 12.6: 'whom the Lord loveth he chasteneth'.

16 **best** Johnson plausibly conjectured this to be compositorial misreading for 'blest', which would reinforce the chiasmus with the following line. Taylor compares 'sacred wills' at *WT* 3.1.7.

20 **mistress; peace** Posthumus addresses the land, already personified in this line, and expresses his underlying loyalty to it as a Briton.

23 **weeds** garments.

24 **a Briton peasant** Posthumus's penance changes not only his side but also his status, from an aristocrat to a poor labourer of the kind that the lost princes presently are (4.4.29–30). The social implications are brought out by Iachimo, who hates being defeated by a 'carl' (5.2.4): at 5.3.86 Posthumus is said to wear 'silly [= rustic] habit'. Some editors provide a direction for Posthumus to change his clothes at this point: conceivably the speech allows it to be done off-stage after the scene has ended, though he does change back again in full view at 5.3.75.

24 **So . . . dedicate** In hoping for death in the ranks of battle, Posthumus seeks suicide without self-slaughter. He wishes to forgo his life but (like Innogen at 3.4.74–6) has proto-Christian scruples that see suicide as sinful: the Roman option is not available. On this point, see Hunter, *Comedy of Forgiveness*, pp. 163–4.

Against the part I come with; so I'll die   25
For thee, O Innogen, even for whom my life
Is every breath a death; and thus unknown,
Pitied nor hated, to the face of peril
Myself I'll dedicate. Let me make men know
More valour in me than my habits show.   30
Gods, put the strength o'th'Leonati in me.
To shame the guise o'th'world, I will begin
The fashion – less without, and more within.   *Exit*

5.2 *Enter* LUCIUS, IACHIMO *and the Roman army at one door, and the Briton army at another,* LEONATUS POSTHUMUS *following like a poor soldier. They march over, and go out.* [*Alarums.*] *Then enter again in skirmish* IACHIMO *and* POSTHUMUS*; he vanquisheth and disarmeth* IACHIMO, *and then leaves him*

IACHIMO The heaviness and guilt within my bosom
         Takes off my manhood. I have belied a lady,
         The princess of this country, and the air on't

---

32 begin] *Theobald;* begin, F   Act 5, Scene 2   5.2 *Scena Secunda.* F   0.3 SD *Alarums.*] *Capell; not in* F

25 **part** side.
28 **Pitied** Neither pitied.
30 **habits** clothes.
31 **th'Leonati** Posthumus lays claim not to his personal name but to his Romanized patronym, and it is as 'Leonatus' that he will be remembered (5.4.143, 201, 441). Fighting less for self than for the clan, he deserves to recover his family in 5.3.
32 **guise** custom.
33 **fashion** a quibble on the relatively recent sense of 'fashion' as 'current mode of dress' (*OED* fashion *sb* 10: as in J. Marston, *Jack Drum's Entertainment*, 1600, B3, 'Her love is as uncertain as an almanac, as unconstant as the fashion'). Posthumus alludes to Jacobean anxieties about the excesses of contemporary aristocratic dress, but his new 'fashion' lies in his inner virtue, not his clothes. This formula revisits and deepens the First Gentleman's glib paradoxes about Posthumus (1.1.22–4).

Act 5, Scene 2
0 SD As F's direction stands, it is more a literary description than a reflection of playhouse practice. Especially, there is no direction for the two armies to engage, and I follow Taylor in supplying alarums (= drum and trumpet calls indicating an attack). Warren suggests that '*They march over*' and the absence of a command to engage indicates that the

battle was staged in a deliberately stylized way, but I doubt any production has ever stuck so literally to the letter of the text. At several points F lacks necessary stage directions (see Textual Analysis); in any case, 5.2's first SD is contradicted by '*The battle continues*' after 10. Taylor divides the scene into a series of three separate units, each marked by an entry; but the action is fluid and continuous, and breaking it up undermines its theatrical integrity.
0 SD 4 **vanquisheth and disarmeth** To disarm one's opponent was a mark of the highest valour. Edelman, p. 169, cites Sir William Segar, *The Book of Honour and Arms*: 'he gaineth the greatest honour that winneth the chief weapon from the enemy, which is the sword, seeing therewith the emperor and kings do create their knights, and the sword is borne before them in sign of authority and regal power'. Compare Guiderius's defeat of Cloten, 4.2.149–51.
2 **manhood** valour (but Iachimo's language, and the loss of his sword, also suggest a more generalized impotence and debilitating sexual guilt).
2–6 **I . . . profession** A specific echo of Beaumont and Fletcher's *Philaster* 4.5.101–2: 'The gods take part against me, could this boor / Have held me thus else?' (*B&F*, I, 457).
3 **on't** of it.

Revengingly enfeebles me; or could this carl,
A very drudge of nature's, have subdued me   5
In my profession? Knighthoods and honours borne
As I wear mine are titles but of scorn.
If that thy gentry, Britain, go before
This lout as he exceeds our lords, the odds
Is that we scarce are men and you are gods.   *Exit*   10

The battle continues, the Britons fly, CYMBELINE *is taken. Then enter to his rescue* BELARIUS, GUIDERIUS, *and* ARVIRAGUS

BELARIUS Stand, stand! We have th'advantage of the ground,
        The lane is guarded. Nothing routs us but
        The villainy of our fears.
GUIDERIUS, ARVIRAGUS   Stand, stand, and fight!

Enter POSTHUMUS, *and seconds the Britons. They rescue* CYMBELINE, *and exeunt. Then enter* LUCIUS, IACHIMO *and* INNOGEN

LUCIUS   Away, boy, from the troops, and save thyself!
        For friends kill friends, and the disorder's such   15
        As war were hoodwinked.
IACHIMO   'Tis their fresh supplies.
LUCIUS   It is a day turned strangely. Or betimes
        Let's reinforce, or fly.   *Exeunt*

5.3 *Enter* POSTHUMUS *and a* BRITON LORD

LORD   Cam'st thou from where they made the stand?
POSTHUMUS   I did,
        Though you, it seems, come from the fliers?
LORD   Ay.

Act 5, Scene 3 **5.3** *Scena Tertia.* F   2 Ay] *Taylor (conj. Craig);* I did F

4 **or** otherwise.
4 **carl** churl.
5 **very . . . nature's** natural born villain (Walker, comparing *R3* 1.3.229, 'The slave of nature').
6–7 **Knighthoods . . . scorn** Although Iachimo is a Roman gentleman, his remark echoes contemporary British anxieties about the inflation of honours. For the discomfort created by James I's indiscriminate conferring of knighthoods and the separation of knightly status from military accomplishment, see Stone, 65–128.
8 **go before** outgo.
13.0 SD *seconds* assists.
16 **hoodwinked** blindfolded. War, personified,

is fighting indiscriminately.
16 **supplies** reinforcements.
17 **Or betimes** Either promptly.
18 **reinforce** obtain reinforcements. A rare transitive use of the verb: *OED* reinforce *v.* 4 gives only one other instance.

Act 5, Scene 3
2 **Ay** F has 'I did', but this is hypermetrical and repeats the preceding line. W. J. Craig (in Dowden) suggests that the copy read 'I' for 'Ay' (see 4.2.207 and note), and that the compositor, reading this erroneously as a first person singular, carried forward 'did' from 1.

POSTHUMUS No blame be to you, sir, for all was lost,
    But that the heavens fought. The King himself
    Of his wings destitute, the army broken,   5
    And but the backs of Britons seen, all flying
    Through a strait lane; the enemy full-hearted,
    Lolling the tongue with slaught'ring – having work
    More plentiful than tools to do't – struck down
    Some mortally, some slightly touched, some falling   10
    Merely through fear, that the strait pass was dammed
    With dead men hurt behind, and cowards living
    To die with lengthened shame.
LORD   Where was this lane?
POSTHUMUS Close by the battle, ditched, and walled with turf,
    Which gave advantage to an ancient soldier,   15
    An honest one, I warrant, who deserved
    So long a breeding as his white beard came to,
    In doing this for's country. Athwart the lane,
    He, with two striplings – lads more like to run
    The country base than to commit such slaughter,   20

3–51 Posthumus's astonishing narrative is in strict theatrical terms a duplication of what we have just seen, and some modern productions (such as the 1989 RSC revival) take this as a signal to skimp on the battle. But this is a serious omission, since by telling us what we already know, the speech focuses attention on the linguistic brilliance with which Posthumus recreates the conflict (like Iachimo's equally elaborate recounting of events at 5.4.153–209). It is the manner, rather than the matter, of his bravura performance which is important.

The episode draws in a general way on the outlines of the battle of Luncarty, near Perth (AD 976), as described in Holinshed's *History of Scotland*. At Luncarty the Scots defeated a force of Danish invaders, the battle being turned by the intervention of a man named Haie and his sons (ancestors of James I's Scottish courtier James Hay). Holinshed provides the overall shape of the encounter, and some of its small details.

4 But Except.
7 strait narrow.
8 Lolling the tongue With tongues hanging out, like hunting dogs.
10 touched wounded.
11 dammed blocked.

12 hurt behind (indicating they were wounded running away.)
13 lengthened shame shame 'extended through the rest of their lives' (*Riverside*).
14 ditched . . . turf 'There was near to the place of the battle, a long lane fenced on the sides with ditches and walls made of turf, through which the Scots which fled were beaten down by the enemies on heaps' (Holinshed, *History of Scotland*, 155). As Sullivan points out, this is emphatically not a Roman road.
16 honest worthy.
16–18 who . . . country 'who, in so serving his country, well deserved the support it had given him during the long life which his beard showed he had lived' (Deighton, substantively). The difficulty in this passage is the slightly skewed sense of 'deserved'. Furness prefers the gloss 'he deserved by his action to be nurtured for as many years as his beard showed him already to have lived', but this requires 'breeding' to mean 'a (future) period of nurture', a sense for which there is no support elsewhere.
20 base a children's game, in which opposed teams, with their own 'bases', try to catch players running out from the other base (*OED* base *sb*³, citing this passage).

With faces fit for masks, or rather fairer
Than those for preservation cased, or shame –
Made good the passage, cried to those that fled,
'Our Britain's harts die flying, not our men.
To darkness fleet souls that fly backwards. Stand,   25
Or we are Romans, and will give you that
Like beasts which you shun beastly, and may save
But to look back in frown. Stand, stand.' These three,
Three thousand confident, in act as many –
For three performers are the file when all   30
The rest do nothing – with this word, 'Stand, stand,'
Accommodated by the place, more charming
With their own nobleness, which could have turned
A distaff to a lance, gilded pale looks;
Part shame, part spirit renewed, that some, turned coward   35
But by example – O a sin in war,
Damned in the first beginners! – 'gan to look
The way that they did, and to grin like lions
Upon the pikes o'th'hunters. Then began

---

24 harts] *Pope 2 (conj. Theobald);* hearts F   24 our] F; her *conj. Thirlby*

---

21 masks women's face coverings, used to protect fair skins from the sun, or for modesty's sake ('for preservation cased, or shame', 22). The boys' complexions are even more delicate than these.

23 Made good Defended; continuing the sense from 'Athwart' (18).

24 harts deer; with a pun on 'hearts'.

24 our The line is explicable as it stands, but Thirlby's conjecture that 'our' should be 'her' may be correct, since the compositor could easily have repeated 'Our' from the beginning of the line.

25 darkness damnation. The souls of soldiers who die flying from the enemy are damned.

26 we are Romans i.e., we will behave like Romans.

27 Like beasts With animal fierceness.

27 beastly in cowardly fashion.

27–8 save . . . frown avert merely by facing the enemy with resolution.

29 Three . . . many With enough confidence for three thousand, and performing as much.

30 are the file practically constitute the whole troop (Onions, comparing *MM* 3.1.136–7, 'the greater file of the subject held the Duke to be wise').

32 Accommodated Favoured.

34 A distaff . . . lance A housewife to a soldier (the distaff, a pole used for spinning thread, being the emblem of domesticity).

34 gilded . . . looks gave colour to those blanched with fear (Deighton). I take 'gilded' to be the main verb governing 28–34 (and looking back to 'These three' at 28), and 'which . . . lance' (33–4) to be a parenthetical clause dependent on 'nobleness'. Alternatively, 'could have turned' and '[could have] gilded' might be parallel constructions, both in apposition to 'nobleness' – in which case the main verb never quite arrives. The syntax of the whole speech is very loose, conveying Posthumus's excitement and the tumultuous events.

35 Part . . . renewed Some (others) were revived by shame, some by courage. In the pace of the narrative, the implied subject has shifted from the three heroes to the fleeing soldiers whom they are addressing. Warren suggests that the subject of 'renewed' continues to be '[t]hese three' (28), so that Posthumus means they renewed a sense of shame in one part of the army, and a spirit of courage in another: but this makes the syntax even more licentious.

36 But by example Only by imitating the others.

37 the first beginners those who set the example.

37 'gan began.

38 they i.e., the three heroes.

38 grin grimace.

A stop i'th'chaser, a retire; anon   40
A rout, confusion thick. Forthwith they fly
Chickens, the way which they stooped eagles; slaves,
The strides they victors made; and now our cowards,
Like fragments in hard voyages, became
The life o'th'need. Having found the back door open   45
Of the unguarded hearts, heavens, how they wound!
Some slain before, some dying, some their friends
O'erborne i'th'former wave, ten chased by one,
Are now each one the slaughterman of twenty.
Those that would die or ere resist are grown   50
The mortal bugs o'th'field.
LORD   This was strange chance:
A narrow lane, an old man, and two boys!

---

42 stooped] *Rowe;* stopt F   43 they] *Theobald;* the F

40 stop a sudden check, used of a horse's movement (*OED* stop *sb*² 21ᵃ, citing *MND* 5.1.119–20: 'He hath rid his prologue like a rough colt; he knows not the stop'), though it could also mean a check to the hounds in hunting (*OED* stop *sb*² 22). The Romans are compared to horsemen hunting an animal which now turns: *pace* Dover Wilson in Maxwell, 'chaser' implies the collective body of the hunters rather than figuring the pursuing Romans as a single horse.

40 retire retreat.

40 anon shortly after.

41–2 they . . . eagles they fly away like chickens along the path they had previously swept over as eagles.

42 stooped swooped down (like Jupiter's eagle at 5.3.180). A technical term from falconry, suitable to the comparison of the Romans with eagles.

42–3 slaves . . . made they retrace like slaves the steps which moments before they took as victors (Deighton, substantively). The victors-turned-slaves comparison reinforces the humiliating eagles-turned-chickens analogy. The whole episode replays the patriotic maxim from Jonson's *Prince Henry's Barriers* (1610), '*Britayne*, the only name, made CAESAR flie' (*Ben Jonson*, VII, 328): see Introduction, p. 41.

44 fragments scraps of food; inconsiderable crumbs which become critical in extreme times

(= 'the life o'th' need').

45–6 Having . . . hearts Probably, 'Finding easy access to the Romans now they had dropped their guard in retreat'. The general sense is clear, though the formula that Posthumus adopts is difficult to gloss exactly. Warren suggests 'hearts' is a metonym for 'fellows' or 'bodies', or is used more specifically to indicate the seat of courage, now abandoned by the resolution that ought to guard it.

47–9 Some . . . twenty A compressed construction which becomes clear once it unfolds. Each successive 'some' describes one category of the British forces who failed under the Roman attack, and refers forward to the main verb 'Are', which is delayed until 49: men who were seemingly dead, or dying, or trampled in the rush, or fled, are now become (in this changed state of affairs) a match for twenty Romans. Maxwell calls 'Some slain' a 'bold hyperbole': in the excitement of the narrative there is no time to register the paradox of dead men reviving to fight again, a contradiction only evident in retrospect.

47–8 some . . . O'erborne probably, some who had been knocked down by their friends in flight. Maxwell suggests F's 'Ore-borne' is a mistake for 'Ore-bore', though this chimes unfortunately with 'before' in 47.

50 or ere before they would.

51 mortal bugs deadly terrors.

POSTHUMUS Nay, do not wonder at it; you are made
           Rather to wonder at the things you hear
           Than to work any. Will you rhyme upon't,   55
           And vent it for a mock'ry? Here is one:
           'Two boys, an old man twice a boy, a lane,
           Preserved the Britons, was the Romans' bane.'
LORD   Nay, be not angry, sir.
POSTHUMUS   'Lack, to what end?
           Who dares not stand his foe, I'll be his friend;   60
           For if he'll do as he is made to do,
           I know he'll quickly fly my friendship too.
           You have put me into rhyme.
LORD   Farewell, you're angry.   *Exit*
POSTHUMUS Still going? This is a lord! O noble misery,
           To be i'th'field, and ask 'What news?' of me!   65
           Today how many would have given their honours
           To have saved their carcasses; took heel to do't,
           And yet died too! I, in mine own woe charmed
           Could not find death where I did hear him groan,
           Nor feel him where he struck. Being an ugly monster,   70
           'Tis strange he hides him in fresh cups, soft beds,

---

53 do not] F; do but *Theobald;* do you *Ingleby*   53 you are] F; Yet you are *Taylor*   64 This is] F; This *Taylor*
(*conj. Ritson*)

53–5 Nay . . . any A confusing moment in which
Posthumus seemingly contradicts himself. Probably
his tone shifts rapidly and sarcastically: Dr Johnson explains that 'Posthumus first bids [the Lord]
not to wonder, then tells him in another mode
of reproach that wonder is all that he was made
for.' Taylor conjectures that 'yet' has dropped out
before 'you' in 53, but this makes a cacophony
of monosyllables, and other possible emendations
(see collation) are disallowed by Posthumus's initial
'Nay'. Posthumus's disdain of the cowardly Lord
recalls Hotspur's anger at the 'popinjay' courtier at
Holmedon (*1H4* 1.3.49).
   55 work any perform any courageous acts.
   55 rhyme upon't compose verses about it.
James, p. 181, compares Posthumus's scornful
riddle to the folk memorials of national antiq-
uities collected in William Camden's *Remains
Concerning Britain* (1605).
   56 vent publish, as in *The Return from Parnassus,* Part 2 (1601): 'What, Jack? Faith, I cannot but

vent unto thee a most witty jest of mine' (Leishman,
p. 284).
   57 twice a boy in second childhood.
   58 bane ruin.
   60 stand withstand.
   61 as . . . do as his nature is.
   62 fly my friendship run away from me.
   64 Still going? Still running away?
   64 This is a lord A redundant 'is' is quite frequent in the Folio, even where the metre requires
a contracted pronunciation: for example, *TGV*
5.4.93, *Shr.* 3.2.1, *MM* 4.2.108, *Lear* 5.3.283; and
Abbott, #461. Taylor omits 'is' as extra-metrical,
arguing that contemporary idiom commonly used
'this' for 'this is'.
   64 noble misery wretched state of one who is
called 'noble' (Maxwell).
   67 took heel took to their heels.
   68 charmed magically protected (by my
'woe' = wretchedness).
   71–2 fresh . . . words i.e., places that seem safe.

Sweet words, or hath moe ministers than we
That draw his knives i'th'war. Well, I will find him;
        [*He changes into Roman costume*]
For being now a favourer to the Briton,
No more a Briton, I have resumed again   75
The part I came in. Fight I will no more,
But yield me to the veriest hind that shall
Once touch my shoulder. Great the slaughter is
Here made by th'Roman; great the answer be
Britons must take. For me, my ransom's death;   80
On either side I come to spend my breath,
Which neither here I'll keep nor bear again,
But end it by some means for Innogen.

        Enter two [BRITISH] CAPTAINS, *and soldiers*

FIRST CAPTAIN Great Jupiter be praised, Lucius is taken.
  'Tis thought the old man and his sons were angels.   85
SECOND CAPTAIN There was a fourth man, in a silly habit,
  That gave th'affront with them.
FIRST CAPTAIN   So 'tis reported,
  But none of 'em can be found. Stand, who's there?
POSTHUMUS A Roman,
  Who had not now been drooping here, if seconds   90
  Had answered him.
SECOND CAPTAIN   Lay hands on him, a dog!

---

73 SD] *this edn; not in* F   83 SD] BRITISH *Theobald (subst.); not in* F   84, 87 FIRST CAPTAIN] *Rowe;* 1 F   86, 91 SECOND CAPTAIN] *Rowe;* 2 F

72 **moe ministers** more agents.
74 **For being now** Because he now is. Some editors think that Posthumus is speaking of himself, but the implied subject is still 'Death'. Still intent on suicide without self-slaughter, Posthumus wonders where he may most reliably encounter Death, and takes him to be acting for the Britons.
75 **Briton** Posthumus turns to himself, and his intention to resume his Roman identity. Lines 74–5 are very compressed and elliptical, and their subject alters almost imperceptibly. Possibly this material was not fully worked out in the manuscript, and it is tempting to adopt Taylor's emendation 'I here resume' for 'I have resumed' (75). But since Posthumus here begins to change back into Roman costume, performance will make the shift of subject apparent.
77 **hind** peasant.

78 **touch my shoulder** arrest me (as a sergeant would, by clapping victims on the shoulder).
79 **answer** retaliation.
79 **be** will be. This word has been queried as ungrammatical (Craig conjectures it should be 'we'), but the shift from 'is' to 'be' voices the difference between already proven facts and facts which are as yet in doubt. Abbott, #299, finds precise parallels in *1H4* 2.4.524–5 ('*Prince.* I think it is good morrow, is it not? / *Sheriff.* Indeed, my lord, I think it be two o'clock') and *Oth.* 3.3.384 ('I think my wife be honest, and think she is not').
81 **On . . . breath** i.e., It doesn't matter which side I die on, so long as I die.
82 **bear** bear away.
86 **silly** rustic.
87 **affront** attack.
91 **answered** supported.

A leg of Rome shall not return to tell
What crows have pecked them here. He brags his service
As if he were of note. Bring him to th'King.

Enter CYMBELINE, BELARIUS, GUIDERIUS, ARVIRAGUS,
PISANIO *and Roman captives. The* CAPTAINS *present* POSTHUMUS
to CYMBELINE, *who delivers him over to a* JAILER.
                              [*Exeunt all but Posthumus and two Jailers*]

FIRST JAILER You shall not now be stolen, you have locks upon you.   95
    So graze as you find pasture.

SECOND JAILER   Ay, or a stomach.

                                              [*Exeunt Jailers*]

POSTHUMUS Most welcome, bondage, for thou art a way,
    I think, to liberty. Yet am I better
    Than one that's sick o'th'gout, since he had rather
    Groan so in perpetuity than be cured   100
    By th'sure physician, death, who is the key

94.0 SD *Exeunt all* . . . JAILERS] Taylor; *Scena Quarta. / Enter Posthumus, and Gaoler.* F   95 FIRST JAILER] Rowe;
Gao. F   95 Rowe; You . . . stolne, / You . . . you: F   96 SD] Rowe; *not in* F

92 **A leg** A metonymy, 'leg' signifying the fliers, those who used their legs to run away. Dowden compared *Dick of Devonshire* (eds. J. McManaway and M. R. McManaway, 1955), p. 734: 'Not so much as the leg of a Spaniard left'.

92 **return** i.e., home to Rome.

93 **brags** (an echo of Caesar's bragging, 3.4.23–4).

94.0 SD F makes a new scene at this point, but the action is continuous, and there seems no reason to assume that Posthumus left the stage. F's directions for exit and reentry are anomalous, and were probably produced by the scribe imposing literary conventions on the theatre text (see Textual Analysis, p. 256). The fluidity of Jacobean stage practice allows Posthumus to pass from the battlefield, to Cymbeline's presence, to prison, by changes in the groups of people around him. He scarcely moves, but the implied location changes, the prison setting being established by the chains put on him at 95. But notwithstanding this continuity, 95–262 is a coherent scenic subset. The centrepiece is the vision, framed by Posthumus's two monologues, with the jailer's dialogue as coda.

95–6 Posthumus is compared to a horse put out to graze with a chain to prevent him being stolen. Thiselton cites *The Return from Parnassus*, Part 2: 'clap a lock on their feet, and turn them to commons' (Leishman, p. 241). The plural 'locks', and 'shanks and wrists' at 103, establish that Posthumus is chained at both his legs and arms.

96 **stomach** appetite.

97–123 The prison monologue explores the penitent sinner's perplexity at the impossibility of ever discharging his burden of guilt. It follows the technical stages laid out in theological discussions of absolution: conviction of sin and contrition (which Posthumus calls sorrow and repentance, 105, 107), and satisfaction (109), for which he offers everything that he has. The problem with this, especially in Protestant theology, is that, because the soul is intrinsically corrupt, Posthumus cannot himself adequately atone for his sins, and so, however penitent, is still dependent on divine mercy for redemption: hence his attempt to bargain with the gods at 109–22. For a full analysis, see Hunter, *Comedy of Forgiveness*, pp. 166–9.

T'unbar these locks. My conscience, thou art fettered
More than my shanks and wrists. You good gods, give me
The penitent instrument to pick that bolt,
Then free for ever. Is't enough I am sorry?   105
So children temporal fathers do appease;
Gods are more full of mercy. Must I repent,
I cannot do it better than in gyves,
Desired more than constrained. To satisfy,
If of my freedom 'tis the main part, take   110
No stricter render of me than my all.
I know you are more clement than vile men,
Who of their broken debtors take a third,
A sixth, a tenth, letting them thrive again
On their abatement; that's not my desire.   115
For Innogen's dear life take mine, and though
'Tis not so dear, yet 'tis a life; you coined it.
'Tween man and man, they weigh not every stamp;
Though light, take pieces for the figure's sake,
You rather, mine being yours. And so, great pow'rs,   120

109 constrained.] *Rowe, subst.;* constrain'd, F

102 **unbar** usually used of bolts or gates, but Shakespeare needs the monosyllable 'pick' for 104.

103 **shanks** legs.

104 **penitent instrument** repentence, which will unfetter his conscience, making him 'free' (105). The 'bolt' is a bad conscience, rather than the bolt of death; nonetheless, once absolved, Posthumus is reconciled to dying.

106 **temporal** earthly.

107 **Must I** If I am to.

108 **gyves** fetters.

109 **Desired . . . constrained** Wished for, rather than compelled.

109 **satisfy** pay my debt; (theologically) atone for my sin (*OED* satisfy *v* 3).

110 **If . . . part** If it is the most important requirement for freeing my conscience.

111 **my all** i.e., my life.

112 **clement** merciful.

113 **broken debtors** bankrupts, whose creditors seize a proportion of their goods, and continue to levy their debt on their reduced resources.

115 **abatement** the diminished amount which is left to them of their principal. Posthumus does not want a temporary reprieve, but to clear his debt in full, even if that means his death.

116, 117 **dear** (1) beloved; (2) valuable.

117 **coined** looking back to the disgusting sexual 'coiner' of 2.5.5; a reversal of Posthumus's earlier position, since he now assumes the gods 'coined' him, rather than some unknown father.

118 **'Tween . . . man** In ordinary monetary exchanges.

118 **stamp** coin: referring to the images with which they are stamped and which give them their currency. What counts is not the metal's absolute weight, which might accidentally vary between pieces, but the symbols by which they are authorized. The worth of individual coins is in the 'stamps' which they bear.

119 **light** (1) short weight; (2) morally imperfect.

120 **You . . . yours** i.e., You may accept my 'coin' all the more readily, since its figure is made in your image.

If you will make this audit, take this life,
And cancel these cold bonds. O Innogen,
I'll speak to thee in silence.   [*He sleeps*]

Solemn music. Enter, as in an apparition, SICILIUS LEONATUS, *father to*
POSTHUMUS, *an old man attired like a warrior, leading in his hand an ancient
matron, his wife and* MOTHER TO POSTHUMUS, *with music before them. Then
after other music, follows the* TWO YOUNG LEONATI, *brothers to* POSTHU-
MUS, *with wounds as they died in the wars. They circle* POSTHUMUS *round as
he lies sleeping*

---

121 make] *Hudson 2 (conj. Daniel);* take F   124 SD *He sleeps*] *Rowe; not in* F

121 **make** Daniel's emendation (F: take)
strengthens this line, presenting Posthumus's audit
as not merely offered but settled: he surrenders
his life, and his debt is discharged. The compositor could have anticipated 'take' from later in the
same line, or from 116 and 119. In *The Textual
Companion* Taylor compares *Mac.* 1.6.27: 'To
make their audit at your Highness' pleasure'; and
Cor. 1.1.144: 'Yet I can make my audit up'.
122 **bonds** (1) legal bonds; (2) bonds of life; (3)
Posthumus's literal shackles. 'Death pays all debts'
is proverbial (Dent, D148).
123.0–214 Generations of critics believed that
the ritualized action and doggerel verse of Posthumus's vision could not be Shakespearean, and no
production between the late seventeenth and mid
twentieth–centuries bothered to include it. But
since Knight's defence (*Crown*, pp. 168–202), its
authenticity has been accepted, and structurally
its integrity is clear: this good dream is the
counterpart to Innogen's nightmares in 2.2 and
4.2. The ghosts' speeches are written in archaic
fourteeners (iambic heptameter lines) that hark
back to the aural world of Elizabethan dramatic
romances, such as *Clyomon and Clamydes*, on which
Cymbeline's plot is partly based (see Introduction, pp. 14–15): they heighten the ghosts' mys-
tery, locating them in a different, more primitive universe. In F most of the ghosts' lines are
split into trimeter and tetrameter units, but the
compositor probably did this because fourteeners
would not fit in the Folio's narrow columns: in just
seven cases he squeezed in a whole verse line (see
the discussion by Hunt). Modern editors follow F, but this edition restores the verses

to their probable original form. The absence
of capitalization for most of F's short lines
suggests they appeared as fourteeners in the
manuscript.
123.1 *Solemn music* This links Posthumus's
dream with the rituals staged at Innogen's 'death',
with their 'solemn music' (4.2.186).
123.1 *as in an apparition* Possibly this implies
a device to indicate the ghosts' otherworldliness,
such as the mists that were used in Beaumont and
Fletcher's *The Maid's Tragedy* and *The Prophetess*,
both Blackfriars plays (Wells). The phrase itself,
though, was probably added by the scribe, Ralph
Crane, who twice used it as a direction for dream
sequences in his transcripts of Middleton's *A Game
at Chess*.
123.4 *music before them* musicians in front
of them. Wells suggests that the parents' ghosts
entered through one door and the brothers'
through another; Warren thinks the musicians
stood by the doors as the ghosts circled around
Posthumus. However, the verb 'follows' seems to
imply a single procession, with the ghosts entering in pairs and preceded by musicians (also in
pairs?) who perhaps continued to walk ahead of
them. If so, it would have been similar to the ceremonial masquerade depicted in the 1596 portrait
of Sir Henry Unton (National Portrait Gallery),
in which masquers at a banquet are shown pro-
cessing in pairs with torchbearers between them.
The musicians could have played portable instruments such as recorders, and been supported by
a larger band off-stage. Compare also *Temp.* 3.2,
where Ariel, playing music, leads around Trinculo,
Stephano and Caliban.

SICILIUS No more, thou Thunder-master, show thy spite on mortal
flies.

With Mars fall out, with Juno chide, that thy adulteries   125
Rates and revenges.

Hath my poor boy done aught but well, whose face I never
saw?

I died whilst in the womb he stayed, attending nature's law,

Whose father then – as men report, thou orphans' father
art –

Thou shouldst have been, and shielded him from this earth-
vexing smart.   130

124–56 *line division this edn;* F *divides thus:* No . . . Master / shew . . . Flies: / With . . . Adulteries / Rates . . .
Reuenges. / Hath . . . well, / whose . . . saw: / I . . . staide, / attending . . . Law. / Whose . . . report, / thou . . . art) /
Thou . . . him, / from . . . smart. / *Moth* . . . ayde, / but . . . Throwes, / That . . . ript, / came . . . Foes. / A . . .
pitty. / *Sicil* . . . Ancestrie, / moulded . . . faire: / That . . . World, / as . . . heyre. / I.*Bro* . . . man, / in . . . hee /
That . . . parallel? / Or . . . bee? / In . . . deeme / his dignitie. / *Mo* . . . mockt / to . . . throwne / From . . . her, /
his . . . one: / Sweete *Imogen?* / *Sic* . . . Italy, / To . . . ielousy, / And . . . vilany? / 2 *Bro* . . . came, / our . . . twaine,
/ That . . . cause, / fell . . . slaine, / Our . . . maintaine. / I *Bro* . . . hath / to . . . perform'd: / Then . . . adiourn'd /
The . . . turn'd? / *Sicil* . . . looke, / looke . . . exercise / Vpon . . . iniuries: / *Moth* . . . good, / take . . . miseries. /
Sicil . . . helpe, / or . . . cry / To . . . Deity. / *Brothers* . . . appeale, /and . . . flye.

124–58 Parker (193–4) compares the ghosts'
complaints with Virgil's *Aeneid* I, 229–53, in which
Venus, Aeneas's mother, appeals to Jupiter to
explain her son's sufferings: 'Sir, you govern the
affairs of gods and men / By law unto eternity,
you are terrible in the lightning: / Tell me, what
wrong could my Aeneas or his Trojans / Have done
you, so unforgivable that, after all these deaths, /
To stop them reaching Italy they are locked out
from the whole world? / Verily, you had promised
that hence, as the years rolled on, / Troy's renaissance would come, would spring the Roman people
/ And rule as sovereigns absolute over earth and
sea. / You promised it. Oh my father, why have
you changed your mind? / That knowledge once
consoled me for the sad fall of Troy: / I could balance fate against fate, past ills with luck to come.
/ But still the same ill-fortune dogs my disaster-
ridden / Heroes. Oh when, great king, will you let
their ordeal end? . . . / Is this the reward for being
true? Is it thus you restore a king?' (transl. C. Day
Lewis). Jupiter's reply predicts the recovery of old
Troy in new Rome, and universal peace after Julius
Caesar's conquests.

124 Thunder-master one of Jupiter's customary denominations: so in *Lear* 2.4.227, 'I do not
bid the thunder-bearer shoot'; and Heywood's *The
Silver Age* (pr. 1613), 'The Thunderer thunders'
(*Dramatic Works*, I: 122).

124 mortal flies Reversing *Lear* 4.1.36: 'As flies
to wanton boys are we to the gods.'

125–6 Juno's anger at her husband's various
adulteries is described in many stories, but this may
be a direct borrowing from Homer's *Iliad*, V, 864–
98, in which Jupiter rebukes Mars for interfering at
Troy and blames Juno's example. For 'chide' (125),
compare Chapman's recent (1610) translation of
Book 5: 'Just of thy mother Juno's moods, stiff-
necked and never yields, / Though I correct her
still and chide' (*Iliad*, V, 887–8; and see Root,
p. 84). Juno's revenges on Jupiter's son Hercules
are a main concern of Heywood's *The Silver
Age*, also sometimes regarded as a source for this
scene.

126 rates rebukes.

127 aught anything.

128 attending . . . law 'awaiting birth in accor-
dance with nature's decree' (*Riverside*). An echo
of *WT* 2.2.57–9: 'The child was prisoner to the
womb, and is / By law and process of great Nature
thence / Freed and enfranchis'd.'

128 orphans' father echoing Psalm 68.5, 'He
is a father of the fatherless' (Dover Wilson, in
Maxwell).

130 earth-vexing smart suffering that plagues
the life of mortals (Sicilius speaks from a ghost's
point of view).

MOTHER   Lucina lent not me her aid, but took me in my throes,
That from me was Posthumus ripped, came crying 'mongst
his foes,
A thing of pity.

SICILIUS   Great nature, like his ancestry, moulded the stuff so fair
That he deserved the praise o'th'world, as great Sicilius' heir.   135

FIRST BROTHER   When once he was mature for man, in Britain
where was he
That could stand up his parallel, or fruitful object be
In eye of Innogen, that best could deem his dignity?

MOTHER   With marriage wherefore was he mocked, to be exiled, and
thrown
From Leonati seat, and cast from her his dearest one,   140
Sweet Innogen?

SICILIUS   Why did you suffer Iachimo, slight thing of Italy,
To taint his nobler heart and brain with needless jealousy,
And to become the geck and scorn o'th'other's villainy?

SECOND BROTHER   For this, from stiller seats we come, our parents
and us twain,   145
That striking in our country's cause fell bravely and were
slain,
Our fealty and Tenantius' right with honour to maintain.

FIRST BROTHER   Like hardiment Posthumus hath to Cymbeline
performed.
Then Jupiter, thou king of gods, why hast thou thus
adjourned

144 geck] F *(geeke)*   144 come] *Dyce 2 (conj. Walker)*; came F

131 **Lucina** Juno Lucina, goddess of childbirth.
For Juno's hostility to the women in Posthumus's
life see 3.4.164. This traumatic birth is reversed at
5.4.368–70 by Cymbeline's image of himself as a
happy mother.
131 **took . . . throes** i.e., I died in the act of
giving birth.
133 **A thing of pity** Compare *Mac.* 1.7.21:
'pity, like a naked new-born babe'. Like Mac-
duff, Posthumus was 'from his mother's womb /
Untimely ripp'd' (*Mac.* 5.8.15–16).
134 **Great . . . ancestry** Nature and his family
stock, working together.
134 **the stuff** the substance (compare 1.1.23,
'such stuff within').
136 **mature for man** fully grown.
137 **fruitful object** object producing love's fruits
(Capell).

138 **deem his dignity** judge his worth.
140 **Leonati seat** The seat of the Leonati;
Abbott, #22, has other instances of proper nouns
used adjectivally. Here it probably means 'the family honour' rather than a specific place (Warren);
compare 'stiller seats' (145).
142 **suffer** permit.
142 **slight** worthless.
143 **geck** dupe. Nosworthy compares 'geck and
gull' (*TN* 5.1.351).
144 **stiller seats** i.e., the Elysian Fields where
blessed spirits live.
144 **come** (came: F) Walker's emendation corrects an easy foulcase error. It improves the sense
and avoids a came/twain clash.
147 **fealty** loyalty (to our king Tenantius).
148 **hardiment** valiant deeds.
149 **adjourned** postponed.

> The graces for his merits due, being all to dolours turned?   150
> SICILIUS Thy crystal window ope; look out; no longer exercise
> Upon a valiant race thy harsh and potent injuries.
> MOTHER Since, Jupiter, our son is good, take off his miseries.
> SICILIUS Peep through thy marble mansion, help, or we poor ghosts
> will cry
> To th'shining synod of the rest against thy deity.   155
> BROTHERS Help, Jupiter, or we appeal, and from thy justice fly.
>
> JUPITER *descends in thunder and lightning, sitting upon an eagle; he throws*
> *a thunderbolt. The ghosts fall on their knees*
>
> JUPITER No more, you petty spirits of region low,
> Offend our hearing. Hush! How dare you ghosts
> Accuse the Thunderer, whose bolt, you know,
> Sky-planted, batters all rebelling coasts?   160
> Poor shadows of Elysium, hence, and rest
> Upon your never-withering banks of flowers.
> Be not with mortal accidents oppressed;
> No care of yours it is; you know 'tis ours.
> Whom best I love, I cross; to make my gift,   165
> The more delayed, delighted. Be content.
> Your low-laid son our godhead will uplift;

---

151 look out] F2; looke, / looke out F

150 **dolours** sorrows.
151 **crystal** transparent, as crystal is. See 177 below.
152 **race** family.
155 **synod** assembly. Used elsewhere by Shakespeare of the gods, e.g., *Ant.* 3.10.4–5, 'Gods and goddesses, / The whole synod of them'. The gods meet in synod in *The Rare Triumphs of Love and Fortune*, one of *Cymbeline*'s sources.
156 **appeal** i.e., from your justice to the whole tribunal.
156.0 SD The play's spectacular high point, especially since Jupiter descends on an eagle, rather than a throne as in other theophanies. The actor would have been lowered on a mechanism worked from a winch hidden in the roof above the Globe stage. Such effects were uncommon at the indoor Blackfriars playhouse and more in vogue at the open-air theatres. For example, in Thomas Heywood's *The Golden Age* (c. 1609–11), staged at the Red Bull, Jupiter and Ganymede ascend to heaven on an eagle; in *The Silver Age* (c.1610–12)

he 'descends in his majesty, his thunderbolt burning', though not on an eagle (Heywood, III, 78, 154). Stage thunder was created by rolling a cannon ball in a groove above the ceiling; the technique for lightning was to send a rocket down a wire.
157 **region low** Jupiter's position in the heavens is elevated beyond the ghosts. His language, too, is more heightened and Latinate.
160 **Sky-planted** Positioned in the heavens.
160 **coasts** regions (*OED* coast *sb* 6).
163 **mortal accidents** human events.
165 **Whom . . . cross** A key aphorism in tragicomedy, voicing the apparently providential discovery of happy purposes beneath seeming misfortune. Compare Lucius's compressed formulation at 4.2.403; see also *Per.* 5.1.245–8, and Guarini's *Pastor Fido*: 'what we imagine is / Our greatest cross, may prove our greatest bliss' (cited in Harris, p. 223). There may be an echo of Hebrews 12:6, 'whom the Lord loveth he chasteneth'.
166 **The . . . delighted** The more delightful for being delayed.

His comforts thrive, his trials well are spent.
Our jovial star reigned at his birth, and in
Our temple was he married. Rise, and fade.   170
He shall be lord of Lady Innogen,
And happier much by his affliction made.
                    [*He gives the ghosts a tablet*]
This tablet lay upon his breast, wherein
Our pleasure his full fortune doth confine,
And so away! No farther with your din   175
Express impatience, lest you stir up mine.
Mount, eagle, to my palace crystalline.   *Ascends*
SICILIUS He came in thunder; his celestial breath
Was sulphurous to smell; the holy eagle
Stooped, as to foot us. His ascension is   180
More sweet than our blest fields. His royal bird
Preens the immortal wing and claws his beak,
As when his god is pleased.
ALL GHOSTS   Thanks, Jupiter.
SICILIUS The marble pavement closes, he is entered
His radiant roof. Away, and to be blest   185
Let us with care perform his great behest.

172 SD] *not in* F   182 Preens] F *(Prunes)*   182 claws] F *(cloyes)*   183 ALL GHOSTS] *All* F

168 **comforts** consolations.

168 **well . . . spent** are well-nigh over (Nosworthy).

169 **Our jovial star** The planet Jupiter, presiding over Posthumus's horoscope.

169–70 **in . . . married** Jupiter resolves any doubts over Posthumus and Innogen's marital status: they have undergone a formal ceremony, and his fatherly sponsorship authorizes their union.

173 **tablet** a small book or single page, in rich binding (see 197–9 below).

174 **confine** contain.

177 **crystalline** made of crystal; alluding to the transparency and beauty of the heavens. Jupiter mentions 'our christall pallace' in *The Silver Age* (Heywood, III, 98); in Kyd's *Spanish Tragedy* Hieronimo sends his prayers to 'the window of the brightest heavens . . . But they are placed in those empyreal heights / Where, counter-mured with walls of diamond, / I find the place impregnable' (3.7.13–18). Warren notes that in Ptolemaic cosmology the 'crystalline heaven' was one of the universe's outermost spheres, next to the firmament.

179 **sulphurous** Perhaps suggesting that

perfume effects were used with Jupiter's descent (compare 123.1 above); or that the fireworks used for lightning left a sulphurous smell.

180 **Stooped** Swooped down; see 5.3.42 and note.

180 **as to foot us** as if to seize us in its talons.

181 **our blest fields** the Elysian Fields.

182 **Preens** Trims (its feathers, with its beak).

182 **claws** Taylor takes F's 'cloyes' as the same as 'clye', one of several variant but now obsolete forms of 'claw' = to scratch (used of an animal). On 'clye' OED quotes from M. Grove, *The Most Famous and Tragical History of Pelops and Hippodamia* (1587): 'Her head was grown so high / Above my pate, that able she was it with nails to clye.'

184 **marble pavement** floor of the heavens. Like 'palace crystalline', 'marble' alludes to the heavens' beauty and colour, but in the Globe there would literally have been a trapdoor in the roof through which Jupiter came down and which 'closed' on his ascent. The Globe ceiling may have been painted to resemble the heavens, with marbled cloud effects.

186 **behest** command.

[*The ghosts and musicians*] *vanish*

POSTHUMUS [*Wakes*] Sleep, thou hast been a grandsire, and begot
　　　　　A father to me; and thou hast created
　　　　　A mother and two brothers. But, O scorn,
　　　　　Gone! They went hence so soon as they were born;　　　190
　　　　　And so I am awake. Poor wretches that depend
　　　　　On greatness' favour dream as I have done,
　　　　　Wake, and find nothing. But, alas, I swerve.
　　　　　Many dream not to find, neither deserve,
　　　　　And yet are steeped in favours; so am I　　　　　　　195
　　　　　That have this golden chance, and know not why.
　　　　　What fairies haunt this ground? A book? O rare one,
　　　　　Be not, as is our fangled world, a garment
　　　　　Nobler than that it covers. Let thy effects
　　　　　So follow to be most unlike our courtiers,　　　　　　200
　　　　　As good as promise.

(*Reads*) 'Whenas a lion's whelp shall, to himself unknown,
without seeking find, and be embraced by a piece of tender air; and
when from a stately cedar shall be lopped branches
which, being dead many years, shall after revive, be jointed to　　205
the old stock, and freshly grow; then shall Posthumus end his
miseries, Britain be fortunate and flourish in peace and plenty.'

186 SD] *this edn; Vanish* F　　187 SD] *Theobald; not in* F　　192 greatness'] *Theobald; Greatnesse,* F

187–9 **Sleep . . . brothers** It is notable that although Posthumus recalls dreaming of his family, he cannot remember Jupiter, as if that part of the vision is inaccessible to him. Hence he will read the tablet but not understand it.

189 **O scorn** An exclamation of disappointment.

192 **greatness** great men at court, whose patronage was sought by clients looking for assistance or employment ('favour'): another of the play's satirical reflections more reminiscent of Jacobean England than Cymbeline's Britain, continued at 199–201.

193 **swerve** err.

194 **dream . . . find** do not dream of finding anything.

194 **deserve** i.e., deserve to find anything.

196 **golden chance** ideal good fortune (looking back to the 'Golden lads' of 4.2.262). Posthumus is amazed at the disparity between his vision and his sense of his own deserts.

197 **rare** fine (referring to the binding).

198 **fangled** given over to finery (Onions).

201 **As . . . promise** Actually carrying through what outwardly they promise.

202–7 As Moffet explains, the riddle is a tissue of biblical echoes, especially from the prophetic visions in Ezekiel. Ezekiel 19 describes a lion's whelp that is cast into imprisonment, and chapter 17 has a great cedar which has fallen into decay; God restores it by breaking off branches and transplanting them, so that they flourish, with birds and animals dwelling in their shade. There are further echoes of Genesis 49.9 ('Judah, the lion's whelp') and Romans 1.16–24 (which compares God's providence to a farmer cutting bad branches from an olive, but grafting them back again when they deserve restoring). There are less certain analogies with Edward the Confessor's deathbed vision, of a dead tree bearing fruit: Shakespeare encountered this when working on *Macbeth* (Rogers).

202 **Whenas** When.

202 **whelp** cub.

205 **jointed** grafted.

206 **stock** trunk.

'Tis still a dream, or else such stuff as madmen
Tongue, and brain not; either both, or nothing,
Or senseless speaking, or a speaking such   210
As sense cannot untie. Be what it is,
The action of my life is like it, which
I'll keep, if but for sympathy.

Enter [FIRST] JAILER

JAILER Come, sir, are you ready for death?

POSTHUMUS Over-roasted rather; ready long ago.   215

JAILER Hanging is the word, sir. If you be ready for that, you are well
cooked.

POSTHUMUS So if I prove a good repast to the spectators, the dish
pays the shot.

JAILER A heavy reckoning for you, sir. But the comfort is, you shall be   220
called to no more payments, fear no more tavern bills, which are as
often the sadness of parting as the procuring of mirth. You come
in faint for want of meat, depart reeling with too much drink;

212–13 *Johnson;* The . . . keepe / If . . . simpathy. F   213 SD FIRST] *Dyce; not in* F   221 are as] *Maxwell (conj. Collier 2); are* F

208 **stuff** rubbish.

209 **Tongue . . . not** Speak without understanding what it means. 'Tongue' and 'brain' are here nouns used as verbs.

209 **either** i.e., both dream and madness. Conceivably there could be a comma after 'either': 'either dream or madness, or both, or neither'. Posthumus's confusion on waking is like Innogen's state at 4.2.291–307.

210 **senseless speaking** speech without meaning.

211 **sense** reason.

211 **Be** 'Be it' is implied (Abbott, #404).

212 **which** (the tablet).

213 **but for sympathy** merely for the sake of its similarity (to my life).

214–59 This half-comic, half-philosophical dialogue introduces a minor character who, though arriving late in the play, foreshadows the turn towards comedy and – like the groom in *R2*, the Apothecary in *Rom.* and the clown in *Ant.* – provides a new perspective on the action (see Mahood, pp. 88–92). It is possible that in Shakespeare's theatre, for reasons of economy, the jailer would have been doubled by the actor who played Cloten, an arrangement which is occasionally adopted in

modern times (for example, by the RSC in 1989). If the roles are doubled, this is the only on-stage episode in which Posthumus and Cloten actually meet (so to speak).

216 **Hanging** Punning on the sense of 'curing raw meat by leaving it to hang' (*OED* hang *v* B.1b). 'Ready', 'over-roasted' and 'hanging' are culinary quibbles that see Posthumus as meat being prepared for death's table.

218–19 **the dish . . . shot** the food meets the bill (the 'shot').

220 **reckoning** quibbling on two senses: 'paying a tavern bill' and 'making an atonement'.

220–30 **But . . . follows** The Jailer's gallows humour reiterates the pre-Christian moral of the dirge in 4.2, that death is an absolute end. There is a strong tension between his earthy wisdom and Posthumus's more transcendental replies, which hints at the play's hidden awareness of the 'fact' that Christ was born in Cymbeline's reign (see Introduction, p. 11).

221–2 **as often** Collier's conjecture greatly improves the parallelism of this sentence. The omission could easily have arisen from accidental compression of 'are as'.

sorry that you have paid too much, and sorry that you are paid
too much; purse and brain both empty: the brain the heavier for   225
being too light, the purse too light, being drawn of heaviness. Of
this contradiction you shall now be quit. O the charity of a penny
cord! It sums up thousands in a trice. You have no true debitor and
creditor but it: of what's past, is, and to come, the discharge. Your
neck, sir, is pen, book, and counters; so the acquittance follows.   230

POSTHUMUS I am merrier to die than thou art to live.

JAILER Indeed, sir, he that sleeps feels not the toothache; but a man
that were to sleep your sleep, and a hangman to help him to bed,
I think he would change places with his officer; for look you sir,
you know not which way you shall go.   235

POSTHUMUS Yes indeed do I, fellow.

JAILER Your death has eyes in's head then; I have not seen him so
pictured. You must either be directed by some that take upon
them to know, or take upon yourself that which I am sure you do
not know, or jump the after-enquiry on your own peril; and how   240
you shall speed in your journey's end, I think you'll never return
to tell on.

POSTHUMUS I tell thee, fellow, there are none want eyes to direct them
the way I am going, but such as wink and will not use them.

---

226 Of] *Globe;* Oh, of F   230 sir] F2; Sis F   239 or take] *Capell (conj. Heath);* or to take F   242 on] *Nosworthy (conj.*
Maxwell); one F

224 **paid** (1) made payment; (2) overcome [by
wine] (*OED* paid *ppl a* 1ᵇ).
225 **heavier** sleepier (through intoxication).
226 **drawn** emptied (of the coins that made it
weighty).
226 **Of** F's 'Oh' is redundant and creates a repetition with the following exclamation, of which it
is probably a compositorial anticipation.
227 **quit** released.
227 **charity** beneficence.
228 **sums up** (1) pays off; (2) disposes of.
228–29 **debitor and creditor** terms used for the
parallel columns in an account book. *OED* cites the
title 'A Profitable Treatise . . . to learn . . . the keeping of the famous reckoning, called . . . Debitor and
Creditor' (1543); and compare *Oth.* 1.1.30–1, '[I]
must be belee'd and calm'd / By debitor and creditor – this counter-caster'. The Jailer sees death as
the great leveller: all men are equal in its account
book.
229 **discharge** written acquittance.

230 **counters** metal discs, used for accounting.
232–3 **but a man . . . to** if a man was destined
to (Abbott, #367).
234 **officer** executioner.
238 **pictured** (death usually being presented as
a hollow skull).
238–40 **You . . . peril** The Jailer queries the
serenity with which Posthumus faces death.
Posthumus's alternatives are to follow others'
advice, presumably theologians or philosophers; to
rely on his own knowledge of the afterlife (of
which he is inevitably ignorant); or to be heed-
less about it. At 240 F's 'to take' is probably an
accidental repetition from 'to know', immediately
before.
240 **jump** hazard. Compare *Mac.* 1.7.7, 'We'd
jump the life to come.'
242 **on of it** (Abbott, #182).
244 **wink** shut their eyes. Maxwell compares
the proverb 'Who so blind as he that will not see'
(Tilley, S206).

JAILER What an infinite mock is this, that a man should have the best   245
use of eyes to see the way of blindness! I am sure hanging's the
way of winking.

Enter a MESSENGER

MESSENGER Knock off his manacles, bring your prisoner to the King.
POSTHUMUS Thou bring'st good news, I am called to be made free.
JAILER I'll be hanged then.   250
POSTHUMUS Thou shalt be then freer than a jailer; no bolts for the
dead.
                                      [*Exeunt Posthumus and Messenger*]
JAILER Unless a man would marry a gallows and beget young gibbets,
I never saw one so prone. Yet, on my conscience, there are verier
knaves desire to live, for all he be a Roman – and there be some   255
of them too that die against their wills; so should I, if I were one.
I would we were all of one mind, and one mind good. O, there
were desolation of jailers and gallowses! I speak against my present
profit, but my wish hath a preferment in't.   [*Exit*]

252 SD] *Theobald; not in* F   259 SD] F2; *Exeunt.* F

245 **mock** jest.
246 **of** The implied '-s' (of's = of his) is probably elided for the sake of euphony, though F is careless with such terminations, e.g., 1.6.167, 'Half all men['s] hearts'.
246 **blindness** (1) ignorance; (2) darkness, to which the Jailer thinks Posthumus is headed.
249 **made free** i.e., through execution, but perhaps echoing John 8.32, 'the truth shall make you free', or Galatians 5.1, 'Stand fast therefore in the liberty wherewith Christ hath made us free, and be not entangled again with the yoke of bondage' (Simonds, 328).
251 **bolts** manacles.
253–59 F's SDs leave a doubt whether this speech is a monologue or not, and in view of the uncertainty of other SDs in Act 5, it seems reasonable to assume that it was designed as a solo speech. Taylor objects that the Jailer is told to bring Posthumus along himself, but there are several ways this could be managed. Perhaps the Second Jailer reentered with the Messenger to escort Posthumus out at 253: his presence was established at 96, but he has no

other function to perform. It does not strain credibility to allow the Jailer a solo moment, for his speech reads like clown's patter, and cannot comfortably be spoken in Posthumus's hearing.
254 **prone** ready in mind; eager (*OED* prone *sb* 7, citing this passage).
255 **for ... Roman** even though he's a Roman, there are much worse people: 'a non sequitur typical of Shakespeare's common folk' (Maxwell).
255–6 **there ... wills** alluding to the Romans' fabled stoicism, which enabled them to face death with equanimity. Lucius will be an exemplary stoic at 5.4.80–1; but the Jailer's scepticism anticipates the final scene's retreat from Roman values.
258 **desolation of jailers** the ruin of jailers (because they would have no work to do).
258 **gallowses** a contemporary plural form, though not elsewhere in Shakespeare.
259 **my ... in't** presumably, because were crime to cease he would get a better job, but also hinting at an underlying proto-Christian intuition.

5.4 *Enter* CYMBELINE, BELARIUS, GUIDERIUS, ARVIRAGUS, PISANIO
and LORDS

CYMBELINE Stand by my side, you whom the gods have made
    Preservers of my throne. Woe is my heart
    That the poor soldier that so richly fought,
    Whose rags shamed gilded arms, whose naked breast
    Stepped before targes of proof, cannot be found.   5
    He shall be happy that can find him, if
    Our grace can make him so.
BELARIUS   I never saw
    Such noble fury in so poor a thing,
    Such precious deeds in one that promised naught
    But beggary and poor looks.
CYMBELINE   No tidings of him?   10
PISANIO He hath been searched among the dead and living,
    But no trace of him.
CYMBELINE   To my grief, I am
    The heir of his reward, which I will add
        [*To Belarius, Guiderius and Arviragus*]
    To you, the liver, heart, and brain of Britain,
    By whom, I grant, she lives. 'Tis now the time   15
    To ask of whence you are. Report it.
BELARIUS   Sir,
    In Cambria are we born, and gentlemen.
    Further to boast were neither true nor modest,
    Unless I add we are honest.
CYMBELINE   Bow your knees.
    Arise my knights o'th'battle. I create you   20

Act 5, Scene   5.4 *Scena Quinta.* F   13 SD] *Rowe; not in* F

Act 5, Scene 4
  4 shamed put to shame.
  4 naked unarmed.
  5 targes of proof tested shields. 'Targes' is a
monosyllable (targ's): compare *Ant.* 2.6.39: 'Our
targes undinted'.
  13 heir . . . reward inheritor of the reward that
properly belongs to him.
    14 liver . . . brain the vital organs.
    15 grant acknowledge.

  20 knights . . . battle The knighting of the
three is anachronistic in Cymbeline's time, but in
keeping with the play's neochivalric aspect. In 1610
there would have been an implicit contrast with
the changing conventions of courtly honour, in
which knighthood was a mark of status increasingly
divorced from military service. The link between
the heroes' knightly reward and their valour has
sensitive social implications: they are emphatically
not carpet knights. See Stone, pp. 71–82.

Companions to our person, and will fit you
With dignities becoming your estates.

Enter CORNELIUS *and* LADIES

There's business in these faces. Why so sadly
Greet you our victory? You look like Romans,
And not o'th'court of Britain.

CORNELIUS   Hail, great King.   25
To sour your happiness, I must report
The Queen is dead.

CYMBELINE   Who worse than a physician
Would this report become? But I consider
By med'cine life may be prolonged, yet death
Will seize the doctor too. How ended she?   30

CORNELIUS With horror, madly dying, like her life,
Which, being cruel to the world, concluded
Most cruel to herself. What she confessed
I will report, so please you. These her women
Can trip me if I err, who with wet cheeks   35
Were present when she finished.

CYMBELINE   Prithee, say.

CORNELIUS First, she confessed she never loved you, only
Affected greatness got by you, not you;
Married your royalty, was wife to your place,
Abhorred your person.

CYMBELINE   She alone knew this,   40
And but she spoke it dying, I would not
Believe her lips in opening it. Proceed.

CORNELIUS Your daughter, whom she bore in hand to love
With such integrity, she did confess
Was as a scorpion to her sight, whose life,   45
But that her flight prevented it, she had

21 **Companions . . . person** Cymbeline's version of the Jacobean office of Gentlemen of the Bedchamber, personal attendants on the king who served him on intimate terms: compare Posthumus's court place at 1.1.42. In Jacobean England this would be the highest mark of favour; in Cymbeline's reformed court the honour goes to the worthiest men.
  21 **fit** equip.
  22 **estates** (new) rank.

31–3 For the similarities between the Queen's death and that of Cecropia in Sidney's *The Arcadia*, see Introduction, pp. 10–11.
  35 **trip** correct.
  38 **Affected** Desired.
  38 **by** through.
  41 **dying** on her deathbed.
  42 **opening** revealing.
  43 **bore in hand** professed (*OED* bear v^1 3^e, citing this passage).

Ta'en off by poison.
CYMBELINE   O most delicate fiend!
Who is't can read a woman? Is there more?
CORNELIUS More, sir, and worse. She did confess she had
For you a mortal mineral which, being took,   50
Should by the minute feed on life and, ling'ring,
By inches waste you. In which time she purposed
By watching, weeping, tendance, kissing, to
O'ercome you with her show; and in time,
When she had fitted you with her craft, to work   55
Her son into th'adoption of the crown;
But failing of her end by his strange absence,
Grew shameless-desperate, opened in despite
Of Heaven and men her purposes, repented
The evils she hatched were not effected; so   60
Despairing died.
CYMBELINE   Heard you all this, her women?
LADIES   We did, so please your highness.
CYMBELINE   Mine eyes
Were not in fault, for she was beautiful,
Mine ears that heard her flattery, nor my heart
That thought her like her seeming. It had been vicious   65
To have mistrusted her; yet, O my daughter,
That it was folly in me thou may'st say,
And prove it in thy feeling. Heaven mend all!

Enter LUCIUS, IACHIMO, [*the* SOOTHSAYER] *and other Roman prisoners,*
with [POSTHUMUS] *behind, and* INNOGEN, [*all guarded*]

Thou com'st not, Caius, now for tribute. That

54 in time] F; in fine *Taylor*   58 shameless-desperate] *Capell;* shamelesse desperate F   63 SH LADIES] F *(La.)*   64
heard] F3; heare F   68 SD] *Enter Lucius, Iachimo, and other Roman prisoners, Leonatus behind, and Imogen* F

47 **delicate** subtle.
50 **mortal mineral** deadly poison.
51 **by the minute** minute by minute.
53 **watching** nursing through the night.
53 **tendance** attention.
54 This line may be corrupt, as it is slightly short and repeats 'in time' from 52; Taylor proposes that 'in time' should be 'in fine' (= 'in the end'). But the language of the opening section of this long scene is deliberately low-key: Shakespeare

reserves his fireworks for later.
55 **fitted** moulded.
56 **th'adoption . . . crown** recognition as heir to the crown.
58 **opened** confessed.
65 **seeming** appearance.
68 **thy feeling** the suffering that you feel.
68 SD Probably the Jailer is one of the characters who should enter here, but he is overlooked in the direction because he has nothing to do or say.

The Britons have razed out, though with the loss   70
Of many a bold one, whose kinsmen have made suit
That their good souls may be appeased with slaughter
Of you their captives, which ourself have granted;
So think of your estate.

LUCIUS   Consider, sir, the chance of war; the day   75
Was yours by accident. Had it gone with us,
We should not, when the blood was cool, have threatened
Our prisoners with the sword. But since the gods
Will have it thus, that nothing but our lives
May be called ransom, let it come. Sufficeth   80
A Roman with a Roman's heart can suffer.
Augustus lives to think on't; and so much
For my peculiar care. This one thing only
I will entreat: my boy, a Briton born,
Let him be ransomed. Never master had   85
A page so kind, so duteous, diligent,
So tender over his occasions, true,
So feat, so nurse-like; let his virtue join
With my request, which I'll make bold your highness
Cannot deny. He hath done no Briton harm,   90
Though he have served a Roman. Save him, sir,
And spare no blood beside.

CYMBELINE   I have surely seen him;
His favour is familiar to me. Boy,
Thou hast looked thyself into my grace,
And art mine own. I know not why, wherefore,   95
To say, 'Live, boy'. Ne'er thank thy master. Live,
And ask of Cymbeline what boon thou wilt,

---

70 razed out scraped out (as ink is scraped off a document to revise it).

71 made suit requested.

74 estate condition (of your souls). The action proposed here repeats the opening action of *Titus Andronicus*, in which Roman soldiers take vengeance on captured prisoners to appease the souls of their comrades who died in battle.

79–80 that . . . ransom i.e., that the only acceptable ransom is our deaths.

80 Sufficeth It suffices.

82 lives . . . on't will take care of it (by revenge).

83 peculiar care personal concerns.

87 tender over sensitive to. Compare *WT* 2.3. 128, 'You, that are thus so tender o'er his follies'.

87 occasions requirements; or, perhaps, business as a page (if 'his' means Fidele's rather than 'the master's').

88 feat deft.

92 And Even if you.

93 favour countenance.

94 looked . . . grace won my favour merely by your looks. In 1607 Robert Carr, the future Earl of Somerset but then a mere page, won favour when he caught King James's attention at a tilt.

95–6 I . . . boy 'I do not know why I should say "Live, boy", yet I do say it.'

96 Ne'er . . . master i.e., because it is my inexplicable instinct, not his plea, which has saved you.

         Fitting my bounty and thy state; I'll give it,
         Yea, though thou do demand a prisoner
         The noblest ta'en.
INNOGEN   I humbly thank your highness.   100
LUCIUS   I do not bid thee beg my life, good lad,
         And yet I know thou wilt.
INNOGEN   No, no, alack,
         There's other work in hand; I see a thing
         Bitter to me as death. Your life, good master,
         Must shuffle for itself.
LUCIUS   The boy disdains me,   105
         He leaves me, scorns me. Briefly die their joys
         That place them on the truth of girls and boys.
         Why stands he so perplexed?
CYMBELINE   What wouldst thou boy?
         I love thee more and more; think more and more
         What's best to ask. Know'st him thou look'st on? Speak,   110
         Wilt have him live? Is he thy kin, thy friend?
INNOGEN   He is a Roman, no more kin to me
         Than I to your highness, who, being born your vassal,
         Am something nearer.
CYMBELINE   Wherefore ey'st him so?
INNOGEN   I'll tell you, sir, in private, if you please   115
         To give me hearing.
CYMBELINE   Ay, with all my heart,
         And lend my best attention. What's thy name?
INNOGEN   Fidele, sir.
CYMBELINE   Thou'rt my good youth, my page;
         I'll be thy master. Walk with me, speak freely.
         [Cymbeline and Innogen walk aside]
BELARIUS   Is not this boy revived from death?

119 SD] *Theobald; not in* F

98 **state** condition, rank.
98–100 **a . . . noblest** the noblest prisoner.
103 **a thing** the ring that Iachimo wears.
105 **shuffle** shift.
106–7 **Briefly . . . boys** proverbial: Dent, L526, 'Love of lads and fire of chats is soon in and soon out.' Compare *Lear* 3.6.18–19, 'He's mad that trusts in the tameness of a wolf, a horse's health, a

boy's love, or a whore's oath.'
107 **truth** loyalty.
108 **perplexed** distressed. A word suggesting stronger emotion than in modern English, according to Maxwell, who compares *Oth.* 5.2.345–6: 'One not easily jealous, but being wrought, / Perplexed in the extreme'.
113 **vassal** subject.

ARVIRAGUS   One sand another   120
          Not more resembles that sweet rosy lad
          Who died, and was Fidele. What think you?
GUIDERIUS The same dead thing alive.
BELARIUS Peace, peace, see further. He eyes us not, forbear.
          Creatures may be alike. Were't he, I am sure   125
          He would have spoke to us.
GUIDERIUS   But we see him dead.
BELARIUS Be silent; let's see further.
PISANIO [*Aside*]   It is my mistress.
          Since she is living, let the time run on
          To good or bad.
CYMBELINE [*Coming forward*] Come, stand thou by our side,
          Make thy demand aloud. [*To Iachimo*] Sir, step you forth.   130
          Give answer to this boy, and do it freely,
          Or by our greatness and the grace of it,
          Which is our honour, bitter torture shall
          Winnow the truth from falsehood. On, speak to him.
INNOGEN My boon is, that this gentleman may render   135
          Of whom he had this ring.
POSTHUMUS [*Aside*]   What's that to him?
CYMBELINE That diamond upon your finger, say,
          How came it yours?
IACHIMO Thou'lt torture me to leave unspoken that
          Which, to be spoke, would torture thee.

---

121 lad] *Hanmer;* lad: F   127 SD] *Rowe; not in* F   129 SD] *Theobald (subst.); not in* F   130 SD] *Rowe; not in* F   134 On,] F3; One F   136 SD] *Capell; not in* F

120–2 One . . . Fidele As the text stands, this is a radical ellipsis in which two parallel constructions are run together: this page resembles Fidele, and one sand does not more resemble another. The compression has troubled editors, and the commonest emendation, following Johnson, is to add punctuation before 'that', treating the last nine words as a separate phrase ('resembles: . . . Fidele!'). Walker thinks that some material had dropped out after 'resembles', through eyeskip caught from the two comparative constructions ('Not more resembles [than . . .] that sweet rosy lad'); there is also irregularity in 120, which is over-length. However, Arviragus's compression might well be generated by his amazement. Antipholus of Syracuse uses a similar metaphor at *Err.* 1.2.35–6: 'I to the world am like a drop of water, / That

in the ocean seeks another drop.'

126 But . . . dead But we see him even though we know him to be dead. Some editors emend 'see' to 'saw', but this misrepresents Guiderius, who is contradicting Belarius, not agreeing with him. Belarius says that it can't be Fidele; Guiderius replies that it has to be.

134 Winnow separate (as in threshing grain).

135 render declare.

139–40 Thou'lt . . . thee i.e., the truth, once you learn it, will torture you so much that you will want to torture me to make me unsay it. Iachimo opens with a remark that signals the bravura rhetorical performance which he is about to undertake, a narrative so elaborate it almost upstages the recognitions to follow. As Freer observes (p. 129), this is the longest speech in the play.

CYMBELINE   How, me?   140
IACHIMO I am glad to be constrained to utter that
         Torments me to conceal. By villainy
         I got this ring. 'Twas Leonatus' jewel,
         Whom thou didst banish, and – which more may grieve thee,
         As it doth me – a nobler sir ne'er lived   145
         'Twixt sky and ground. Wilt thou hear more, my lord?
CYMBELINE All that belongs to this.
IACHIMO   That paragon, thy daughter,
         For whom my heart drops blood, and my false spirits
         Quail to remember – give me leave, I faint.
CYMBELINE My daughter? What of her? Renew thy strength.   150
         I had rather thou should'st live while nature will,
         Than die ere I hear more. Strive, man, and speak.
IACHIMO Upon a time – unhappy was the clock
         That struck the hour! – it was in Rome – accursed
         The mansion where! – 'twas at a feast – O would   155
         Our viands had been poisoned, or at least
         Those which I heaved to head! – the good Posthumus –
         What should I say? He was too good to be
         Where ill men were, and was the best of all
         Amongst the rar'st of good ones – sitting sadly,   160
         Hearing us praise our loves of Italy
         For beauty that made barren the swelled boast
         Of him that best could speak; for feature, laming
         The shrine of Venus or straight-pight Minerva,

---

142 Torments] *Hudson² (Ritson);* Which torments F

142 **Torments** F's 'Which torments' is probably
compositorial, caught from the beginning of 140.
148 **and** 'and whom' is implied.
151 **while nature will** for the length of your
natural life.
153–60 F's punctuation (here rendered as dashes)
indicates that Iachimo's narrative begins as broken
fragments. It suggests a mind working under emotional pressure, though it is, too, part of the artistry
of his narrative.
156 **viands** food.
157 **heaved to head** raised to my mouth.
160 **rar'st** most exceptional.
160 **sadly** reservedly.
162 **made . . . boast** reduced even the most
inflated boasting to fruitlessness.

163 **feature** looks, or physical shapeliness (compare *R3* 1.1.19, 'Cheated of feature by dissembling
nature').
163 **laming** rendering deformed (by comparison).
164 **shrine** literally, a structure containing a
deity's image, but here referring to the image itself.
For similar figurative usages, see *Mer.* 2.7.40 ('To
kiss this shrine, this mortal breathing saint') and
Rom. 1.5.93–4 ('If I profane with my unworthiest
hand / This holy shrine').
164 **straight-pight** straight-pitched; tall and
erect (*OED*'s only instance of this compound).
164 **Minerva** goddess of arts and war.

Postures beyond brief nature; for condition,   165
A shop of all the qualities that man
Loves woman for; besides that hook of wiving,
Fairness, which strikes the eye –

CYMBELINE   I stand on fire.
Come to the matter.

IACHIMO   All too soon I shall,
Unless thou wouldst grieve quickly. This Posthumus,   170
Most like a noble lord in love and one
That had a royal lover, took his hint,
And not dispraising whom we praised – therein
He was as calm as virtue – he began
His mistress' picture, which by his tongue being made,   175
And then a mind put in't, either our brags
Were cracked of kitchen-trulls, or his description
Proved us unspeaking sots.

CYMBELINE   Nay, nay, to th'purpose.

IACHIMO Your daughter's chastity – there it begins.
He spake of her as Dian had hot dreams,   180
And she alone were cold; whereat I, wretch,
Made scruple of his praise, and wagered with him
Pieces of gold 'gainst this which then he wore
Upon his honoured finger, to attain
In suit the place of's bed and win this ring   185
By hers and mine adultery. He, true knight,
No lesser of her honour confident
Than I did truly find her, stakes this ring –

168–9 I . . . matter] *Rowe 2; one line in* F   177 cracked] F (crak'd)

165 **Postures** Forms.
165 **beyond . . . nature** exceeding nature's hasty
workmanship (Warburton): perhaps with the implication that all natural beauty fades.
165 **condition** character.
166 **shop** storehouse.
167 **hook of wiving** bait of marriage.
172 **hint** cue.
177 **cracked** boastfully uttered. F's 'crak'd' is
merely a variant form: see *OED* cracked *v* 6.
177 **kitchen-trulls** kitchen wenches.
178 **unspeaking** incapable of adequate expres-

sion. Characteristically, the competitive Iachimo
feels himself threatened by Posthumus's way with
words, as well as his mistress.
180 **as Dian** as if Diana (goddess of chastity).
182 **Made scruple of** Made a doubt about.
185 **In suit** By courtship.
186 **hers . . . adultery** her adultery and mine.
For pronominal adjectives placed before the noun,
see Abbott, #238.
187–8 **No . . . her** i.e., his confidence in her
chastity was no less than I subsequently found it
to be worth.

And would so, had it been a carbuncle
Of Phoebus' wheel, and might so safely, had it   190
Been all the worth of's car. Away to Britain
Post I in this design. Well may you, sir,
Remember me at court, where I was taught
Of your chaste daughter the wide difference
'Twixt amorous and villainous. Being thus quenched   195
Of hope, not longing, mine Italian brain
'Gan in your duller Britain operate
Most vilely; for my vantage, excellent.
And to be brief, my practice so prevailed,
That I returned with simular proof enough   200
To make the noble Leonatus mad,
By wounding his belief in her renown
With tokens thus, and thus: averring notes
Of chamber-hanging, pictures, this her bracelet –
O cunning, how I got it! – nay, some marks   205
Of secret on her person, that he could not
But think her bond of chastity quite cracked,
I having ta'en the forfeit. Whereupon –
Methinks I see him now –

---

197 operate] F2; operare F   205 got it] F2; got F

189 would so; 190 might so would have done
so; might have done so.
189–90 carbuncle . . . wheel ruby on Phoebus's
chariot wheel (the chariot of the sun). In Ovid's
Metamorphoses the chariot glitters because of the
precious stones which stud it: 'The spokes were
all of sylver bright, the Chrysolites and Gemmes /
That stood uppon the Collars, Trace, and hounces
in their hemmes / Did cast a sheere and glim-
mering light, as Phoebus shone thereon' (Ovid,
p. 35). The image recurs in *Ant.* 4.8.28–9: 'He
has deserv'd it [a suit of golden armour], were it
carbuncled / Like holy Phoebus' car.'
191 all . . . car the value of his whole chariot.
192 Post Hasten.
196 longing desire.
197 duller Britain alluding to the scientific idea
that national mental constitutions were determined
by factors relating to climate, so rendering northern
nations more slow-witted than southern. This the-
ory goes back to Aristotle, but in the Renaissance it
was widely taken as fact: see, for example, T. Nashe,
Preface to Greene's Menaphon, 1589: 'Tush, say our
English Italians, the finest wits our climate sends

forth are but drie brained dolts in comparison of
other countries' (*Works*, III, 322).
198 vantage profit (*Cor.* 1.1.160, 'to win some
vantage').
199 practice treachery.
200 simular pretended. Iachimo refers not to
the evidence, which was real enough, but the coun-
terfeited arguments which it could support (Furness). Compare *Lear* 3.2.54, 'thou simular of virtue
/ That art incestuous', where 'simular' means
'hypocrite, dissembler'.
202 renown reputation.
203 averring notes avouching evidence (Dowden). *OED* aver *v* 5, citing this passage, glosses
'asserting the existence of', but Dowden is nearer
the mark.
207 cracked broken: a commercial metaphor
that continues in 'bond' and 'forfeit' (208; =
the penalty incurred by the breach of an agreement). But 'forfeit' also carries the suggestion that
Iachimo enjoyed Innogen's sexual favours: his language intensifies the shame of the slander by representing her chastity as an object to which his false
report does material damage.

POSTHUMUS [*Coming forward*] Ay, so thou dost,
        Italian fiend! Ay me, most credulous fool,   210
        Egregious murderer, thief, anything
        That's due to all the villains past, in being,
        To come! O give me cord, or knife, or poison,
        Some upright justicer! Thou King, send out
        For torturers ingenious: it is I   215
        That all th'abhorrèd things o'th'earth amend
        By being worse than they. I am Posthumus,
        That killed thy daughter – villain-like, I lie –
        That caused a lesser villain than myself,
        A sacrilegious thief, to do't. The temple   220
        Of virtue was she; yea, and she herself.
        Spit and throw stones, cast mire upon me, set
        The dogs o'th'street to bay me. Every villain
        Be called Posthumus Leonatus, and
        Be 'villain' less than 'twas! O Innogen!   225
        My queen, my life, my wife! O Innogen,
        Innogen, Innogen!
INNOGEN   Peace, my lord, hear, hear–
POSTHUMUS Shall's have a play of this? Thou scornful page,
        There lie thy part. ⟜ linked to theatre
        [*Striking her, she falls*]

---

209 SD] *Rowe; not in* F   **225** 'villain'] *Maxwell;* villany F   **228–9** *Hanmer;* Shall's . . . this? / Thou . . . part.   **229** SD]
not in F

211 Egregious Flagrant. The word harks back
to Iachimo's precursor, Iago, 'making [Othello]
egregiously an ass' (*Oth.* 2.1.309).
   211 anything i.e., any name.
   213 cord rope (to hang myself).
   214 justicer judge. Shakespeare's only other use
of this word is in *Lear* (quarto text), 3.6.21 and
56, and 4.2.78 ('This shows you are above, / You
justicers').
   216–17 That . . . they i.e., I am so vile that
all the world's vilest things are improved by being
less vile than me. Compare *3H6* 5.5.53–55 and *John*
4.5.51–6.
   218 villain-like (because gentlemen do not lie).
   220 sacrilegious (anticipating the comparison
of Innogen to a temple).
   221 she herself virtue herself. Virtue is personified, or imagined to be a venerated female image
(like Iachimo's conceits at 163–5).
   225 villain The thought repeats 215–17: 'so
unsurpassable is my villainy that the word "villain"
will seem less serious in future'. Maxwell suggests

that F's 'villainy' was a misreading of 'villaine': an
easy error, especially in Ralph Crane's hand. Walker
(*Critical Examination*, #58) gives several examples
of *villain/villanie* entanglements. There is an analogous error at 1.4.57 (a *Britane/Britanie* confusion).
   229 There . . . part 'Play your part there, by
lying on the ground' (Deighton). Posthumus's gratuitous anger with Innogen echoes the violence suffered by heroines of other tragicomedies, whose
vulnerability is often central to the plot: for example, Polixenes' threat to scratch out Perdita's beauty
(*WT* 4.4.425–6), the wounding of Arethusa in *Philaster* (*B&F*, I, 000), and the rejection of Chariclea
in Heliodorus's *Ethiopica* (see Introduction, p. 9).
See also *TGV* 5.4.87, where Julia, disguised as a
boy, faints in very similar circumstances. Posthumus limits the shock by talking about playing a part
even as he strikes Innogen, so acknowledging it is
only theatre, but his blow nonetheless unleashes
upon her, if only for a moment, the violence which
the rest of the action has threatened. It is a capsule
version of the whole play.

PISANIO   O gentlemen, help!
        Mine and your mistress! O my lord Posthumus,   230
        You ne'er killed Innogen till now! Help, help!
        Mine honoured lady.
CYMBELINE   Does the world go round?
POSTHUMUS How comes these staggers on me?
PISANIO   Wake, my mistress!
CYMBELINE If this be so, the gods do mean to strike me
        To death with mortal joy.
PISANIO   How fares my mistress?   235
INNOGEN O, get thee from my sight,
        Thou gav'st me poison. Dangerous fellow, hence,
        Breathe not where princes are.
CYMBELINE   The tune of Innogen.
PISANIO Lady,
        The gods throw stones of sulphur on me, if   240
        That box I gave you was not thought by me
        A precious thing. I had it from the Queen.
CYMBELINE New matter still.
INNOGEN   It poisoned me.
CORNELIUS   O gods!
        I left out one thing which the Queen confessed,
        Which must approve thee honest. 'If Pisanio   245
        Have,' said she, 'given his mistress that confection
        Which I gave him for cordial, she is served
        As I would serve a rat.'
CYMBELINE   What's this, Cornelius?
CORNELIUS The Queen, sir, very oft importuned me

239–40 *Malone; one line in* F   245 Pisanio] *Pasanio* F

230 **Mine and your** Your mistress and mine.
Compare 186 and note.

233 **comes** singular verb with plural subject, a
normal Shakespearean usage where the subject is
still in the future (Abbott, #335).

233 **staggers** giddiness, unsteadiness.

235 **mortal joy** joy so great it is deadly. Warren suggests that F's speech-heading is wrong,
the 'combination of ecstasy and violence' sound-
ing more like Posthumus, but this perhaps under-
estimates the extent to which Cymbeline is the
centre of the scene, Posthumus's reunion with his
wife being only one element in a more complex

scenario.

237–8 **Dangerous . . . are** Innogen's anxiety
about the safety of princes possibly echoes the con-
temporary response to the assassination of Henri
IV of France by François Ravaillac, on 4 May 1610.
For the event's significance in dating the play, see
Introduction, pp. 5–6.

239 **tune** voice, accent; perhaps responding to
the imperiousness of Innogen's anger.

240 **stones of sulphur** thunderstones. Compare
Jupiter's sulphurous breath (5.3.179).

245 **approve** testify.

246 **confection** compound.

To temper poisons for her, still pretending   250
The satisfaction of her knowledge only
In killing creatures vile, as cats and dogs
Of no esteem. I, dreading that her purpose
Was of more danger, did compound for her
A certain stuff which, being ta'en, would cease   255
The present power of life, but in short time
All offices of nature should again
Do their due functions. Have you ta'en of it?

INNOGEN Most like I did, for I was dead.

BELARIUS   My boys,
There was our error.

GUIDERIUS   This is sure Fidele.   260

INNOGEN Why did you throw your wedded lady from you?
                    [*Embracing Posthumus*]
Think that you are upon a rock, and now
Throw me again.

POSTHUMUS   Hang there like fruit, my soul,
Till the tree die.

259–60 My . . . error.] *Hanmer; one line in* F   261 from] *Rowe;* fro F   261 SD] *Malone; not in* F   262 rock] F; lock *conj.* Dowden

250 **temper** mix.
250 **still** always.
254 **of more danger** more hurtful than that.
255 **cease** arrest. The verb is used transitively: compare *Shr.* Ind. 2.13: 'Heaven cease this idle humor in your honour'; and Milton, 'Ode on the morning of Christ's nativity' (1629): 'He her fears to cease, / Sends down the meek-eyed Peace.'
257 **offices of nature** natural faculties.
260 **sure** true. Used as an adjective; compare 'very Cloten' (4.2.107), 'true Guiderius' (5.4.358), and Abbott, #16.
261 **from** F's 'fro' is probably a compositorial compression caused by the difficulty of accommodating a long line within the column.
262 **rock** emblematic of fortitude, patience or endurance. Many editors are attracted by Dowden's suggestion that the manuscript read 'lock' = a wrestling hold, similar to an embrace, from which the participants might 'throw' one another; but the resulting image seems grotesque and excessively literal-minded. However, an l/r misreading is possible (it occurs at *1H6* 4.4.16, 'Regions' for 'legions'), and *OED* lock *sb* 12 has several seventeenth-century examples of 'upon a lock' used metaphorically, including Oliver Cromwell's 'being indeed upon this lock, hoping that the disease of your army would render their work more easy' (Cromwell, III, 40), and Roger L'Estrange's 'He was now upon the same lock with Balbinus' (*Twenty-Two Select Colloquies of Erasmus,* 1699).
263–4 **Hang . . . die** The implied image is a vine supported by an elm, commonly used as an emblem of marriage or friendship unto death: the vine goes on producing fruit even after the tree dies. The image appears in Geoffrey Whitney's *A Choice of Emblems,* 1586, p. 62, with verses explaining that it 'shows we should be link'd with such a friend, / That might revive and help when we bee old' (quoted by Simonds, p. 259). Simonds finds further examples in the emblem books of Alciati (1531) and Camerarius (1559). Both Jonson and Milton use it to betoken a good marriage (*Ben Jonson,* VII, 237; *Paradise Lost,* V, 215–19). It is notable that in this case the female partner is the supportive elm and the male the fruitful vine, rather than (as we might have expected) the reverse.

CYMBELINE   How now, my flesh, my child?
                   What, mak'st thou me a dullard in this act?   265
                   Wilt thou not speak to me?
INNOGEN   [*Kneeling*]   Your blessing, sir.
BELARIUS [*To Guiderius and Arviragus*] Though you did love this
                   youth, I blame ye not,
                   You had a motive for't.
CYMBELINE   My tears that fall
                   Prove holy water on thee! Innogen,
                   Thy mother's dead.
INNOGEN   I am sorry for't, my lord.   270
CYMBELINE Oh, she was naught, and 'long of her it was
                   That we meet here so strangely. But her son
                   Is gone, we know not how nor where.
PISANIO   My lord,
                   Now fear is from me, I'll speak truth. Lord Cloten,
                   Upon my lady's missing, came to me   275
                   With his sword drawn, foamed at the mouth, and swore
                   If I discovered not which way she was gone
                   It was my instant death. By accident
                   I had a feignèd letter of my master's
                   Then in my pocket, which directed him   280
                   To seek her on the mountains near to Milford,
                   Where, in a frenzy, in my master's garments,
                   Which he enforced from me, away he posts
                   With unchaste purpose, and with oath to violate
                   My lady's honour. What became of him,   285
                   I further know not.
GUIDERIUS   Let me end the story:
                   I slew him there.

---

266 SD] *Rowe; not in* F   267 SD] *Pope; not in* F   274 truth] F *(troth)*   286–7 Let . . . there.] *Pope; one line in* F

265 **dullard** insensible oaf; bystander.   275 **missing** being missed.
265 **act** performance   277 **was** Taylor speculates that 'was' is a mis-
268 **motive** reason.   take for 'had', anticipating 'was' in the follow-
269 **holy water** water of blessing. *Lear* uses the ing line. F has several instances of auxiliary verb
same phrase ironically, to denote court flattery ('O   substitution.
nuncle, court holy-water in a dry house is better   279 **feignèd letter** the false letter in which
than this rain-water out o' door', 3.2.10–11).   Posthumus pretended to be at Milford, given to
271 **naught** worthless, wicked.   Cloten at 3.5.100.
271 **'long** because.   280 **directed** guided.
272 **strangely** as strangers (Warren).   283 **posts** rushes.

CYMBELINE   Marry, the gods forfend!
I would not thy good deeds should from my lips
Pluck a hard sentence. Prithee, valiant youth,
Deny't again.
GUIDERIUS   I have spoke it, and I did it.   290
CYMBELINE He was a prince.
GUIDERIUS A most incivil one. The wrongs he did me
Were nothing prince-like, for he did provoke me
With language that would make me spurn the sea,
If it could so roar to me. I cut off's head,   295
And am right glad he is not standing here
To tell this tale of mine.
CYMBELINE   I am sorrow for thee.
By thine own tongue thou art condemned, and must
Endure our law. Thou'rt dead.
INNOGEN   That headless man
I thought had been my lord.
CYMBELINE   Bind the offender,   300
And take him from our presence.
BELARIUS   Stay, sir King.
This man is better than the man he slew,
As well descended as thyself, and hath
More of thee merited than a band of Clotens
Had ever scar for. [*To Guard*] Let his arms alone;   305
They were not born for bondage.
CYMBELINE   Why, old soldier,
Wilt thou undo the worth thou art unpaid for

---

297 sorrow] F; sorry F2   299–300 That . . . lord.] *Pope; one line in* F   305 SD] *Theobald; not in* F

287 **forfend** forbid it.

288 **good deeds** (in the battle).

290 **Deny't again** Speak again and deny it (as in *MND* 1.1.181, 'that fair again unsay').

292 **incivil** ill-mannered, uncouth: Cloten's behaviour was nothing like a prince's should be. Elsewhere in Shakespeare the adjective is always 'uncivil', but possibly this form is cognate with 'incivility'.

297 **tell . . . mine** to tell my story, but with the roles reversed.

297 **sorrow** Emendations to 'sorry' are unnecessary as 'sorrow' is a predicate, a remnant of older grammatical usage. There is a parallel case at 5.4.2, 'Woe is my heart'. Compare also *Temp.*

5.1.139, 'I am woe for't'; *The White Devil*: '[we] are inly sorrow' (Webster, I, 217); and Abbott, #230.

299 **dead** condemned to death.

302 **This man** Taylor prints 'This boy', conjecturing that the repetition of 'man' in a single line is a compositorial contamination. But although Belarius calls the princes 'boys' in private (259), publicly he calls them 'gentlemen' or 'gentleman' (17, 328, 359); and the word underlines that in the battle the princes have grown to manhood (see Introduction, p. 52). Guiderius is probably about fifteen years younger than Cloten.

305 **Had . . . for** Ever deserved through their wounds in battle.

By tasting of our wrath? How of descent
As good as we?
ARVIRAGUS   In that he spake too far.
CYMBELINE And thou shalt die for't.
BELARIUS   We will die all three   310
But I will prove that two on's are as good
As I have given out him. My sons, I must
For mine own part unfold a dangerous speech,
Though haply well for you.
ARVIRAGUS   Your danger's ours.
GUIDERIUS And our good his.
BELARIUS   Have at it then, by leave: 315
Thou hadst, great King, a subject who
Was called Belarius.
CYMBELINE   What of him?
He is a banished traitor.
BELARIUS   He it is that hath
Assumed this age; indeed a banished man,
I know not how a traitor.
CYMBELINE   Take him hence.   320
The whole world shall not save him.
BELARIUS   Not too hot.
First pay me for the nursing of thy sons,
And let it be confiscate all, so soon
As I have received it.
CYMBELINE   Nursing of my sons?
BELARIUS I am too blunt and saucy. Here's my knee.   325

                              [*Kneeling*]

Ere I arise I will prefer my sons;
Then spare not the old father. Mighty sir,
These two young gentlemen that call me father,

---

311 on's] F (one's)   317–18 What . . . traitor.] *Capell; one line in* F   325 SD] *not in* F

308 **tasting** of feeling.
310 **thou** apparently addressed to Belarius.
311 **But I** If I do not. F has a comma after 'three' in 310, and Nosworthy (understanding 'But' as 'even so') takes 'We will die all three' as a statement of collective readiness to die; but the first phrase seems conditional on what follows.
311 **on's** of us.
312 **given out him** declared Guiderius to be.
313 **For . . . part** i.e., My speech will be danger-

ous only to me (an adverbial transposition, Abbott, #419a).
315 **by leave** with your permission.
319 **Assumed . . . age** Acquired this aged appearance.
323 **confiscate** confiscated (accented on the second syllable).
323 **all** completely.
323–4 **so . . . it** the very moment I receive it.
326 **prefer** advance.

And think they are my sons, are none of mine.
They are the issue of your loins, my liege,   330
And blood of your begetting.
CYMBELINE   How, my issue?
BELARIUS So sure as you your father's. I, old Morgan,
Am that Belarius whom you sometime banished.
Your pleasure was my mere offence, my punishment
Itself, and all my treason; that I suffered   335
Was all the harm I did. These gentle princes,
For such and so they are, these twenty years
Have I trained up; those arts they have, as I
Could put into them. My breeding was, sir, as
your highness knows. Their nurse Euriphile,   340
Whom for the theft I wedded, stole these children
Upon my banishment; I moved her to't,
Having received the punishment before
For that which I did then. Beaten for loyalty
Excited me to treason. Their dear loss,   345
The more of you 'twas felt, the more it shaped
Unto my end of stealing them. But, gracious sir,
Here are your sons again, and I must lose
Two of the sweet'st companions in the world.
The benediction of these covering heavens   350
Fall on their heads like dew, for they are worthy
To inlay heaven with stars.
CYMBELINE   Thou weep'st, and speak'st.
The service that you three have done is more

334 mere] *Rann (conj. Tyrwhitt);* neere F   335 treason;] *Pope;* Treason F   339–40 *Johnson;* Could . . . (Sir) / As . . .
Euriphile F   351 like] F2; liks F

333 **sometime** once.
334–6 **Your . . . did** 'My whole offence, the punishment it received and the treason I was supposed to have done, were simply what it pleased you to believe; the only wrong I had anything to do with was the consequent suffering that I underwent' (after Deighton). Belarius's rather cryptic explanation perhaps reflects his need to show respect for Cymbeline's authority while expressing his sense of injury, and to present his theft of the children in a manner that diminishes his own responsibility and blame.
337 **such and so** i.e., both princes and gentle

(an example of chiasmus).
338 **arts** accomplishments.
343 **before** in advance.
344 **Beaten** My having been beaten.
346 **of** by.
346–7 **shaped . . . of** fitted my purpose in.
352 **To . . . stars** To be cut like stars in heaven. An echo of the customary hyperbole of court masques, in which courtiers masqueraded disguised as demigods. Compare also *Rom.* 3.2.22–4, 'Take him and set him out in little stars. / And he will make the face of heaven so fine / That all the world will be in love with night.'

Unlike than this thou tell'st. I lost my children;
If these be they, I know not how to wish   355
A pair of worthier sons.
BELARIUS [*Rising*]   Be pleased awhile.
This gentleman, whom I call Polydore,
Most worthy prince, as yours, is true Guiderius;
This gentleman, my Cadwal, Arviragus,
Your younger princely son. He, sir, was lapped   360
In a most curious mantle wrought by th'hand
Of his queen mother, which for more probation
I can with ease produce.
CYMBELINE   Guiderius had
Upon his neck a mole, a sanguine star;
It was a mark of wonder.
BELARIUS   This is he,   365
Who hath upon him still that natural stamp.
It was wise nature's end in the donation,
To be his evidence now.
CYMBELINE   Oh, what am I,
A mother to the birth of three? Ne'er mother
Rejoiced deliverance more. Blest pray you be,   370
That after this strange starting from your orbs,
You may reign in them now! O Innogen,

---

356 SD] *Warren; not in* F

354 **Unlike** Incredible (i.e., your attested achievements are so astounding, that this story, though amazing, seems easier to credit).

356 There is no indication in F as to where Belarius stands up; Warren suggests that this is the best place, as he needs to present the princes to Cymbeline.

356 **Be . . . while** Permit me a few more moments.

361 **curious** exquisitely made.

362 **his . . . mother** his mother the queen.

362 **probation** proof. The marshalling of testimony to identity is conventional in the recognition scenes of romance plots. In *WT* the evidence of Perdita's identity includes a 'mantle' belonging to her mother (5.2.32–3).

364 **mole** The same birthmark that Iachimo uncovered on Innogen. In *TN*, 5.1.242–6, a mole is used to prove the twinship of Viola and Sebastian.

364 **sanguine** blood-red.

365 **of wonder** wonderful.

367 **end . . . donation** intention in giving it to him; partially recollecting the ghost's testimony to Nature's power at 5.3.134.

370 **Rejoiced . . . more** Felt more joy at her moment of delivery. For Cymbeline's male motherhood as a fantasy of parthenogenesis, see Adelman, p. 202.

371 **starting . . . orbs** displacement from your spheres. The princes are compared to stars or planetary bodies which, in Ptolemaic cosmography, occupied positions on the fixed concentric spheres, from where they exerted influence over human affairs, hence 'reign' at 372 (= a technical term for the exercise of astral power). There is a comparable image in *Ant.* 3.13.145–7: 'When my fixed stars, that were my former guides, / Have empty left their orbs, and shot their fires / Into th'abysm of hell'.

Thou hast lost by this a kingdom.

INNOGEN   No, my lord,
I have got two worlds by't. O my gentle brothers,
Have we thus met? O never say hereafter   375
But I am truest speaker. You called me brother
When I was but your sister; I you brothers,
When ye were so indeed.

CYMBELINE   Did you e'er meet?

ARVIRAGUS Ay, my good lord.

GUIDERIUS   And at first meeting loved,
Continued so, until we thought he died.   380

CORNELIUS By the Queen's dram she swallowed.

CYMBELINE   O rare instinct!
When shall I hear all through? This fierce abridgment
Hath to it circumstantial branches which
Distinction should be rich in. Where, how lived you?
And when came you to serve our Roman captive?   385
How parted with your brothers? How first met them?
Why fled you from the court, and whither? These,
And your three motives to the battle, with
I know not how much more should be demanded,
And all the other by-dependences,   390
From chance to chance. But nor the time nor place
Will serve our long inter'gatories. See,
Posthumus anchors upon Innogen,

---

378 ye] *Rowe;* we F   386 brothers] *Rowe 2;* Brother F   387 whither? These] *Theobald;* whether these? F   392
inter'gatories] *Steevens-Reed (conj. Tyrwhitt);* Interrogatories F

373 **Thou ... kingdom** i.e., because the title to the crown passes first to the king's male children: the brothers' return 'corrects' Cymbeline's lineage problems. See Introduction, p. 34.

374 **worlds** (alluding to the idea of man as a microcosm, and correcting Cymbeline's threat against Belarius, 321).

376 **But** Anything other than.

378 **ye** I follow Rowe's emendation, though F's 'we' is comprehensible and tinkering perhaps reflects a misplaced desire for perfect logic. Innogen's 'we' might be apt since she is still dressed as a boy: Malone glosses 'when we were brothers and sister'.

382 **fierce abridgement** drastically compressed summary. *OED* has no exact parallel for 'fierce',

but the underlying meaning is probably 'violent'. In rhetoric an 'abridgement' is a plan for a narrative, hence the 'circumstantial branches' (383) which Cymbeline anticipates.

384 **Distinction ... in** 'as they are distinguished should prove to be abundant' (*Riverside*).

388 **your three motives** the motives of you three.

390 **by-dependences** side-issues; circumstances that hang on these.

391 **chance** event.

392 **inter'gatories** Used by Shakespeare as a five-syllable word. Compare *MV* 5.1.300, where F prints 'intergatory'.

393 **anchors** fastens his looks.

And she, like harmless lightning, throws her eye
On him, her brothers, me, her master, hitting   395
Each object with a joy; the counterchange
Is severally in all. Let's quit this ground,
And smoke the temple with our sacrifices.
[*To Belarius*] Thou art my brother; so we'll hold thee ever.
INNOGEN You are my father too, and did relieve me   400
        To see this gracious season.
CYMBELINE   All o'erjoyed,
Save these in bonds. Let them be joyful too,
For they shall taste our comfort.
INNOGEN [*To Lucius*]   My good master,
        I will yet do you service.
LUCIUS   Happy be you!
CYMBELINE The forlorn soldier that so nobly fought,   405
        He would have well becomed this place, and graced
        The thankings of a king.
POSTHUMUS   I am, sir,
        The soldier that did company these three
        In poor beseeming. 'Twas a fitment for
        The purpose I then followed. That I was he,   410
        Speak, Iachimo. I had you down, and might
        Have made you finish.
IACHIMO [*Kneels*]   I am down again,
        But now my heavy conscience sinks my knee,

---

399 SD] *Rowe; not in* F   403 SD] *not in* F   403–4 My . . . service.] *Pope; one line in* F   405 so] F2; *no* F   412 SD] *Theobald; not in* F

---

394 **throws her eye** In Galenic physiology the eye was believed to emit beams of light that illuminated the object of vision and transformed the air into an optical instrument.

395 **her master** Lucius.

396–7 **counterchange . . . all** each person's looks reciprocate with every other person's.

398 **smoke** fill with smoke, from sacrifical fires.

400 **relieve** succour.

403 **taste . . . comfort** feel our mercy.

405 **forlorn soldier** soldier who fights at the most dangerous position, at the front of the army (see *OED* forlorn *sb* 2). Some editors gloss 'forlorn' simply as 'lost' or 'wretched', but for the military meaning see E. E. Duncan-Jones in *N&Q* 202, 1957, 64, and compare *1H6* 1.2.19, 'Now for the honor of the forlorn French'.

406 **becomed** an irregular past participle (Abbott, #344). Compare *LLL* 5.2.758: '[It] Have misbecomed our oaths and gravities'.

407–9 **I am . . . beseeming** In all productions of the play, this statement never fails to raise a laugh. This is the point at which the scene's prolonged emotional tension is at last allowed to relax.

408 **company** assist.

409 **beseeming** appearance (*OED*'s only example).

409 **fitment** device (Nosworthy). The word in this sense is unknown outside Shakespeare, and his sole other use of it is rather different. In the brothel in *Pericles*, 4.6.6, the bawd says Marina 'should do for clients her fitment, and do me the kindness of our profession': here it seems to mean 'what is fitting'.

412 **finish** die.

As then your force did. Take that life, beseech you,
Which I so often owe; but your ring first,   415
And here the bracelet of the truest princess
That ever swore her faith.

POSTHUMUS [*Raising him*]   Kneel not to me.
The power that I have on you is to spare you,
The malice towards you to forgive you. Live,
And deal with others better.

CYMBELINE   Nobly doomed!   420
We'll learn our freeness of a son-in-law:
Pardon's the word to all.   *Forgiveness as structurally /
dramatically
significant*

ARVIRAGUS [*To Posthumus*]   You holp us, sir,
As you did mean indeed to be our brother.
Joyed are we that you are.

POSTHUMUS Your servant, princes. Good my lord of Rome,   425
Call forth your soothsayer. As I slept, methought
Great Jupiter, upon his eagle backed,
Appeared to me with other spritely shows
Of mine own kindred. When I waked I found
This label on my bosom, whose containing   430
Is so from sense in hardness, that I can
Make no collection of it. Let him show
His skill in the construction.

LUCIUS   Philarmonus.

SOOTHSAYER Here, my good lord.

LUCIUS   Read, and declare the meaning.

SOOTHSAYER (*Reads*) 'Whenas a lion's whelp shall, to himself   435
unknown, without seeking find, and be embraced by a piece of

---

422 SD] *Capell; not in* F   436 SH] *Capell;* F *omits the speech-heading and centres 'Reades' above the oracle*

415 **often** many times over.
415–16 **ring, bracelet** Iachimo brings the play full circle, returning the love tokens that were exchanged in its first significant action.
417–20 **Kneel . . . better** Posthumus's forgiveness is a radical change to the wager plot as Shakespeare's sources transmitted it; see pp. 24–5 above.
420 **doomed** judged.
421 **freeness** generosity.
422 **holp** helped (a now-archaic past participle).
423 **As** As if.
427 **backed** riding.
428 **spritely shows** ghostly appearances.

430 **containing** contents.
431 **from sense** remote from meaning; difficult to understand.
432 **collection** inference, deduction (*OED* collection *sb* 5).
433 **construction** interpretation.
433 **Philarmonus** 'Lover of harmony', from the Greek *philo-harmonia*. The Soothsayer's name, not mentioned until this moment, signals that he is a diviner of arcane connections, and a fit person to preside over a reconciliation. Taylor modernizes the spelling to Philharmonus, but F's version probably indicates its pronunciation.

tender air; and when from a stately cedar shall be lopped branches
which, being dead many years, shall after revive, be jointed to the
old stock, and freshly grow; then shall Posthumus end his miseries,
Britain be fortunate and flourish in peace and plenty.'   440
       Thou, Leonatus, art the lion's whelp;
       The fit and apt construction of thy name,
       Being *leo-natus*, doth import so much.
       [*To Cymbeline*] The piece of tender air, thy virtuous daughter,
       Which we call *mollis aer*, and *mollis aer*   445
       We term it *mulier*; [*to Posthumus*] which *mulier* I divine
       Is thy most constant wife, who even now,
       Answering the letter of the oracle,
       Unknown to you, unsought, were clipped about
       With this most tender air.   450
CYMBELINE   This hath some seeming.
SOOTHSAYER The lofty cedar, royal Cymbeline,
       Personates thee, and thy lopped branches point
       Thy two sons forth, who, by Belarius stol'n,
       For many years thought dead, are now revived,
       To the majestic cedar joined, whose issue   455
       Promises Britain peace and plenty.

---

443 *leo-natus*] Capell; *Leonatus* F   **444** SD] Theobald; *not in* F   **446** SD] Capell; *not in* F   **447** thy] Capell; this F

443 *leo-natus* lion-born (Latin).

443 *import* signify.

445 *mollis aer* tender air (Latin).

446 mulier woman (Latin). Today this explanation seems more picturesque than convincing, but it was current in several contemporary Latin reference works: see the examples in Baldwin, I, 720. Caxton's *Game of the Chesse* (*c.* 1474) explained it to English audiences: 'For the Women ben lykenede unto softe waxe or softe ayer, and therefore she is called Mulier whiche is as moche to say in latyn as mollis aer and in englissh softe ayer' (cited by F. C. B. Terry, *N&Q* 108, 1888, 105). Shakespeare used the pun in *Son.* 1, 'His tender heir might bear his memory'. Some Renaissance writers regarded ingenious etymologies as testimony to the truth of a word's hidden meanings: H. Etienne, *A World of Wonders*, 1607, praised the analysis of 'mulier' as showing the ancients' 'good dexterity in giving etymologies' (cited by W. A. Wright, *N&Q*, 7th series, 2, 1886, 85).

446 divine interpret.

447 thy Capell's emendation of F's 'this' is nec-
essary, given that at 451 the subject of 'were' is suppressed. It will become clear on stage that 448–50 are addressed to Posthumus. Vaughan suggested that 'were' was a mistake for 'wert'.

448 Answering the letter Corresponding to the literal sense.

449 clipped about embraced.

451 cedar an emblem of sovereignty, especially in the Bible where it is the patriarch among trees. See Psalm 104.16, 'The high trees are satisfied, even the cedars of Lebanon'; and Ezekiel 17.23, 'Even in the high mountain of Israel will I plant it: and it shall bring forth boughs and bear fruit, and be an excellent cedar, and under it shall remain all birds, and every fowl shall dwell in the shadow of the branches thereof.' See Simonds, 241–3. James I is imaged as a cedar in Cranmer's prophecy of the future in *H8* 5.3.53; the image was also used of him in the 1604 Union debates (see Jordan, 83, and Introduction, p. 40). For 'lofty cedar', see also Jonson's *Sejanus*, 5.242, used to describe the Roman Germanicus.

452 Personates Represents.

CYMBELINE   Well,
My peace we will begin. And Caius Lucius,
Although the victor, we submit to Caesar
And to the Roman empire, promising
To pay our wonted tribute, from the which   460
We were dissuaded by our wicked Queen,
Whom heavens in justice both on her and hers
Have laid most heavy hand.
SOOTHSAYER The fingers of the powers above do tune
The harmony of this peace. The vision   465
Which I made known to Lucius ere the stroke
Of this yet scarce-cold battle, at this instant
Is full accomplished. For the Roman eagle,
From south to west on wing soaring aloft,
Lessened herself, and in the beams o'th'sun   470
So vanished; which foreshowed our princely eagle,
Th'imperial Caesar, should again unite
His favour with the radiant Cymbeline,
Which shines here in the west.

467 this yet] F3; yet this F

457 **My peace** The personal pronoun strengthens the conclusion's Jacobean associations, since
James always sought to present himself as the peace-
able monarch, pursuing stability at home and reconciliation overseas. His peace credentials were especially strong in 1609–10, when he brokered the
Twelve Years' Truce between Spain and Holland.
See Introduction, p. 40.
460 **wonted tribute** tribute we used to pay.
462 **hers** i.e., Cloten.
463 **hand** strictly speaking, the grammar
requires 'hand on', but this is obviated by 'on hers'
in 462.
464–5 **The . . . peace** (the world is seen as an
instrument played on by the hands of the gods – the
so-called *musica mundana*).
466 **made known** explained (at 4.2.347–53).
467 **this yet** F's 'yet this' is comprehensible
but gives a strange word order, and is probably a
compositorial transposition, like the parallel case at
4.4.2.
469 **west** understood in classical geography as
the location of Britain, and so used in early modern
panegyric as shorthand for the island; in his corona-
tion pageantry James was called 'Great Monarch
of the West' (Dekker, II, 279). The underlying

thought in this passage extends the Virgilian idea
of an empire moving progressively westwards: just
as (in the *Aeneid*) fallen Troy is remade at Rome, so
Rome's empire will be translated to British Troynovant. Compare Drayton's *Poly-Olbion*, 1612, on
Brute's arrival in Albion: 'Where, from the stock
of Troy, those puissant Kings should rise, / Whose
conquests from the West, the world should scant
suffice' (Drayton, IV, 11).
470–1 **in the . . . vanished** A combination of two
myths about the eagle: that it could look directly
at the sun (see 1.4.9 and note), and that it renewed
itself every ten years (though usually by flying into
the sea). See Spenser, *The Faerie Queene* 1.11.34, 'As
Eagle fresh out of the Ocean waue, / Where he hath
left his plumes all hoary gray, / And deckt himselfe with feathers youthly gay'; and Isaiah 40.31,
'they that wait upon the Lord shall renew their
strength: they shall mount up with wings as eagles'.
The eagles' self-renewal was understood to symbol-
ize rejuvenation or resurrection, but in the present
context it expresses the translation of empire from
Rome to Britain, as the eagle seemingly shrinks in
size, and becomes female.
470 **Lessened herself** (by disappearing into the
distance).

CYMBELINE   Laud we the gods,
And let our crookèd smokes climb to their nostrils
From our blest altars. Publish we this peace
To all our subjects. Set we forward. Let
A Roman and a British ensign wave
Friendly together. So through Lud's Town march,
And in the temple of great Jupiter   480
Our peace we'll ratify, seal it with feasts.
Set on there. Never was a war did cease,
Ere bloody hands were washed, with such a peace.

Exeunt

483 SD] *Exeunt. / FINIS.* F

474 **Laud** Praise.
475 **crookèd** curling.
476 **Publish we** We announce.
477 **Set** Go.

478 **ensign** flag.
480 **temple of great Jupiter** where Innogen and Posthumus were married (5.3.169–70).

LONGER NOTES

2.5.27–32 In F this passage is obviously disturbed:

> All faults that name, nay, that Hell knowes
> Why hers, in part, or all: but rather all For euen to Vice
> They are not constant, but are changing still;
> One Vice, but of a minute old, for one
> Not halfe so old as that.

Two syllables are missing from 27, and 28 has four syllables too many, cramming *For even to vice* into the space at the end of an already full line. It looks very much as though in the copy these words were part of either an addition or a correction. This impression is reinforced by the shift in Posthumus's argument, as he suddenly moves from speaking of *her* to *them*, *woman* to *women*. Probably these lines represent some second thoughts, which have been incompletely integrated into the printed text.

F's version of 27 is defensible if *name* is understood as a verb meaning 'have a name' or 'are capable of being named', but the construction is strained and it is difficult not to suppose that something is missing. I have followed Taylor's conjecture that 'earth can' has dropped out before 'name', which makes good sense and creates a plausible antithesis between what 'earth names' and 'hell knows': compare *R3* 4.4.167, 'Thou cam'st on earth to make the earth my hell.' Other plausible suggestions include 'that man may name' (Walker), 'that name may name' (Vaughan), 'that have a name' (Dyce). The problem with the following line could be solved by deleting 'but rather all', on the assumption that Shakespeare intended 'For even to vice' to replace it rather than to be added to it. Editorial tradition usually preserves the whole line but adjusts it by relineating, treating 'For even to vice' as a hanging half-line. This can be explained as a symptom of Posthumus's intense passion, but a possible solution is that the manuscript included complex corrections that were incorrectly reproduced by the scribe.

3.4.85–91 In F this passage has difficulties that suggest that the text has been imperfectly transmitted:

> Stands in worse case of woe. And thou *Posthumus*,
> That didd'st set vp my disobedience 'gainst the King
> My Father, and makes me put into contempt the suites
> Of Princely Fellowes, shalt heereafter finde
> It is no acte of common passage, but
> A straine of Rarenesse:

There are several problems with this. In the third line 'makes' is clearly wrong, while 'It' in the fifth line is hard to explain: it is far from clear what its referent is, since Innogen seems to be talking about two things, her disobedience to Cymbeline and her contempt for her wooers. Lines 2 and 3 also present lineation difficulties. They can just about be scanned, but both are too long, and the second line has an unhappy huddle of unaccented syllables. A more natural scansion is to treat 'That didst set up' as a hanging half-line, and divide the following words at 'father, / And', which creates two regular iambic pentameter lines. This combination of problems suggests that the scribe or compositor was unable to decipher the copy at this point. Possibly Shakespeare made alterations *currente calamo* and left it to the scribe to make sense of them. Conjecturally, he might first have written 'And thou Posthumus / That mad'st me put into contempt the suits / Of princely fellows . . .', but turned back to stitch in the clause about Innogen's disobedience to her father so as to develop further the topic of treason discussed elsewhere in this scene. This might have involved a messy correction of 'mad'st' to 'make', which the scribe misread as 'makes', thus producing the specific verbal error.

4.2.234–41 The boys' reluctance to sing the dirge Many editors have felt that this passage – seemingly so gratuitous and at odds with the normal convention of singing over a grave (as in *Ado* 5.3) – may signal a change of plan, with Shakespeare wanting the dirge sung but finding himself without actors who could do it justice. Taylor remarks that '[i]f anything in the canon is a theatrical interpolation due to exigencies of casting, these lines are a chief candidate' (*Textual Companion*, pp. 607–8). But if that is so, the device is very clumsy and hardly fulfils its objective, for it draws attention to a little local difficulty by building it centrally into the dialogue. This solution creates more problems than it solves.

In the text the dirge is called 'our song' (253) and preceded by the heading 'SONG'. As Warren notes, the heading is probably a scribal interpolation. It is just the kind of presentational refinement that Ralph Crane was wont to supply in his manuscripts, and has no value as evidence that Shakespeare originally intended the lyric to be sung. The dirge is all the more sonorous for being spoken: its simplicity and materialism contrast starkly with the often overelaborate artifice of the pastoral scene in which it is embedded. G. K. Hunter, 146–7, compares the effect with Kyd's *The Spanish Tragedy*, where Hieronimo chooses to speak a dirge over his son as 'singing not fits this case' (2.5.66), and Marston's *Antonio's Revenge*, where Pandulpho refuses to sing for his son since ''twill be vile out of tune' (4.2.88–90). The boys' inability to sing their dirge emphasizes that their grief is tragically serious, and that singing would be too affected a response to such intense feelings. Moreover, it allows Shakespeare to draw attention to their newly broken voices, which show that they are adolescents for whom the loss of a 'brother' is their first taste of adult sorrow. If, far from stepping around a problem, Shakespeare positively wanted to foreground the boys' position as young adults taking leave of their childhood, the rationale for seeing this passage as a change of mind evaporates (see Introduction, p. 52).

4.2.331 SD
Enter Lucius, Captaines, and a Soothsayer.
Cap. To them, the Legions garrison'd in Gallia

As it stands 332 does not need emendation, but it is arguably overlength and some editors speculate that the first two words originally belonged to the preceding stage direction and were incorporated into the dialogue in error. An anonymous conjecture reported in the 1863–6 Cambridge edition suggests that the SD originally read '*Enter Lucius, Captaines, and a Soothsayer to them*', and that the last two words were mistaken by the scribe or compositor for the Captain's opening remark. English dramatic texts of this period often used the formula '*Enter to them X and Y*' to mark the arrival of characters joining other figures already on stage, or entering a scene already in progress. Maxwell compares 'To them a Messenger' in *Cor.* 1.4.0, but he rejects any parallel with *Cymbeline* on the grounds that the Soothsayer does not join the dialogue until fourteen lines later. But perhaps the 'them' referred to were Innogen and Cloten, in which case 'to them' could have migrated from a position near the head of the SD. If it was inserted as an afterthought and placed below the line, it could easily have been accidentally absorbed into the following speech: '*Enter <to them> Lucius, Captaines and a Soothsayer*'.

'HARK, HARK, THE LARK'

A contemporary setting of 'Hark, hark, the lark' survives in a collection of songs owned by the Bodleian Library, MS Don. c.57, a volume that was probably copied *c.* 1648–50. The setting has been plausibly, though not certainly, attributed to Robert Johnson (*c.* 1582–1633); the manuscript has seven other Johnson songs, including 'Where the bee sucks'. The relevant part of the manuscript is reproduced by Willa McClung Evans in 'Shakespeare's "Harke Harke ye Larke"', *PMLA*, 60 (1945), 95–101.

Johnson was a lutenist and composer closely associated with Shakespeare's company. The son of a lutenist to Queen Elizabeth, he followed his father into royal service, becoming lutenist to James I in 1604, and later holding positions in the music of Prince Henry and Prince Charles. His connection with the Chamberlain's/King's Men may have come through Baron Hunsdon, in whose household he served his musical apprenticeship: Johnson was indentured to Hunsdon for the years 1596–1603, which was precisely the period that, as Elizabeth's Lord Chamberlain, Hunsdon was the patron of the Chamberlain's Men. Johnson's extensive work for the company includes song settings for *The Winter's Tale* (1610), *The Tempest* (1611), *Valentinian* (*c.* 1611), *The Captain* (1612), *The Duchess of Malfi* (1614), *The Witch* (*c.* 1614), *The Mad Lover* (1616), *The Devil is an Ass* (1616) and *The Lover's Progress* (1623). He would also have played in court masques, and he wrote incidental music for some, including *Oberon* (1611), *The Memorable Masque* (1613), *The Masque of the Inner Temple and Gray's Inn* (1613) and *The Gipsies Metamorphosed* (1621). Music historians associate his songs with those of Alfonso Ferrabosco and Nicholas Lanier in the development of the 'declamatory air'. This freer and more dramatic manner of writing departed from the melodic and polyphonic style associated with Elizabethan song and culminated a generation after *Cymbeline* in the work of Henry and William Lawes: see Robert Johnson, *Ayres, Songs and Dialogues*, ed. Ian Spink (*The English Lute Songs*, 2nd series, 17; revised edn, 1974), pp. iii–iv.

The song is transcribed here (by David Lindley) substantially as it appears in the manuscript. No attempt is made to elaborate the accompaniment or to take account of changes in pitch since the seventeenth century, as such editorial interventions inevitably court controversy. The manuscript's textual overlay has been modernized, but its scribal variations have been retained. It will be seen that the text set by Johnson does not correspond at all points with that printed in F: in particular, two lines are omitted. Given the manuscript's late date, it is impossible to be confident that it accurately reflects how the song was performed in Shakespeare's theatre. However, since some of Johnson's other settings have verbal differences from the printed texts, it is possible that in performance F's words did undergo some alteration.

Longer notes   [254]

Collation (by bar numbers)
1–3 Hark, hark, hark, hark, hark] Hark, hark F
5 heav'n] heaven's F
6–7 at heav'n gate sings] *not in* F
9 to rise] arise F
9–10 F *adds* His steeds to water at those springs / On chaliced flowers that lies
10 The] And F
20–22 my Lady sweet arise] *not in* F

Hark, hark, the lark

?Robert Johnson

TEXTUAL ANALYSIS

Cymbeline was first printed in the 1623 Folio of Shakespeare's plays (hereafter F). This is the sole textual authority, and all subsequent editions derive from it. The text is relatively clean, and emendation is only occasionally needed. There are about seventy-five substantive errors, and forty instances of incorrect lineation or confusion between verse and prose. However, the punctuation is very heavy, and does require extensive correction. As Shakespeare's holographs were probably lightly punctuated, the pointing suggests that printing-house copy was some kind of scribal transcript.

Cymbeline is the last play in F and was placed at the end of the Tragedies, occupying signatures zz3–bbb6, with the verso blank. The final page, bbb6r, carries the colophon for the whole volume. By comparing the box rules used to frame the final pages of *Cym.* with those used for F's Catalogue (sig. πA6), Charlton Hinman established that the Preliminaries were set up immediately after *Cym.* This suggests that once *Cym.* was printed the volume was regarded as complete.[1]

Cymbeline's position among the Tragedies has sometimes been thought of as inappropriate, and has fuelled speculation that the copy reached the printer late.[2] But had Jaggard felt uneasy about placing it with the Tragedies, he could have inserted it at the end of the Comedies, as had already been done with *The Winter's Tale*. Further, copy for *Cym.* must have been available in cast-off form before *Antony and Cleopatra* was fully set, since in signature zz the beginning of *Cym.* overlaps with the end of *Ant.*, the paired leaves zz2–5 and zz1–6 (which contain parts of both plays) being composed simultaneously. Unlike *Troilus and Cressida*, which was delayed over copyright, there were no problems with *Cym.*'s ownership, and it was entered in the Stationers' Register on 8 November 1623, shortly before publication, in a portmanteau entry with fifteen other plays 'as are not formerly entred to other men'.[3] The involvement in its printing of the apprentice Compositor E, who was not usually allowed to handle manuscript copy (see below, p. 266), suggests that, at this late point in its production, F was being hastily prepared.

---

[1] Although, in fact, one more play was yet to be added, *Troilus and Cressida*, which was printed as a separate gathering at the head of the Tragedies, but not listed in the Catalogue. See Charlton Hinman, *The Printing and Proof-Reading of the First Folio of Shakespeare*, I (1963), p. 170; and W. W. Greg, *The Shakespeare First Folio: Its Bibliographical and Textual History* (1955), pp. 445–9.

[2] Principally by Nosworthy, ed., *Cymbeline* (1955), p. xiii; and Greg, *The Shakespeare First Folio*, pp. 80–81n. If, as argued below, Ralph Crane prepared the copy for *Cymbeline*, it may have been done well before the end of printing, since the bulk of Crane's other work for F relates to the earliest plays in the volume.

[3] Greg, *The Shakespeare First Folio*, p. 59.

The copy underlying F (1)

F was set up from a scribal transcript at one or possibly two removes from the text as it left its author. W. W. Greg thought it derived from the playhouse promptbook,[1] but the evidence points towards a literary transcript and has little to suggest preparation for playhouse use. An impressive variety of data indicates that the underlying manuscript was a transcript deriving from the author's papers.

1. There is a recurrent uncertainty about the names and numbers of minor characters, which bespeaks a text whose author had not sorted out details that would need regularizing before performance. Two 'ghost' characters, a Dutchman and a Spaniard, are listed at the beginning of 1.4 but do not subsequently speak: presumably Shakespeare began the scene by listing the characters he thought he might need, but forgot to delete them once the scene was complete.[2] There is uncertainty about how many jailers have custody of Posthumus in 5.3. Only one is mentioned at 5.3.94SD, but a second jailer speaks at 5.3.96, and possibly returns at 5.3.248 (see note to 5.3.254–60). The text is vague about whether the Lady attending Innogen in 2.2 is the same Lady who encounters Cloten at 2.3.71. One is called Helen and the other Dorothy: perhaps these are different women, but they could be a single attendant appearing under alternative names, an inconsistency that Shakespeare overlooked.[3] Similarly, Philario's name is spelled 'Filorio' at its first occurrence (1.1.97), a variant that suggests uncertainty in the process of composition, and although Philarmonus is named at 5.4.433, he always appears in SDs and speech-headings as 'Soothsayer', suggesting that Shakespeare did not name him until the dialogue made it needful. Also, the Queen never acquires a personal name at all.[4]

2. Stage directions do not supply all the information that is needed in performance. Entrances for minor characters are missing at 2.3.48 and 5.3.94, and possibly at 5.4.68 (First Jailer). Exits are negligently treated: they are missing at 1.4.138, 2.3.80, 2.3.143, 4.2.70, 4.2.253 and 5.3.96, and possibly 1.1.176 and 5.3.253. At 2.1.45/59 exit and exeunt directions are reversed, and although Innogen enters '*in her Bed*' in 2.2.0, no exit direction is supplied at the end of the scene. Some are oversights due to complex stage business, and unnamed characters tend to be overlooked: other examples include 1.1.158, 2.3.27, 3.5.34 and 3.5.53. On the whole the text is inattentive to

---

[1] Greg, *The Editorial Problem in Shakespeare* (1942), p. 150; *The Shakespeare First Folio*, p. 414. Greg's judgement was partly due to his reluctance to accept the vision of Jupiter as authentic, agreeing with E. K. Chambers that it was 'a spectacular theatrical interpolation'. This led him to see the text as a playhouse adaptation, though he also suggested an intermediate position, that Shakespeare's text might first have 'contained a vision in dumb-show only' (*The Shakespeare First Folio*, pp. 413–14 and note). But if the vision is accepted as authentic, the argument for prompt-copy becomes less pressing. The converse also holds, that pre-theatrical provenance testifies to the vision's authenticity.

[2] There are similar 'ghost' characters in the opening direction of *Ado* (the quarto text of which is thought to derive from foul papers).

[3] The text is inconsistent about how many women Innogen has: at 2.3.132 she speaks of 'Dorothy my woman' (and compare 3.2.75) but Posthumus mentions 'attendants' (2.4.124). The uncertainty about whether Pisanio attends on Posthumus or Innogen may reflect a comparable inconsistency: see note to 1.1.169.

[4] The misspellings of *Cymbaline* at 2.3.27SD *Paladour* at 3.3.86, and *Pasanio* at 5.4.245 are not authorial variants but obviously compositorial.

supernumeraries, whose movements would need thinking through more carefully in the playhouse than in the author's papers.[1]

3. The directions fail to supply other information that would have been needed in the playhouse. Props are carelessly treated. In 2.2 no provision is made for Iachimo's trunk, nor for the removal of Innogen's bed. Belarius and his family enter '*from the cave*' at 4.2.0, but the cave is unmentioned in their entry at 3.3.0, even though the dialogue indicates it is needed. Pisanio enters '*reading of a letter*' at 3.2.0, but the directions ignore the letters that Innogen throws away at 3.4.78. They also ignore the removal of Cloten's corpse (4.2.402), the manacling of Posthumus (5.3.94), and the tablet left by Jupiter (5.3.172) – details which are self-evident, but have to be inferred. Music cues are also rare. '*Solemn music*' is specified at 4.2.185 and 5.3.123, but directions are missing at 2.3.16, and the only other off-stage sounds mentioned are a clock (2.2.50) and thunder and lightning (5.3.156). The hunting-horn (3.3.98) is overlooked, and although Guiderius says 'The noise is round about us' at 4.4.1, there is no sound cue. 'Alarums' are missing at 5.2.0 SD, and in the theatre more flourishes would have been used in the court scenes, notably in the state entry at 3.1.0. Perhaps some of these cues were present in Shakespeare's drafts but edited out by whoever transcribed it: see 'The Nature of the Transcript', below.[2]

4. The character of the SDs varies: they are laconic in the first half, but fuller towards the end. This may mean that the copy was composite (discussed below), but even the more elaborate directions fall short. The most striking instance is the contradictory direction at 5.3.94, where F prints '*Enter Posthumus, and Gaoler*', even though they were unmentioned in the previous exit. This anomaly was perhaps produced by a scribe trying to arrange complex stage business into a more literary format, but the absence of adequate exits also suggests that the transition between scenes is imperfectly managed: maybe second thoughts were involved. The elaborate direction at 5.2.0 also falls short, failing as it does to order the armies to engage. There are further uncertainties about business at 5.3.253, and the Jailer is perhaps omitted at 5.4.68. The directions also ignore the costume changes at 5.1.22 and 5.3.73 (as throughout the play), and often their wording is more descriptive than would arise in playhouse texts. Four SDs take the readerly form '*Enter x alone*' (1.6.0, 3.6.0, 4.1.0, 5.1.0; and compare '*Enter Pisanio, reading of a letter*', 3.2.0). In the vision the long direction at 5.3.123 gives information about the identities and appearance of the ghosts calculated for a readership, and the SDs instructing that '*the ghosts fall on their knees*' (5.3.156) and that Posthumus enters '*behind*' (5.4.68) help to create the stage picture for the reader by explaining the action. Such phrases reflect not playhouse practicalities but an author or scribe attempting to represent business for a reader.

Two passages have sometimes been thought to suggest that the manuscript originated in the playhouse. One is the dialogue in which Arviragus and Guiderius excuse themselves from singing the dirge (4.2.238–41), which some scholars think shows that

[1] Greg's comment 'Half a dozen unimportant exits are unmarked' (*The Shakespeare First Folio*, p. 413) understates the shortfall.
[2] See Wells and Taylor, *A Textual Companion* (1987), p. 604; and E. A. J. Honigmann, *The Texts of 'Othello' and Shakespearean Revision* (1996), p. 72.

the text was altered because of casting problems at some early stage. On inspection, this supposed production change proves to be imaginary (see Longer Notes, p. 251, and Introduction, p. 52). The other is the vision of Jupiter: this was once thought to be a playhouse interpolation, but since Wilson Knight's defence of its integrity (see note to 5.3.123–214), few critics would want to question it. In any case, the consequence of rejecting the vision is disintegration on a grand scale, since if that goes, the Soothsayer's speech at 5.4.435–56 cannot stand, and then his earlier appearance at 4.2.333–53 has to come into question, and so on.

The nature of the transcript

So F was probably based on a scribal transcript deriving from Shakespeare's papers and was unaffected by playhouse adaptation. Two further claims have been made about it: that it was (at some level) a composite involving the work of more than one scribe; and that its preparation for the Folio was the work of Ralph Crane, a scrivener closely associated with the King's Men, whose work has some highly idiosyncratic features.

Ralph Crane's part in *Cymbeline* requires extensive consideration. Crane was a professional scrivener who had a close working relationship with the King's Men.[1] His surviving work consists mostly of transcripts of plays and masques produced for a literary readership *c.*1618–27, but he prepared at least one promptbook for the company, and transcribed the copy for *Othello* and for the first four plays printed in the Shakespeare Folio. J. C. Maxwell was the first to suggested that *Cym.* was another play printed from a Crane transcript.[2] A great deal is known about the effect of Crane's working habits on the texts that he transcribed, and Crane features are apparent in *Cym.*, if more thinly spread than in the other six plays.

1. The systematic marking of acts and scenes is characteristic of Crane. Acts and scenes are consistently distinguished, and with a formula ('*Actus Secundus. Scena Prima*', etc.) that Crane uses elsewhere. That the divisions are scribal is shown by the errors in marking new scenes at 1.1.69 and 3.6.27. At each of these points, although the stage is momentarily cleared, the action is continuous at the same location, but the scribe has regularized his copy by beginning a new scene. He also creates a double anomaly at 5.3.94 by making a new scene and inserting an entry for Posthumus and the Jailer when the characters are not meant to leave the stage – an intervention where the desire to produce a tidy reading text has overridden theatrical logic.

2. The descriptiveness of the stage directions is characteristic of Crane's literary transcripts. Crane tended to elaborate SDs in line with his sense of what readers required, and he may have added information that he recollected from performances.[3] In *Cymbeline* the full directions in Act 5 may be signs of his hand, though they are less

---

[1] The fullest account of Crane's work is by Trevor Howard-Hill, *Ralph Crane and some Shakespeare First Folio Comedies* (1972).

[2] Taylor also argues the case in the Oxford Shakespeare (*Textual Companion*, p. 604); and in G. Taylor and J. Jowett, *Shakespeare Reshaped 1606–1623* (1993), it is regarded as virtually established (pp. 240, 250).

[3] See Howard-Hill, *Ralph Crane*, pp. 21–7; and Jeanne Addison Roberts, 'Ralph Crane and the text of *The Tempest*', *S.St.*, 13 (1980), 213–33.

developed than the SDs in *The Tempest*, and earlier SDs in *Cym.* are less elaborate. However, one direction uses parentheses (5.3.123), a feature associated with Crane and which is almost completely absent from other SDs in F.[1] This SD also has a phrase, '*as in an apparition*', which Crane used in an SD in his transcript of Middleton's *A Game at Chess*. Middleton's autograph manuscript reads 'like an Apparition', but Crane's revised phrasing, combined with the parentheses, is identical to the wording in *Cym.*[2]

3. Some support for Crane's hand comes from spelling. The surviving transcripts tell us a great deal about Crane's preferred spellings, but in the printed texts compositorial preferences inevitably predominate. In *Cymbeline* just one uncommon spelling stands out: 'dampn'd', in the uncorrected state of 1.6.104 – a Craneism which was spotted during printing and corrected.[3] Other rare spellings include the unusual form 'ghesse' (1.1.60), found in the early Crane-based comedies but otherwise not widely used in F;[4] 'prime-rose' for 'primrose' (1.5.83), occurring elsewhere in F only in *The Winter's Tale*, another Crane text;[5] 'powre(s)'(1.6.179, 3.5.24, 4.3.31, 5.4.256, 418, 464); and 'guift' (1.4.68, 69, 2.4.102, 3.6.83, 5.3.165). It is worth noting that the confusion between 'villain' and 'villanie' (see 5.4.225) corresponds with a recurrent difficulty in Crane's hand.[6] In print such orthographical survivals are necessarily rare, and even sparse occurrences are disproportionately significant. In this regard the evidence in *Cym.* is similar to that in F's other Crane-based plays.[7]

4. Much the most substantial evidence comes from the punctuation, the density and preferences of which are very reminiscent of Crane. Crane's pointing has been fully examined by Trevor Howard-Hill, who analyses the frequency of punctuation use proportionate to the number of words per play in five Folio Comedies associated with Crane. The following table compares the punctuation in *Cymbeline* to Howard-Hill's figures derived from *The Tempest*, *The Two Gentlemen of Verona*, *The Merry Wives of Windsor*, *Measure for Measure* and *The Winter's Tale*.[8] Each line compares ratios for full stops, question marks, colons, semicolons, commas, parentheses, apostrophes (i.e., marks of elision only), hyphens and capitals (i.e., words capitalized arbitrarily

---

[1] This point is strongly made by Wells and Taylor, *A Textual Companion*, p. 604.

[2] Crane's full direction in Bodleian MS Malone 25 is 'Musique: The B^l.B^ps. Pawne (as in an Apparition) Comes richely habited' (N. W. Bawcutt and K. Duncan-Jones, eds., 'Ralph Crane's transcript of *A Game at Chess*', *Malone Society Collections*, 15, 1993, ll. 926–9). Middleton's own version in the Trinity manuscript reads 'Musique, enters the Iesuite in rich attire like an Apparition presents himselfe before the Glasse, then exit' (*A Game at Chess*, ed. T. H. Howard-Hill, 1990, ll. 1576–9).

[3] A connection made by G. Blakemore Evans in *The Riverside Shakespeare*, p. 1561. The word occurs on a page now known to have been set by Compositor E; it was corrected to 'damn'd'. In his transcript of Middleton's *The Witch* (eds. W. W. Greg and F. P. Wilson, 1950), Crane wrote 'dampnation' at l. 2019; he used 'dampnation' in his transcript of Fletcher and Massinger's *Sir John van Oldenbarnavelt* (ed. T. H. Howard-Hill, 1980), l.588; and 'dampnably' in his transcript of Fletcher's *Demetrius and Enanthe* (eds. M. M. Cook and F. P. Wilson, 1951), l.2037.

[4] Crane used the spelling 'ghesse' at l.921 of *Demetrius and Enanthe*. The spelling 'guesse' is dominant throughout the Folio, but *ghesse* appears in *TGV* 2.1, *MM* 4.4, *WT* 1.2 and *R2* 2.3.

[5] See *WT* 4.4.122 ('Prime-roses'). *Cym.*'s example is weakened, though not nullified, by the appearance of 'Primrose' at 4.2.221.

[6] See Greg's note to *The Witch*, l. 280.

[7] Howard-Hill offers only very limited orthographical evidence (thirty rare spellings across five plays) in *Ralph Crane*, pp. 100–1.

[8] Howard-Hill, *Ralph Crane*, p. 82.

within the dialogue, not speech-headings, names or the beginnings of sentences). Each figure represents the proportion of occurrence (total occurrences divided into total words, rounded to the nearest whole number). The final column is Howard-Hill's average derived from the five Comedies. The final line is the global ratio of words to punctuation (including the handful of rarely occurring marks which I have not tabulated because the ratios they generate are so vast as to be meaningless: exclamations, dashes and quotation marks).

Punctuation	Cym.	Temp.	TGV	Wiv.	MM	WT	Average
.	25	23	21	24	23	26	24
?	87	88	60	57	66	81	70
:	41	29	34	23	34	31	30
;	192	122	104	127	135	147	127
,	12	10	11	11	11	10	11
()	182	170	130	99	290	69	151
'	31	30	46	50	44	26	39
-	193	121	144	62	243	98	134
Caps	12	15	21	15	19	12	16
Words:punc	3.4	3.2	3.5	3.1	3.7	3.0	3.3

Crane's pointing was dense and idiosyncratic. Howard-Hill describes him as preferring colons to semicolons, and question marks to exclamations; he was heavy-handed with parentheses and hyphens; his hyphenation and elisions are also distinctive. These details are visible in the printed texts, but they appear all the more clearly in comparisons with other texts based on non-Crane transcripts. The average density of 3.3 for these five comedies compares strikingly with an average of 4.1 for five non-Crane Comedies, which are much more lightly pointed.

It will be seen from the chart that *Cym.*'s pointing broadly corresponds to the pattern of other Crane-derived texts.[1] The colon/semicolon inequivalence is strongly apparent, even though these marks are less frequent in *Cym.* than in the five Comedies. *Cym.* also prefers interrogations over exclamations, though the recurrence of question marks is below average, and there is a higher recurrence of exclamation marks.[2] This makes the practice with colons, semicolons, question marks and exclamations seem in line with Crane's, if pushing against his parameters. The lesser indicators (capitals, commas and stops) appear as we might expect. With parentheses the proportions are lower than the Crane norm for a transcription made from an authorial draft,[3] though still more lavish than in non-Crane texts (Howard-Hill's figure for five non-Crane Comedies is

[1] Of course, all these figures are affected by the habits of the different compositors, and an inexact match would not preclude a Crane attribution. The early Comedies include no pages set by Compositor E; conversely, *Cymbeline* was set by B and E only.

[2] I count twenty exclamation marks in *Cym.*, in comparison with four in *Temp.* and none at all in *TGV*, *Wiv.*, *MM* and *WT*. But the quantities are so small as to be statistically insignificant.

[3] I am setting aside the figure for *MM*, which is out of line with the other four, and regarded as such by Howard-Hill in 'Ralph Crane's parentheses', *NQ*, 210 (1965), 334–40.

1 parenthesis in 923 words). They look more typical when one adds that there is a difference of around three to one between nonvocative and vocative parentheses, which is very close to the ratio in *Temp.*[1] Moreover, Honigmann has argued that a strong test for Crane is a high frequency of brackets enclosing single words, of which *Cym.* has 32, a figure close to *Oth.* and the other Crane texts. Of the five nonvocative single words in brackets, two ('happily' and 'alas') are bracketed elsewhere by Crane.[2]

With elisions and hyphens, the case is more complex. Crane used both very frequently, though he had some distinctive habits that *Cym.* does not consistently exhibit. The recurrence of apostrophes is well in line with the Comedies, and some Crane forms are well represented, such as 'i'th" (1.6.39, 41 etc.) and 'o'th" (1.2.8, 1.3.1, etc.). The elision 'ha's' (for 'has,' 1.5.2, 33, 36, 59; 4.2.288) may be Crane's, though it occurs elsewhere in F. However, the so-called Jonsonian elisions that Crane frequently used (in which the apostrophe indicates elided syllables though the words are fully spelled out) are entirely absent. Still, the evidence from the Comedies is equally tentative.

Cym.'s hyphenation is lighter than in the Comedies,[3] though its 152 occurences of 138 hyphenated words or phrases are sufficiently frequent to be distinctive. Some of the unusual hyphenations to which Crane was addicted are present. There are several instances of his adjective+noun form ('not-fearing-Britain', 2.4.19; 'rejoycing-Fires', 3.1.32; 'Salt-water-Girdle', 3.1.77; 'Rich-ones', 3.6.12;[4] 'rich-left-heyres', 4.2.225; 'scarse-cold-Battaile', 5.4.467). The unusual compound 'wing-led' (2.4.24) is probably a misreading (for 'mingled') by a scribe constitutionally inclined towards compounds. On the other hand, the text lacks Cranean compounds such as verb+pronoun ('box-me', 'peg-thee', etc.) or verb+preposition ('tears-up', 'falls-off', etc.; but compare. 'out-stood', 1.6.207 and 'vnpayd-for', 3.3.24). These hyphenations are less common in contemporary printed texts than adjective+noun forms, and would have been a clearer sign of his hand. However, a lot depends on the compositors' willingness to transmit hyphenation, and these forms are also rare in *Temp.*, *TGV* and *MM.*[5] Howard-Hill notes as well that the high frequency of hyphenated prefixes in *Cym.* ('a-foot', 'a-while', 'fore-end', 'o're-throw', 'sur-addition', 'up-cast', etc.) corresponds with other Crane-based texts.[6]

5. The relatively infrequent indication of off-stage sounds aligns *Cym.* with the other Crane texts, where they are usually omitted. *Cym.* does have a few sound cues, but nowhere near the number that performance would require, and their suppression may reflect Crane's habits.

---

[1] See ibid. The ratio for *Temp.* is 3:1; for *Cym.* 3.2:1. *Cym.* has 163 parentheses in all (including three from which the opening bracket is missing), of which 38 enclose vocative phrases.

[2] Honigmann, *The Texts of 'Othello'*, pp. 59–63, 161–5. The figure could have been higher had the whole play been set by Compositor B: of the 32 'swibs', only one occurs on one of Compositor E's pages.

[3] Again, some exceptions have to be made. *MM* is somewhat out of line, while the exceptionally high ratio for *Wiv.* was generated by the high proportion of prose, and the greater stylistic flexibility which that involves.

[4] Compare 'blind-ones', *WT* 4.4.836; 'Great-ones', *Oth.* 1.1.8, 3.3.273; and Honigmann, *The Texts of 'Othello'*, p. 66.

[5] See Howard-Hill, *Ralph Crane*, pp. 106, 114, 128.

[6] T. H. Howard-Hill, 'Shakespeare's earliest editor, Ralph Crane', *S. Sur.*, 44 (1991), 128n.

6. The handling of the dirge, which is titled 'Song' even though the lines are spoken, reflects Crane's habit of 'improving' the presentational features of his transcripts.

7. Finally, a small sign of Crane might be the compositorial failure to distinguish prose from verse at 1.2.4, 12 and 24–5, and the ambiguity over the lineation at 3.1.11–14 (rough verse in F but considered by Nosworthy to be prose: though perhaps affected by revision – see below). Since Crane did not always run prose fully into the right-hand margin, prose/verse confusions are frequent in texts set from his transcripts and, in a play with little prose, these are the few instances.[1]

To summarize: the case for Crane is plausible. Most of the indicators that one would look for occur, albeit not as emphatically as in attested Crane texts. If the presence of his hand is not absolutely certain, there is sufficient evidence to deem it probable.

E. A. J. Honigmann was the first to notice an inconsistency in the text around the spelling of the exclamation O (Oh).[2] In the first third of the play (roughly Acts 1 and 2), the spelling is exclusively O (17 occurrences), but after 2.4.152 it is predominantly Oh (56 occurrences, to 6 of O). This shift is all the more impressive given that it is unaffected by the stints of the two compositors who set the text. This demonstrates that it does not originate in the printing house but was present in the manuscript, and Honigmann took it to indicate that the underlying copy was in two hands. It is supported by a parallel shift in the naming of Cloten. Cloten's name is spelled in full twenty times. The first four times he is 'Clotten' (the last being 3.1.0); on the fifth (3.5.0) and subsequent occasions he is 'Cloten', the single exception being 4.1.0 SD. An exotic or unfamiliar name is precisely the kind of detail that was open to scribal misreading, and the difference suggests that two hands were involved in producing the copy, the division of labour coming around the end of Act 2 and beginning of Act 3.[3]

Gary Taylor and John Jowett have attempted to reinforce the case for two hands by adding to Honigmann's Ohs seventeen pairs of variant spellings taken from the two halves of the text.[4] However, this list is problematic, since hardly any of the pairs recurs frequently enough to be confidently taken as a pattern. More than half appear only two or three times; some do not conform to the anticipated division;[5] and some are affected by compositorial spellings.[6] The one pair which does recur extensively, Britaine/Brittaine, does not fit the pattern, since 'Britaine' is used throughout all parts

---

[1] Howard-Hill, *Ralph Crane*, pp. 36–7.

[2] E. A. J. Honigmann, 'On the indifferent and one-way variants in Shakespeare', *The Library*, 5th series, 22 (1967), 189–204.

[3] There is also a change in the speech-headings for Pisanio, who before Act 3 is overwhelmingly designated as '*Pisa.*' but is thereafter three times more likely to be called '*Pis.*' (Taylor and Jowett, *Shakespeare Reshaped*, p. 255).

[4] Ibid., p. 254. One pair not included by Taylor and Jowett is 'ceiz'd' (2.2.7) and 'seiz'd' (3.5.60) – though this may be due to compositorial preference.

[5] For example, the claim made for 'breast' at 2.4.134 as an alternative spelling to 'brest' at 5.3.173 and 5.4.4 is weakened by 'brest' at 2.2.37; and the claim for 'briefe' at 1.1.101 as an alternative to 'breefe' at 3.4.164, 5.4.165 and 5.4.199 is weakened by 'briefely' at 5.4.106. Taylor and Jowett emphasize the narrowness and relative unreliability of their data, especially in comparison with *King John*, where a similar case can be made much more emphatically.

[6] For example, the division between 'lips' and 'lippes' is subject to the different preferences of Compositors B and E, since at 1.6.100 and 105 the two spellings recur within five lines of one another, at the end of a Compositor E stint and beginning of a Compositor B stint.

of the text, and the variant form is found both towards the beginning (1.6.113) and towards the end (3.5.65 and 5.4.478, as 'Brittish' in each instance). So the case for composite transcription continues to rest on Honigmann's Ohs and Clotten/Cloten. Nonetheless, it does reinforce the earlier observation that the SDs seem to change in the second half. Taken together, these changes might indicate the presence of more than one scribe.

The copy underlying F(2)

We can now return to the question of copy for F. Given that the copy shows signs of Crane's involvement and of being composite, how many stages intervened between Shakespeare drafts and the copy from which the printers worked? Did Crane copy a composite manuscript, or was he one of the two scribes?

Punctuation analysis suggests that Crane's characteristic pointing increases after Act 2. The frequency of question marks increases by 10%, parentheses by 20% and semicolons by 30%. This could signal that his hand is clearer after Act 2 than before. There is also the problem of the inconsistencies over Cloten/Clotten and the Pis./Pisa. speech-headings, where one would have expected Crane to standardize. However, other indications tell against this: hyphenations and single words in brackets are evenly spread; the uncommon spelling 'dampn'd' occurs in Act 1; and Crane's marking of acts and scenes is present throughout. Additionally, on the crucial issue of O/Oh, Crane had no preferences but tended to reproduce the spelling in front of him, so that a composite manuscript copied by him would exhibit the evidence of its origin.[1] So it may be correct to posit a manuscript in two hands, from which Crane made a fair copy for printing-house use. Possibly one of the two hands was Shakespeare's, in the form of an authorial fair copy from the final draft. If, for example, Crane transcribed Acts 1 and 2 directly from authorial copy, this could explain the abruptness of the SDs and the preference for O rather than Oh, which Taylor and Jowett see as characteristic of Shakespeare.[2] Against this is the point that the one verbal error that seems to derive from a misinterpretation of a Shakespearean spelling comes in the second half.[3]

This scenario is in line with Crane's work for the King's Men as now understood, and his importance to the Folio project. He appears to have been given the task of transcribing the first four plays ready for use as print-copy, and he may also have prepared *Oth.* and *2H4*. In making these transcriptions he operated not merely as a slavish copyist but as an editor, tidying up and even expurgating his texts, and establishing their formal

---

[1] Taylor and Jowett, *Shakespeare Reshaped*, pp. 256–59.
[2] Ibid., pp. 248–56.
[3] At 4.2.58, the word 'patience' is incorrectly reproduced as 'patient'. This may indicate that at one stage it was spelled as 'patienc', a characteristic Shakespeareanism, the suffix '-enc' appearing three times in the one surviving holograph, Addition D of *Sir Thomas More* ('obedyenc', l. 39; 'insolenc', l. 81; 'obedienc', l. 94). An 'enc/ent' misreading from Shakespearean copy may underlie F's reading 'present' for 'presence' in *Temp.* 1.1.22 (also a Crane text), and 'Ace' for 'Ate' in *John* 2.1.63. A clearer Shakespearean spelling in *Cym.* is 'Iarmen' (= 'German' at 2.5.16), which can be paralleled in *2H4* 2.1.145 (Q1: as 'Iarman'), *Wiv.* 4.5.87 (F; 'Iamanie' misprinted for 'Iarmanie') and *LLL* 3.1.190 (Q: as 'Iermane').

features as they were to be transmitted into print.[1] It is not surprising, then, that *Cym.* should have come down in a relatively clean form, with most of its loose ends purged away. F transmits a text that has already been thoroughly worked over with readers in mind.

There are, nonetheless, confusions and false starts which indicate ultimate origin in Shakespeare's foul papers. One or two loose ends perhaps preserve plot initiatives that Shakespeare failed to develop as the writing progressed. At 2.1.35–44 a meeting between Cloten and Iachimo seems to be envisaged, but this never comes about. In 3.4 there is some improvisation around Pisanio, who begins the scene with no plans for Innogen but then produces a page's disguise from nowhere. The time scheme is not fully satisfactory through 3.4–3.5, since at the end of 3.4 Pisanio is somewhere on the road to Wales, yet he is back at court by 3.5.80, and Innogen has only just been missed. There does not seem to be enough time to get Innogen on the road and Pisanio back to court, making this migratory section feel as if all its problems have not been adequately solved. At 3.5.145–7 further episodes between Cloten and Pisanio seem to be in mind, and at 4.3.43–4 Pisanio talks about proving himself in battle, but none of this subsequently happens. Many of these problems relate to Pisanio's awkwardly asymmetrical role, since after 3.5 he has nothing to do but wait, but they might indicate material still being compressed into shape, with all its consequences not finally tied together. There is also some carelessness over repeated detail. The passage which Pisanio reads from Posthumus's letter at 3.2.17–19 does not correspond with 3.4.21–9, and the 'feignèd letter' mentioned at 5.4.279 does not square with what we have seen, though such details are not troublesome in performance. Roger Warren has also suggested that the command 'bring him to th'King' (5.3.94), the confusion in the subsequent SD, and the slightly clumsy dumbshow may indicate that Shakespeare originally intended to move straight from Posthumus's capture into the final scene, but turned back to insert the prison scene and vision as an afterthought.[2] Given the prison scene's integral relation to the rest of the play, and the arc of Posthumus's three big speeches in 5.1 and 5.3, I find it hard to believe that so major a change can have been made very late, and prefer to suppose that the confusion reflects the consequences of Crane's mistaken decision to start a new scene. Still, the possibility that Shakespeare changed his mind early on, and left an unresolved join in the manuscript, cannot be entirely discounted.

More interesting is the evidence of fossilized verbal revision, the most striking of which is some seeming expansion to Cloten's part. The clearest example comes at 3.1.34–43, where the continuity between the Queen's incomplete line 33 and Cymbeline's fragmentary line 44 suggests that the intervening prose dialogue between Cloten and Cymbeline has been added in as an afterthought. Possibly Cloten's unmetrical interruption to his mother's speech at 11–14 is also an addition, in which case Shakespeare may originally have written the whole scene as a confrontation between Lucius, Cymbeline and the Queen only, and turned back later to give Cloten a place in it.

---

[1] See Howard-Hill, 'Shakespeare's earliest editor'.
[2] Warren, ed., *Cymbeline* (1998), pp. 74–5.

In turn, this makes more plausible the suggestion that Cloten's reflections at 2.3.61–71 on the power of gold, which interrupt a continuous sequence of dialogue and are enclosed within a pair of repeated lines, may also be an addition: the clown's role is that part which is most commonly open to unpredictable expansion. There may be further signs of revision in the uncertainties over the handling of scene ends at 3.3.99–107 and 4.2.395–402. In the first case, doubled phrases and nine huddled lines of exposition probably indicate that in going over an early draft Shakespeare added in material which he subsequently found was needed. In the second case, some awkwardness in the concluding passage suggests second thoughts about how to dispose of Cloten's headless trunk. Other possible revisions are the disturbances at 2.5.27–31 and 3.4.86–8, which perhaps indicate changes that were incomplete or imperfectly interpreted by the scribe. And further revision must have taken place before the play was staged, since the performed version would have needed some technical adjustments and cutting. At 3,000+ lines, *Cymbeline* is one of F's longest plays, and (then as now) it is unlikely that it would have been performed in its entirety. So F seems to represent a fair copy of a penultimate draft, with the play complete except for its finalizing for performance.

The treatment of copy in F

It is now known that F was set up by two compositors working in tandem, and not, as Hinman thought, by one alone. Compositor B, one of Jaggard's most experienced workmen (and who set much of the Tragedies), composed the bulk of *Cym*. But in 1980 Trevor Howard-Hill argued that Hinman's orthographical tests failed to disclose the work of the apprentice Compositor E, whose spelling habits, over time, became virtually identical to B's, and he invented alternative tests for E.[1] The most dramatic is a variation in the spacing of internal commas in short lines: B tended to insert a thin space after an internal comma, E to leave commas unspaced. This simple test (combined with other, more complex indicators) readily reveals that, while B was solely responsible for quire bbb, E set five pages in zz and aaa: sigs. zz4v (1.4.15–123), zz5v (1.6.1–104), zz6v (2.1.3–2.3.5), aaa1v (2.3.115–2.4.64) and aaa3 (3.2.4–3.3.38). This coincides with Hinman's discovery of stop-press corrections in sigs. zz4v, zz5v, zz6, zz6v, aaa3 and (possibly) aaa6v, showing that this section of the Folio was carefully proofed. Hinman was surprised that B's reliable work should have been closely inspected, but it is now apparent that Compositor E was the reason. My own analysis of damage to the running-titles shows that a single skeleton was used, and that setting proceeded in a regular manner in each quire from inner pages to outer.[2] Compositor E worked at a third of

---

[1] T. H. Howard-Hill, 'New light on Compositor E of the Shakespeare first Folio', *The Library*, 6th series, 2 (1980), 156–78.

[2] See M. Butler, 'Running-titles in *Cymbeline*', *The Library*, 7th series, 1 (2000), 439–41. Only if one arranges the running-titles according to the assumptions described does a regular pattern appear. The skeleton can be distinguished by three anomalies which occur regularly in one of the paired running-titles. One reads 'The Tragedie of Cymbeline' (whereas its pair reads 'The Tragedy of Cymbeline'), and has damage to the swash 'T' in 'The'; there is also an error in 'Cymbeline', which on five appearances carries a roman rather than italic 'i'. Hinman was puzzled by the presence of this rogue letter in zz3v, suggesting as it seemed to

the rate of Compositor B, setting one page in each leaf of quires zz-aaa while B set the remaining three pages (with the exception of aaa2–5, set entirely by B).

The characteristics of B and E have been widely discussed. Briefly, B was a reliable worker, though hardly errorfree. His attitude towards the text could be high-handed and his errors are sophistications rather than straightforward misreadings. E, by contrast, followed copy more slavishly and committed more elementary mistakes. He had a higher rate of inaccuracy, though his mistakes are all the more obvious. Normally he was trusted only to set up text from print-copy, but towards the end of the volume, with *Ant.* and *Cym.*, he handled scribal copy.

The differences between the compositors are apparent in their stints in *Cym.* E set only five pages but committed nearly 30% of the substantive errors: his error rate was almost twice as high as B's. He made trivial mistakes of substitution or omission, for example: adding or omitting '-s' at the ends of words – 'thousand⟨s⟩' (1.4.103), 'desire⟨s⟩' (1.6.7), 'take⟨s⟩' (1.6.28), 'garment⟨s⟩' (2.3.131), 'courage⟨s⟩' (2.4.60), 'leave[s]' (2.4.60); overlooking prepositions in prose – 'if I offend [not]' (1.4.37), 'I could not [but] believe' (1.4.59), 'come to court [to-]night' (2.1.30); and introducing uncertainty over minims – for example, 'Britaine/Britanie' (1.4.57), 'mingled/wing-led' (2.4.24). He was responsible for the three worst errors, radical misreadings of the copy with little concern for the nonsense that it produced: 'Fiering' (for 'Fixing', 1.6.104), 'Sleepe' (for 'Stoope', 3.3.2) and 'Babe' (for 'Bribe', 3.3.23). On one occasion, at 2.1.55–6, he introduced two errors in the process of correcting one. As Brooks suggests (in Nosworthy), the stop and capital T in 55 are really required in 56: the second line must have been marked for proof correction, but E replaced the wrong stop and capital letter.

Compositor B produced more complex errors of substitution. He replaced correct readings with nearly similar words, in which the sense is superficially meaningful: 'with his [this] eye or ear' (1.3.9), 'base and illustrious [illustrous]' (1.6.109), 'it is a voyce [vyce] in her ears' (2.3.25), 'Monsters her accuse [accuser]' (3.2.2); 'to th'lowd [lowd'st] of noise' (3.5.44), 'sluggish care [crare]' (4.2.204). He tended to confuse pronouns, prepositions and verbal forms, through anticipation or repetition of the incorrect form elsewhere in the same line: 'Glad at [of] the thing they scowle at' (1.1.15); 'vnder her Breast / (Worthy her [the] pressing)' (2.4.134–5); 'gaine the Cap of him, that makes him [them] fine' (3.3.25); 'Thou diuine Nature; thou [how] thy selfe' (4.2.169); 'Mightst [Might] easilest' (4.2.205); 'When they heare their [the] Roman horses' (4.4.17). At two points he substantially reordered his copy, apparently on the assumption that it was incorrect: 'Since the true life on't was –' for 'Such the true life on't was.' (2.4.76), and 'To winter-ground thy Coarse –' for 'To winter-ground thy corse.' (4.2.228). In

---

do that this page was set up last in the quire, rather than first as the running order otherwise indicated (Hinman, *Printing and Proof-Reading*, II, pp. 315–16). But its appearance is entirely logical in sequence. It was set up as the first running-title for quire zz, but the word '*Cymbeline*' was taken out and set aside during the printing of the remaining pages, which are the titlepage of *Cym.*, and four pages of *Ant.*: the broken swash 'T' and the spelling 'Tragedie' remain on zz2v and zz1v. Then, when the printing of aaa commenced at aaa3:4 (inner), the type for '*Cymbeline*' was restored, with its incorrect 'i'. This remained unnoticed until aaa2 (outer) had been printed, at which point the letter was corrected. Thereafter running-titles appear as they should.

each case he assumed that a difficult reading was an incomplete remark by the speaker, and added dashes (these are almost the only dashes in the text).

The most substantial disturbances are the loss of lines at two points, both in 4.2. At 4.2.49–51 the speech-heading *Arui.* appears twice in succession. It is just possible to rearrange the dialogue to give reasonable sense, but it leaves one long and one short line. Probably a speech has been overlooked and is now irrecoverable. A clearer case arises at 4.2.286–8, where the absence of a rhyming pair for 287, and a momentary hiatus in the sense, indicate that at least one line has dropped out. There is also a difficulty with 284, which seems to have been incorrectly read, and the whole passage is cramped into the bottom of the column, as though the compositor was under pressure of space. This is the one point that could be an error in casting-off copy. There is also a possible mislining of prose as verse at 3.1.11–14. But, generally, the text as we have it is reliable.

Finally, Charlton Hinman found forty-three stop-press corrections in the six pages that were proofed. Most of these are accidentals and nonsubstantive errors. Only two are substantive variants: 'riuete' corrected to 'riueted' at 2.2.43, and 'to go do od seruice' corrected to 'to do good seruice' at 3.2.14. One change of punctuation conceivably affects the sense at 1.4.102 ('safe,' corrected to 'safe.').

READING LIST

This is not a comprehensive list of books and articles cited in the Introduction and Commentary, but a selection of some of the critical works that might be of interest to those who wish to undertake further study of the play.

J. Adelman, *Suffocating Mothers: Fantasies of Maternal Origin in Shakespeare's Plays*, 1992

A. Barton, 'Wrying but a little: marriage, law and sexuality in the plays of Shakespeare' in *Essays, Mainly Shakespearean*, 1994, pp. 3–30

C. Belsey, *Shakespeare and the Loss of Eden*, 1999

D. S. Brewer, *Symbolic Stories*, 1980

J. P. Brockbank, 'History and histrionics in *Cymbeline*', *S.Sur.*, 11 (1958), 42–8

J. Carr, '*Cymbeline* and the validity of myth', *SP*, 75 (1978), 316–30

J. E. Curran, 'Royalty unlearned, honor untaught: British savages and historiographical change in *Cymbeline*', *CompD*, 31 (1997), 277–303

L. Danson, '"The catastrophe is a nuptial": the space of masculine desire in *Othello*, *Cymbeline*, and *The Winter's Tale*', *S.Sur.*, 46 (1997), 69–79

M. Floyd-Wilson, 'Delving to the root: *Cymbeline*, Scotland and the English race', in D. J. Baker and W. Maley, eds., *British Identities and English Renaissance Literature*, 2002, pp. 101–15

R. A. Foakes, *Shakespeare: The Dark Comedies to the Last Plays*, 1971

C. Freer, *The Poetics of Jacobean Drama*, 1981

N. Frye, *A Natural Perspective: The Development of Shakespearean Comedy and Romance*, 1965

C. Gesner, '*Cymbeline* and the Greek romance: a study in genre', in W. F. McNeir, ed., *Studies in English Renaissance Literature*, 1962, pp. 105–31

B. Gibbons, *Shakespeare and Multiplicity*, 1993

J. Goldberg, *Voice Terminal Echo*, 1986

H. Granville-Barker, *Prefaces to Shakespeare*, ed. M. St. Clare Byrne, 1930

D. B. Hamilton, *Shakespeare and the Politics of Protestant England*, 1992

B. Harris, '"What's past is prologue": *Cymbeline* and *Henry VIII*', in J. R. Brown and B. Harris, eds., *Later Shakespeare*, 1966, pp. 203–33

J. Hartwig, *Shakespeare's Tragicomic Vision*, 1972

T. Hawkes, *Shakespeare in the Present*, 2002

N. K. Hayles, 'Sexual disguise in *Cymbeline*', *MLQ*, 41 (1980), 230–47

R. Henke, *Pastoral Transformations: Italian Tragicomedy and Shakespeare's Late Plays*, 1997

G. Hill, '"The true conduct of human judgment": some observations on *Cymbeline*', in D. Jefferson, ed., *The Morality of Art*, 1969, pp. 18–32

R. G. Hunter, *Shakespeare and the Comedy of Forgiveness*, 1965

H. James, *Shakespeare's Troy*, 1997

E. Jones, 'Stuart *Cymbeline*', *EiC*, 11 (1961), 84–99

C. Jordan, *Shakespeare's Monarchies: Ruler and Subject in the Romances*, 1997

C. Kahn, *Roman Shakespeare: Warriors, Wounds, and Women*, 1997

A. C. Kirsch, *Jacobean Dramatic Perspectives*, 1971

A. C. Kirsch, *Shakespeare and the Experience of Love*, 1981

G. W. Knight, *The Crown of Life*, 1947

W. W. Lawrence, *Shakespeare's Problem Comedies*, 1931

L. S. Marcus, *Puzzling Shakespeare: Local Reading and its Discontents*, 1988

D. R. C. Marsh, *The Recurring Miracle: A Study of 'Cymbeline' and the Last Plays*, 1962

C. Marshall, *Last Things and Last Plays: Shakespearean Eschatology*, 1991

T. Marshall, *Theatre and Empire: Great Britain on the London Stages under James VI and I*, 2000

J. Mikalachki, 'The masculine romance of Roman Britain: *Cymbeline* and early modern English nationalism', *SQ*, 46 (1995), 301–22

R. S. Miola, *Shakespeare's Rome*, 1983

R. Moffet, '*Cymbeline* and the nativity', *SQ*, 13 (1962), 207–18

H. Nearing, 'The legend of Julius Caesar's British conquest', *PMLA*, 64 (1949), 889–929

C. T. Neely, *Broken Nuptials in Shakespeare's Plays*, 1985

R. Nevo, *Shakespeare's Other Language*, 1987

M. Novy, *Love's Argument: Gender Relations in Shakespeare*, 1984

T. G. Olsen, 'Iachimo's drug-damn'd Italy and the problem of British national character in *Cymbeline*', in H. Klein and M. Marrapodi, eds., *Shakespeare and Italy*, 1999, pp. 269–96

S. Palfrey, *Late Shakespeare: A New World of Words*, 1997

P. Parker, *Literary Fat Ladies: Rhetoric, Gender, Property*, 1987

P. Parker, 'Romance and empire: anachronistic *Cymbeline*', in G. M. Logan and G. Teskey, eds., *Unfolded Tales: Essays on Renaissance Romance*, 1989, pp. 189–207

P. A. Parolin, 'Anachronistic Italy: cultural alliances and national identity in *Cymbeline*', *S.St.*, 30 (2002), 188–215

D. L. Peterson, *Time, Tide and Tempest: A Study of Shakespeare's Romances*, 1973

H. M. Richmond, 'Shakespeare's Roman trilogy: the climax in *Cymbeline*', *SLI*, 5 (1972), 129–39

L. G. Salingar, *Shakespeare and the Traditions of Comedy*, 1974

M. M. Schwartz, 'Between fantasy and imagination: a psychological exploration of *Cymbeline*', in F. Crews, ed., *Psychoanalysis and Literature*, 1970, pp. 249–83

J. R. Siemon, '"Perplexed beyond self-explication": *Cymbeline* and early modern/postmodern Europe', in M. Hattaway, B. Sokolova and D. Roper, eds., *Shakespeare in the New Europe*, 1994, pp. 294–309

P. M. Simonds, *Myth, Emblem and Music in Shakespeare's 'Cymbeline': An Iconographic Reconstruction*, 1992

M. Skura, 'Interpreting Posthumus' dream from above and below', in M. M. Schwartz and C. Kahn, eds., *Representing Shakespeare: New Psychoanalytic Essays*, 1980, pp. 203–16

R. Smallwood, 'We will nothing pay for wearing our own noses', in M. T. Jones-Davies, ed., *Shakespeare: Cosmopolitisme et Insularité*, 1994, pp. 97–113

G. A. Sullivan, *The Drama of the Landscape*, 1998

H. D. Swander, '*Cymbeline*: religious idea and dramatic design', in W. F. McNeir and T. M. Greenfield, eds., *Pacific Coast Studies in Shakespeare*, 1966, pp. 248–62

H. D. Swander, '*Cymbeline* and the "blameless hero"', *ELH*, 31 (1964), 259–70

A. Thompson, '*Cymbeline*'s other endings', in J. I. Marsden, ed., *The Appropriation of Shakespeare*, 1991, pp. 203–20

W. B. Thorne, '*Cymbeline*: "Lopp'd branches" and the concept of regeneration', *SQ*, 20 (1969), 143–59

R. C. Tobias and P. G. Zolbrod, eds., *Shakespeare's Late Plays*, 1974

R. Warren, *Cymbeline* (Shakespeare in Performance), 1989

R. Warren, *Staging Shakespeare's Late Plays*, 1990

V. Wayne, 'The career of *Cymbeline*'s manacle', *Early Modern Culture*, 1 (2000), 1–21

R. S. White, *"Let Wonder Seem Familiar": Endings in Shakespeare's Romance Vision*, 2nd edn, 1985

G. Wickham, 'Riddle and emblem: a study in the dramatic structure of *Cymbeline*', in J. Carey, ed., *English Renaissance Studies*, 1980, pp. 94–113

L. Woodbridge, 'Palisading the body politic', *Texas Studies in Language and Literature*, 33 (1991), 327–54

F. A. Yates, *Shakespeare's Last Plays: A New Approach*, 1975